THE FOUNDING OF THE AMERICAN REPUBLIC

VOLUME II

THE WAR OF INDEPENDENCE AMERICAN PHASE

THE WAR OF INDEPENDENCE

American Phase

BEING THE SECOND VOLUME OF
A HISTORY OF THE FOUNDING
OF THE AMERICAN REPUBLIC

BY

CLAUDE H. VAN TYNE

PROFESSOR OF HISTORY IN
THE UNIVERSITY OF MICHIGAN

BOSTON AND NEW YORK
HOUGHTON MIFFLIN COMPANY
The Riverside Press Cambridge
1929

The Riverside Press
CAMBRIDGE • MASSACHUSETTS
PRINTED IN THE U.S.A.

TO
WILLIAM LAWRENCE CLEMENTS

PREFACE

WITH the progress of this work a change, perhaps only an extension, has become necessary. The history of the actual War of Independence, with its political, diplomatic, and military aspects, has demanded two volumes rather than one. When William L. Clements purchased and made available the Sir Henry Clinton Papers and the Lord George Germain Papers, the very expansion of our knowledge of many phases of the war forced some change of proportions. Moreover, the voluminous printed sources made available by E. C. Burnett's scholarly and indefatigable efforts, and the recent publication of the letters of King George III, have introduced new problems or more extended treatment of old ones. All these things changed my original perspective.

A natural division of the war period seems to be just after France openly embraced the American cause, which she had aided secretly from the first, and when America was no longer left to struggle desperately alone against the most powerful of nations. That American phase of the war is quite different from the later phase when England was battling against fearful odds in nearly every part of the world. After Burgoyne's defeat and the French alliance, the stage is no longer merely the Atlantic seaboard, but the seven seas and danger points in many lands.

Without repeating the obligations acknowledged in the earlier preface, I wish to thank Dr. R. G. Adams, custodian of the William L. Clements Library, and the devoted members of his staff, Miss Steere, Miss Vosper, and Miss Mallory, for the thousand kindnesses which have shortened and smoothed my labor there. That collection of Americana, the Mecca of all historians of the American Revolution, has been my greatest resource. Miss Helen Bates, my research assistant during the past year, has checked all of my references except those to manuscripts. Her faithful, scholarly work, in other directions also, has been of the greatest service. Miss Jane Clark, archivist in Mr. Clements' home, where the Clinton and Germain papers still repose, has rendered the most unstinted aid by her amazing knowledge of that mass of manuscript material. As in every undertaking of my life, my wife's devoted help has been the chief of my obligations.

C. H. V.

June, 1929

CONTENTS

THE WAR OF INDEPENDENCE

American Phase

THE WAR OF INDEPENDENCE

American Phase

∴

CHAPTER I

THE FIRST FRUITS OF LEXINGTON

WITH the eighteen miles of fighting on that interminable nineteenth day of April, 1775, began the American phase of the war for independence. When that old friend of America, Thomas Pownall, heard in England the first rumors of Concord and Lexington, he wrote in alarm 'the die is cast and more mischief will follow.' [1] Samuel Adams had warned Gage six months earlier that a clash between his soldiers and the people of Massachusetts would leave a wound which would never be healed.[2] Armed rebellion, indeed, then took the place of a war of the quill. Muskets in the hands of angry men superseded efforts to coerce the British Government by injury to British commerce. Things had happened under the bright sun on that chill, windy day of April, which gave all the advantage to the colonial radicals. Cool-headed men who kept calm became objects of scorn, enemies of their country, and 'ministerial tools.' The radicals agreed with the English reformer, who cried,

[1] Hist. MSS., Com., *Various MSS.*, VI, 118. Just one year before this historic battle was fought, Lord North solemnly sent to King George a report of the vote, 182 to 49, of the Commons refusing to consider a repeal of the Tea Act. *Corres. of King George III*, III, 95.

[2] *Letters of Members of the Continental Congress* (ed. Burnett), I, 69.

'Don't tell me of a moderate man, he is always a rascal.' Rumor with its thousand tongues drowned the quiet voice of truth. Indeed, it was said that in the colonies only the Whig stories of Lexington and Concord could circulate, because the post was stopped, mails broken open, and Tory accounts extracted.[1]

The Massachusetts Government hastened the issue of a flaming poster with forty black coffins at the top. Underneath each was the name of one of the patriot slain. The American fondness for alliteration appeared in the heading, 'Bloody Butchery by the British Troops or the Runaway fight of the Regulars.' The American version followed in fine print, and, circulating far and wide, fixed the American tradition for generations to come.[2]

From that day on, things that never happened, mere atrocities of the mind, creations of a maddened fancy had as great influence as facts. A legendary history grew which embittered each side, British and American, more than what actually occurred. On the crucial matter as to the firing of the first shot, and as to whether there was pillage, vandalism, atrocities, and scalping of victims, two clashing stories grew up supported by affidavits, the testimony of eye-witnesses, who flatly contradicted each other.[3] To-day we can read the conflicting stories

[1] *The Remembrancer,* I, 58; Hist. MSS., Com. Report. *Dartmouth MSS.*, II, 299, 301.

[2] *Broadside* (WLCL).

[3] The best critical analysis of all this testimony is in Allen French, *The Day of Concord and Lexington,* and in Harold Murdock, *The Nineteenth of April.*

with cool indifference, but not so then.[1] Reason had fled; men only felt, and they believed what they wished to believe. The shock which Lexington gave the New England mind was greater because for one hundred years no one had been killed by an enemy within many miles of Boston, not since King Philip's War. No shadow of death and destruction terrified their memories, and they were realizing anew that war was not made with rosewater.[2]

Stories grew with the flying hours. By evening of the nineteenth of April, Amos Farnsworth was ready to believe that he 'went into a house where Blood was half over Shoes.' Men's names were blackened in a day, and were not to be cleared of infamy for several generations. That 'true and gallant gentleman,' as his fellow officers described Major Pitcairn, the British commander at Lexington, was, in the mind of Captain John Parker, leader of the minutemen there, the chief villain of that tragic meeting on Lexington Common.[3] The retreat to Boston came also to have two utterly different aspects. In England, funds were collected for the support of the widows of soldiers 'inhumanly and wantonly butch-

[1] Manuscript affidavits of Americans are in the W. L. Clements Library. An important contemporary account, W. Sutherland's, is in the *Clinton Papers* (W.L.C.L.). Important new points are: (1) The British troops heard rumors that 1000 men were gathered at Lexington. (2) One patriot tried to fire at them before they reached Lexington. (3) British officers rode among the Americans *before* there were any shots. (4) W. Sutherland says, 'some villain fired from behind a hedge,' and then the British fired. This has now been published for the Club of Odd Volumes, 1927, with an introduction by Harold Murdock.

[2] French, *The Day of Concord and Lexington*, 82.

[3] *Ibid.*, 124–28.

ered' by rebels 'while marching peaceably' to and from Concord.[1] Acts of war on both sides, though easily defensible, were twisted into vandalism or barbarities. Embattled farmers had made fortresses of private houses, and that aided their attack, but it also gave Earl Percy the right to send soldiers to clear these houses, even to burn and destroy. Discipline was thus relaxed, and looting followed. Moreover, the British soldier was not the only one who had a chance to plunder.[2] In each case the robberies seem to have been in spite of their officers, and on the whole the British officers seem to have acted on the famous retreat like gentlemen rather than the brutes they were charged with being. The men they led were the flower of the British army, the grenadiers and light infantry.

Atrocities were charged and denied. Powder was stored in the Reverend Jonas Clark's meeting-house, provincial soldiers were gathered near, and the British impiously sent a cannon ball through it. This was loudly denounced as 'desecration,' but the British officers feared to leave it standing. What was 'wanton vandalism' in the provincial mind was just as logically 'military necessity' in the British mind. Those 'ruthless hirelings of the Crown, whose hands were stained with American blood,' were reported to have abused aged, unarmed men, but they in turn were filled with rage by the story that at Concord, colonials scalped their victims, tore out

[1] *Journal of Society of Army Historical Research*, VI, 1, 3.

[2] See Harold Murdock, *The Nineteenth of April*; French, *The Day of Concord*, 266–69, 249–50.

their eyes, and cut off their ears.[1] There was but one dubious case of each of these rumored atrocities, but a thousand American minute-men passed on to willing ears one story, and a hundred British soldiers spread the news of the scalping atrocity. There were also yarns of colonial duplicity. Earl Percy told them; General Gage told them. They were even discussed later in Parliament.[2] As these stories waxed with the telling, the conviction grew in many British minds that the only good American was one over whom there was a canopy of stone, and Americans thought of a British soldier as little better than a follower of Attila.

Though there was no radio to spread the story of Lexington and Concord to the uttermost parts of America, it traveled fast enough from town to town, from hamlet to hamlet, until breathless horsemen carried it even into the upland regions of North and South Carolina. On April 23, it reached New York, and within a few hours the city was in the hands of a mob led by the hotheads, Lamb and Sears. They broke into the arsenal, seized the muskets, formed volunteer corps, and for a week ruled the

[1] M. W. Willard, *Letters on the American Revolution,* 77, 78; J. Macpherson, *The Rights of Great Britain . . .* (1776), 59.

[2] The best critical analysis of these charges is in Harold Murdock's *Nineteenth of April, 1775;* French, *The Day of Concord and Lexington,* 211–14. The friendly *London Magazine* was inclined to give more credence to the American than to the British accounts. (June, 1775, p. 323.) American enterprise in sending their story by a ship in ballast, while Gage sent his by a loaded merchant ship, got the colonial story first to London. Even Germain said the Bostonians were 'right to make the King's troops the aggressors.' *Germain Papers* (W.L.C.L.).

city.[1] Philadelphia got the news a day later, and before another sun it was at Baltimore. Then the committees of correspondence sent it on to Williamsburg in Virginia, and to Williamstown in North Carolina, and Cornelius Harnett's exhortation, 'For God's sake, forward it by night and by day,' was not needed to send it on South and West even to the settlements beyond Savannah. Wherever the news went, 'the people,' Gage wrote, 'were as mad as they are here in Boston.' 'The infamous false reports,' snarled Governor Martin, took 'deep root in the minds of the vulgar . . . confirming the seditious,' and bringing over the 'fickle, wavering, and unsteady multitude.'[2] In the city of Savannah the Committee of Safety got the news on May 10. Next day they broke open the Government's powder magazine and removed six hundred pounds of 'the King's powder' to garrets and cellars where it could be ready for the use of the Sons of Liberty.[3] As Seabury declared, after Lexington the colonists rushed headlong down the precipice of rebellion.[4]

New England was first to rally to the aid of the Massachusetts men who swarmed to the siege of Boston. Nathanael Greene, fresh from the 'Lives' of Plutarch and the 'Commentaries' of Cæsar, led eager Rhode Island men. John Stark, who was much more than the husband of Molly, came with

[1] C. L. Becker, *Political Parties in New York*, 193; Colden, *Letter-Book*, II, 288.

[2] Governor Martin complained that the rebel leaders got the news a month before he did. North Carolina, *Colonial Records*, x, 44.

[3] C. C. Jones, *History of Georgia*, II, 175.

[4] Samuel Seabury, *The Congress Canvassed* (1775), 21–22.

men from New Hampshire, while the reputed 'wolf-slayer,' Israel Putnam, riding the same horse one hundred miles within eighteen hours, arrived to lead the patriot-swarm from Connecticut. The Massachusetts Congress authorized a provincial army of 13,600 men, and asked the other New England States to raise that number to 30,000. A great help to enlistment was the fact that numerous sailors, riggers, longshoremen, and ropemakers had been thrown out of work by the operation of the Boston Port Bill, and their idleness now became more widespread because of the outbreak of war. In general, New England reorganized its militia, and put it on a war footing.[1]

The first Continental Congress, indeed, in the preceding September had advised the people to elect officers, to appear under arms at least once a week, and with the utmost diligence to acquaint themselves with the art of war.[2] This 'treasonable vote,' Galloway declared, laid the foundation of military resistance throughout America.[3] It did beyond question provide a great number of half-equipped, ill-trained men ready at a minute's notice to gather in an armed camp about Boston. It had also encouraged the Massachusetts Assembly to buy twenty field pieces, four mortars, twenty tons of shot, five thousand muskets, seventy-five thousand

[1] Schlesinger, *Colonial Merchants*, 542, note 1.

[2] *Journals of Congress*, I, September 17, 1774. In February of 1775, train-bands in Massachusetts towns were choosing officers and taking covenant to attend military duty. *Boston Evening Post*, February 6, 1775.

[3] Galloway, *Historical and Political Reflections* . . . (1780), 69.

flints, to which later the Committee of Public Safety added a thousand wooden mess bowls, some peas and flour, as a small beginning of the warlike stock with which if need be they would fight the most powerful nation in the world of that day.

The Loyalists bitterly reproached the British Government that the flame of rebellion spread with more rapidity in a province under the eye of His Majesty's army than in any other. It did not seem to occur to them that the presence of the army was the reason for the flame. For, as Bacon wrote, 'they are the most dangerous discontents where the fear is greater than the feeling.' Real fear was in the breasts of those who swarmed about Boston, but they were bent on refuting Charles Fox's pessimistic assertion that no people, whatever their principles, can make a successful resistance to military discipline, that standing armies had made slaves of all mankind. They would prove, if possible, that *men* did not make so sad a figure against soldiers, as Fox feared.

All were there 'to revenge Massachusetts' slaughtered sons upon the venal, servile instruments of tyranny.' Those who had taken part in shedding the blood of the soldiers of King George were filled with desperation. Their best prospect was a laurel wreath, their worst a hempen cord; they were either patriots or traitors. 'We may as well die by the sword as be hanged like rebels,' was their slogan. Those who came to their aid were emboldened by the belief in the story spread far and wide that, between Lexington and Boston, 'three hundred intrepid, rural sons of freedom drove before them more than five times their number of regular well-appointed troops.'[1] Believers in this wild tale of inequality of courage explained that 'one fights for 3 shillings 5 pence per week, the other fights for his altar and his fires' — for 'his religion, his wife, his children, his house, his property, his liberty.'[2]

Though actually in arms against their King's legal representative, few of the members of the gathering train-bands would admit that they were rebels. It was deeply resented when the King's friends declared that 'Rebellion had reared its head high above the dictates of reason.' In the pamphlets of the time there were eloquent arguments to the effect that 'Passive obedience is all a mistake, and instead of being a duty to suffer oppression 'tis a Glorious act to resist it, and instead of leaving Injuries to be redressed by God, we have a natural right to relieve ourselves.'[3] John Adams expressed clearly what was merely a fog in many a duller brain. 'Resistance by arms against usurpation and lawless violence,' he wrote, 'is not rebellion by the law of God or the land.' He even enumerated the heroes whom he thought he was imitating. 'Hampden, Russell, Sidney, Somers, Holt, Tillotson, Burnet, Hoadley, etc., were not tyrants or rebels, although some of them were in Arms, and others undoubtedly excited resistance against the tories.' No, the citizens of New

[1] *Essex Gazette*, May 18, 1775. See facts in A. French, *The Day of Concord and Lexington*, 211–70.

[2] Pamphlet entitled *Right of Britons*, 74.

[3] *An Essay upon Government — Lawfulness of Revolutions Demonstrated*, 7; British Museum, *Egerton MSS.*, 2659, F 141.

England were merely fighting to preserve their rights. In Chaplain Duché's words, their 'hedges of liberty were broken down, their vineyard no longer secure.'[1] There were good precedents in English history for armed resistance to a government not observant of the constitution, or which made a threat to liberty.

The news of Lexington — like a fire-bell in the night — roused the American leaders to greater efforts. Committees of Correspondence and of Safety, organs of the radicals, already wholly disloyal to the established colonial government, began to discipline their opponents, the Loyalists, and to hasten all military preparations. Defense associations sprang full-armed from committees lately created only to enforce the continental association as to commerce. Now all their powers were spent on binding men by oath to take up arms. A pledge to fight for the cause was a better test of patriotism than a mere pledge not to trade with the British oppressor, and public attention was quickly centered on military resistance. Forced by excited committeemen to take oaths of allegiance to the colonial cause, men bound themselves by the 'ties of religion, honor and love of country' to adhere to radical measures not yet even passed by the Provincial or Continental Congress. Faced with the menace of war, Massachusetts, and other colonies fearful of attack, began to stop all exports even before September 10, the date set for that action by the First Continental Congress in the Association. The

[1] Duché, *The American Vine* (1775), 20.

folly of impoverishing and cutting themselves off from articles of daily need, not made in America, was a measure of the passion of the moment.[1] James Madison told long after how embarrassed he was by the theft of his conical hat which the non-importation laws made it almost impossible for him to replace. But the colonists thought only of the 'ruin infallible' which they hoped to wreak on British commerce and manufactures.[2]

Moderates everywhere began to take to cover. In Georgia, to avoid more violent measures, they hastened to adopt the Continental Association, and to play with fire by pledging that colony to defend 'the violated rights of America.' The radicals thus placed in the saddle were described by Governor Wright as a 'parcel of the Lowest People, Chiefly Carpenters, Shoemakers, Blacksmiths.' From his point of view there were only a few men of 'real abilities, Gentlemen or Men of Property,' in the radical tribunals.[3] To his loyal eyes it seemed 'truly Terrible . . . that Such People should be suffered to overturn the Civil Government . . . and sport with Other Mens Lives, Liberties and Properties.' It was

[1] The folly of it was sung by 'Bob Jingle,' in the Association, etc., of the Delegates of the Colonies, at the Grand Congress held in Philadelphia, September 1, 1774. *Versified and adapted to Music, Calculated for Grave and Gay dispositions, with a Short Introduction, by Bob Jingle, esq., Poet Laureate to Congress*, Philadelphia, 1774, p. 22 (Carter Brown Library).

[2] R. H. Lee, *Letters*, I, 133; Griggsby, *Va. Const. Convention*, 36.

[3] Ga. Hist. Soc., *Collections*, III, 228. We are told, in Smyth's *Tour in America* (II, 274), that the Committee of Frederickton, Va., consisted of 'a Taylor, a leather-breeches maker, a shoemaker, a ginger-bread-baker, a butcher and two publicans —' most of them being Germans.

his belief that great numbers, the greater part of the province, were intimidated to sign the Association. At last, Government, he declared was 'totally Annihilated,' the 'Poison has Infected the whole Province,' he wrote. Congresses, Councils and Committees ruled everywhere with 'the greatest Acts of Tyranny.' [1]

Indeed, it was true everywhere after Lexington that the committees, lately given powers to observe and inspect with the aim of enforcing the Continental Association, became engines for crushing loyalist opinion, employing either mob action or military organizations.[2] These committees, sensitive to public opinion, snuffing it with rebel nostrils, obedient to the electric waves of mass passion, responded with the greatest accuracy to the unexpressed, but no less resistless, will of the radical multitude. Committees sometimes directed the mob, sometimes merely gave it free rein. In Portsmouth, New Hampshire, the mob, four months before Lexington, having overpowered the King's soldiers in Fort William and Mary,[3] carrying off the powder and small arms for use against their royal master at a subsequent time, ventured again some six months later to rifle the government treasury of nearly two thousand pounds and to carry it off in triumph. A Rhode Island mob broke windows, entered houses, and threatened Captain Wallace of the

[1] Ga. Hist. Soc., *Collections*, III, 205, 213.

[2] Schlesinger, *Colonial Merchants*, 552.

[3] C. L. Parsons, *The Capture of Fort William and Mary*, in reprint from N.H. Hist. Soc., *Proceedings*.

ship Rose with tar and feathers.[1] Another furious crowd, suspecting a merchant of buying food for government use, stopped his carts, and threw out the flour. When a King's officer brought one hundred men ashore, the 'rebels' came in shoals, armed with bayonets, sticks, and stones, and only retreated when the officer threatened to put them to the sword.[2] In Connecticut, while four hundred soldiers marched with horns and drums and fifes, and thousands looked on, many from the housetops, two hundred pounds of tea was put in the middle of the road, with tar-barrels, shavings, and wood all about, and the whole was fired. Two blackened fellows threw the tea about until all was consumed and then all gave a great hurrah![3] In Delaware one who had 'as lief be under a tyrannical King as a tyrannical Commonwealth, especially if the d——d Presbyterians had the rule of it' was forced to recant. Another man in Virginia who believed his eyes, and declared 'this Country is in a state of rebellion and aims at a state of independence,' was forced to express deep sorrow for such heretical ideas.[4] At Williamsburg, on a large pole, hung a bucket of tar and a bag of feathers — Archibald Cary's idea of a hint to the King's friends.[5] In New York, 'rebel' soldiers from Connecticut destroyed Rivington's presses, because they had been too busy printing

[1] *Calendar of State Papers* (Home Office), XI (1773–75).

[2] *Ibid.*, XII (1773–75).

[3] Conn. Hist. Soc., *Collections*, VII, 113.

[4] Force, *American Archives* (4th Series), III, 644.

[5] *Magazine of American History* (1906), III, 136.

loyal literature, and fifteen hundred Gothamites stood and huzzaed in approbation.[1] In the same city, one Sears, a leader in the destruction of Loyalists' property, refused bail, was jailed, rescued by the mob, and carried in triumph through the city to a stage in the fields, whence he harangued the mob, asking 'whether a son of liberty should give bail.'[2] Civil authority was prostrate there as in Boston, save under General Gage's eye.

Edmund Burke, friend of the colonists but enemy to mob rule, was to write long after, apropos of the French Revolution: 'In a democracy the majority of citizens are capable of exercising the most cruel oppression upon the minority, whenever strong divisions prevail in that kind of policy, as they often must; and that oppression of the minority will extend to far greater numbers, and will be carried on with fury, than can almost ever be apprehended from the domination of a single scepter. In such a popular persecution individual sufferers are in a much more deplorable condition than in any other. Under a cruel prince they have at least the balmy compassion of mankind to assuage the smart of their wounds; . . . but those who are subjected to wrongs under multitudes are deprived of external consolations; they seem deserted by mankind and overpowered by a conspiracy of their own species.' What Burke feared in the ominous rise of mass rule was being realized in this breaking up of the old political system in America.

[1] *Essex Gazette*, December 7, 1775.

[2] British Museum, *Egerton MSS.*, 2135, F 5. *Calendar of Home Office Papers* (1773–75), Preface, vi–vii.

Jonathan Boucher, friend of Washington, but a firm opponent of revolution, and who was finally compelled to fly to England for refuge, paid his respects long after to the mass action of 1775. The Whig mobs were in his eyes 'Those numerous swarms of restless men who are as naturally engendered in free governments as serpents and other fierce and noxious animals are in warm climates.' 'Their taste,' he declared, 'is directed only to pulling down and their reforms terminate only in destruction.'[1] To the Loyalist overwhelmed by this blind mass resentment of all opposing views, no other opinion was possible. It is enough to explain Boucher's spleen if we know that on a Sunday morning he found his church filled with two hundred armed men under command of one Osborne Sprigg, who warned him not to preach. When Boucher ascended the pulpit with a sermon in one hand, and a loaded pistol in the other, friends pinioned his arms and tried to remove him. While factions in the congregation disputed among themselves, Boucher seized Sprigg, put a pistol at his head, and marched him out while a mischievous drummer played the Rogues' March.[2] Another arch-Loyalist, Joseph Galloway, who, had the Revolution failed, might have taken the place in the hearts of his countrymen now occupied by George Washington, believed that America had now come to be governed by 'the barbarian rule of frantic folly, and lawless ambition — freedom of speech suppressed, liberty of

[1] J. Boucher, *A View* (1797), vi, vii.

[2] *Ibid., Reminiscences* . . . 121–23.

press destroyed, voice of truth silenced, a lawless power depriving men of their natural rights, property taken without law — America arming east and west and pushing on with madness in the high road of Sedition and Rebellion.' [1]

Lord Dunmore in Virginia described the activities of Whig Committees with vivacity if not with sympathy. 'A committee has been chosen in every County,' he wrote, 'whose business it is to carry the association of the Congress into execution, which committee assumes an authority to inspect books, invoices and all other secrets of the trade and correspondence of Merchants: to watch the conduct of every inhabitant, without distinction and to send for all such as come under their suspicion into their presence: to interrogate them respecting all matters which, at their pleasure, they think fit objects of their inquiry; and to stigmatize, as they term it, such as they find transgressing what they are now hardy enough to call the Laws of the Congress, which stigmatizing is no other than inviting the vengeance of an outrageous and lawless mob to be exercised upon the unhappy victim.' [2] Even Henry Laurens, a moderate Whig, thought it 'abhorrent and detestable' to hold all persons 'inimical to liberty,' who refused to sign the Association, though he himself was ready to sign with his hand and seal with his blood. [3]

[1] Galloway, *A Candid Examination*, iii–iv.

[2] Force, *American Archives* (4th Series), I, 1061–62. Governor Martin drew the same picture in North Carolina. *Colonial Records*, X, 49, 232, 244.

[3] Wallace, *Life of Henry Laurens*, 207, 209.

William Eddis, a surveyor of the customs in Annapolis, paid these committees his compliments. 'I am heartily disgusted with the times. The Universal cry is Liberty, to support which, an infinite number of petty tyrannies are established, under the appelation of committees; in every one of which a few despots lord it over the calm and moderate, inflame the passions of the mob, and pronounce those to be enemies of the general good, who may presume any way to dissent from the creed they have thought proper to impose.' [1] Samuel Seabury, the Tory 'Westchester Farmer,' cried, 'If I must be enslaved let it be by a king at least and not by a parcel of upstart, lawless committee men.' He preferred being devoured 'by the jaws of a lion' to being 'gnawed to death by rats and vermin.' General Gage, too, regarded the system with horror.[2]

There was, however, a more charitable way to look at it. John Adams, in after years, looked back upon it in rapture, 'What an engine! France imitated it and produced a revolution.' R. H. Lee recommended it to all colonies.[3] It was a tyranny the people had erected themselves. And there was some truth in the assertion of a Massachusetts Whig that in his province 'Four Hundred thousand are in a state of nature and yet as still and peaceable as ever they were when government was in full vigor.'

[1] William Eddis, *Letters from America,* 210. Eddis was a recent comer, arriving in 1769.

[2] *Calendar of Home Office Papers* (1773–75), Preface, vii.

[3] J. Adams, *Works,* x, 197. R. H. Lee, *Letters,* I, 84. One can see the machine at work in *Calendar of Home Office Papers* (1773–75), Preface, ix, and Am. Antiquarian Soc., XXI (n.s.), pt. 1, p. 73.

There were no officers save 'a multitude chosen by the people and exercising . . . more authority and spirit than ever any did who had commissions from a governor.' [1]

These 'flaming patriots,' 'without property,' with 'only impudence' — had long made wretched the life of the opponents of the radical cause. Those who obeyed the voice of 'our Lord the King,' or 'bowed down to the Tea Chest,' sold arms to Tories, or refused to provide arms for themselves; those who belittled the Patriot generals, cursed the honorable Continental Congress, or were even apathetic to it, and those who even held that British wrong did not justify the bitterness of American opposition, were haled before 'pragmatical committee men' and, if not 'by force and oppression compelled to be free,' were denounced as Ministerial tools, 'dastardly low-spirited court sycophants,' 'Jacobites,' 'Sons of Despotism,' and enemies to America. Those who talked of leaving the regulation of the state to those competent in the matter, or who spoke of George III as an 'ornament of the human species,' the 'provident father of all of his people,' preachers who declined to preach sermons asking charity for the sufferers in Boston, and all those who 'planted seeds of dissension' by disagreeing with their Whig neighbors, were hushed by this 'lawless power.' Whoever loved ease and madeira better than liberty and strife learned soon that he must perforce accept the rejected horn of the dilemma. None could retire from this blind mass movement against government.

[1] *The Remembrancer*, I, 101.

Those erstwhile Whigs, whose noble rage for political principles had been checked by the thoughts of civil tumult, and perhaps war; those whom 'the word rebellion had frozen up like fish in a pond,' were hurried along toward the end they hated by fanatical committees bent upon American unity.

CHAPTER II

LOYALISTS AND PATRIOTS

To be loyal to the King, to wish to preserve the British Empire, became very dangerous virtues in New England in 1775. Even before Lexington, all who had a good word for the British Government had found comfort in the military force under Gage in Boston.[1] After that affair it was the only safe place in Massachusetts for loyalty. In Boston were huddled the Episcopalian ministers and wardens, as well as the thirty-three citizens of Marblehead who had sent a gracious address to the retiring Governor Hutchinson, odious to all Massachusetts Whigs, who regarded him as a villain, though few men ever less deserved the title. There, too, came the unrepentant Suffolk County Justices of the Peace who addressed and greeted General Gage as one come to still the waves of public commotion. No other place was so safe for the one hundred and twenty-three subscribers to an address which welcomed Gage and sped Hutchinson. These, while regretting the rigor of Boston's punishment, were meek enough to be ready to pay for the cost of the Boston Tea Party. For months thereafter these subscribers were kept busy signing recantations in the public press.[2] Boston, too, was the refuge for twenty-four bar-

[1] It is not far wrong to say that a genuine Loyalist party did not exist in the colonies until commercial war failed and real war began.

[1] See *Essex Gazette*, September 4 and 14, 1775, for examples.

risters and attorneys, and some merchants of Boston, as illustrious men as Massachusetts could boast, who had likewise written themselves down as Tories — to be held up, like all other "addressers," for the next seven years as traitors and enemies to their country.[1] All 'Addressers' led 'a devil of a life,' wrote an approving Whig.

Not only were 'Addressers' in bad odor, but also 'Protesters' and 'Mandamus Councillors.' When Joseph Warren sent through all the towns of Massachusetts a 'Solemn League and Covenant,' putting a ban on all trade with Great Britain, the Tory merchants of Boston protested it as a 'base, wicked and illegal measure.' As provided in the Massachusetts Regulating Act, Gage appointed by 'Mandamus' some thirty-six Councillors, chosen for their loyalty to their King, but against whom the rage of the populace turned at once. Old and infirm Israel Williams for that offense was 'smoked to a Whig' when the doors and chimney of his house were closed by a mob. Thomas Oliver was besieged by three or four thousand armed men and compelled to recant. Later, he and Mr. Hallowell and Deacon Edson, all councillors, fled into Boston. Some like Colonel Saltonstall met the 'flagiticious disturbers of American liberty and loyalty' with splendid courage, but all sooner or later became refugees. Gentle Samuel Curwen, the writer of as charming a book of letters as that generation of Americans produced, whose

[1] In the lists of these sinful 'addressers' one finds the familiar and respectable names of Brattle, Faneuil, Winslow, Amory, Loring, Holmes, Murray. See *Essex Gazette*, November 2, 1775.

heart overflowed with love for America and loyalty to his King, became an outcast, wandering unhappy in London and longing for the land of his birth.

To Curwen, and his fellow refugees, the Patriot persecutors were those 'who, when the bands of society are unhappily loosened and the laws are forced into silence, do not neglect to avail themselves of those times to run riot against peace, order, and security, the most valuable blessings of social and civile life.' [1]

Samuel Seabury, able Tory pamphleteer, destined after the Revolution to be the first Episcopalian Bishop in America, paid his compliments to the radicals in his 'Congress Canvassed': 'People who talk so very feelingly, and with so much pleasure about revolutions, and who are ever ready to justify the most violent and the most needless opposition to government by the example of the great revolution in England seem to me too fond of revolution to be good subjects of any government on earth.' 'Tar and feathers,' he wrote, 'may silence the pusillanimous' and 'loud cries of liberty may catch the ignorant and beguile the unwary,' [2] but he would not admit that the use of these were the proofs of patriotism. To the Loyalists 'the whole human race, root and branch,' was sliding willingly down again into 'the gulf of primæval chaos.'

Between the radicals and the conservatives the chasm was widening. Just as each new act of war or wild rumor made reconciliation with England less

[1] Curwen, *Journal and Letters*, 177.

[2] S. Seabury, *The Congress Canvassed*, 16, 44. (A. W. Farmer.)

likely, so untoward events and words spoken in rage made civil war between Whig and Tory inevitable. Peter Oliver, shut up with the 'Duke of Alva' in Boston, wrote in despair: 'If we may judge from the conduct of the colonies etc., it won't appear the least probable that we poor disconsolate refugees will be able to visit our once peaceable habitations these two or three years without the greatest danger and not until these rebel breed are entirely demolished. . . . Hanging people wont pay me for what I have suffered, nothing short of forfeited estates will answer and after my damages are sufficiently compensated then hang all the Massachusetts rebels by dozens if you will.' [1] Madame Higginson wanted to ride through American Whig blood to the hubs of her chariot wheels.[2] A Loyalist furnished officers and soldiers of His Majesty's troops with lists, later published in the papers, bearing the names of Samuel Adams, Dr. Cooper, James Bowdoin, John Hancock, and other Whigs, urging that they be the first victims of the mischief they had wrought; that they be put to the sword, their houses destroyed, their goods plundered. Some wanted the rebels to swing for it, or wished to see the blood streaming from the hearts of the leaders. Temple Bar was the proper place for the 'patriotic noddles of the Boston Saints.'

Whig opinion of Tories was no more charitable. Loyal efforts to save the British Empire were depre-

[1] Boston, December 7, 1775. British Museum, *Egerton MSS.*, 2659, F 190.

[2] *New England Historical and Genealogical Register* (1872), 431.

cated as 'dark and criminal designs.' Would-be saviors of the Union of English-speaking people were 'infamous betrayers of their country,' not 'one hundred per cent Americans.' They were left at the mercy of mobs, deprived of all legal rights, jailed, exiled, and threatened with death. Franklin denounced them as 'Judases ready to betray their Country for a few Paltry Pieces of Silver.'[1] Even Washington declared his purpose to root out and secure 'such abominable pests of society,' and he heartily approved of the confiscation of their estates, a process which began early and continued late in the war.[2] To this state of utter intolerance came erstwhile friends, neighbors, and even members of the same family.[3]

In the mutual recriminations by Whigs and Tories we find that they agree in general as to the social position in which members of each faction were commonly found. The Whigs published lists of 'Protesters' and 'Addressers,' stressing the fact that they were rich merchants, crown officials, great landowners, and their relatives. A Tory judge, with a great wig, and looking like an oiled and curled Assyrian bull, was designated as a good type of these patricians who upheld despotic power. Benjamin Thomson, a Loyalist of New Hampshire, who, as Count Rumford, was to become a great figure in the scientific world, was known as one who always had a

[1] Franklin, *Works* (Smyth, ed.), VI, 88.

[2] Van Tyne, *Loyalists*, 211, 223, 281.

[3] John Lovell, Boston Loyalist, had a brother in the Continental Congress.

kick ready for the underdog. The great Cuvier pronounced him no democrat. 'His services to his fellow men,' wrote Cuvier, 'were rendered them without loving them or even thinking well of them. He felt that the common people could not be trusted with the care of their own well-being. He loved slavery as if he were the owner of a plantation and China seemed to him to have a nearly perfect government because its common people were absolutely in the power of its men of education.' [1] His reputation was not different in his humbler days in New Hampshire.

Much was made by the Whigs of any titles, like that of Sir William Pepperell, and it was insinuated that the remarkable number of chaise-makers, portrait-painters, bookbinders, jewelers, goldsmiths and lapidaries who signed loyal addresses to the King's governors were those whose best trade came from the aristocrats, wealthy merchants, rich officers, and that thrift would follow fawning.[2] Even in rebellious Massachusetts Samuel Adams had little confidence in the merchants, and, indeed, most of them returned his dislike with interest. The rich Quakers of Pennsylvania, some great landowners in the Hudson Valley, like the De Lanceys, certain great planters of South Carolina and Georgia and the Scotch merchants of Virginia and the Carolinas, were pointed at with the finger of scorn as haughty

[1] *The New England Quarterly,* I, 531. The future Count was not above being a spy for the British Government when he was in the American army in Cambridge. R. G. Adams, *The Papers of Lord George Germain,* 18–19.

[2] Mass. Hist. Soc., *Proceedings* (1869–70), 392.

betrayers of the cause of the people.[1] The Whigs did not consider their argument weakened by the fact that John Hancock and George Washington were two of the richest and most aristocratic men in America. They were only the exceptions that proved the rule.

On the other hand, the Tories were at one in denouncing the Whig leaders as 'the once meaner people' who had of late risen from the social mire. The Whigs of the Massachusetts House of Assembly were, asserted Peter Oliver, 'inn-keepers, retailers and yet more inferior orders of men.'[2] The 'rebels' were 'ignorant and destitute of means,' he declared, and Galloway agreed with him that even the best of them were 'men of bankrupt fortunes, overwhelmed in debt to British merchants.'[3] The 'noisy blustering and bellowing patriots' were the 'refuse and the dregs of mankind.'[4] James Otis, though a Whig, said of the Revolution, 'When the pot boils the scum will arise.' Even European commentators gained the impression that the 'rebels' were Jack Straws and Wat Tylers, needy lawyers, pettifogging attorneys, and word-spouting cobblers. Benedict Arnold was a horse-dealer, Putnam an innkeeper, General Sullivan a breeches-maker, Knox a blacksmith, and Wayne a tanner's boy, wrote one European student of the situation.[5] The Tory satirist had

[1] Galloway claimed that the Loyalists 'possessed the greatest fortunes in America.' *Historical and Political Reflections*, 66–67.

[2] British Museum, *Egerton MSS.*, 2671, F 17, and 2659, F 141.

[3] Galloway, *Historical and Political Reflections*, 66.

[4] Tyler, *Literary History of the American Revolution*, II, 57–58.

[5] *Letters from America* (Pettengill trans.), 251–52. Colonel Von

much to say of mob-chosen upstarts, 'Colonel Shoe-Black' and 'General Convict,' of the quacks and vile rebel priests, the barbers and pettifoggers, strutting with sword and pike into battle for their rights. Thomas Cushing, Speaker of the Massachusetts House was a 'distiller of Spirits,' and most of the other members of the House were of lowly origin, according to a Loyalist's list prepared for a London paper.[1] Samuel Curwen believed the world turned upside down and that the poor were riding in coaches.[2] Members of Congress were the special object of the Tory lampoon.

> 'Down at night a bricklayer or carpenter lies,
> Next sun a Lycurgus, a Solon doth Rise,'

wrote one Tory verse-monger.[3] In this way did the Loyalists rail against the 'wretched banditti' upon whom they had been wont to look down throughout a past in which their wealth, cultivation, and social position had never been in question. If some of their own faction were of humble origin and estate, they thought it no detraction from the general truth of their characterization.

There was much of truth in the opinions which each faction held of the other. A statistical study of such Whigs as attained sufficient fame in the Congress, in the military or diplomatic service, or in the

Heeringen sneered at Lord Stirling, who was 'no lord at all,' and declared that most American officers were 'mere mechanics, tailors, shoemakers, wig-makers.' See J. G. Rosengarten, *The German Soldier* (ed. 1890), 65–66. Also *Letters from America* (Pettengill trans.), 251.

[1] Mass. Hist. Soc., *Proceedings* (2d Series), XII, 139.

[2] Curwen, *Journal*, 235–36.

[3] Moore, *Diary of the Revolution*, II, 22.

governments of the several States — of whom the necessary facts have been recorded — reveals certain generalizations, remarkable if we bear in mind that it was the colonial custom to leave political activities to men of established social position.[1] About one half came of the middle or lower class in colonial society, and yet these were the leaders of the revolutionary party. The strength of the revolutionary party lay in the plain people. About one third of these leaders were college graduates, the great majority from Harvard, Yale, Princeton, and William and Mary. Only the men who attained the greatest prominence in the Revolution could be included in these statistics, and the great mass of their followers must have been of far humbler origin and conditions.

Another revelation of these statistics is that it was youth which espoused rebellion; age tended to cling to the old or, at least, to go slowly. Jonathan Boucher thought that 'the chief abettors of violence' — patriots we call them to-day — were 'young men of good parts, but spoiled by a strange, imperfect, desultory kind of education which has crept into fashion all over America.'[2]

The lists of refugees, banished Loyalists, and persons sent to places of detention during the war read often like bead-rolls of the finest and oldest colonial

[1] It was possible in only three hundred and twelve cases to get the necessary data, and then, of course, the classification of the position in society involved personal judgment upon which no two students of the matter would always agree.

[2] *Germain Papers* (W.L.C.L.), Boucher to Germain, November 27, 1775. He thought the 'northern academies' — 'seminaries of sedition' — led the way.

families. The culture, the dignity, the official rank, the inheritors of wealth tended to support the old order. As one pores over Sabine's biographical dictionary of Loyalists, or the thousands of names included in the manuscript lists compiled by the British Government, one is impressed with the frequency of names of great merchants, landholders, Episcopalian ministers, lawyers, judges, great officials, and the socially elect of the old colonial régime.[1] So high was the social position of some Loyalists that even their open dislike of the Patriot cause was endured. The first gentleman of Virginia, William Byrd of Westover, remained peacefully on his beautiful estate until his death in the midst of the war. Lord Thomas Fairfax, owner of a vast estate in Virginia, continued to the war's end to live there in quiet, and likewise unmolested lived the Reverend John Camm, president of William and Mary.[2] Goodly lists might be made of Revolutionary Fathers who were aristocrats in the colonial days, but such lists would not be as impressive as these rolls of the heroes of the lost cause. Moreover, it must not be forgotten that John Jay, John Dickinson, Robert Morris, and other famous Patriots wavered when decision was necessary and only narrowly missed turning to the Loyalist cause.

[1] A few Loyalists' names at random illustrate the point: J. L. McAdam, inventor of McAdamized roads; Count Rumford; J. Andrews, Provost of the University of Pennsylvania; Curwen, Galloway, Boucher, Daniel Leonard, Andrew Allen, Copley, Samuel Seabury. But one must read them by the hundreds to be duly impressed. See Sabine, *American Loyalists*.

[2] Eckenrode, *The Revolution in Virginia*, 129. A descendant of Byrd was the first aviator to reach the North Pole.

To understand why the prosperous and privileged classes tended to embrace the British cause, one must remember that they were the people to whom the dream of empire would most appeal. They conjured up a vision of an English-speaking people dominating the sea, the vast resources of India, the seaboard and the fertile interior valleys of America. Imagination pictured for them a world empire, rivaled by none, paramount over all, mingling everything that was best of East and West, a noble dominion bringing peace, freedom, and industrial growth over all the globe. It was this gorgeous prospect which they refused to abandon for an iridescent dream of independence and perhaps wild disorder. Some held the belief of Daniel Leonard that, 'after many more centuries shall have rolled away, long after we, who are now bustling on the stage of life, shall have been received to the bosom of mother earth, and our names are forgotten, the colonies may be so far increased as to have the balance of wealth, numbers and power in their favor; the good of the empire may make it necessary to fix the seat of government here, and some future George, equally the friend of mankind with him that now sways the British sceptre, may cross the Atlantic and rule Great Britain by an American parliament.'[1]

The proportions of social aristocrats and democrats in Whig and Tory factions differed widely in different provinces. Virginia, named in honor of Spenser's 'most high, mighty and magnificent Empresse,' had, perhaps, a larger percentage of aristo-

[1] *Massachusettensis* (1776), 43–44.

crats in her Whig party than any other colony. The pride of her great planters in having the 'Old Dominion' rule herself was higher, possibly, than in any similar group in the other provinces. Certainly, more of the top rank socially entered heartily upon the revolutionary road than did the like rank elsewhere. In Philadelphia, New York, and Boston, the socially elect were in the main cold toward rebellion. In the South, the great planter, not having the New England preoccupation with local politics, had a greater comprehension of the imperial problems of the British Government, and, being less affected by the British commercial policy, could listen to argument aimed at preserving the old order of things. Such men easily became Loyalists or, like Henry Laurens, conservative Whigs.

Some of the noblest characters in America were active Whigs, but there are many contrasts between Whig and Tory which give pause to one who wishes to think that the choicest of American spirits went with the Revolutionary party.

In a dual biography, 'Two Men of Taunton,' the heroes are Daniel Leonard, Loyalist, and Robert Treat Paine, Patriot. It was a quaint conceit to compare the two, but if the author wished to serve a patriotic purpose his comparison was ill chosen, for Leonard is ever the better man, more charming in person, more pleasing in spirit, more gallant in manner. He, quite naturally, when the time came, chose the Loyalist side, the aristocratic side, the conservative side, where his character and breeding naturally placed him. With many of his kind he fled to

England, and there practiced law until near the end of the war when he was made Chief Justice of Bermuda. Paine, the Patriot, was a very ordinary man, who could give an impromptu blessing at a dinner party, discuss theology over the tea-cups, serve as a pallbearer, or be the moderator of a town meeting, but had he not been merely the biggest man of revolutionary tendencies in a very small community at the time of a great political upheaval, he would have cut a very diminutive figure in this big world. And there are many other like contrasts which one could make only at the peril of his repute as a true patriot.

It was with party and class feeling aroused to this degree that the New England Minute-Men swarmed about Boston. Oliver thought them possessed by a 'strange infatuation,' unparalleled, in which no absurdity in politics was too gross to be accepted without question. Not only were the Whig masses enraged against the British Ministry, but they were even more bitter against their fellow countrymen, who seemed bent on betraying their cause. The letters of James Warren and of the 'brace of Adamses' show, during the ten years before Independence was resolved upon, a deeper hate of Bernard and the Hutchinsons and Olivers — rulers of Massachusetts under the old colonial régime — than of the British Ministry. The Adamses believed that the Hutchinsons and Olivers put the British Government up to Stamp Acts, and all other oppressive measures. It was such men, declared Charles Lee, who totally poisoned the mind of Gage until he could no longer discern facts 'as manifest as the noon-day sun,' leaving him 'consummately ignorant of the principles, temper, disposition and force of the colonies.'[1] Place-men and sycophants they seemed, whose base motives ought to be exposed to the scorn of all good men and lovers of America. While favorites of fortune like the Hutchinsons and Olivers stood in their path, the Adamses could not hope to rise as their talents warranted, and the motive to destroy the prestige of those court sycophants, the ruling aristocracy of Massachusetts, became as great as that to reduce the power of George III. Thus the question who should rule at home had become as vital as the question of 'home rule.'[2] Out of this fact rose much of the rancor against the aristocratic Loyalists, governors, councillors, secretaries, attorneys-general, chief justices, or those, at least, through wealth and social graces, admitted to their caste.

There was, of course, much more stirring in a Patriot's breast than jealousy of fortune and envy of power. There were sincere hopes for a better world, one where the rich and the socially elect would not control government for the good and increase of their privileges, but where the poor man would have his voice and the sick and weary would be at rest under rulers with a benevolent interest in their welfare. Such men dreamed of sweeping away the political evils of their day and setting up a better and purer state.

One of them, Samuel Adams, had dreams which democracy has never realized. He scorned those

[1] Fonblanque, *John Burgoyne,* 164.

[2] *American Historical Review,* XXIX, 345.

'men who are afraid of a free government, lest it should be perverted, and be made use of as a cloke for Licenciousness. The Fear of the People's abusing their Liberty is made an argument against their having the enjoyment of it,' he wrote with a sneer.[1] He dreamed of a democratic Utopia where 'corrupt men may be kept out of places of public trust.' He warned his friends, nevertheless, that demagogues would 'put on the appearance and even speak boldly the language of patriots,' hoping to get the loaves and fishes. But, he cautioned, 'we must examine their views and pretensions. Jealousy is necessary in this degenerate state of mankind.' Also, he urged, 'prevent a plurality of places' being given one man. Here is the 'golden opportunity of restoring the ancient purity of principles and manners in our own country.'[2] To the Continental Congress especially Adams wanted the best men sent — 'men of moderate abilities, especially when weakened with Age, are not fit to be employed in *founding Empires.*' To realize this political dream of Alnaschar, he believed the wheels of Providence to be in their swiftest motion, that the age of George III would produce the 'grandest revolution the world had ever seen.'[3] Adams was not alone in having these dreams. John Marshall, with a much sounder mentality, remembered long after what crazy ideas he entertained at the time.[4] Into the Patriot party went men with

[1] Samuel Adams, *Writings*, III, 244 (December 26, 1775).
[2] *Ibid.*, III, 230 (October 29, 1775).
[3] *Ibid.*, III, 234–35 (November 4, 1775).
[4] *Atlantic Monthly*, July, 1920.

these golden dreams along with much of a far baser alloy.

Nor were political Utopias the only dreams that fired the Patriot zeal for an independent future. There were visions of economic potentialities to be exploited solely by Americans. As they gazed westward and over their continent they foresaw the 'vast Desert,' 'residence of Wild Beasts,' broken up. Arts and sciences would anon change the face of nature. Stone from vast quarries would be piled into great cities. Inestimable treasures of gold and silver, 'Huge mountains of Iron Ore,' more useful than gold, were vast stores that would employ millions of hands in future generations. Not only the 'martial sword' and the peaceful plowshare, but an infinity of utensils would be wrought. 'Ye unborn Inhabitants of America' were called upon to note that all this had been foreseen long before the Revolution.[1] To exploit this fairest of created worlds Americans must be able to guide their own destinies. The events of Lexington and Concord freed all the contents of Pandora's box. British and American charges and countercharges, false rumors spreading through all the colonies, the hastening of military preparations everywhere, the free use of that noxious word 'rebellion,' the loosing of the Whig mobs, and the revealing of class hate, dreams of political and economic millenniums, all set up such a train of events as made war for independence, unconscious at first, the inevitable end.

[1] Nathaniel Ames, *Almanac for 1758.*

CHAPTER III

BUNKER HILL AND CONGRESS FAN THE FIRES OF REBELLION

FEELING ran to fever height as the armed farmers gathered about Boston. The 'Minute-Men,' nevertheless, having come at the signal of danger, and having chased the British into Boston, felt no obligation to remain longer. The besieging force began to melt away before the Provincial authorities got their breath and resolved to enlist a more permanent army. Men who had come in the clothes they had happened to wear when they left the plow, and who had not a farthing in money, were in no frame of mind to stay. All was confusion and turmoil. With some sixteen thousand soldiers to be fed and bedded, with no commissariat or military order, and with men whose training was made up of a few short drills, a day or so of musketry practice,[1] and a sham battle or two, there was not perfect promise in the fact that the individuals were brave, accustomed to long journeys, and used to firing guns at game in a semi-wild country.

At first there was a commandeering of kettles and food to put in them until the Provincial stores could be delivered. Disobedient soldiers had to be threatened, thieving soldiers had to be whipped. Grogshops were put under restrictions to stop the drunkenness, which even thirty-nine lashes and discharge

[1] *Dartmouth MSS.* (W.L.C.L.), *passim.*

from the army would not cure. There were also efforts to make a God-fearing army. Orders were issued that on Sunday no drums were to be beaten after the parson was on the stage, and 'Prophain Cursing and Swearing and all Indesant Language' was not tolerated.[1] Most of the army lived in huts made of boards, turf, stones, or even brush, the Rhode Island troops alone dwelling in tents. Discipline was little heeded in the relation of officers and soldiers, even the pay being sometimes the same and privates often choosing their commanders, stoutly insisting, too, upon social equality.[2] It was June before there was around Boston anything like a permanent force, and the army had meanwhile been in a constant state of flux.

The officers were mostly veterans of the French and Indian wars — now some ten years in retrospect — or, perhaps, mere popular leaders. General Artemas Ward, an Indian war veteran, had risen from a sick-bed and galloped over a rough road from Shrewsbury to Cambridge to take command, under the Committee of Safety, of the besieging forces.[3] Such troops as came from New Hampshire, Rhode Island, and Connecticut were under their Provincial leaders. This motley collection of soldiers — some sixteen thousand men in all [4] — was extended from

[1] L. C. Hatch, *The Administration of the Revolutionary Army*, 1–3; Conn. Hist. Soc., *Collections*, VII, 13, 15, 20, 28, 48.

[2] Hatch, *Administration of the Revolutionary Army*, 1–3.

[3] C. Martyn, *Artemas Ward*, 89.

[4] The number of soldiers actually in camp *all* the time was, perhaps, not so large, but whenever there was an action, General Howe wrote, the whole country came in. *Correspondence of King George III*, III, 223.

Jamaica Plain to Charlestown Neck, with special strength behind the narrow isthmus to the south of Boston, which alone in that day connected the town with the mainland. Headquarters were at Cambridge, where academic interests gave way to military needs, and Harvard College halls became barracks. The ambition of the army was to drive the British out of Boston, and, if not into the sea, at least into their ships. Capture was out of the question, for the British enjoyed then, as throughout the war until the fatal day at Yorktown, control of the sea, which enabled them to rescue hard-pressed commanders if they but kept in touch with the salt water.

Within the town of Boston were huddled not only the British army, but all the Loyalist refugees, and there was much misery. 'You who riot in pleasure in London,' wrote Peter Oliver, 'know nothing of the distress in Boston, you can regale upon delicacies whilst we are in the rotations of Salt Beef and salt pork one day and the next chewing upon Salt Pork and Salt Beef. The very rats are grown so familiar that they ask you to eat them, for they say that they have ate up the sills already and they must now go upon the clapboards.'[1] Indeed, there was constant complaint from British officers in America of the stores sent to them from the corrupt British War Office — even the tents being reported so bad that they would not turn the rain, thus leaving the men constantly wet.[2]

[1] British Museum, *Egerton MSS.*, 2659, F 141.

[2] P.R.O., *War Office, In Letters*, 2, *passim.*

After the reënforcements which arrived with three major-generals, Howe, Burgoyne, and Clinton, on May 24, Gage had on paper over thirteen thousand men.[1] In spite of bitter complaint by the Whigs against the 'savage barbarity' of these 'lawless free-booters,' this 'banditti,' this 'hellish gang,' let loose to rob and rape and murder, making it 'unsafe to walk the streets at noonday,' [2] the British army in Boston seems to have behaved about as well as any army in like position of which there is historical record. A few facetious officers at a play had made the people chorus 'God save the King' and 'Rule Britannia.' They confessed to having been '*un peu énivrés*,' and were no doubt supercilious, and had a trying air of tranquil superiority, but conscious of the fifty thousand pounds a year which their regiments brought to America plus the labor of their soldiers, they could not imagine themselves unendurable.[3] Nevertheless, Hannah Winthrop believed Gage's cruelties 'made human nature shudder,' and that there never was 'but one parallel Tyrant, Cæsar Borgia,' but she was thinking of a 'tender husband detained in cruel captivity from the wife of his bosom.' [4] Gage believed as firmly that the people of Massachusetts were 'the infatuated Multitudes' long led by well-known 'Incendiaries and Traitors' until they were in a state of rebellion.[5]

[1] *William Howe's Orderly Book* (1775), xvi.
[2] Moore, *Diary of the Revolution,* 54–55.
[3] British Museum, *Egerton MSS.,* 2659, F 16.
[4] *Warren-Adams Letters,* i, 102.
[5] *Essex Gazette,* June 15, 1775.

Earl Percy, serving under Gage and soon made major-general, found the Boston people 'quick and violent,' rash and timid, and 'like all other cowards . . . cruel and tyrannical.' By the time this friendly and liberal officer had been in their midst four months, he despised them completely.[1]

This young nobleman was impressed, as many of his fellow officers were, by the folly of a rebellion in this prosperous land, more free than England itself. As Earl Percy rode about Boston, he noted the landscape beauties, delightfully varied, 'the hills, rising from the valleys by gradual and gentle ascents, interspersed everywhere with trees . . . and the small lakes of water with which the country abounds,' adding to the richness of the scene. He thought a landscape gardener useless in a land where Nature had dressed the ground in a way no art could equal, and all the countryside was like a park finely laid out.[2] It was in his eyes a paradise where only man was vile.

The only people of Massachusetts with whom the British officers had anything in common were the Tory aristocrats, who came pouring into Boston with tales of persecution by Whig mobs. About the firesides in loyal homes the British listened in horror to terrified men and women telling of boycotts, threats of tar and feathers, mutilated cattle, battered and ruined homes. The British officer thought it sheer nonsense that a people who had done these barbarous things to neighbors, guilty, perhaps, only

[1] *Letters of Hugh, Earl Percy* (Bolton ed., 1902), 28, 29.

[2] *Ibid.*, 32.

of signing an 'Address,' should set up an uproar about 'slavery and oppression.' On the whole, they were very contemptuous of the 'ragamuffins,' and doubted whether anything but 'drunkenness or madness' would force them to molest the British army. In England, the Government journals had declared that only rum and the belief that 60,000 citizens of London, armed in America's behalf, were encamped on Blackheath under Wilkes, the Lord Mayor, had emboldened the farmers to fight at Lexington and Concord.[1] British officers, in general, agreed with Gage that Americans would be lions only while the British were lambs. The rebellious Bostonians were 'men in a high fever,' and bleeding would 'bring them to their senses.'[2]

This was the British state of mind when a sudden resolution of the besieging army brought on the event which goes down in history as the Battle of Bunker Hill. The British occupation of Boston could be threatened from two elevations, Bunker Hill and Dorchester Heights, across the waters to the northeast and the southwest. From no other points could the town be made untenable by the artillery of that day. Immediately after Lexington, Admiral Graves had proposed seizing and fortifying the heights of Charlestown, but the idea was rejected as rash.[3] Upon the arrival of Howe, Clinton,

[1] *London Chronicle*, July 13, 18, 1775, August 15, 1775, *Gloucester Journal*, July 10, 1775.

[2] *Letters of Hugh, Earl Percy*, 35, 62. *Correspondence of George III to Lord North.* (Donne ed.), *passim.* Hist. MSS. Com., *Various MSS.*, VI, 117.

[3] British Museum, *Add. MSS.* (L. C. Trans.), 14038, F 50.

and Burgoyne, it was, however, planned by Gage with his increased force to extend his lines to the menacing hills. Proclaiming pardon to all rebels except Hancock and Samuel Adams, Gage was about to strike terror to all men in arms against him, when he was forestalled at the northern danger point, on Charlestown Peninsula, by the 'rebel' leaders with some twelve hundred men seizing and fortifying, June 16, in the evening, Breed's Hill, even nearer to Boston than Bunker Hill.

The nature of the American force and the actual chief of command has been a controversial matter for generations. Charles Lee, who at least had a soldier's eye if not his honor and character, said the 'Americans were composed in part of raw lads and old men, half armed, with no practice or discipline, commanded without order, and God knows by whom.'[1] Though pride and prestige alone kept the British at Boston, since New York was the real strategic center of America, yet it was resolved at once to seize the six-foot redoubt which Colonel Prescott's regiment with the aid of others had raised on Breed's Hill during the night.[2] The American advance so far from Charlestown Neck, their only

[1] H. Murdock, *Bunker Hill*, 79.

[2] A list of the regiments, portions of which took part in the battle, is found in Frothingham's *Siege of Boston*, 401–04. Chapters IV–VII have a full account of the battle of Bunker Hill. The British sentries on the Boston side had heard the Patriots at work all night, and made *no report* of it. Gage heard nothing of it until the ships began firing on the breastwork in the morning. See remarkable letter of General Howe's describing the whole battle in *Correspondence of King George III*, III, 220–24. Harold Murdock's *Bunker Hill* is the best critical study, and is very good reading as well.

exit from the peninsula, was a piece of folly easily fatal but that it was matched by equal British folly. With complete control of the sea, the British had only to seize the causeway over which Prescott had come, and the whole American force was shut up in the peninsula as in a bag, but, instead, the weight of opinion in the council of war was in favor of a direct attack.[1] Prescott had thrust his head in the lion's mouth, but the beast was too proud to close his jaws.[2] Under General Howe's command, the British set about driving the 'peasants' out of the trap with three thousand veteran soldiers.

It was shining noon of a beautiful June day before the British troops began to cross the river in boats. Meanwhile, Connecticut and New Hampshire men, and eager individuals like Joseph Warren and Israel Putnam, had passed the light barrage which British ships laid across the causeway and had joined Prescott at Breed's Hill. It was three of the afternoon before the British were ready to attack. Thereupon began a spectacle rivaled only by a twentieth-century football game in a huge stadium, for, the air being clear and dry, it was possible for thousands of eager onlookers on the housetops, in

[1] Only one good practical reason can be seen. The British army did not have 'proper boats for landing troops.' *Correspondence of King George III*, III, 216.

[2] C. F. Adams, *Studies in Military and Diplomatic History*, 3, 18, 19. See also *American Historical Review*, I, 401. Mass. Hist. Soc., *Proceedings* (1910), Vol. 44, p. 96. The only valid argument against the seizure of the Neck and then Bunker Hill was the danger of putting the British troops between two parts of the American army. The *Detail and Conduct of the American War* (ed. 1780), 14. A British officer, in a letter of July 5, 1775, shows clearly how the Americans could have been shut up 'as in a bag.'

the windows of Boston, and on the very church steeples, to watch every figure in this fateful combat. They could see the cannon on Copp's Hill in Boston playing upon Charlestown and upon Prescott's redoubt on Breed's Hill. They could see the Lively and the Falcon reënforcing that fire with shells. Howe and Pigot were visible leading their redcoated soldiers, burdened with heavy knapsacks,[1] the first, straight against Prescott's redoubt, the other, leading his men against a stone and rail fence behind which Stark and Putnam sought to prevent a British flank movement to get possession of Bunker Hill in Prescott's rear. The protected Patriot troops were seen to hold their ground until the British were not fifty yards distant, and then to fire a deadly volley, mowing down the front rank as with the swish of a modern machine gun.[2] The line was seen to break but probably did not, as tradition has it, retreat in haste to their boats. It staggered, reformed, and marched on toward its goal.[3]

Before the astonished spectators in Boston could get breath, Charlestown was seen to have been fired by the shells of the fleet or from Copp's Hill, because the British were badly galled by fire from its wooden houses.[4] Nearly four hundred wooden houses went

[1] If, as Stedman declares, the equipment of the British soldier weighed one hundred and twenty-five pounds (*American War*, I, 128), the wonder is that they climbed the hill at all.

[2] Frothingham, *Siege of Boston*, 141. H. Murdock, *Bunker Hill*, 68–71.

[3] *Ibid*, 70–72.

[4] *The Detail and Conduct of the American War* (3d ed.), 14. In some undated notes in Clinton's wretched handwriting (*Clinton Papers*), he seems to state positively that Howe and the admiral gave orders

up in flame and smoke. Meanwhile, the watchers beheld the plucky British columns advance again. General Howe, leading wherever he asked his men to go, seemed to bear a charmed life that day, standing alone at times among the slain. Once more his men met at thirty yards the murderous fire. Another halt, a long delay, and the brave 'Redcoats' thrilled the Boston observers by doggedly continuing the attack.

This time Sir Henry Clinton, a volunteer, bringing some five hundred men, came into the action, 'spiriting on the troops in the noblest manner,' only to get a letter in due time from his influential cousin, the Duke of Newcastle, calling him an 'idle wanton volunteer' and chiding him for forgetting his children. Though Clinton's 'happy pride' was almost crushed at the time, the noble Duke repented his foolish letter in a few months, and doubtless used his powerful influence to get Clinton made commander of the ill-fated expedition against Charleston in the following year.[1] Moreover, military opinion at the time of Bunker Hill complimented his judgment, coolness, and decision, and gave him general applause for saving the day.[2]

'to fire the town of C. by carcass.' Howe gives the same testimony. *Correspondence of King George III*, III, 222. Further proof is in British Museum, *Add. MSS.* (L. C. Trans.), 14038, I, f. 64, p. 120.

[1] *Clinton Papers* (W.L.C.L.), Grosvenor Street, Saturday, 1775, and April 3, 1776. General Phillips to Duke of Newcastle (copy) and General Phillips to Clinton.

[2] *Clinton Papers* (W.L.C.L.), Howe to Clinton, October 1, 1775. *Ibid.*, Gage to Clinton, October 16, October 19, 1775. Howe seems to have been too general in his report of this gallant episode at the time, and much ill-feeling grew out of it. Clinton made a sketch of Charlestown, the hill, his place of landing, and the position of the ships, which is among the *Clinton Papers*.

As the British again resumed the charge up the hill, it was plain that the Patriot powder-horns were empty; the shots from behind the breastworks were few and scattered, and the British entered the redoubt, drove the half-armed soldiers out, and pursued them a short way toward their gateway of escape. Their retreat was 'no flight; was covered with bravery and even military skill,' wrote Burgoyne, and they went no farther than the nearest hill, where they took a new post and entrenched again.[1] Among the Americans slain was Joseph Warren, a leader of great promise, whose loss was heavy to bear.

Gage, reporting the Bunker Hill battle to Lord Barrington in the War Office, said, 'This action has shown the superiority of the King's troops who under every disadvantage attacked and defeated above three times their own number, strongly posted and covered by breast-works.'[2] The relative numbers were almost exactly the reverse of his estimate, and if the American supply of powder had held out, there is grave doubt as to whether Prescott could have been dislodged except by a complete change of tactics. Gage did admit that 'the rebels were not the despicable rabble' he had supposed,[3] and that

[1] *Correspondence of King George III*, III, 225.

[2] P.R.O., War Office, *In Letters*, II, F 243. General Howe had the same exaggerated idea of the 'rebel' numbers. *Correspondence of King George III*, III, 223. For William Howe's report to Gage see document from the *Firle Papers*, quoted in full in H. Belcher, *First American Civil War*, I, 196–98.

[3] Gage's return to the War Office of killed and wounded was:

Dead: Colonels, 1; Majors, 2; Captains, 7; Lieutenants, 9; Sergeants, 15; Drum Officers, 1; Rank and file, 191.

Wounded: Colonels, 2; Majors, 3; Captains, 27; Lieutenants, 32; Ensigns, 8; Sergeants, 40; Drum Officers, 12; Rank and file, 706.

Public Record Office, War Office, *In Letters*, II, F 243.

the killed and wounded were greater in number than he could afford. Lord North wrote that he would 'abandon the contest' were he not 'most intimately convinced' in his conscience that the British cause was just and important. 'The number of wounded and killed makes my heart bleed,' he wrote.[1]

Burgoyne, however, thought nothing had happened at Bunker Hill that raised the American soldiers 'one jot above the level of all men expert in the use of firearms. Corsicans, Miquelets, Croats, Tartars, mountainers and borderers have in almost all countries . . . done much more hardy things than defend one of the strongest posts that nature and art combined could make, and then run away.' He thought it all nonsense to compare their courage with Sparta and Athens. In Burgoyne's opinion the battle reëstablished 'the ascendency of the King's troops in public opinion.' We can now rest on our arms, he wrote, even close the war, leaving a good impression as to English power. Since the safety of states in general depends, he reflected, on the idea that trained troops are invincible against any number or any position of 'undisciplined rabble,' the results of Bunker Hill will restore 'the general repose of mankind' so sadly shaken by the 19th of April.[2]

Yet in spite of Burgoyne's cheerful optimism, the British army, first under Gage and then under Howe, remained nine mortal months after Bunker Hill, shut up in Boston. Among Sir Henry Clinton's

[1] Hist. MSS., Com., *Report*, x, App., part 6, p. 10.

[2] *Germain Papers* (W.L.C.L.), Burgoyne to Germain, August 30, 1775.

papers lie many plans for bombarding the 'rebels,' trying their mettle, sorties against weak points in their lines, ventures of the fleet up the Mystic, up the Charles River, yet all ended with the flow of ink, the consuming of paper, but final inaction. Nevertheless the loss of 1054 out of some 3000 men engaged, and with a far too great proportion of officers, was too high a price to pay for scarce enough territory to bury the slain. More such victories would ruin the army.[1] The American loss, concealed from the enemy, 'in the Indian style,' was, in killed and wounded, 449 out of some 1500 engaged.[2]

The moral victory of the colonists brought more joy than sorrow in London, judging from the newspapers. The news found the members of the Ministry scattered all over the kingdom, only the Chancellor being in London. They had never taken the war seriously enough to consult with military men, leaving all military preparations to Lord Barrington. Soldiers were writing each other about the Ministry's 'shameless supineness and ignorance.' [3] Friends of America in England asked the Government with a sneer: 'Is every redoubt which the Americans can throw up in a short summer night to be demolished at this expense? How many such victories can we bear?' Even in Lord Sandwich's circle — and none was more scornful of the colonies — there was less talk about 'undisciplined and spiritless Yankees,'

[1] Arthur Lee, *A Second Appeal* (1775), 6. General Phillips to Clinton, *Clinton Papers*, August 2, 1775. 'Too dearly bought,' wrote Howe, *Correspondence of King George III*, III, 223.

[2] Hist. MSS. Com., *14th Report, Rutland MSS.*, III, 3.

[3] *Clinton Papers*, Phillips to Clinton, October 2, 1775.

ardor in the breast of that dashing young Connecticut officer, Benedict Arnold, he sought and secured a commission to recruit a force for the purpose of taking by surprise the ill-guarded forts.[1] Hastening on alone toward the scene of action, he found that Ethan Allen, a bold frontier spirit among the settlers in the New Hampshire Grant, had been inspired with the same idea, and had already enlisted his hardy Green Mountain boys for the desperate venture. Arnold joined as a volunteer, and the company hastened on to Lake Champlain, which they crossed in such boats as were found. By stealth they entered the fort, surprised the commandant, and Allen, as he recorded four years later, demanded a surrender 'in the name of the Great Jehovah and the Continental Congress,' [2] though, in truth, he had no commission from either of those high authorities, and other witnesses reported something about a challenge to a 'd——d old rat' to come out,[3] which was more like the big, rough frontiersman who swaggered and roared oaths famous the country round. Allen's brandished sword convinced the officer of the wisdom of surrender. Although, as Allen relates, his followers began at once to 'toss round the flowing bowl,' yet enough discipline remained so that Crown Point passed into his hands

[1] J. H. Smith, *Our Struggle for the Fourteenth Colony*, I, 117–19.

[2] Ethan Allen, *Narrative*, 1779 (Burlington ed., 1849, p. 98). It is noteworthy that Arnold was the only one who took the pains to apprise the Continental Congress of the capture, and his messenger said that Arnold and men from Connecticut had taken Ticonderoga. *Letters of Members of Continental Congress* (Burnett, ed.), I, 93.

[3] W. C. Todd, *Biography and other Articles*, 104; Goodhue, *Sharham*, 14.

two days later, and when fifty recruits joined Arnold, he placed them on a schooner, sailed north, and took Fort St. John on the Sorel.[1] Over three hundred cannon were taken in these bold ventures, and great stores of warlike supplies which brightened American prospects not a little. They would no longer have to echo Schuyler's cry for 'cutlasses, stinkpots and hand-grenades.'

Even while the curtain was rising on this dramatic act, the Second Continental Congress, chosen by colonial legislatures or lower houses of them and by conventions or congresses of irregular and unconstitutional nature, had come together in Philadelphia.[2] The Bostonian delegates, already wearied with triumphal processions along the whole way, with escorts of militia and sentinels at their doors, were given a grand public entry, being met six miles out of the Quaker city by some five hundred militia officers with drawn swords, and gentlemen on horseback.[3] From two miles out, companies of riflemen and of infantry, headed by a band, escorted them through the streets at a slow, solemn pace amidst the plaudits of fifteen thousand people and all the bells of the city ringing and chiming. Of the whole affair Adams declared no martial tale could equal

[1] J. H. Smith, *Our Struggle for the Fourteenth Colony*, I, 156–57.

[2] *Journals of the Continental Congress* (Ford, ed.), II. Delaware, Rhode Island and Pennsylvania by legislatures; South Carolina, New Jersey and Virginia by lower houses, and the remainder by congresses and conventions.

[3] When the people wished to take the horses from the carriage and drag it, Hancock rather wished the experience, but Samuel Adams would not let his fellow citizens 'degrade themselves into beasts' and threatened to get out and walk. L. Sears, *J. Hancock*, 175.

it.[1] Galloway, the Loyalist, it was reported, had fled; Dr. Franklin had returned from London, sure that there was no getting on with the mother country; and it was plain that this Congress was more radical than the last. At once, wrote John Adams, 'such a vast Multitude of Objects, civil, political, commercial and military, press and crowd upon us . . ., that We know not what to do first.' [2] Absolute secrecy was agreed upon, and the famous Congress began its fateful work.

John Adams found that the general sense of the Congress was 'to prepare for defensive War, but at the Same Time to keep open the Door of Reconciliation — to hold the Sword in one hand and the olive Branch in the other — to proceed with Warlike Measures, and conciliatory Measures Pari Passu.' Adams himself was for a major operation at once, because the 'cancer was too deep rooted,' but he admitted that Congress must go slowly because the continent was a vast, unwieldy machine; [3] or, changing his figure, he likened it to 'a large fleet sailing under convoy. The fleetest sailers must wait for the dullest and slowest.' As a result there was necessary a 'strange Oscillation between love and hatred, between War and Peace.' [4] Nearly all, however, approved when Duché, their chaplain, preached

[1] Moore, *Diary of the Revolution*, 77; *Letters of . . . Continental Congress* (Burnett, ed.), I, 90; Curwen's *Journal*, May 10, 1775. *Diary of C. Marshall*, 25, shows that Southern delegates were met with like ceremony.

[2] *Warren-Adams Letters*, I, 51.

[3] *Letters of . . . Continental Congress* (Burnett, ed.), I, 118, 132.

[4] *Ibid.*, I, 152.

from the text, 'Stand fast therefore in the liberty wherewith Christ hath made us free.' [1]

With no purpose of fighting for independence, therefore, the Congress continued for at least six or seven months to take every warlike measure, duly mixed with efforts at reconciliation, as would bring the King and his Ministers to the American terms of living within the Empire. It is curious that after Lexington and Concord, after Crown Point and Ticonderoga, even after the bloody fight at Bunker Hill, the Congress went on palliating non-importation and non-exportation as a peaceful means of getting American rights. It went on 'raising armies' because of an 'ardent desire for harmony.' It continued 'cheerfully bleeding' in a righteous cause, because it wished 'reconciliation.' It explained that in taking up arms, it was not seeking disunion. While 'forcing Britain to terms,' it asserted that its followers were 'trying to be obedient subjects.' [2] And the most amazing thing about this apparent inconsistency, all these resolves were in perfect good faith as far as the majority mind was concerned.

As the historian pores over the journals of the Congress, or the letters and diaries of its members, he finds that the word 'gunpowder' sprinkles every page, that sulphur and saltpeter and guns are of absorbing interest, and that Congress preferred to issue floods of paper money rather than propose

[1] Duché, *Sermon*, 1.

[2] *Journals of Continental Congress* (Ford, ed.), II, 87, 88, 139, 154, 160, 171, 198, 205, 217; III, 321, 489; IV, 137, 138, 142, 146. July 6, 1775.

taxation to a people imbued with the idea that they were making war to avoid a tax. Men feared that there was not virtue enough in the country to bear heavy taxes with patience. One of the big problems was to adapt to the new war conditions the Continental Association, with its non-importation already in effect and its non-exportation to be enforced after the 10th of September. They were, they confessed, 'between hawk and buzzard,' puzzling themselves between warlike and commercial opposition. Some day they must decide between a reconciliation with Great Britain or the means of carrying on war. That they did delay so long proves the unreason of those who charged them with the original intention of seceding from Great Britain and forming an independent empire. They at last approved the secret importation of munitions (July 15, 1775) in spite of the Association,[1] and, indeed, as the months wore on, they practically annulled the prohibitions of both outgoing and incoming commerce. The Bermudas were given food in exchange for munitions, and even some export was allowed to Great Britain and her West Indian Isles, if in exchange some munitions were acquired. At last (January, 1776) even dry goods and merchandise were likewise admitted.[2] A month earlier, Congress had authorized the seizure of British ships carrying troops and supplies to America, hoping to increase the colonies' scanty stores by confiscation of goods and munitions sent

[1] *Journals of Continental Congress* (Ford, ed.), II, 184; III, 306; *Letters of . . . Congress* (Burnett, ed.), I, 437.

[2] Schlesinger, *Colonial Merchants*, 567–68.

to accomplish their own subjugation.[1] Agricultural America could not auspiciously open the gates of the Temple of Janus unless they could admit the products of the manufacturing world.

As the dreaded day set for ceasing exportation drew near, the merchants discounted its effects by increasing their outward-bound trade. There was a forty per cent increase for the colonies as a whole during the year that preceded September 10, 1775. So little did commerce take account of the military needs of the country that General Greene declared the merchants in general 'a body of people whose God is gain,' and who wanted public measures to square with their private interests.[2] In the last week of open trade, all was bustle at the ports and fifty-two vessels sailed from Philadelphia, leaving hardly a ship behind. Additional water transport could not be had for any price, and millers who had hurried their flour to the wharves offered reckless bargains in vain.[3] Hovering British warships, enforcing a 'Restraining Act' of Parliament, aided the enforcement inadvertently, and though there was some smuggling, yet the non-exportation regulations were well kept. After some four months of non-exportation, however, the cries of distress from the mercantile and agrarian interests became so loud that, early in 1776, Congress began to talk of opening the ports to all the world. Repudiate the Navigation Act and all acts of trade, cried the radicals,

[1] *Journals of Continental Congress* (Ford, ed.), III, 437.

[2] *Greene Papers* (W.L.C.L.), Greene to Ward, October 23, 1775; December 18, 1775; December 31, 1775.

[3] Schlesinger, *Colonial Merchants*, 570–72.

militia besides, and music playing. Even Hancock wrote of Washington to New England friends, 'He is a fine man,' a 'gentleman you will all like'; and Eliphalet Dyer, though fearing Washington was too modest, believed him 'discreet and Virtuous, no harum scarum ranting swearing fellow but sober, steady, and calm.'[1] With such recommendations Washington arrived at Cambridge on July 2, and on the following day took command of his army which was still at a high pitch of excitement over the events of Bunker Hill.

At once there was a change in the conduct of the army. Greene saw joy visible in every countenance, for Washington was 'universally admired.' The spirit of conquest seemed to breathe through the whole army, wrote Greene, and he hoped now for a better order and strictness of discipline which would insure victory.[2] The father of Ralph Waldo Emerson wrote at the time: 'There is a great over turning in the camp, as to order and regularity. New lords, new laws. The Generals Washington and Lee are upon the lines every day. New orders from his excellency are read to the respective regiments every morning after prayers. The strictest government is taking place, and great distinction is made between officers and soldiers. Every one is made to know his place and keep it, or be tied up and receive thirty or forty lashes, according to his crime. Thousands are at work every day from four till eleven o'clock in the morning. . . . All the lands, fields, orchards, laid

[1] *Letters of . . . Continental Congress* (Burnett, ed.), I, 128.

[2] *Greene Papers* (W.L.C.L.), July 14, 1775.

common — horses and cattle feeding in the choicest mowing land, whole fields of corn eaten down to the ground, and large parks of well-regulated locusts cut down for firewood and other public uses.'[1] When Washington rode through the camp, Thacher thought it was not difficult to distinguish him from the military men about him. 'His personal appearance is truly noble and majestic, being tall and well proportioned. His dress is a blue coat with buff colored facings, a rich epaulette on each shoulder, buff under dress, and an elegant small sword, a black cockade in his hat.'[2] Abigail Adams thought the gentleman and soldier agreeably blended in him; that modesty marked every line and feature of his face, where was dignity, ease, and complacency.[3]

Washington needed all his complacency, for he found corruption, jealousy, provincial rivalry, and lack of discipline which neither lashes, fines, the pillory, the wooden horse, nor even drumming out of camp would cure. Men seemed to wish to be bribed into the preservation of their liberties, and Washington declared that one army was actually disbanded and another raised in the very sight of the enemy in Boston. 'Such dearth of public spirit,' he cried, 'and want of virtue, such stock-jobbing, and fertility in all the low arts to obtain advantages of one kind or another . . . I never saw before and pray

[1] Washington, *Letters* (Sparks, ed.), III, 491.

[2] James Thacher, *A Military Journal* (2d ed.), 33.

[3] Adams, *Familiar Letters*, July 16, 1775. She recalled Dryden's lines: 'Mark his majestic fabric, he's a temple — sacred by birth, and built by hands divine; His soul's the deity that lodges there; Nor is the pile unworthy of the god.'

God I may never witness again.' He wondered that he did not retire to the back-country and live in a wigwam, and doubted whether one could search the volumes of history through and find a case similar to his. General Greene fully agreed with him.[1] No conventionally trained soldier would have tried with armed farmers to drive Gage with well-drilled soldiers out of Boston. According to all the books on war, it could not be done. But all Washington's moral intuitions told him that to abandon this task — however madly undertaken — would be a fatal blow to the cause. 'Battles are won in the hearts of men,' and Washington must dare even the impossible rather than risk any blow to the faith of his army.

While Washington's 'hasty concourse' of men, being drilled into an army, was holding the British penned up in Boston, Congress had decided upon an invasion of Canada, on the assumption that the people there might wish, as a fourteenth province, to join the rebellious colonists, and with the conviction also that the strategic importance was great. If the British could control the line of water communications from the St. Lawrence through Lake Champlain, Lake George, and on down the Hudson, they might form in Canada an expedition which would cut the colonies along that line, isolate the New England colonies, and conquer them at leisure. Moreover, it was believed that in the hands of the British, led by so able a general as Sir Guy Carleton, it would enable them to inflame all the

[1] Washington, *Writings* (Ford, ed.), III, 246–47, November 28, 1775. Frothingham, *Siege of Boston*, 285–86.

Indians in America, and to pour down regulars and Canadians as well as savages upon the northern borders.[1] By autumn two American expeditions, under the supreme command of General Schuyler, were bound northward to seize Montreal and Quebec.[2] Young Richard Montgomery, an Irish officer, who had become enamored of the Patriot cause, led one expedition. His army took advantage of the possession of Crown Point and Ticonderoga and pushed, by the Lake Champlain route, to Montreal, which it captured in November. This it accomplished, though the troops, as Montgomery wrote, 1775, were 'exceedingly turbulent, even mutinous,' the 'privates all generals.'

The other expedition, under Benedict Arnold, made an heroic march, with incredible hardships — a march 'Hannibal might have admired' — from the Kennebec through the almost impenetrable Maine forest, reaching the St. Lawrence in November, ready to coöperate with Montgomery in an attack on Quebec. The leaders of both armies did all that heroes could do, but on the last day of 1775 their desperate assault failed, Montgomery fell before the walls of Quebec, and though Arnold, urged by Washington and Congress, clung to the task for several months, it had at last to be abandoned.[3] It was an heroic episode, never to be for-

[1] *Letters of . . . Continental Congress* (Burnett, ed.), I, 355.

[2] Schuyler soon became ill and was obliged to return, leaving Montgomery in actual command.

[3] The best and fullest account of this expedition is J. H. Smith, *Our Struggle for the Fourteenth Colony*, 2 vols. C. H. Jones, *History of the Campaign for . . . Canada*, is useful.

gotten as an example of desperate valor and almost invincible spirit on the part of the leaders, but it had few results except to divide Howe's army in 1776, and to delay the British offensive, bound to come from the Canadian direction as soon as the North Ministry fully grasped the size of its problem. An ill effect for the American cause was that it aroused great wrath in England, because it carried war into another province of the Empire. Minds too dull to be awakened by Lexington and the siege of Boston were stirred to action by this 'treason to the empire.' Moreover, it aroused the lethargic Ministry, which was so alarmed for the safety of Quebec that it warned all vessels leaving England in January, 1776, not to venture up the St. Lawrence unless they were sure Quebec had not fallen. All orders sent out from December to March provided a successor to Carleton, should he be killed or taken prisoner.[1]

The reasons for the failure of the expedition, upon the success of which, Washington believed, the interests and salvation of 'our bleeding country' in a great degree depended, are hard to draw from the tangle of interweaving and contrary forces. Some have thought that the Quebec Act kept the mass of the Canadians loyal, but in some cases the effect of that most unfortunate of well-meant laws — fostered, it would seem, by some malign genius — was alienation, especially when misrepresented and misunderstood. The Act was associated in American minds with the Boston coercive measures, and, on

[1] P.R.O., *Colonial Office*, Class 5–123, p. 95, and Class 5–253, p. 213.

the other hand, was easily represented to the Canadian peasantry as again setting up the compulsory tithe system. That Act of Parliament, passed doubtless for the good of the French Canadians, became often the object of their discontent and dislike. Yet, in spite of all the propaganda, the promises and threats of the Congress agents, the simple-minded Canadian peasants knew that under the British rulers they could worship freely, that their old ways of life were unchanged, their priests unmolested, and a spirit of tolerance brooded over all.

Before the American invasion began, an act of vandalism in Montreal suggested the state of the *habitant's* loyalty to his British sovereign. The King's bust in a park was disfigured, and about its neck was hung a chaplet of potatoes with a wooden cross and a label, 'Le pape de Canada ou le sot Anglais.' [1] Yet, if the Catholic Canadians could not love their conquerors, the British Redcoats, neither could they embrace the older, more hated enemy, the bigoted New-Englander. They were not unready to listen to General Washington's address which urged their 'brethren' to unite with the colonies 'in an indissoluble union' and to 'run together to the same goal,' [2] yet their credulity was not equal to

[1] *American Catholic Historical Research* (n.s.), v (January), 86–87. Nevertheless, Baron de Kalb found in Canada few people with any affection for France. They were happy under the new government, taxes less, lands worth more, their conscience free, and they shared in their own rule. Bib. Nat'l. MSS., *Fr. Nouvelle Acq.*, 9435, F 375.

[2] *Essex Gazette*, September 28, 1775. Dr. Johnson exposed the inconsistency of the American protest against the Quebec Act, giving religious freedom to the Papists there, and Congress's appeal to

believing that the old religious prejudice was quite blown away by the breath of freedom.

The masses, therefore, were quite neutral, and only the clergy, and the French *noblesse*, much favored by the English Government, and encouraged to hope for a renewal of their old privileges, were faithful to the British rule at this crisis. The Roman clergy, thought Condorcet, preferred to be tolerated, but protected, by the British Government, rather than to see established 'a liberty of opinion always so alarming to men accustomed to dominate men's souls.' [1] To them, moreover, the New-Englander was raising to empire and independence a confederacy of bigots and enthusiasts, who might perhaps burn Catholics at the stake or oblige them to give up their religion.[2] The clergy, at least, read not only the Congress address to Quebec, which bridged the religious chasm with a disingenuous phrase, but also the earlier address to the British people with its abuse of 'Popery,' and the discrepancy was so gross and palpable that they scorned the 'perfidy of Congress.'

The testimony of Schuyler, Arnold, and Montgomery all agrees, however, that at first the Canadians were friendly and joined in great numbers, but that was at a time when the British were weak

Quebec Catholics to join the thirteen colonies in resistance to 'British tyranny.' *Taxation no Tyranny* (4th ed., 1775), 57–59.

[1] *Éloge de Franklin* (Paris, 1791), 26.

[2] *A Letter from a Gentleman*, etc. (pamphlet, 1775, in W.L.C.L.), 6. Congress made great promises about rights of conscience and free enjoyment of religion, but the memory of the past bigotry of New England could not be wiped out. *Letters of . . . Continental Congress* (Burnett, ed.), I, 227.

and the invaders sweeping swiftly and easily up to the walls of Quebec. Carleton, the British commander, spoke at that time of the stupid baseness of the Canadian peasantry, actually serving with the Americans in every quarter, yet in fact about as many took up arms with the British as with the invaders. Only a few hundred men joined the American standard even at the high tide of success. 'Terrified or corrupted,' Carleton cried, there was no dependence to be placed on them. Yet the masses were neutral, not in opposition. They favored the Americans some until the disaster at Quebec, and even thereafter seemed favorable but timorous. Montgomery would gladly have waited until April to make his attack, when the Quebec garrison would be distressed for food. He attempted the desperate assault in December for the moral effect on the Canadians, who would not relish union with the colonies until they saw the whole country in American hands, 'no longer in danger of falling under the Ministerial lash.' [1] Those 'peasants' who followed the 'rebels,' wrote Burgoyne, did not follow 'the cry of liberty, but the belief of strength.' They used to be subjects of France, 'they were since so to England, they would be the same to the Emperor of Morocco.' [2] They were very kind to the Americans even on the retreat, gave every assistance, and would, perhaps, still have joined an enterprise of vigor.

[1] *Continental Congress Papers* (*Schuyler Letters*), no. 153, I, 394 (Montgomery to Schuyler, December 18, 1775).

[2] *Germain Papers* (W.L.C.L.), Burgoyne to Germain, June 22, 1776.

When Commissioners Charles Carroll, Samuel Chase, and Benjamin Franklin were sent by Congress, in March of 1776, to try their blandishments on the Canadians, they found a surprising change, but thought the Canadian allegiance might even yet be regained. Even later, General Sullivan was affected to see the banks of the Sorel lined with men, women, and children, leaping and clapping their hands for joy 'to see the Americans arrive.' They weakened when moved by fear or the desire of being on the stronger side; and, when their priests refused absolution to those joining the invaders, it was no wonder that they cooled. Nevertheless, there was throughout the Revolution a popular leaning to the American cause, a sympathy, perhaps only skin-deep.[1] The 'better sort of people' wish 'to see our throats cut,' wrote a competent American officer.

One reason why the Americans failed to make a successful Canadian alliance was that the mismanagement and misconduct of officers and men impressed the Canadians with their incapacity. The wonder was that the peasantry kept any degree of respect for an army which by ill-treatment drove them to neutrality if not actual hostility.[2] In spite of Washington's entreaties to use all tact, the Canadians were often treated not even as neutrals, but rather as irreconcilable enemies. In Washington's own army he was obliged to issue an order against

[1] The ablest analyses of this whole Canadian fiasco are in chapter VI of V. Coffin, *The Province of Quebec and the Early American Revolution*, and in R. Coupland, *The Quebec Act*, 160–73, and there are important differences of opinion.

[2] J. H. Smith, *Our Struggle for the Fourteenth Colony*, II, 225–27.

'the ridiculous and childish custom of burning the effigy of the Pope'[1] — a ceremony not likely to convince the Catholic Canadian of American friendship. Schuyler declared, that there was 'disorganization and lawlessness everywhere.'[2] 'The licentiousness of our troops is not easy to be described.' The men were disorderly and disobedient to officers, as in all half-trained armies. There were 'scandalous excesses,' and, as Sullivan wrote, court-martials were in vain where officers connived at the depredations of the men. Promises to pay for the supplies freely furnished were disgracefully repudiated, even before lack of money began to be a cause of failure. The peasants, naturally skeptical of the value of Continental paper money, were dragooned and forced to furnish wood below the current price, and then the price was not paid, or paid only in paper money. Even the clergy, Schuyler wrote, were neglected and sometimes ill-used. Indeed, the priests and the *seigneurs* were bitter enemies of the American invaders, and they were by no means without influence.

General Montgomery thought New England troops 'the worst stuff imaginable for soldiers. They are homesick, their regiments have melted away; there is such an equality among them that officers have no authority . . . the privates are all generals but not soldiers.'[3] Schuyler added his testimony to

[1] Washington, *Letters* (Sparks, ed.), III, 144.

[2] *Continental Congress Papers* (*Schuyler Letters*), no. 153, I, 52.

[3] Lossing, *Schuyler*, I, 427. *Boston in 1775* (S. B. Webb to his brother).

'the scandalous want of subordination . . . ruinous to the army, destructive to the service and disgraceful to those in command.' Greedy officers returned false payrolls and escaped military punishment by timely resignation before discovery.[1] The Commissioners sent by Congress agreed that words could not describe the 'confusion, the unfeeling flight and return at this juncture of the soldiers and the greater part of the officers . . . entitled to be discharged.' Men excused from duty because of pretended illness 'were foremost in flight and carried off such burdens on their backs as hearty and stout men would labour under.'[2] Hearing of these things, John Adams, safe within the four walls of Independence Hall, remembered that 'Flight was unknown to the Romans. I wish it was to Americans. There was a flight from Quebec, and worse than a flight at the Cedars. If we do not atone for these disgraces we are undone.'[3] It was not disease, and short terms merely, but, as Washington said, 'want of discipline and proper regard to the conduct of the soldiers' was the cause of failure.

Perhaps the greatest of all reasons for failure was the utter want of trained organization. It hampered all the early operations of the American armies. Schuyler on his way to Canada, wrote from Ticonderoga, 'not one earthly thing has been done to enable one to move.' 'I have neither boats nor

[1] *Continental Congress Papers* (*Schuyler Letters*), no. 153, I, 20, 351, 352, 367.

[2] *Carroll's Journal*, 38. (Maryland Hist. Soc., 1876.)

[3] *Letters of . . . Continental Congress* (Burnett, ed.), II, 57.

materials to build them.' The ordered stores had not arrived, no nails, no pitch, no oakum. None of the gunpowder, ordered weeks before, had been delivered; the desperate leader was obliged to depend upon getting some at St. John's, 'when we take it.' There was little ammunition, not a gun carriage, and few guns; one poor armorer and no tools for him. In July there were one hundred sick and no hospital stores.

After a month's delay, Schuyler had boats and powder and stores so that he could move one thousand men, and, meanwhile, two hundred had gone off. Disputes and jealousies among the 'Green Mountain boys' had prevented them organizing at all.[1] Meanwhile, Schuyler was in wretched health, writing generously that it was Montgomery who did everything. At last he was obliged to give up altogether, 'not able to hold a pen.' When he had recovered and, in February, 1776, was again in charge of the Northern army, he was driven to desperation by the conduct of the army about Albany and the needs of the forlorn troops still clinging to a few points in Canada. He was 'ashamed of the conduct' of the soldiers stationed near Albany. 'Tories and Whigs are indiscriminately the object of plunder.' 'I have given orders, I have entreated the officers to prevent such scandalous depredations,

[1] *Continental Congress Papers* (*Schuyler Letters*), no. 153, I, 52–128. See especially letter of September 8. Schuyler could not get the Commissary to keep records because he was too ignorant to understand the forms. *Ibid.*, 103.

All the causes of failure are carefully weighed in Coupland, *The Quebec Act.*

but all in vain.' There were many arms taken in the captured garrisons in Canada. Where are they now? Stolen and taken home; only the unfit left in forts. Of the new troops sent to bolster the failing cause, the men from Pennsylvania were 'greatly infected with venerial desease,' fourteen were in the hospital and the medicine all gone. Others from that State had mutinied, and their leaders had been court-martialed and punished. All had arrived in the dead of winter with no mittens or moccasins, their powder supply 'vastly short.' Finally, though the troops in Canada — not at that time quite one thousand — needed everything from shoes to ammunition, he had nothing for them. To cap it all, the Indians were now tormenting him from every quarter, and all his Indian goods to buy their favor were gone.[1] Such was the inglorious close of a venture that in its early, heroic glow had rarely been outshone in history.

Before this tragic failure at Quebec had been consummated, the Boston drama came to a happy ending for the Patriot forces. It was preceded, however, by months of corroding anxiety for the American leaders. 'My situation,' wrote Washington, in September, 1775, 'is inexpressibly distressing — to see the winter fast approaching upon a naked army, the time of their service within a few weeks of expiring,' and no provision made against it. A spell of rain or cold weather, and the whole army would disperse, he feared. General Greene found his soldiers weary of camp life, and 'so home-sick that I

[1] *Continental Congress Papers* (*Schuyler Letters*), no. 153, I, 505, 506–08, 512–14; II, 45.

fear the greater part, and the best part' will go home.[1] 'The military chest,' wrote Washington, 'is totally exhausted; the paymaster has not a single dollar in hand.' Credit for the subsistence of the army was usually strained to the utmost, and the greater part of the troops were 'in a state not far from mutiny,' because of a pay reduction. Washington was almost hopeless, early in 1776. We are 'without any money in our treasury, powder in our magazines, arms in our stores . . . and by and by, when we shall be called upon to take the field, shall not have a tent to lie in.'[2] The one necessity, of which there was usually plenty, was food — fair rations of fresh or corned beef, pork, salt fish, rice, flour and Indian meal, butter, peas and beans, potatoes, onions and turnips and spruce beer for drink.

There were times when Washington was obliged to conceal the state of his army from his own officers. Two thousand men were without flints, while gunpowder was so scarce at times that the army must submit to cannonading without reply because the little in hand must be kept for muskets. In a land of forests, Washington found different regiments on the point of cutting each other's throats for a few standing locusts near their encampment.[3] Only the fortunate capture of the British brig Nancy, by Captain Manly, made possible even an unrealized

[1] *Greene Papers* (W.L.C.L.), December 10, 1775.

[2] Washington, *Writings* (Ford, ed.), III, 342.

[3] *Greene Papers* (W.L.C.L.), December 10, 1775 (9th page). Greene says the soldiers had to eat provisions raw for want of fuel to cook them.

plan of assault on Boston.[1] The army rejoiced over this capture, this 'instance of divine favor,' as if each grasped victory in his hand. While matters were at their worst, the Commander-in-Chief was bombarded by the 'ardor of the Chimney-corner heroes' to make an assault on Boston. It was hard, he wrote, 'to have the eyes of a whole continent fixed with anxious expectation' on the army, 'and while its commander was restrained in every military operation, for want of necessary means to carry it on.' Then there were the soldiers themselves, 'void of fear,' and 'daily raving for action,' but who knew not the gaunt resources. The worst was, wrote Washington, that the means used to conceal his weakness from the enemy concealed it also from his friends. With such conditions the best he could do was to hover like an eagle over his prey, and wait for a favorable opportunity to pounce upon it.[2]

Fortunately for Washington, the British army 'ignominiously cooped up' in Boston also had its troubles. British officers there were twitted even by their own friends in London with their 'inclosed scene,' 'so useless, so impotent,' so disgraceful; penned up by enemies they proposed to conquer, yet unable to make a move to that end. 'You may be Lyons, but you are Lyons confined in a den, and the provincial rebels are your keepers.'[3] There were

[1] The booty was 2000 muskets, 1,000,000 flints, 30,000 round shot, 30 tons of musket shot, a 13-inch brass mortar. Washington, *Writings* (Ford, ed.), III, 179.

[2] *Letters of . . . Continental Congress* (Burnett, ed.), I, 275, 283. December 13 and 21, 1775. Congress barely missed ordering Washington to storm Boston.

[3] *Clinton Papers,* Phillips to Clinton, September 14, 1775.

still over six thousand inhabitants left in the town, and the army numbered 13,600. The Ministry had counted too much on abundant provisions in the theater of operations, but bad roads, indifferent if not actually hostile country people, and foraging parties swept off, if they but showed their noses to the Yankee sharpshooters, made it necessary to draw mainly from England. After Bunker Hill, Gage was called home, but let down easy, and Howe, 'in fashion' at court, took his place, and inherited his troubles.

The new commander appealed to Lord Barrington, 'We are in want of every necessity here,' send a ship with them, 'the sooner the better.' [1] The fleets from Cork, the central British provision dépôt, if not seized by American privateers, were delayed by storms and contrary winds. Ships sailing from Plymouth, early in 1776, were driven back or run ashore by tempestuous weather. 'The Elements have certainly warred against us most cruelly,' wrote the head of the Admiralty to the King.[2] Moreover, so large a percentage of the transported food was damaged, vermin or worm-eaten, lost from flimsy bags and barrels, stolen by rascally stevedores, or inedible before it left the warehouses of dishonest contractors, that General Howe 'trembled' when he thought of the state of provisions, and at one time could see food for only thirteen days ahead. Even

[1] P.R.O., *War Office, In-Letters*, 2, F 282. *Clinton Papers*, Phillips to Clinton, October 2 and December, 1775.

[2] *Correspondence of King George III*, III, 329; E. E. Curtis, *The British Army in the American Revolution*, 120–34.

when there was enough food, there was a lack of *fresh* provisions, so that scurvy was a constant menace. Indeed, it was one of General Greene's hobbies that the best way to fight the British was to strip the islands of Boston Bay of all fresh provisions and leave the 'Red Coats' to die of scurvy. He hoped for a 'prodigious mortality.'[1]

Not only in Boston but often, later in the war, the British forces were on the verge of starvation. Besides all the corruption and rascality which honeycombed the administrative fabric, there were constant quarrels between the Treasury and the Admiralty boards which often rendered the Commissary-General desperate.[2] If the bread supplied was mouldy, the biscuit weevily, the butter rancid, the beef maggoty, and the peas worm-eaten, the Commissary-General might reject hundreds of barrels of it, but that did not hush the clamor for food.[3] Hungry men would eat pork four or five years old, and break with a cannon ball biscuits taken from the French in the Seven Years' War, rather than starve.

[1] *Magazine of History* (May and June, 1914), 232–41. (Article by E. E. Curtis.) *Greene Papers* (W.L.C.L.), Greene to Ward, October 23, 1775. British Museum, *Add. MSS.*, 14038, I F 64, p. 111.

[2] The Treasury had reason to complain. The Government regularly lost fifteen per cent on bills drawn for specie on England by the forces in America, but when it rose to twenty-three per cent the Government protested, for by this financial juggling one fourth of its supplies were swallowed up. Hist. MSS. Com., *American MSS.*, I, 15.

[3] All the beef, pork, bacon, oatmeal, rice, peas, butter, cheese, raisins, even the potatoes, parsnips, cabbages, and onions for the hospital, and the antidotes for scurvy, porter, claret, malt-vinegar, had to come from Cork. Only beer and rum were shipped from the West Indies.

In these dire straits there was amazing adherence to legal forms, bordering, it would seem, on sheer stupidity. As late as August 2, 1775, a solemn meeting was held in Boston, attended by Gage, Clinton, Burgoyne, Earl Percy, Admiral Graves, Chief Justice Oliver, and half a dozen lesser personages. They were asked by the customs officers whether they still adhered to their decision — at a similar meeting in the previous May — to maintain the Boston Port Act, which permitted no incoming vessels to unload their cargoes at Boston. Since rebellion had closed Plymouth and Marblehead, the incoming vessels had been allowed to stand in the harbor under guard, though they were loaded with provisions of which the army and inhabitants of Boston were in dire need. After due consideration it was unanimously agreed to allow the vessels to dispose of their cargoes to supply necessities to the army, navy, and citizens.[1] Thus, nearly four months after Lexington, and six weeks after Bunker Hill, the Gordian knot was cut. Obedience to law, one of the finest traits of British character, would seem in this case to have been carried a little far.

By September of 1775, the army was reported 'diminishing every day by disease, and beginning to lose men by desertion,' though Burgoyne assured the Ministry that except a few 'rascally recruits' taken out of the Irish jails, the privates had not deserted. Not even the rumor that the aid of twenty thousand Russians had been secured raised

[1] *Clinton Papers* (W.L.C.L.), Boston, August 2, 1775. British Museum, *Add. MSS.*, (L. C. Trans.), 14038, I, F 64, p. 111.

the morale.[1] Through subsisting on salt provisions, 'the town was very sickly,' and not the more happy because subject to continual alarms and cannonading since Washington took command of the besiegers. Perhaps this accounted for the one bit of praise Burgoyne would allow the British army, that it was 'exasperated against the enemy.'[2] The barracks-master complained that the soldiers could not even rest comfortably at night because 'a combination among the provinces has deprived us . . . even of straw for filling the soldiers' "pallasses,"' and 'flocks,' or ground wool, must be got from England to soften the men's beds. Added to this discomfort, they were camped with no shade on the hot Boston Common and in bad tents furnished by dishonest contractors.[3] Little wonder that there was too great use of rum, a quart of which might be bought for a sixpence. Though it took one thousand gallons to supply ten thousand men for thirty days, yet the British commissary proved equal to that.[4] If rum could make one forget poor beds and the summer's heat, a new logic could make it give warmth when winter came with no adequate supply of wood, so that even the Liberty Tree, for which the King's troops

[1] Hist. MSS., *Various MSS.*, VI, 121; *Germain Papers*, Burgoyne to Germain, August 30, 1775.

[2] *Germain Papers*, Burgoyne to Germain, August 30, 1775.

[3] Royal Hist. Com., *Report on American MSS.*, I, 21. Indeed, King George was told, there were not enough horses for the artillery or baggage, little forage, hay or corn, no wagons or harness for horses except some made on the spot, no 'fascines or pickles, only three or four thousand pounds in the military chest.' *Correspondence of King George III*, III, 216.

[4] P.R.O., *State Papers, Domestic*, no. 19, p. 17.

could not be expected to have any sentiment, was ruthlessly chopped down. Among other deprivations even money could no more be got 'than the gold of Ophir,' for Congress had forbidden Americans to take the officers' bills, leaving them 'in great distress.' [1]

The British army was not wretched alone in Boston. The citizens who were afraid to leave lest their effects be plundered by the soldiery; the Loyalists glad to find refuge there out of reach of 'Tory hunters,' and the poor who had no means to go elsewhere, suffered the same deprivations. The Provincial Assembly tried to care for the poor, and relief was sent from every colony. When Samuel Adams returned from Philadelphia in September, he delivered to Moses Gill sums of thirteen ounces, fourteen pennyweight, and twenty grains of gold, given him by Thomas Jefferson from the Patriots of Lancaster County, Virginia, and other donations of pounds, ounces, pennyweights of gold and silver sent from other counties and provinces by the hands of Patrick Henry, Peyton Randolph, and others.[2] But all this, and many loads of provisions, did not prevent them feeling sorely the pinch of famine. They were also agonized in mind to see sacred places defiled. Old South Church was made a riding-school, Deacon Hubbard's beautifully carved pew, with silk upholstery, taken down and made a pigsty, and the Old North Chapel pulled down for fuel.[3] If patriotic

[1] *P.R.O., State Papers, Domestic,* no. 19, p. 17.

[2] *Writings of Samuel Adams,* III, 223.

[3] *Sir William Howe's Orderly Book,* 200. As soon as coal arrived, the tearing down of old buildings for fuel ceased. While the Patriot army

persons were punished for making signals from the church steeples, or for printing what Gage called 'treason' and 'sedition,' a great outcry went up about Nero and other tyrants of antiquity.

Though there was much complaint about the licentiousness of the soldiery, the most critical study of the facts makes it certain that the discipline of both Gage and Howe was good, and rogues were flogged unmercifully, if they were caught.[1] This was all the more creditable to Gage, since he believed Boston the place where 'the arch rebels formed their scheme long ago,' and that the whole rebellion was due 'to the deep designs and dark contrivances of Ambitious men to raise themselves from obscurity to power and emoluments.' For this they had deceived and betrayed the 'infatuated multitude,' getting them to try 'to avert evils that exist only in imagination,' and thus 'for liberty to erect tyranny.'

When the winter came on, and there was less work on the New England farms, Washington's army filled up.[2] For a time in early December the barracks progressed, firewood came in, the soldiers were comfortable and easy, but then at the end of the month all was dark again, soldiers hurrying home when their terms were out, and the army saved only by the devotion of its commander. On the last day of the service of the old recruits, December 31, 1775,

kept Howe's army from getting fuel from the woods, it could hardly be expected that the army would be allowed to freeze rather than tear down old houses to furnish wood.

[1] Frothingham, *Siege of Boston*, 281.

[2] Washington, *Writings* (Ford, ed.), III, 243; *Greene Papers* (W.L.C.L.), December 10, 1775, December 18, 1775.

General Greene wrote that nothing but confusion and disorder reigned, so large a number of soldiers were going home. History did not, he vowed, afford an example of so dangerous a maneuver as that of disbanding an old army and forming a new one within point-blank shot of the enemy.[1] He was glad to learn that people were refusing provisions to the home-going soldiers, and he hoped they might be shamed into returning. Unjust as it was, Washington had to retain the guns of the soldiers who were leaving, though they were private property. Often without bayonets and of different-sized bores, yet they were all that could be had.[2] The need for ammunition was even greater. 'Old Put' was 'crying out for powder — powder — ye gods, give us powder!' and toward the end of February, the cry was answered, through captures by privateers and by raiding the King's stores. When an ordinance brig was taken by the Americans, Sir Grey Cooper wrote in alarm that, if Boston and the British camp there should be burned by the bombs, sent from England to burn Roxbury and Cambridge, the 'saints of predestination' will say that the Lord has delivered us into their hands.[3]

The enterprise of Colonel Knox brought from Crown Point and Ticonderoga, over snows and frozen lakes, more than fifty cannon, mortars, and howitzers. Then after several days of diverting the British attention to points north and west of Boston, on the night of March 4, redoubts were erected on

[1] *Greene Papers*, Greene to Ward, December 31, 1775. [2] *Ibid.*

[3] Hist. MSS. Com., *Various MSS.*, vi, 122.

Dorchester Heights, as if by 'the Genii belonging to Aladdin's Wonderful Lamp.' Howe was 'much amazed' in the morning with 'the forwardness of their work,' and swore they could not have employed less than twelve or fourteen thousand men.[1] When several days of severe storm prevented a British effort to retake those heights before they were made too strong, an officer wrote, 'Adieu balls and masquerades!' There was meat for only fourteen days. Howe had long been desperate for provisions. As far back as January, the troops had been put on short rations. The fleet could now no longer stay in the harbor under fire from Dorchester Neck. Howe made the only logical deduction.[2] The army was no longer to be entertained; Boston must be evacuated.

Sir Henry Clinton had urged Gage early in August to give up Boston and go to New York, an island easily protected by the fleet, and where Loyalists abounded and fresh provisions were easily obtained.[3] As far back as September of 1775, former Governor Hutchinson wrote from London, where he enjoyed inside information, that Boston was to be deserted. A month later, the British commanders were being urged in letters from London to give up 'that damned Boston.'[4] Now, with the guns out of Ticon-

[1] *Clinton Papers* (W.L.C.L.), Howe to Clinton, March 21, 1776. Indeed, Washington had caused all the militia from near-by towns to be called in for brief service and thus greatly swelled his numbers. Washington, *Writings* (Ford, ed.), III, 437.

[2] *Letters written by Ebenezer Huntington*, p. 31. *Clinton Papers*, March 31, 1776. Mass. Hist. Soc., *Proceedings* (1st Series), VII, 240–41 (Diary of E. Pierce). *Colonial Office*, 5–253, pp. 173–76.

[3] *Clinton Papers* (W.L.C.L.), Clinton to Gage, August 7, 1775.

[4] British Museum, *Egerton MSS.*, 2659, F 177 (T. Hutchinson to

deroga frowning down upon the city from Dorchester Heights, its evacuation became a necessity and no longer a matter of debate. Clinton records a conversation with Howe three months earlier wherein he warned the Commander-in-Chief that the Americans would try to burn Boston from the Dorchester side, but Howe was sure they never would attempt that.[1]

After the Ministry, months before, had advised, even authorized Howe to remove his army southward, he had dallied, and now he must ungracefully leave in a hurry. He had in fact been leisurely gathering transports, but the hour of need came so suddenly that even the means of departure were deficient. It was too great a hazard to leave in separate divisions; the whole army must be embarked at once. Howe's decision to go north, rather than south to Rhode Island or New York, was defended on the ground that Halifax was friendly and that it was 'a season for rest.'[2] Well-bred European soldiers did not fight in the winter season. Moreover, it ought to be added, Howe's army was not large enough at that time for the conquest of New York — hardly more than forty-three hundred actual fighting men.[3] It sounded well for Howe to report that he judged it most conducive to the interest of His Majesty's service to proceed with the army to

his son in Boston). *Clinton Papers* (W.L.C.L.), Phillips to Clinton. October 2, 1775. *Colonial Office*, 5–253, p. 153.

[1] *Clinton Papers* (W.L.C.L.), Sunday, December 3, 1775.

[2] P.R.O., *State Papers, Domestic, Military*, 19, no. 9, p. 53.

[3] *Clinton Papers* (W.L.C.L.), Howe to Clinton, March 21, 1776.

Halifax [1] — 'a cursed, cold, wintry place,' as an officer wrote; but the British were glad of an informal understanding with Washington that they could go in peace on condition of leaving the town undamaged.

Soon all was 'uproar and confusion; carts, trucks, wheel-barrows, coaches, chaises . . . driving as if the devil was after them.' [2] Only with difficulty were the soldiers kept from plunder and drink. A thousand Loyalists, fearing to face the enraged Patriots, were forced to go, bringing about, as Harrison Gray Otis wrote, 'a total subversion of the social structure' in Boston.[3] Howe's fleet carried to Nova Scotia the greater part, perhaps, of the aristocrats who had ruled the society of Massachusetts for the last generation. Families distinguished from the days of Winthrop and the Mathers were swept away with all their cultivation and political experience — a great loss not made up by the return of some after the war, for their fortunes were ruined, their influence gone.

Though Howe complained that he was 'much pinched for ship room,' some ships were said to be wholly filled with the household goods of the refugees. Yet General Robertson protested to Howe that ships, said to be loaded, were really light; that,

[1] P.R.O., *War Office, In-Letters*, II, F 759. Force, *American Archives* (4th Series), III, 642 (September, 1775).

[2] *Memorial History of Boston*, III, 164. No one can have any doubt as to the haste of the departure who reads the inventory of stores, vessels, etc., left by the British army. Frothingham, *Siege of Boston*, 406–08.

[3] Morison, *Harrison Gray Otis*, I, 18.

if the holds of the vessels had been well stored, all the stores and goods might have been carried away. Ships and stores left behind were not even destroyed, declared Robertson, and at least one ship was afterward used by the Americans as a privateer.[1] Abigail Adams counted from Penn Hill 'upwards of 170 sail,' the masts looking 'like a forest.' The fugitive fleet lay for some days in Nantucket Road and greatly worried Washington, who feared a surprise.[2] As March was the most tempestuous month on the American coast, it was thought a miracle that this wretched fleet was not dispersed or lost. If the delay was for the purpose of warning belated transports, it did not wholly avail. A transport with one hundred and eight men, which blundered into Boston Harbor, having no news of Howe's departure, was surrounded in a dead calm by five privateers, and surrendered after expending every shot.[3]

All this trouble, wrote one of the sufferers, was owing to Great Britain being 'fast asleep.'[4] Howe's enemies were very bitter, their prayer being that he might 'be safe in the belly of the whale, like another Jonah,' but the Ministry was the chief object of criticism. The Ministerial papers in London dis-

[1] The King ordered Howe to remove all the merchandise and put it in store so that British merchants might recover their property which had never been paid for, but there was a lack of ships. *Germain Papers, Military Despatched,* January 5, 1776. *Clinton Papers* (W.L.C.L.), Howe to Clinton, March 21, 1776.

[2] Washington to Josiah Quincy, March 24, 1776 (W.L.C.L.).

[3] P.R.O., Colonial Office (L. C. Trans.), 5–140, p. 9.

[4] *Remembrancer,* III, 107.

guised the facts, holding that the army had gone away of its own free will; that the King had the same men, in the same ships, but only in another place, and with no loss of glory; but the Opposition was not deceived.[1] The Duke of Manchester in the House of Lords pointed out with sarcasm that the same London paper which announced the evacuation of Boston announced that His Majesty had appointed commissioners to receive the submission of the Bostonians. 'Since when have the fugitives been respected and obeyed by their conquerors? Are the men who have chased you out of their country going to ask your pardon for chasing them? Isn't it a bit ridiculous? Couldn't they have chosen a better time for announcing commissioners?'[2] Stung by such taunts, the British Government resolved that there should be no turning back. America, too, from that moment thought less of war for the restoration of its rights, and turned ever with firmer decision toward war for Independence.

[1] *Broadside* (W.L.C.L.), Edinburgh, 1776. *Archives des Affaires Étrangères, Angleterre,* vol. 515, no. 21 (secret report of Debates in House of Lords). Also in different form in *Hansard.*

[2] *Ibid.*, vol. 516, no. 28.

CHAPTER V

BRITISH PREPAREDNESS

After the evacuation of Boston, there was little doubt in the minds of British or American leaders that a war to the finish was before them. The colonists were no longer merely resisting 'tyranny' with arms, but they were actually at war with one of the most powerful of nations, the only one whose sea-power was equal to carrying on a struggle three thousand miles from home. On either side speculation was rife as to the outcome. There were certain facts as to the respective strength of the combatants upon which we can look coolly to-day and reason logically enough where Victory would place her wreath. But there were also opinions, delusions, prejudices, which deeply affected the logic of thoughtful men on either side, and determined their actions quite as much as facts. It is not only real resources but fancied strength which steels a people to engage in war.

It was literally true, as Daniel Webster was to declare half a century later, that the 'American colonists raised their flag against a power to which, for the purposes of foreign conquest and subjugation, Rome, in the height of her glory, was not to be compared; a power which had dotted over the surface of the whole globe with her possessions and military posts; whose morning drumbeat, following the sun, and keeping company with the hours, circled the earth daily with one continuous and unbroken strain of the martial airs of England.' It was true that the population of the British Isles was five times that of British America. Great Britain had a hundred times the sea-power, a veteran navy lately come from sweeping the seas of all enemies, in all quarters of the globe.[1] Her veteran army, too, had lately come from carrying conquest wherever it carried colors. In the matter of money Britain had perhaps a thousand times the wealth convertible into the instruments of warfare. And finally, there was the prestige of world-wide victory, only a decade before. How is it possible, was asked in Parliament, 'that the American people, without arms, ammunition, money or navy, should dare to brave the foremost among all the powers on earth?'

There were many aristocratic Englishmen to give advice to the rash Americans. Sir John Dalrymple warned them that their destruction was inevitable. 'No people situated as you are, can hope for success in war, unless they are possessed of four things . . . fortified towns to secure the persons of their people, and intercept the incursions and advances of their enemies; a disciplined army to defend their lands; a navy to protect their seas and rivers; and not only a great annual revenue, but the capacity of funding

[1] Sir J. Dalrymple, *Address to the Inhabitants of America* (1775), 4. For an interesting list of the ships in the English fighting marine see *Correspondence of King George III*, III, 306–11. The list was in the King's own handwriting. Indeed, the extent to which the King, personally, added up his kingdom's resources gives reality to the old nursery line about the king in his counting house 'counting out his money.'

it.... And this last article is perhaps in modern times of more importance than all the others put together, because in modern times the success of war depends more on the longest purse than on the longest sword.' And Sir John went on, in the most affable way, talking down to their meaner understandings, and pointing out that the colonists 'had not a single walled town, nor a single disciplined regiment, nor a single ship of war, nor a single fund on which monied men would lend them a month's expense of an armament.' [1] What nation would dare supply them while Great Britain was their enemy? [2] Much was made, and very reasonably, too, of America's lack of money. What was their trifling revenue perhaps seventy-five thousand pounds a year, against that of a nation which had a sinking fund of two or three million pounds a year, and which during its last war spent seventeen millions in a single twelvemonth? [3]

The American Loyalists joined lustily in the chorus of warning voices. President Myles Cooper, of King's College, writing in the dark of anonymity, a pamphlet, 'What think ye of Congress now?' begged his countrymen to remember that they were without fortresses, without discipline, without military stores — the work of an age to remedy. Daniel Leonard, masking as 'Massachusettensis,' predicted that nothing short of a miracle could gain America a

[1] Sir John Dalrymple, *Address to the Inhabitants of America* (1775 ed.), 3–4.

[2] *A Letter from a Gentleman* (W.L.C.L.), 6–7.

[3] *Ibid.*, 5.

single battle. Had not British arms already reaped immortal honors in the iron harvest of the field? Let Americans stop before their feet stumbled on the dark mountains. Governor Bernard, in a published letter to Lord Camden, made much of his conviction that the Americans were unable to defend themselves by sea, and therefore for a century to come could not even exist, let alone fight, except under the protection of some powerful naval state.[1] If abandoned by England, cried Myles Cooper, they would be exposed to every maritime power in Europe.[2] Indeed, a noble lord thought 'the little state of Genoa or San Marino may soon overrun them' if the British withdrew protection.[3]

This was a gloomy prospect, indeed, but there were also encouraging factors. It was true, granted the British opponents of an American war, that England had great financial resources, but she had vast debts too — more than a hundred and thirty millions sterling — hanging about the neck of the British public. Already the interest on that debt, plus the peace establishment, exhausted the existing revenues. If now the cost of only thirty thousand men, and a train of artillery, and necessary ships, were added, the expense would be some seven million pounds. Would the British people bear it? The Reverend Gordon, preaching courage to his Boston flock, thought not. Vividly he pictured a

[1] *A Letter to Lord Camden* (W.L.C.L.), 30.

[2] M. Cooper, *What think ye of Congress now?* 25. J. Adams admitted it was Quixotic to talk of coping suddenly at sea with Great Britain. *Letters of . . . Continental Congress* (Burnett, ed.), I, 220.

[3] Hansard, *Parliamentary History*, XVI, 177.

load of taxes, an exhausted treasury, a decaying trade, while the British poor were multiplying, and their provisions growing less.[1] In Parliament the Duke of Richmond reminded the First Lord of the Admiralty — who talked lightly of the cost of the portended war, 'a mere bagatelle,' 'ten or twelve million sterling' — that the noble lord judged the affluence of the nation by that which reigned in his palace, whereas all was want, all famine in the house of the citizen.[2] Let not Great Britain then presume too much upon her wealth! It is a fact that the wealthy landholders, who were most bent on coercing America, were least willing to be taxed therefor. Had this governing class been willing to pay its proportion of the taxes, it is conceivable that England might have won the war.

But grant that England had the money and the ships and men, it must not be ignored that she would be obliged to fight three thousand miles from her base of supplies. It was 'mere romance' to expect to subdue three millions of people at that distance, thought some men of excellent judgment.[3] All munitions and most of the food must traverse that watery waste. To sail that distance in those days was like steaming from San Francisco to Australia in our generation, but with far less certainty of arriving. Between August and November during the siege of Boston, only one supply ship passed in

[1] Gordon, Sermon on 'Religious and Civil Liberty,' 24. (W.L.C.L.). *New England Chronicle*, May 23, 1776 (quoting an English pamphleteer).

[2] *Archives des Affaires Étrangères, Angleterre*, vol. 515, no. 21.

[3] *William and Mary Quarterly*, XVIII, 43, 44.

safety,[1] and as if the stars in their courses fought for America, the weather that winter was severe almost beyond the memory of men, as Germain wrote Howe. It greatly obstructed the naval service.[2] The last dispatches Howe received from home before he evacuated Boston on March 17, 1776, were dated October 22 of the preceding year! [3]

Transport ships in that day were a terror to all who had either experience or imagination. As a result of embezzlement, thievery, swindling, or at the best, of official carelessness in the dockyards, the transports were often little better than floating charnel houses.[4] Of thirty-four ships, said by the Admiralty to be in prime condition, Keppel on one occasion found only six 'fit to meet a seaman's eye.' [5] During the seven years after 1775, seventy-six ships capsized or were wrecked. Of the ships that figured in the Bunker Hill fight, both the Falcon and the Lively were cranky and undermanned. The British regiments that fought in the battle had in some cases been carried to America in leaky and worm-eaten boats whose bows, like those of the Patna in Conrad's 'Lord Jim,' had to be raised well out of the

[1] Hist. MSS. Com., *Report on American MSS.*, I, 46.

[2] *Germain Papers, Military Despatched* (W.L.C.L.), February 1, 1776.

[3] *Ibid.*, May 3, 1776. Nor had any supplies come, which might have been fatal had the army remained in Boston. Yet North had assured King George that all needed supplies would reach Boston before the end of October, 1775. *Correspondence of King George III*, III, 255–56 (September 9).

[4] Lord Howe complained also of 'the unfortunate defection of the shipwrights' in the summer of 1775. *Germain Papers*, July 29, 1775.

[5] Belcher, *First American Civil War*, I, 289.

water to keep them from being wave-crushed.[1] And it must be realized that even when those boats were seaworthy, the tonnage was so light that four or five vessels were needed to bring over an average regiment. Within a given time a single vessel of the Lusitania or Leviathan type could in our day carry more troops from England to America than could all the British fleets have done in the days of Lord North. It was little wonder that men, storm-tossed in such cockleshells, wrote of the waves as 'forbidding chains of mountains,' and declared that the ship 'flew like a ball, now among the clouds, and now as swift as an arrow into the trough of the sea.'[2]

But the size and ill condition of the ships was not the only terror of the voyage. It was an age of the world when aristocratic officialdom had little mercy in its heart for the common man. To-day more sympathy is bestowed on dumb brutes that are freighted by sea or land than was given to the common sailor or soldier in the late decades of the eighteenth century. Soldier or sailor, started perhaps on this woeful journey by the press-gang, or, like David Balfour, kidnaped, suffered from the first under official rapacity or carelessness. Terror, embodied in the cat, the rattan, the rope's end, ruled on the voyage. From morn to eve men were apt to be caned and kicked by the mate, the corporal, or the sergeant. Every morning except Sunday there was like to be flogging at the gangway. Men who escaped being branded, pilloried, starved, or hanged were sure at

[1] *Barham Papers*, I, 60, 254.

[2] *Narrative of J. C. Buettner* . . . 23.

the voyage's end to be pitilessly robbed by paymaster or purser. These men treated like animals became riotous and licentious, and then they were denounced as the 'scum of the earth.' The King's Navy cried aloud for another Pepys to render it the simple service of honest attention. The careless and immoral character of the high officials was reflected in the shamelessness of the men.[1] Their protests against the worst of abuses were interpreted as the unrest of their wicked hearts.

Sailors and soldiers alike suffered at sea from the pestilential scourge of scurvy, when a little acid fruit, green vegetables, or even, as we now know, fresh fish might have saved them. In 1779, the British fleet in the West Indies had two thousand men down, mostly with scurvy. They had been refused the simple anti-scorbutics, sugar, coffee, and chocolate.[2] If a man came down with either scurvy or some other disease, the only care was by a ship's surgeon, wretchedly paid, who, incredible as it may seem, had to furnish his own medicines. If the sick man died, his body was sewed up in a bit of sailcloth, tied to a bag of sand, and buried in the waves of the sea.

Those who escaped the scourge and death were not in consequence happy in their lot. There is an amazing likeness in all the letters and diaries of the time as to the miseries of the voyage on a transport. The daily bread, for which they prayed if they did not eat, was often full of vermin, and the other food ruined by the heat of the hold where it had lain,

[1] *Barham Papers*, I, 299. [2] *Ibid.*, I, 75.

perhaps, eighteen months. The Commissary at Cork was almost 'shocked to death' at Howe's report that the bread was bad. He vowed he had tasted all the bread himself, and hoped to be 'hanged above all men alive' if he passed any not good. Yet it *was* bad, mixed with sand, unfit for use.[1] Oatmeal, sour and weevily, boiled in rotten ship-water, was served mornings out of the ship's 'coppers.' Hessian soldiers, being floated to the American shambles, ate bacon, four or five years old, black at the outer edges, yellow a little deeper, and drank putrid water 'heavily sulphured' which 'lay in deep corruption,' and was full of worms which must be filtered out through cloths.[2] It tasted like ink, almost undrinkable except with rum. The meats, old and poor, had been in salt for years. Such food, furnished by war-profiteers to a careless Government official, had prepared the soldier's body for the ordeals of the American campaign.[3]

Not only the food but the quarters were intolerable, from a modern point of view. It was common to place the pigsties, source of the fresh pork for the officers' mess, under the forecastle, the seamen's quarters. On transports, the soldiers, 'pressed and packed like salted herrings,' lay in bunks between

[1] *Barham Papers*, 74. Contractors went even to the lengths of putting sand in their bread, and were always ready with glib excuses for rotten flour and ill-provided cattle ships. Hist. MSS. Com., *Report on American MSS.*, I, 37, 38, 47–48, 54, 64, 82.

[2] A. Pfister, *The Voyage of the First Hessian Army* (Heartman Hist. Ser. no. 3), 30–31.

[3] Hist. MSS. Com., *Report on American MSS.*, I, 54, 64. See the excellent chapter on 'Provisioning the Army,' in E. E. Curtis, *The British Army in the American Revolution*, chap. IV.

decks, one row above another, so shallow, to save room, that none could sit upright.[1] When a storm heaved and pitched the ships, the decks and port-holes were made tight, and men found it like being 'buried alive in coffins,' gasping for light and air. Even the windswept deck was pervaded with odors, especially after barrels of water were opened there. In the cabins, wrote one storm-tossed victim, though all articles were tied fast, they broke loose, went 'helter-skelter, bruising men in the agony of sea-sickness.'[2] Soldiers who ventured on deck were dashed into the hold by giant waves. Even the supplies in the hold did not escape. Beds were broken up in storms, and cartridges eaten by the rats which infested every ship. It was under these conditions that such armies as Britain might muster would have to be flung three thousand miles to the scene of action. No wonder the Government found difficulties in filling the ranks of an army to serve far from home.[3] Dread of the journey would deter all to whom rumor, imagination, or actual experience conveyed any idea of its miseries. Perhaps in addition to lack of experience or imagination was the fact that the conditions of industrial life in England made many workmen conceive that it was better to fly to evils that they knew not of. Howlett, one of the few in that callous age who cared, wrote: 'If war

[1] Pfister, *The Voyage of the First Hessian Army*, 29.

[2] *Ibid.*, 12, 13.

[3] Chalmers, *Estimate* (ed. 1776), 119, said the British army was made up of 'convicts, vagabonds'; but even if that had been truer than it was, the significance in that day was very different from what it would be to-day.

can tell its dismal tale of thousands slain on the field . . . arts and manufacturers can present as long a catalogue — of our fellow creatures suffocated in mines and pits, or gradually poisoned by the noxious effluvia of metals, oils, powders, spirits, etc., used in their work, and can exhibit as mournful a scene of blinded and lame, of enfeebled, decrepit, asthmatic, consumptive wretches, panting for breath and crawling half-alive on the surface of the earth.'[1] It was to escape such lives that unhappy wretches might take the King's service even if they knew its conditions.

Nor were distance and the service conditions the only obstacles to the exercise of England's vast military powers. Having transported her armies, in spite of all the infelicities of the voyage, her commanders would find in America large inaccessible areas defying military conquest. Governor Bernard wrote Lord Camden deploring any attempt to march through the wilds, any thought of storming the woods and lakes of the continent.[2] It was a land of fastnesses where defeat was ruin, where ground must be won by inches. Lord Cornwallis swore there

[1] *Gentleman's Magazine,* LII, 526. Edmund Burke wrote, in 1756: 'I suppose that there are in Great Britain upward of 100,000 people employed in lead, tin, iron, copper and coal mines; these unhappy wretches scarce ever see the light of the sun; they are buried in the bowels of the earth; there they work at a severe and dismal task, without the least prospect of being delivered from it; they subsist upon the coarsest and worst of fare; they have their health miserably impaired and their lives cut short by being perpetually confined in the close vapours of these malignant minerals.' E. R. Turner, in *American Historical Review,* XXVII, 1–23.

[2] *Letter of T. Bernard to Camden* (W.L.C.L.), 27. *New England Chronicle,* May 23, 1776.

never was a stronger country or one better calculated for the defensive. It was 'rugged, hilly, woody,' a bad fighting ground.[1] Turgot's vivid imagination saw the colonists flee and disperse themselves in the immense wilderness behind their settlements. 'European armies will attempt in vain to pursue them.'[2] Moreover, American settlement was too dispersed to conquer. Pitt taunted the Ministry, that after two years of effort, they held nothing in America but stations.[3] Even the methods of a Sherman or a Sheridan would be in vain. A Bismarck could not bleed it white. Attack would find only empty spaces. One might sooner 'pluck the moon from her sphere than conquer such a country.' It was 'beyond the reach of humanity.' English generals could not do it, declared Lord Ellibank.[4] It was 'an ugly job . . . a damned affair indeed,' wrote Harvey. There was no one place of government, as General Howe was to learn, and no place of military concentration which might be seized. All reasoning based on European warfare was in vain; Napoleon had not yet had his fatal venture in the Russian fastnesses. Colonial seaports were scattered, and the one strategic center, New York, was dangerous for fleets, especially in winter. Summer heat in the South, winter severities in the North, malaria in Virginia, prevented continuous

[1] P.R.O., *State Papers, Domestic*, no. 18, pp. 3, 39.

[2] Archives Nationales, K. 1340, no. 10. *Plain English* (*to the King*), (W.L.C.L.), 1775, 16.

[3] Hansard, *Parliamentary Debates*, XIX, 317.

[4] *Germain Papers* (W.L.C.L.), January 12, 1776.

military effort. Ill-charted, badly marked seacoasts, uncertain currents and winds endangered both the blockading and transport fleets. These conditions, too, upset all calculation on the time needed for the transfer of troops and supplies. Nature with her uncertain moods and freaks of temper fought in the main on the rebellious side.

Unmindful of these clogs upon British sea strength, 'one of the principal dowries of that kingdom,' there were statesmen who thought the navy was the only proper instrument for pressing the war in rebellious America.[1] Lord Barrington, Secretary of War, held from the first that only disaster and disgrace could come from an effort to fight the colonists on land. Leave it to the navy, he urged. Withdraw the troops to Canada, and with a naval force, Burke's 'winged ministers of vengeance,' reduce Massachusetts to submission without a drop of blood.[2] He never changed his opinion, and he had never liked the quarrel; yet for three years his orders sent out all the troops who fought in America. Perhaps the chief reason why his advice remained unheeded was that already there was a British army in America which for honor's sake must be extricated with dignity.

Pamphleteers warned Americans of this peril of blockade. 'Your towns are built all on the edge of

[1] F. Osborn (5th Duke of Leeds), *A Short Hint*, 11.

[2] W. Shute, *Life of William W. Wildman, Viscount Barrington* (1814), 140–52. *Correspondence of King George III*, III, 250. Harvey, the Adjutant-General, wrote: 'To attempt to conquer it [America] internally by our land force is as wild an idea as ever controverted common sense.' 'Our army will be destroyed by damned driblets.'

deep water,' wrote one, 'so as to be within reach, not only of common shot but even of pistol shot.' He pointed out that their country houses and estates lay on the banks of deep rivers, and that these and their towns on two thousand miles of coast might in a summer be reduced to ashes by ships of war.[1] Their trade might be annihilated, their vessels and seamen captured. Indeed, three twenty-gun ships and three sloops stationed off the Virginia capes and Albemarle Sound could lock up the coast of six hundred miles of extent and two of their noblest provinces.[2] Others proposed controlling all American exports in this way, stopping all trade not useful to Great Britain. To jest as did a British Minister that fishermen were not otters, and could live without fish, was no good answer to the proposal to close the port of Boston and bring its people to terms by starvation.[3] Yet there were English friends of America who held a philosophy, to which Thomas Jefferson later subscribed, that commerce only saps a country's virtue, happiness, and vigor. Let Americans then adopt non-importation and non-exporta-

[1] Americans expected this. See *Letters on the American Revolution* (Willard, ed.), 101. J. Dickinson's reply to this was: 'Our towns may be destroyed, but they will grow again. We compare them not with our rights and liberties.' Force, *American Archives* (4th Series), II, 443.

[2] Indeed, the eastern counties of Virginia were raided so successfully and profitably by the British war vessels in 1775 and 1776 that the Committee of Safety seriously considered depopulating Norfolk and Princess Anne Counties, and did compel all Loyalists to move into the interior at least thirty miles. Eckenrode, *The Revolution in Virginia*, 140–41.

[3] J. Dalrymple, *Address to the Inhabitants of America* (W.L.C.L.), 5, 6; Loch, *Essays on Scotland* (W.L.C.L.), 78; *London Evening Post*, January 10, 1778.

tion forever, they urged. They will as a result be the greatest as well as the happiest people under Heaven. There will then be a country to which all can fly and enjoy the rights of man after luxury and vice have brought European ruin. This vision of a happy Arcadia in America was one given to many idealists both in Europe and in the colonies.[1] John Adams declared that if Parliament should build along the Atlantic a wall of brass at low-water mark, America might bear it forever. Habits must be changed, he admitted, prejudices, palates, tastes in dress, furniture, equipage, architecture, but Americans could live and be happy, though barred from the luxuries of Europe. They must give up coffee, wines, silks, punch, sugar, and molasses. Dress would not be so elegant, because silks, velvet, and lace would be wanting; but what were these trifles in a contest for liberty?[2]

[1] *New England Chronicle and Essex Gazette*, May 18, 1775. Mahatma Gandhi's philosophy suggested the same idea for freeing India in 1921.

[2] *Letters of ... Continental Congress* (Burnett, ed.), I, 236, 239.

CHAPTER VI

AMERICAN PREPAREDNESS

BUT after all the speculations of the publicists and the dreams of the idealists, the outcome of the struggle was to be determined by knock-down facts like the actual man-power and defensive strength of the colonies, and the attitude of jealous European powers toward Britain, the hated mistress of the seas. On the matter of population and defenses, Lord Dartmouth, Colonial Secretary, had gathered official estimates from the governor of each province less than two years before the clash on Lexington Green.[1] In what the Secretary learned there was little to alarm the British Ministry by reason of the state of preparedness of their rebellious subjects. Perhaps no war in history was fought with less preparedness than that waged for American Independence. As John Hancock replied in desperation, when Congress was blamed for the unsatisfied needs of the army, 'the unprepared State of the Colonies on the Commencement of the War, and the almost total Want of every thing necessary to carry it on, are the true sources from whence all our Difficulties have proceeded.'[2] Though paper estimates showed some three hundred thousand militiamen in the colonies, their period of training varied from two to

[1] *Dartmouth MSS.* (W.L.C.L.), I.

[2] *Letters of . . . Continental Congress* (Burnett, ed.). I, 437.

four days out of each year, while such arms as they had were their private property.[1]

With the potential three hundred thousand militiamen, estimated by British Government officials,[2] Washington was never able to gather for any one battle over eighteen thousand men, and he never had in his army at one time over twenty-two thousand. In the first flush of rebellion the greatest number enlisted,[3] and then patriotism cooled as the demand for labor and the war-time opportunities for getting rich made their appeals to human cupidity and avarice. The difficulty of enlistment increased with each year of war, and, when the French army arrived, became worst of all. The army actually in arms was always meager, yet the militia, farmers and laborers of the neighborhood, wary of long service, were always ready to fight a few days, as at Bennington, for their altars and their fires. That was the nebulous, incalculable and yet mighty force which the British had to meet.

The report in detail from each colony showed that no militia had ever been established in Pennsylvania, the Quaker colony, and the New Jersey militia law was unavailing in the west of that colony, because the exponents of brotherly love refused obedience.[4] In Massachusetts for several years some regiments had been without officers. In New Hampshire each

[1] *Dartmouth MSS.* (W.L.C.L.), Answers to Question 15. In Georgia, a sort of military buffer colony, the militia trained *six* days of the year.

[2] *Rights of Britons* . . . (W.L.C.L.), 84 (ed. 1775).

[3] (Gray), *Rights of Britons* (pamphlet, W.L.C.L.), 84. In the first year Congress *summoned* 89,600 men.

[4] *Dartmouth MSS.* (W.L.C.L.), I (N.J. Query 15).

militiaman at his own cost, and with no pay, must equip with a knapsack, a flintlock, a hatchet, one pound of powder, and twenty bullets; while each town must have a barrel of powder, two hundred pounds of bullets, and three hundred flints for each sixty soldiers. This was fairly typical for all other colonies, and even with these regulations there was little compliance.[1] So scarce was gunpowder that in August, 1775, the Massachusetts House urged the citizens of that province not to fire a gun at beast, bird, or mark without real necessity.[2] Washington at that time found that instead of four hundred and eighty-five quarter-casks on which he had counted, there was only half a pound of powder to each of his men. 'He was so struck that he did not utter a word for half an hour,' wrote Sullivan.[3] The most popular prescription in America was the recipe for making 'villainous saltpeter.'

How agricultural America, severed from its customary source of ammunition and industrial supplies, muddled through the first two years of war is a desperate story.[4] When the first shot was fired on Lexington Green, there was little powder in America beyond what had lain in colonial magazines since Wolfe climbed to the Plains of Abraham. Since that day the mills had decayed; the art of making powder was almost lost. As war-clouds gathered, the re-

[1] *Dartmouth MSS.* (W.L.C.L.), I (N.J. Query 15).

[2] *New England Chronicle and Essex Gazette*, August 17, 1775.

[3] Amory, *Military Services of J. Sullivan*, 16. *Writings of Washington* (Ford, ed.), III, 54, 64.

[4] O. W. Stephenson's article in *American Historical Review*, XXX, 271–81.

volting colonists hastened to seize the Crown stores, ten thousand pounds at Portsmouth, six hundred at Savannah, and twelve thousand more from one of King George's ships there, other thousands here and there — something like eighty thousand pounds altogether. Half of this was early sent to help blow the British out of Boston, and there spent in reckless fashion, so that Washington found little left on his arrival late in June. All the cannon were silent, he wrote, except a small nine-pounder. By Christmas the want of powder was 'inconceivable.' [1] In spite of every effort — seeking 'mines of saltpeter' under every stable, dove house, cellar, vault — the entire original supply was gone in nine months, as well as what was imported. Meanwhile, each colony encouraged by laws the erection of public and private saltpeter and powder mills, Massachusetts and Pennsylvania getting the best results. The total colonial production, by the fall of 1777, was about 115,000 pounds of powder, perhaps the maximum of American resources.[2] This quantity would have been wholly inadequate but for the far greater quantities imported.

By the fall of 1777, nearly half a million pounds of saltpeter, often disguised as tea chests or rice barrels, was slipped by the cordon of British ships, and nearly 700,000 pounds of gunpowder made out of it, while imports of about 1,500,000 pounds of powder already fabricated brought the total near

[1] *Writings of Washington* (Ford, ed.) III, 100–01, 299.

[2] *American Historical Review*, XXX, 271–81. (Stephenson's thesis, typewritten, giving full details, is in the University of Michigan Library.)

to 2,200,000 pounds derived from foreign sources. Probably nine tenths of the ammunition used at Saratoga in the defeat of Burgoyne was from foreign sources. Dutch, French, and even English merchants were selling explosives and guns to the agents of Congress. As early as August of 1775, the British Government was alarmed at the extent of this trade, which began, declared Admiral Graves, as early as December, 1774.[1] Powder was being carried to America even from the coast of Africa, whither it had been sent in the course of trade. Saltpeter came in Dutch vessels from distant Bengal. British war vessels were sent to guard Government stores in Bermuda and the Bahamas.[2] By January, 1776, King George was urging Lord Sandwich to convert even coal vessels into ships of war, and to 'cover the Sea with Vessels,' so as to stop the Americans from getting gunpowder from St. Eustatius, the Dutch port, on which they relied for these supplies so necessary to the next campaign.[3] Of all sources the French came to be the most important, before the end of 1776. When 85,000 pounds of

[1] British Museum, *Add. MSS.*, 14038, I. *North Carolina Colonial Records*, x, 233. January 5, 1775. *The Boston Evening Post* had an account of British men-of-war going to the Texel to stop the trade in arms. P.R.O., *Colonial Office*, 5–250, pp. 229–30, 234, 235, 236, 244. British ship captains were caught using flint stones for ballast. *Ibid.*, 257.

[2] P.R.O., *Colonial Office*, 5–250, pp. 245, 246, 247, 272. (There were seven hundred barrels in the Bermudas, six hundred barrels in the Bahamas.) Edler, *Dutch . . . and American Revolution*, 41.

[3] *Correspondence of King George III*, III, 332. When there was a profit of 120 per cent on such cargoes, the Dutch figured they could afford to lose two cargoes out of every three and still make money. Edler, *Dutch . . . and American Revolution*, 40.

powder were shipped in two days from Amsterdam to France — more than ever before in time of war — the British Government had little doubt that America was its final destination.[1] The French Government encouraged the Danish and the Dutch, and connived at the activities of its own merchants who ventured out from L'Orient and Nantes, and evaded the patrol of British warships by pretending a trade with the West Indies, especially St. Eustatius.[2] There, and at Cape Nicholas Mole in Hispaniola, they were met by American vessels, which took on the French produce, arms, and ammunition in such quantities as to alarm the British Ministry and General Howe. A British spy, personal agent of Lord George Germain at St. Eustatius, saw with his own eyes twelve vessels from South Carolina, loaded with rice and indigo, which were exchanged for ammunition. Admitting that English frigates could not watch the French islands without offending that powerful nation, he urged watching the Dutch and Danish islands.[3] There poured in also upon the British Ministry harassing reports of American

[1] F. Edler, *Dutch . . . and the American Revolution*, 39–40. Hist. MSS. Com., *Report, Dartmouth MSS.*, II, 405.

[2] *American Historical Review*, XXX, 279. *Correspondence of King George III*, III, 227; P.R.O., *Colonial Office*, 5–140, pp. 63, 65. In the American press there appeared from day to day cheering items such as 'yesterday, a schooner from Guadaloup, with about seven tons of powder,' arrived in Philadelphia. *Boston Gazette*, April 22, 1776. There were also inventories of captures from 'the King's stores' and ships. *New England Chronicle*, April 25, 1776, May 23, 1776.

[3] P.R.O., *Colonial Office*, 5–123, p. 17, and 5–253, p. 174 (L. C. Trans.). *Ibid.*, 5–78, pp. 181–201. *Letters of . . . Continental Congress* (Burnett, ed.), I, 303.

ships, loading at Bordeaux, Saint-Malo, Havre de Grâce with ammunition which they carried to the French islands, and thence to American ports.[1] The worst blow to British pride was the report that vessels carrying provisions from Cork to the British army in America slipped away from the convoy in the night, sailed to Bordeaux, and sold their provisions to aid American privateers.[2]

But supplies of ammunition were not all that flowed in streams into American ports. Mr. Kelly, Germain's eyes in the West Indies, thought too much stress was laid on stopping the importation of powder and ball; the real trouble was woolens. If cloth could be kept from America, the 'rebels' would be near perishing, for the severity of American weather made wool a necessity. Stop the 'Golden Fleece from England, coarse Dutch cloth, warm jackets and wool stockings and Washington's army is done for,' declared Kelly. All American supplies of any consequence had come in the main through two or three West Indian islands, while the British navy paraded at home, he sneered, rather than serve in the Caribbean. If Britain had exerted herself, he said, one twentieth part as much between the tropics as she had in America, Congress could not have carried on the war.[3]

The report to Lord Dartmouth on fortification was dismal reading for an American Patriot. Penn-

[1] P.R.O., *Colonial Office*, 5–139, p. 14 a.b. 74 b (L. C. Trans.).

[2] *Ibid.*, 5–140, p. 155.

[3] P.R.O., *Colonial Office*, 5–78, pp. 181–201. For the extent of French trade with New England, up to June, 1776, see *Archives des Affaires Étrangères, États Unis*, 2, no. 178, Fol. 345–49.

sylvania had kept up no forts since 1763. There was a stone fortification on an island in the Delaware, ten miles below Philadelphia, to keep off pirates and privateers, but it was left unfinished. 'Not one fort now,' was Virginia's reply, and New Jersey's report was like unto it. Portsmouth, New Hampshire, had a castle built of stone, turfed within, and two batteries, but they were officially described as quite ruinous. The barracks were maintained with the greatest parsimony, and though the King had ordered three thousand stand of arms, there were only seventy. In Massachusetts the only fortress, Castle William in Boston Harbor, was in need of repair. Batteries at other seaport towns were all ruinous. Connecticut boasted a small battery at New London. Georgia, a point of danger, had four forts in fair condition, and New York made the best impression of all with a fort in good order at the seaport, ranges of batteries guarding East River, and forts defending Albany and Schenectady. Even there the stockades and blockhouses had decayed since 1763; and of the four frontier forts, Stanwix, Oswego, Edward, and Niagara, the latter only was garrisoned.[1] Such an array of fortification had no terror for the British Ministry except that of losing the colonies to any European nation ready to pounce upon such easy prey.

But mere statistics of man-power and fortified places only half-revealed the colonial military con-

[1] For all above reports on fortifications see *Dartmouth MSS.* (W.L.C.L.), I. (Query 16.) *Letters of ... Continental Congress* (Burnett, ed.), I, 100, Duane's summary.

ditions. Few civilized people had worse military traditions. John Adams faced the facts when he declared: 'A more exalted love of their country, a more enthusiastic ardor for military glory, and deeper detestation, disdain, and horror of martial disgrace must be excited among our people, or we shall perish in infancy. I will certainly give my voice for devoting to the infernal gods every man, high or low, who shall be convicted of bashfulness on the day of battle.'[1] In few Western peoples was there greater prejudice against the necessary discipline of war. Few resented the needed taxation more fiercely. From the first, Washington pleaded in vain for long-term enlistments, for a standing army, and described the militia as more hurtful than serviceable, 'a broken staff,' the cause of all misfortunes. Greene fully agreed with him.[2] Just before the battle of Bemis Heights, at the crisis of the Revolution, Stark's militia joined Gates in the morning and left before noon because their time of service had expired! Few events in the war so proved the utter failure of the militia system.

Men could not be brought to the right degree of subordination, Washington cried, in a day, a month, or even a year. 'Men just dragged from the tender scenes of domestic life,' he wrote, 'unaccustomed to the din of arms, totally unacquainted with every kind of military skill . . . are timid and ready to fly from their own shadows. Besides, a sudden change

[1] *Letters of . . . Continental Congress* (Burnett, ed.), II, 57, August 19, 1776.

[2] *Continental Congress Papers* (L.C.), *Greene Letters*, December 7, 1776. Washington's *Writings* (Ford, ed.), III, 344; IV, 77.

in their manner of living, particularly in their lodging, brings on sickness in many, impatience in all, and such an unconquerable desire of returning to their respective homes that it not only produces shameful and scandalous desertions among themselves but also infuses the like spirit in others.'[1] There was so much running home on furlough that Greene even proposed exchanging the Northern and Southern armies to 'cure the itch for going home' — since the soldiers would then have too far to go.[2] The winter season especially increased that 'terrible disorder,' homesickness.[3]

There was little of the glamor of war to lead the Patriot soldier on to glory. He was ill-armed, worse-clothed, often shoeless, 'never such tatterdemalions,' the British declared. Nothing was more rare than the 'buff and blue uniforms' seen to-day in fanciful portraits of Revolutionary ancestors. A hunting-shirt, butternut-stained, was nearer the real uniform, where there was any uniformity. A Hessian, who saw them in training, said they wore the clothes in which they went to field, to church, or to the tavern. They did not have that 'sprightly and foppish' appearance of regular forces 'when nicely powdered.'[4] Washington protested against a use-

[1] Washington, *Writings* (Ford, ed.), III, 344; IV, 77. The public press contained repeated advertisements by American officers for the return of men who had deserted from their companies. For example, see *Boston Gazette*, August 19, 1776, and the files for a month before and after.

[2] *Greene's Papers* (W.L.C.L.), December 31, 1775.

[3] *Continental Congress Papers* (*Schuyler Letters*), 153; III, 307 (October 15).

[4] Soldiers often took great care to have long hair in a powdered

less 'clothier general' where there were no clothes. His own servant in camp was 'indecently and shamefully naked.' Colonel Bland's ragged regiment looked, said Anburey, borrowing Shakespeare's phrase, 'as if the gibbets had been robbed to make it up.' [1] Such ill-clad men having perhaps sold their blankets to get bread, must perforce lie in straw to die of pleurisy and pneumonia. Ebenezer Huntington, 'fighting the Lord's battles, . . . ready for any infliction which God in his all-wise judgment chooses to inflict,' complained bitterly, nevertheless, that he had lain in filthy rags for forty hours on the rain-soaked ground, while his countrymen at home held their purse-strings as though they 'would damn the world rather than part with a dollar.' [2] All such lamentable conditions were the consequences of frontier characteristics, individualism, hatred of taxation, and lack of military experience, except in warfare with the redskin of the forest. The American militia were fitted for border warfare, for farm and village defense, the skirmish and the raid, but for the 'plumed troop and the big wars' they had little flair or fitness.

Added to the other frontier weaknesses, the 'embattled farmers' were ill-armed and ill-officered. The arms were muskets and smoothbore guns, or, in the case of the sharpshooters from the frontiers of Pennsylvania, Virginia, and Carolina, the rifle,

queue, even if their feet were bare. *Letters from America* (Pettengill trans.), 110–12.

[1] Anburey, *Travels*, II, 186.

[2] *Letters written by Ebenezer Huntington*, 30, 88.

brought to America by some of the earlier immigrants from the Austrian Tyrol. The blacksmiths of Maryland and New Jersey were able to make the barrels and stocks for a part of these crude weapons, but in the main the arms must in some way be got from abroad. The custom of loading the muskets with powder, put up in home-made paper cartridges, made handling so slow that the American soldier was often a victim of bayonet charges by an enemy quick to see this weakness.[1] The rifles, too, were muzzle-loading and too slow, but the frontier riflemen were deadly shots at three hundred yards. These riflemen were, however, in a small minority, and in the early stages of the war, at least, the average militiaman was a very poor shot, indeed. In the famous retreat from Concord to Boston, the British suffered only 273 casualties, and as there were at least 3500 Americans shooting at the 'Redcoats' that day, one in ten made his mark upon the enemy.[2] Not only were the small arms ineffective, but such cannon as were not early captured from the King's arsenals were home-made, cast in rude iron furnaces — and most unpopular with military men — or brass artillery, shooting three to twenty-four-pound balls, secured from Europe.[3] Such artillery as they had they rarely used, wrote a competent

[1] E. J. Lowell, *The Hessians* . . . 65. A fine treatment of this is in A. French, *The Day of Concord and Lexington*, 27–34, 255–58.

[2] French, *The Day of Concord and Lexington*, 258.

[3] Colonel von Heeringen wrote that the American artillery at the battle of Long Island was 'wretched, iron pieces, badly served and mounted on ships' carriages.' J. G. Rosengarten, *The German Soldier* . . . 66.

opponent. When they did, they served it 'slowly, but not ill.' [1]

To wrest victory with such weapons from a well-disciplined enemy, Washington had only squads of militia, drilled by the officers they elected, by whom they had been recruited, and from whom they would accept no strict discipline. Yet he frankly said to Congress that 'the government of an army must be a perfect despotism.' [2] As a result of the widespread 'leveling' spirit, the officers must fire with example or whiskey, and win with arguments; they could not command.[3] General Greene wrote in despair, 'we are obliged to relax the very sinews of military government and give a latitude of indulgence to the soldiery incompatible with the security of the camp or country.' [4] Governor Trumbull attributed this insubordination to 'the genius and spirit of our people' whose pulse 'beats high for liberty'! To be popular, officers must pretend to care nothing for titles, must depreciate military salutes, and do menial tasks to show that they were not proud. Washington, the Southern aristocrat, liking as officers none but gentlemen with dignity of character, who could use the tone of authority, was dismayed at the New England officer who barbered his soldiers, and even pooled with them his pay. Such men often lacked not only honor but decency; and Washington confessed early that he had broken one

[1] The Earl of Harrington, P.R.O., *State Papers, Domestic, Military*, 18, no. 6, p. 57.

[2] Hildreth, *History of the United States* (ed. 1880), III, 163.

[3] A. B. Hart, *Contemporaries*, II, 481.

[4] *Greene Papers* (W.L.C.L.), Greene to Ward, December 31, 1775.

colonel and five captains for cowardice, or for drawing more pay and provisions than they had men in their companies.[1] Some of these, wrote Greene, did everything they could to obstruct and retard the recruiting of the new army, that on the ruin of Washington's efforts they might rebuild their own power.[2] In time Washington created a body of efficient, brave, and dependable officers, but he first had his trials with the peasant officer, chumming perhaps with his own wagonmaker, and intriguing like a ward boss for his election to a captaincy. In the early New England armies critics found 'every man a general and not one of them a soldier.' In such an army men were insubordinate even under guard.[3] This aggregation of unmilitary men, ill-clad, poorly armed, undisciplined, it was Washington's task to make fit for a war against professional soldiers.

In doing this, Washington was handicapped by the most unwieldy superior council that ever hampered a military chieftain. Congress, unwilling to trust one-man power, did all the business of a war department through committees whose work was finally reviewed by the whole Congress; and behind that were thirteen selfish political communities which pulled and hauled in different directions, each demanding all the defense it could get. In the actual business of directing the war, the British Ministry had a far better engine, a small group of six men who planned and executed every military measure,

[1] Washington, *Writings* (Ford, ed.), October 8, 1776.
[2] *Greene Papers* (W.L.C.L.), December 31, 1775.
[3] Conn. Hist. Soc., *Collections*, VII, 124.

and secured its means from a Parliament most subservient during all the early years of the war. America had no unity of command except at a few times of supreme peril when Congress yielded Washington a kind of dictatorship.

Americans who realized their lack of forts, of artillery, of discipline, of proper command, and of military traditions, comforted themselves as they could with reflections upon the 'little Swiss cantons,' and the 'small provinces of the Low Countries,' who opposed successfully the tyrants of their day.[1] There was comfort also in the memories of colonial valor at Louisburg, when 'a few raw provincials,' favored by 'the smiles and care of heaven,' beat down strong batteries defended by regulars.[2] They never doubted that the 'God of Hosts' was again with them. The 'heroes of '76' were in a state of mind to believe that the Kingdom of Heaven could be carried by storm.

Moreover, eager Patriots set about acquiring military knowledge, urging aspiring officers to study the works of Müller, Saxe, Count Pogan, M. Vauban, M. Blondell, and M. Belidar. In July of 1775, there was published in Philadelphia 'The Prussian Evolutions,' containing military instructions on fortifications, evolutions, and the art of war in general. Even military academies were proposed, and public exhibits of models of forts, redoubts, ramparts, parapets, scarps, glacis, and esplanades.[3] When Con-

[1] *Boston Evening Post*, July 4, 1774; *Letters of . . . Continental Congress* (Burnett, ed.), I, 100.

[2] William Gordon, *Religious and Civil Liberty*, 17, 30.

[3] *New England Chronicle*, May 9, 1776; *Pennsylvania Evening Post*, August 3, 1775.

gress set about making articles of war, it went a bit against the grain to have to take over the British system almost without change. Yet the British articles were finally voted, because there was, as a member wrote, but one system 'which had carried two empires to the head of mankind.' The British articles were only 'a literal translation of the Roman,' and it would be vain for Americans to try to invent, or try to extract from the records of other warlike nations, a better system of military discipline.[1] Even the proposal of the 'Southern cavalier,' Rutledge, to strike out an article which forbade the sending of challenges, failed, in spite of his fiery argument that the sending of such challenges tended to make officers gentlemen.[2] The articles were finally, therefore, pure British — and Roman. Thus, with French and Prussian books on military art and English articles of war, the Americans accepted the ordeal by battle. There prevailed almost universally the same blind faith in raising disciplined armies between daylight and dark which was to cheer worthy American demagogues for over a century and a half to come.

[1] *Letters of . . . Continental Congress* (Burnett, ed.), II, 55.

[2] *Ibid.*, 56.

CHAPTER VII

GEORGE III BORROWS PART OF HIS ARMOR

FORTUNATELY for the American cause, the preparedness of the British was not what the efficient George III would have desired. For years he had fretted over the 'fatal military economy' of England, its 'injudicious ideas' in times of peace, which left it 'very unable to draw the sword.' Like Cromwell, he was not satisfied that England was 'environed with a great ditch from all the world besides.' Englishmen, to use again 'the Protector's' phrase, must turn their 'ships and shipping into troops of horse and companies of foot,' if England would be safe. In August of 1775, the King wrote Lord North of the misfortune that 'just at the beginning of this American business there has been an unwillingness to augment the army and navy.' Early in the summer he had wished to send 'beating orders' to Ireland which would have made the army three thousand men stronger, but the Cabinet had objected.[1] British prejudice against a standing army had, on the very verge of war, fixed the effective land force at about 17,500 and the sea force at 16,000 men. Next year, 1775, Parliament voted 55,000 soldiers

[1] *Correspondence of George III and Lord North* (Donne, ed.), I, 265, 266. British Museum, *Egerton MSS.*, 982. General Wolfe agreed with George III that England was lazy in times of peace. For the King's own careful counting up of his resources, see *Correspondence of King George III*, III, 305–27.

and 28,000 seamen, but these men were still to be raised, and even when enlisted would be quite inadequate to their task.[1] Pownall, sure that England 'must arm from head to foot,' feared that 'unless it rained men in red coats' the Ministry could not get all the men it needed. At a time when it was estimated that there were 2,350,000 fighting men in Great Britain, Parliament dared not call one twentieth of them to arms to save the Empire.[2] But even had they dared, there is reason to believe that efforts to recruit would have failed. The partisan charge that aversion to the American war prevented enlistments would be hard to prove, but certain it is that all devices failed, and the Ministry had to look abroad for a good part of its armies. England was still dominated by the theory of a volunteer army, though by a system of impressing and kidnaping there was in fact conscription not legalized.[3] The law recognized the conscription only so far as to authorize recruiting agents to impress first of all any idle, unknown, or suspected fellow who could not account for himself, and any fortune-teller or sturdy beggar. Next to be seized were jailbirds, or such as had been summoned before justices of the peace, and finally any 'incorrigible rogue.' Poachers, too, were good prey, the better because they were good

[1] Force, *American Archives* (4th Series), VI, 143; I, 1479. See Belcher, *American Civil War*, I, 259. *Clinton Papers*, Pownall to Clinton, 1775.

[2] Chalmers, *An Estimate of . . . Strength* (1786), 138.

[3] E. E. Curtis, *The British Army in the American Revolution*, chap. III. This chapter on recruiting brings out admirably the difficulties.

shots; and all convicts were suited to fill the ranks.[1] Men not enlisted in this manner were enticed by large bounties, reënforced by copious beer and military music. It would, perhaps, have been fairly easy to raise independent companies and new regiments had King George been willing to encourage certain lords and baronets and gentlemen of leisure who offered to recruit if they might count on a rank in the army proportionate to the number of men they succeeded in enlisting. It was, however, expensive, unfair to the officers of the regular line, and the King, to the end of the war, refused his consent.[2] Yet all these methods failed, because Englishmen were not attracted by the poor pay and harsh discipline, and, moreover, they were affrighted from the service by the ridicule and abuse of a soldier's life with which the provincial press was filled. When Gage was clamoring for twenty thousand men, there were only nine thousand in Boston, and that was almost the only available field force in the Empire.

In this crisis the King, seated on his throne in his royal robes, sent the gentleman usher of the black rod to summon the House of Commons into the House of Lords to hear his most gracious speech wherein he announced the sending of his Electoral troops, four thousand Hanoverians, to the Mediterranean to release an equal number of British troops

[1] If these methods would seem to result in filling the British army with bullies and blackguards, one must recall that eighteenth-century laws made men criminals and stuffed them into prisons for offenses which to-day would be punished with a fine or mere warning and probation.

[2] *Correspondence of King George III*, III; nos. 1614–18, 1628, 1630.

for American service.[1] The Ministry left Ireland, moreover, almost defenseless by reducing its garrisons in order to get a few thousand men for America.[2] In desperation they tried recruiting in Ireland, even accepting Roman Catholics, against all recent precedents. All these resources failed, however, and soon it became manifest that it was cheaper to buy abroad than to buy at home. Turning first to Russia and then to Germany, the needs were partly met, and by the summer of 1776 the anxious Government placed thirty-six thousand British and German soldiers in America.

This army was made up of marines, infantry, artillery, and a few dragoons. In it there was no horse artillery, only the embryo of a medical corps. There was great weakness in the matter of engineers and land transport. Though General Wolfe had declared that England's military education was the worst in Europe, yet it is certain that the British army was finely disciplined, and the British generals were not cursed with short-service men who made off home just as they were trained. Moreover, the British soldiers were much more impressive than the ragged American Continentals. With them was the neighing steed, the shrill trumpet, the spirit-stirring drum, the ear-piercing fife, all the pride and pomp of war. There were real uniforms in which the famous red coat was a dominant feature. Long gaiters and tight shoes tortured the foot soldier, while stocks forced his head up, and a tallowed queue finished

[1] *London Gazette*, October 24, 1775.

[2] P.R.O., *State Papers, Domestic, George III*, 11–88/15c.

his discomfort, but did not better his marksmanship. In addition to the fact that the game laws of England brought it about that the middle and lower classes lacked experience in the use of the musket, the tightly squeezed arms and legs and neck of the soldier completed his incapacity to shoot at anything in particular. Only the occasional poacher redeemed this fault, and furnished the British army with some sharpshooters. The soldier's kit and accouterments overloaded him shamefully, but at least he was properly equipped with arms and ammunition, unless transport failed utterly.

The officers of the British army were apt to be gentlemen with the habit of command, though their efficiency was seriously lowered by the vicious custom of buying and selling commissions. It was even possible for a provident parent to purchase a commission for an infant, though in the book of fate it might be written that he was better fitted for the pulpit than for the field of Mars. This source of weakness in the British army was not remedied for generations thereafter. It is a debatable question whether the British officers in charge of the Crown's armies in America were the equals in military knowledge and training of the German officers in charge of the mercenary troops that largely augmented the British force.

The use of mercenary soldiers by the British Ministry was not such an evidence of their madness as rhetorical pamphleteers of that time, and emotional historians of later years, asserted. Nearly all great European wars up to the time of the French Revolution were carried on with mercenaries. Hanoverians and Hessians went to America to fight for George III, as the German warriors of Tacitus went away with their chiefs to fight in the army of any other people. The eighteenth century saw no harm in any man taking his sword into any service, if the pay and pillage was good. English, Scotch, and Irish soldiers had often served in foreign armies. From the ten thousand Greeks under Xenophon to the Swiss Guard about the august person of Louis XVI, the precedents for such action ran unbroken. The British naturally turned to their old comrades of the Seven Years' War, of even earlier wars, when England had more money than cannon fodder.[1] It was not so novel a fact as Shelburne hinted for British Ministers to go 'with bowed head from court to court begging a morsel of soldiers.' They simply went into the open market rather than make use of crimps and decoys. George III had grace enough not to like doing business with 'man-stealers' or being 'turned into a kidnaper';[2] but soldiers he must have in a hurry, and the Germans were reputed for their aptitude in arms, their endurance, bravery and discipline, their loyalty, if promptly paid. Their leaders asked no moral questions as to the merit of a war, they did not grow sentimental over the battle-field and hospitals, and in an age of frightfulness possessed admirable traits of rapacity and cruelty.[3]

[1] Max von Eelking, *The German Allied Troops* (Rosengarten trans.), 16. In 1702, 1726, 1745, 1755, foreign troops had served in British pay. *Archives des Affaires Étrangères, Angleterre*, 515, no. 2, no. 4.

[2] *Correspondence of George III*, I, 297; *Atlantic Monthly*, XXXV, 136.

[3] For an argument in defense of the system of hiring mercenaries as

Before being assured of an adequate supply of German mercenaries, the British Ministry sought aid from Russia, whose soldiers, fresh from the Turkish wars, were veterans much to be desired. The King was ready if necessary even to grant a subsidy, but 'profusion' must be avoided if possible. Gunning, the British Minister in Russia, came off ingloriously from this effort to secure through Count Panin twenty thousand infantry from Catherine II.[1] The Empress expressed the greatest readiness, urging the British, 'For God's sake put an end to the rebellion as soon as possible.' So sure was Gunning at first that his quest was granted that he wrote home a letter, which induced Lord Dartmouth to write General Howe the joyful news, and which duped George III into writing an autograph letter to 'Madame, my sister,' asking for the soldiers.[2] The King's 'constant affection' and 'ardent wishes' and 'heartfelt sentiment' were not spared in assuring her imperial majesty that nothing could efface from his memory this generous act. Catherine's answer, not 'genteel,' was a clear refusal, maddening to George III, because she had not been polite enough to answer in her own hand, and containing advice, civil, perhaps, 'to a Russian ear,' but not 'to more

suited to the times, and also as a remnant of feudalism, see Max von Eelking, *Leben und Wirken des . . . Riedesel*, II, 3–4.

[1] June 30, 1775, Lord Suffolk authorized this effort. *State Papers, Foreign Office*, 98.

[2] Hist. MSS. Com. *Report on American MSS.*, I, 7. P.R.O., *State Papers, Foreign Office*, 99. The whole amazing story of these negotiations from June 30, 1775, to November, 1775, is found in Gunning's *Correspondence*, in this group of *State Papers*.

civilized ones.'[1] Catherine had been full of excuses and regret. Poland was in a bad state. Such aid might alarm other powers. She had a repugnance to the use of her troops in Canada; had understood that they were to be used against Spain. Could she not help in some other way? If other powers attacked England, she would help at once. All of Gunning's efforts to see her and appeal to her honor and gratitude failed. She became very ill, even on the Grand Duke's birthday. Thus, in humiliation and disgrace, ended England's efforts to get aid from Catherine II. Was it the influence of the French Minister, or did Frederick the Great use his great influence with Catherine to foil the British designs?[2] Catherine was a great admirer of Charles James Fox, and may thus have been led to believe that the British nation did not approve of the King's policy.[3] No more successful was the attempt in November, 1775, to borrow from the Dutch the Scotch brigade relied upon heretofore in time of need.[4] No attention was paid to Lord Ellibank's proposal to give Canada back to the French on the condition of their helping to reduce the rebellious colonies.[5] There was then nothing for it but 'German boars and vassals from twenty hireling states,' to use Burke's unsympathetic phrase.

[1] *Correspondence of George III and North* . . . I, 282. P.R.O., *State Papers, American and West Indies,* 431, F 75.

[2] *American Historical Review,* XXI, 92–93. P.R.O., *State Papers, Foreign Office,* 353, II, no. 97, 99. Gunning doubted Prussia's influence.

[3] P.R.O., *State Papers, Foreign Office,* no. 99.

[4] F. Edler, *The Dutch Republic and the American Revolution,* 28–31.

[5] Hist. MSS. Com., *Stopford-Sackville MSS.,* II, 21.

It was not a new quest upon which Colonel William Faucitt was sent by the Secretary of State for Foreign Affairs. At seven guineas a soldier, contractors in Hamburg had long been accustomed to fill the British ranks, and in 1775 there were a number of petty landgraves and princes eager to gorge their treasuries with British gold. Alchemy and lottery having failed, Prince Charles of Brunswick-Luneberg, brother-in-law to George III, was ready to sell 4300 men at a bargain which in time put £160,000 into his coffers.[1] The ruler of Hanau, with a reputed brood of seventy-four children to support, came in thirst to the fountain of British need. There, too, came the Landgrave of Hesse-Cassel, whose imitation of the French court had cost him dear. Expensive tastes, the cast-off mistress of a French duke, and numerous unlawful progeny had emptied his treasury. Out of 300,000 subjects he managed to get 20,000 soldiers, of whom 17,000 were shipped to America.[2] With the proceeds he founded schools and museums, built marble palaces and rich art galleries, and left to his heirs a full treasury, ample atonement, surely, for any blood and tears his man-market cost his subjects. Six princes[3] in all ministered to Lord

[1] E. J. Lowell, *The Hessians in the Revolution*, 8.

[2] An interesting defense of the Hessians and their prince is in *Pennsylvania Magazine of History*, XXIII, 157–83. A review of the whole literature concerning German mercenaries is found in *Proceedings of the American Philosophical Society*, XXXIX, 129–54, by Rosengarten.

[3] E. J. Lowell, *The Hessians* . . . 20, gives the sum total of the men sent:

Brunswick, 5,723; Hesse-Cassel, 16,992; Hesse-Hanau, 2,422; Anspach-Bayreuth, 2,353; Waldeck, 1225; Anhalt-Zerbst, 1,160; Total, 29,875.

North's needs, and furnished altogether some thirty thousand soldiers for the American war.

In the main these troops were drilled on the Prussian model, and were better equipped than the British troops, at least according to Continental standards. Fighting for a cause they loved, they would have been the best of soldiers, but duped by the submissive spirit of the age, or lured by false promises, they readily became deserters when experience later revealed to them the truth. Moreover, they proved troublesome allies, claiming the merit for all that was done, becoming proud and arrogant if honored, disdaining their 'unsoldierly' allies, sure that the success of a campaign depended upon them alone. The nature, character, and state of mind of the typical mercenary is fairly drawn in 'Barry Lyndon' and George Sand's 'Consuelo.'[1] Those who trafficked in them haggled and chaffered, kidnaped foreigners, committed any crime to fill the regiments, following in this respect the example of their great master, Frederick the Great.[2] Nor were they particular about dealing honestly with their royal customer. Faucitt wrote of the first division inspected, that the front and rear were made up of sound men, but that the center was worthless, some too small,

[1] Thackeray, *Barry Lyndon*, chaps. V, VI, VII; Sand, *Consuelo*.

[2] Read Carlyle's description of the Prussian recruiter in his *Life of Frederick II*, book V, chap. 5. The almost ludicrous caution taken in getting a new recruit to camp revealed the absurdity of the assertion that he was eager to fight for King George. The recruit was disarmed, the agent armed. At night the recruit's clothes were locked up until morning. He was marched in front of the armed agent, never allowed to come near to him, and while he ate, sat between the table and the wall.

'imperfectly grown,' some too old, too feeble to carry a musket, some too young, raw recruits needing months of training. In order to spare their own provinces, the princes' agents had enlisted deserters from neighboring armies, runaway poets and wandering students. John Gottfried Seume was swept into the mass, where he found a monk from Würzburg, a Prussian sergeant, a Hessian major, a bankrupt from Vienna. No one was safe from the sellers of souls. In addition to honest peasant lads there were political malcontents, restless ones, looselivers, spendthrifts and drunkards, all guarded like convicts until safe on the slave ships which took them to America. Though many of these Falstaffian recruits were weeded out, some of the bargains must have been poor, because the terms differed widely, and even the 'duodecimo tyrants' who drove the worst bargains made fortunes.[1] Faucitt was accused of extravagance, but he was told at the outset that expense was less to be considered than great activity, and, moreover, it must be in the reckoning that George III by buying Germans was saved, for years to come, half-pay for British officers and pensions for wounded veterans.[2] Faucitt made every

[1] The exact profits cannot be computed, even the details of payment were kept secret by the British Ministry; but Parliament voted the following sums:

Hesse-Cassel (8 years)	£2,959,800
Brunswick (8 years)	750,000
Hesse-Hanau (8 years)	343,130
Waldeck (8 years)	140,000
Anbach-Bayreuth (7 years)	282,400
Anhalt-Zerbst (7 years)	109,120

Max von Eelking, *The German Allies* (trans.), 18.

[2] *Correspondence of George III* . . . (Donne, ed.), I, 294.

effort to see that the soldiers got a square deal, even insisting upon paying the wages direct to the men, where he distrusted their princely masters.[1]

Though many scornful arrows were aimed at the 'huckster princes' by the British opposition, and by the enraged Americans, it is remarkable how small was the volume of contemporary German criticism of this 'auction of blood and tears.' Few there were moved even by Mirabeau's 'Avis aux Hessois.'[2] Ideas of freedom had touched in Germany only a few of the spiritual heights. Feudal ideas still held sway over the nobles and common people who were used to being inherited like flocks and herds. Even the subjects of the German princes saw foreign money flowing in, reducing taxes in some cases, and they were content. German literature was censored, it is true, but, nevertheless, it is remarkable how most of it was pro-British and the press anti-American throughout the war.[3] Doubtless there was propaganda to that end, as there certainly was among the German soldiers, who nearly all wrote home from America unfavorable accounts of the American rebels. They found them unbearably conceited, and believed that wickedness and pleasure was the cause of the rebellion, that they grew haughty because

[1] E. J. Lowell, *The Hessians* . . . 16. All the essential details of the bargains can be found in Chapter II.

[2] Printed in *Proceedings* of American Philosophical Society, XXXIX, 150.

[3] E. J. Lowell, *The Hessians* . . . 21–22. Yet Rousseau was a hero among the intelligentsia, and Henriette Herz writes at this time, 'I can't remember anybody in my father's circle on the English side.' Royal Historical Society, *Transactions* (3d Series), x, 53. See also *Letters from America* (Pettingill, trans.), 229.

they lived too well.[1] The few Germans who cried 'shame' upon the traffic in men were either idealists like Schiller, living spiritually in a coming age, or selfish rulers like Frederick the Great, animated by a lively concern for his own needs, and by hate of the British Government, which had deserted him during his direst perils in the Seven Years' War. Schiller arraigned the man-selling in his *Kabale und Liebe*, and Frederick sneered at the 'dirty selfishness' of dragging one's subjects to the shambles, but he had in his mind his own need of those subjects in projected wars, and he conveniently forgot that his own agents regularly kidnaped any subject suited to fill the ranks of his armies.[2]

In England, the opponents to Lord North in Parliament made the most of every argument against the German treaties. Besides rhetorical sneers at a German Sancho Panza selling his 'blackamoor subjects,' at 'German slaves' hired to subdue the sons of England and of freedom, and at hirelings sold 'like so many beasts for slaughter,' there were auguries of the danger in sending twelve thousand foreigners into British domains, fears that they would mutiny and desert, and that the employment of Germans would be a bad example to Americans, who would then turn to France and Spain.[3] And

[1] *Letters from America* (Pettingill, trans.), 165, 166, 180, 189, 191, 229.

[2] There is good evidence of collusion between Prussia and France in the matter of preventing German troops being sent to the aid of England. France thanked Frederick and he welcomed that recognition. A. de Circourt, *Histoire . . . de la France et de l'Amérique* . . . 117, 127.

[3] *Parliamentary Register* (1st Series), III, 341–60; V, 174–216. *Archives des Affaires Étrangercs, Angleterre,* 515, no. 4.

how great would be the contrast between England's allies and those of America. 'I search the map of Europe,' cried the Duke of Grafton, 'and I find an almost imperceptible point, and I am told that it is Hesse.' [1] There was scorn for a treaty on equal terms between 'the mistress of the seas' and a petty German landgrave. Worst of all it was a treaty binding England to a defensive alliance. If Hesse is attacked, England must come to the rescue. 'If an enemy destroys its parks, palaces, cascades ... England must compensate.' [2] 'What,' asked the Duke of Richmond, 'has become of the noble statesmanship, what of the magnanimity, the elevated sentiment which was once the admiration of the world?' [3] Some dwelt upon the danger of letting Europe know that England was so exhausted, had so few soldiers that she must hire from petty German rulers who could scarcely care for themselves.[4] Classical scholars as most British statesmen were, we find no one quoting Demosthenes, when Philip threatened Athens: 'Cease to hire your armies. Go yourselves, every man of you, and stand in the ranks, and either a victory beyond all victories in its glory awaits you, or falling you shall fall greatly and worthy of your past.' In the last war, asserted Lord Shelburne, three hundred thousand Englishmen entered British armies; now fifty thousand men was all the Ministry could summon, and a good part of that must be bought from German princes. 'In a

[1] *Archives des Affaires Étrangères, Angleterre,* 515, nos. 4, 18.

[2] *Ibid.*, no. 4. This is a French report of Parliamentary debates.

[3] *Ibid.*, no. 4. [4] *Ibid.*, no. 4.

worthy cause,' was his parting taunt, 'we can get soldiers enough.'[1] During the debate the whole merit of the war was discussed, and withering scorn turned on those who would conquer America with barbarian Russians and mercenary Germans.[2] London critics dwelt upon the folly of using foreign troops and 'papists.' The Mayor and Aldermen of London pleaded with the King against the 'disgrace of hiring foreign mercenaries.'[3] Even Wedderburn, who thought it illegal to send troops from Ireland, would break the law and defy critics rather than seek a foreign force. It would look 'less like a desperate resource.'[4] Where was the logic of refusing the services of excellent Irish officers because they were Catholics, and then accepting the mercenary sword of a Papist German? There was talk of the knout and the bow-string and Janissary law, but no one offered another solution of the real problem as to how else soldiers were to be got if rebellious America was to be conquered. North, luminous on the dangers that threatened, using the argument that to support him was to save the ship, carried the day. He fooled Parliament and the nation into believing that he alone could save its honor.

Perhaps the greatest argument against hiring German soldiers was the wrath it aroused in America. The 'infamous treaties' made by the 'unre-

[1] *Archives des Affaires Étrangères, Angleterre*, no. 4.

[2] Hansard, *Parliamentary History of England*, XVIII, 1016, 1200–28.

[3] Force, *American Archives* (4th Series), III, 1010–14. *State Papers, Domestic, George III*, 11.

[4] Hist. MSS. Com., *Report on American MSS.*, x, Appendix, part VI, 9.

lenting tyrant of Britain' engrossed the attention of Congress as early as May of 1776.[1] No conciliation could be talked of after that unmotherly act. American anger was the hotter because they really feared the Germans. Congress had been startled already when there appeared at their door 'a German Hussar, a veteran in the Wars in Germany, in his Uniform, and on Horse back, a forlorn Cap upon his Head, with a Streamer waving from it half down to his Waistband, with a Deaths Head painted in Front, a beautiful Hussar Cloak ornamented with Lace, and Fringe and Cord of Gold, a scarlet Waistcoat under it, with shining yellow metal Buttons — a Light Gun strung over his Shoulder — and a Turkish Sabre, much Superior to an high-Land broad sword, very large and excellently fortified by his side — Holsters and Pistols upon his Horse — in short the most warlike and formidable Figure,' John Adams ever saw.[2] Throughout the war, Germans were an object of awe and wonder to the simple American farmer. Von Steuben swore that they came to see him as if he were a rhinoceros. All the 'damned curious inhabitants,' whole families with wives and daughters, came to see the German prisoners after Saratoga. One thought that his guard charged admission to see him.[3] The thought of thousands of these terrible fellows invading America

[1] *Letters of . . . Continental Congress* (Burnett, ed.), I, 458, 468, 470, 473. *New England Chronicle*, May 23, 1776.

[2] *Warren-Adams Letters*, I, 75–76, July 11, 1775, Congress authorized the formation of a body of fifty German Hussars who had fought in Germany.

[3] *Letters from America* (Pettingill, trans.) 123.

was alarming and maddening, but it did not frighten men into submission.

Yet, on the whole, the British Government was perhaps strengthened by the mercenaries. England itself must not be stripped of men. Though the sea was still a wall, a moat, 'against the envy of less happier lands,'[1] yet England had vulnerable possessions in the four quarters of the earth. Her greatest weakness was the envy she had aroused in the European world, by the vast expansion of her empire. No sooner was she occupied with rebellion than the other powers of Europe, France, Spain, Prussia, and Russia, began to press for the settlement of standing diplomatic questions, getting more daring and more pressing as England's troubles grew. Like a strong man fighting with many weaker men, danger was all about, safety only in defense at every point. Jealous nations ready to fight were a greater menace than a nation at open war, for the British strong naval force gave an advantage if it could face an open enemy whose wealth could be seized at sea. England was at war with a jealous world as soon as she was at war with America, and it must never be forgotten that France, her envious neighbor, had nearly double the population of the British Isles, so that man-power from abroad was practically a necessity if England was to be safe.

[1] The Duke of Richmond questioned this. 'Almost as often as foreign forces have attempted to land they have succeeded,' he declared, Nov., 1777. Hansard, *Parliamentary History*, XIX, 407.

CHAPTER VIII

DIVIDED PUBLIC OPINION IN ENGLAND

By the end of the year 1775, the British Ministry, and such small part of the British people as possessed any influence on government, were face to face with the greatest crisis in many centuries of a most eventful history. If George III and his Ministers could have obtained from America and have read at first hand only a half of the thousands of protests which came with 'damnable iteration' from politicians, congresses, conventions, meetings in counties and towns, from editorial offices, from every colony, all with like ideas drawn from the same sources, they might have realized that it was not Boston nor New England, but the American continent, that was ablaze with rebellion. They might have seen the folly of Lord George Germain's idea that a pistol accidentally fired occasioned all the mischief. Little minds might account in that way for the rending empire, but more profound spirits would perceive that fatal differences in economic interests, in political theory, in social and intellectual character, and in the basic conceptions of the moral world widened daily the breach in the imperial fabric. Statesmanship that could effectively meet a crisis of this kind was not likely to be born out of such conditions as prevailed then in England. The moral standards of the ruling class were never lower. It was the hopelessness of changing these conditions which early converted John Adams to the idea of Independence. If we 'consider the Education of the sovereign, and that the Lords, Commons, the Electors, the Army, the Navy, the officers of Excise, Customs, etc., have been now for many years gradually trained and disciplined by Corruption to the system of the Court, We shall be convinced that the Cancer is too deeply rooted . . . to be cured by anything short of cutting it out entire.'[1]

We are amazed as we read Lord Malmsbury's diary that so many of his companions at Oxford, Charles Fox, Lord Romney, Lord North, and William Eden, made their way in the world in spite of their wild dissipations and imitations of London high life.[2] One can have no doubt that such men had constitution enough to be wicked. Moreover, the great families whose rakish scions shocked the sterner morals of Puritan America were never dastards in war, never lacking in that courage which sent them to die in India, Germany, America, or on any one of the seven seas which Britain was somewhat vain of ruling. If their morals were weak, their spirits were high, and there was no sign of degeneracy.

Nevertheless, the politically active part of the English people, in numbers small, was drunk with victory and the dissipations of wealth. Government positions were in the hands of placemen, corruption was rampant, not called in merely upon extraordinary emergencies, Junius cried, but glittering in the van, maintaining an army of mercenaries which im-

[1] *Letters of . . . Continental Congress* (Burnett, ed.), I, 118.

[2] Lord Malmsbury, *Diaries*, I, ix.

poverished and enslaved the nation.[1] Chalmers, little given to exaggeration, wrote at the close of the Revolution, 'As we grew more opulent, we became more luxurious, and, as our voluptuousness increased, our industry diminished, till, in the progress of our folly, we found a delight in sacrificing our diligence and economy to the gratifications of a pleasurable moment, during a dissipated age.'[2] Nor was it merely Cowper's nabob, putting the wealth of Indian provinces into his overgorged and bloated purse, who brought on this condition, but fraudulent contractors aided by careless officers who sent rotten ships to sea, caulked with putty, and furnished British soldiers with low-grade powder, and cannon with balls of a different caliber. Worst of all, neither corruption nor profligacy seemed to deprive a public man of the approbations of those in whose hands was the gift of power. If we recall Grafton's career, it was not mere sarcasm when Horace Walpole wrote, 'If I paid nobody and went drunk to bed every morning at six, I might expect to be called out of bed by two in the afternoon to save the nation.' English political society did not reject a leader because he was dissipated, and it only frowned if he was corrupt. Pitt was thought curiously eccentric when he declined irregular profits which his office might have yielded. In the matter of securing votes in Parliament, it was not so much that too many fine gentlemen were 'slipping Lord North's bribes so elegantly under their ruffles' as

[1] *Letters of Junius* (ed. 1799), II, 176.

[2] Chalmers, *Estimate of the Comparative Strength* (1786), 219.

that he and the King knew how to procure the choice of members upon whom they could rely, binding them with the many favors in their power to grant.[1]

The King, by use of the crown lands and hereditary revenues, had the means of gratifying the expectations of all, spending a million pounds when the whole expense of the state was five million. The purposes for which these sums were used were conventional enough at the time, and did not look like corrupt practice to the members of the ruling class.[2] Actual bribes were not necessary, for George III could keep the lords obedient with delectable gifts of office. He could make a peer one of his two Treasurers, a Comptroller, or a Cofferer. If he could not put him in charge of his royal dress as Master of the Robes, he could make him Keeper of the Wardrobe, or of the Removing Wardrobe, and still have left for other obedient nobles the offices of the Groom of the Stole, the King's Valet, or the King's Valet's Deputy.[3] Votes in the House of Commons could be made secure with such offices as those of Tellers of the Exchequers, State Keepers of the Ordnance, Vice-Treasurers of Ireland, Paymasters of the Marines, Rangers of the Royal Forests, Registrars of the Chancery of Barbadoes, Clerks of the Board of Green Cloth, the Grooms of the Bed Chamber, and Lords of Trade.[4] All these

[1] *The Parliamentary Papers of John Robinson* (Laprade, ed.), xix. Stirling, *Coke of Norfolk*, etc., 110–11.

[2] *The Parliamentary Papers of John Robinson* (Laprade, ed.), xix; *Correspondence of King George III*, III, 114.

[3] *Parliamentary Papers of J. Robinson* (Laprade, ed.), 12–13.

[4] *Ibid.*, 9–17.

marched to the King's order. The historian Gibbon was one of the placemen of George III, and he cynically declared that, corruption 'was the most infallible symptom of constitutional liberty,' admitting that he had supported, 'with many a sincere and silent vote, the rights though not perhaps the interests of the mother country.'

Nevertheless, history may not picture George III leading with chains of gold an unwilling people. Few kings have been more popular, at least with those who had the vote in their hands, the landowning squires and those whom we are now pleased to call the *bourgeoisie*. Laying aside his royal robes, he would have found peace and accord in their company. As he more and more firmly grasped the lever of governmental machinery, his control over great sections of the ruling classes increased, but his parliamentary majorities were not gained by corruption alone. Burke blamed 'the good people of England,' who were no longer 'the eager, inquisitive, jealous, fiery people' of old, but partook more and more of the character of that administration they had been induced to tolerate. They did not exactly commend its measures, but their opposition was 'cold, languid,' excited to no passion, prompted to no action. Pitt, too, found the England of his day 'no more like old England, or England forty years ago,' than modern Romans were like the Gracchi or Catos.[1] It was this fact which dashed the hopes of the little band, Burke, Pitt, Camden, Barré, and others, who set out to drive the Government to do the statesmanlike rather than the legal thing.

[1] Chatham, *Correspondence*, IV, 83.

This band and its followers did not escape the charge of 'tossing brands among the rabble,' of encouraging rebellion in America, of creating the opposition to the North Ministry by their unwearied defense of the American claims. People of 'good hearts and weak heads,' said the King's friends, delighted 'to encourage traitors beyond the Atlantic.' [1] Dr. Johnson and others put on them the miseries of the war, and urged vengeance on them for inflaming the Americans.[2] A pamphleteer described their activities: 'They serve to bark at government in the open streets, and keep up the wholesome spirit of clamour in the common people — it is so teazing to a minister, it makes him winch and fret, and go uneasy in his post. — Ah! many a comfortable point has been gained by clamour.' [3] That encouragement from these gentlemen of the Opposition was one of the minor sources of colonial discontent seems likely, in spite of Walpole's assertion that it was the cruelest thing said of the Americans, because the Opposition had so little spirit that one might as well try to light a fire with a wet dish-clout as rebellion with such measures as theirs. It was, indeed, strange that the group, having 'almost all the wit, and popularity, and abilities in the kingdom,' could rarely get a majority in either house of Parliament.

[1] *A Letter from a Gentleman* (W.L.C.L.), 6. John Wesley was one who made this charge in his *Calm Address*, 18; *London Chronicle*, June 13, July 1, 1775; *London Packet*, June 9, 1775.

[2] *Taxation no Tyranny* (4th ed.), 87; *An Appeal to the Unprejudiced* (Oxford, 1776), 6, 42, 43; *The Honour of the University of Oxford Defended* (1776), 10.

[3] Lind, *Three Letters to Dr. Price* (1776), title-page.

Americans, indeed, greatly overestimated the resources of their English friends. They, nevertheless, doted on approval by these prominent Englishmen.[1] In that day they showed that sensitiveness to the opinion of the outside world which was a marked trait for a century thereafter. Flattery they lapped up greedily, and when Pitt, Burke, Wilkes, Barré, Hartley, and the Bishop of St. Asaph paid them a compliment they almost grovelled in appreciation. In 1775, Franklin proposed resolutions in Congress thanking Chatham, Burke, Hartley, and the Bishop of St. Asaph for their pleas in America's behalf.[2] Ten years earlier, Virginians expressed deep gratitude for the support of Lord Shelburne and Barré, accepted a portrait of Pitt, and had subscribed money for a picture by Reynolds or West of Lord Camden, who actually promised to sit, but forgot about it![3]

Nor were they always so choice in their selection of heroes. It is one of those strange freaks of history that the Puritanical leaders of New England, who were shocked by the merely compliant morality of Dr. Franklin, should exalt as a hero and martyr John Wilkes, who spent his days cheek by jowl with the most dissolute companions, wrote obscene verse, and abandoned himself to vicious pleasures which would have kept him in the stocks in New England. Yet we know that James Otis, Samuel

[1] Every approval by individuals or by bodies of Englishmen was eagerly printed in American newspapers. See *Essex Gazette*, June 22, 1775, September 14, 1775, October 26, 1775.

[2] *Letters of . . . Continental Congress* (Burnett, ed.), I, 105.

[3] *Letters of R. H. Lee*, I, 21, 22–24, 26, 35–37, 41.

Adams, John Hancock, Joseph Warren, Josiah Quincy, and other prominent citizens of Massachusetts, carried on an extended correspondence with John Wilkes, and Virginians, smoking 'Wilkes and Liberty' pipes, enjoyed them the more for the inscription.[1] The South Carolina Legislature called him 'that intrepid patriot,' and carried on for years the 'Wilkes Fund' dispute with the British Government, insisting on their right to send money for his defense during his prosecution for his scandalous writings in number 45 of the 'North Briton.' For this cause, too, they risked inebriation, drinking forty-five bowls of punch under forty-five candlelights on certain convivial occasions.[2] The forty-five Boston Patriots who sent him the 'Farmer's Letters' and addressed him as the 'incorruptible honest man, reserved by Heaven to bless and save a tottering empire,' would have found him, on intimate acquaintance, irresponsible, clever, witty, reckless, with no pretense at morality; one who, like a hero of Victorian fiction, 'from being brazen became brass.' Samuel Adams, who wrote [3] Wilkes that he knew no character with a 'stronger lustre,' would, perhaps, have half-approved this agitator, adventurer, able to make a noise, and create rancor, but he would have agreed with Walpole that he was wanton, a martyr indifferent to his cause.[4] William Palfrey, asserting that the fate of Wilkes and America 'must

[1] *Letters of R. H. Lee*, I, 73; British Museum, *Add. MSS.*, 30870, F 19–222.

[2] Wallace, *H. Laurens*, 154–66.

[3] British Museum, *Add. MSS.*, 30870, F 45.

[4] *Ibid.*, 30870, F 51.

stand and fall together,' would have found that 'to laugh and riot and scatter firebrands' was his hero's idea of liberty.[1] Samuel Adams and Wilkes exchanged platitudes about liberty, but Adams was never so puerile, stilted and banal on that subject as Wilkes. Spirit and firmness Wilkes urged upon his American adorers, while he himself made an adventure of life and a game of politics.[2] A man of genius, earnest, no doubt, for liberty, knowing how to assume the garb of liberal ideas and make them the fashion, yet he disappointed his admirers by failing utterly to take the place in Parliament that he had held in the market-place. Friends claimed that he preserved an essential privilege of English liberty, that he had a powerful influence on the spirit of the age; but others as honest coldly doubted whether Liberty, about which he wrote little that lives, owed much to Wilkes.[3] The trifles which he wrote so well, but with so much scurrility, seemed not to offend American taste, and his letters from the King's Bench prison, arraigning the Townshend Act as 'Asiatic despotism,' warmed the hearts of the Boston committee.[4] Up to the outbreak of the war, his home in London was a rendezvous where Arthur Lee and Beaumarchais could come together and plot French aid to the American cause. It is at least significant that American leaders drew such solace from cordial

[1] British Museum, *Add. MSS.*, 30870, F 114, 172; *American Historical Review*, XXIII, 620.

[2] British Museum, *Add. MSS.*, 30870, F 45.

[3] H. W. Bleackley, *Life of Wilkes, passim.*

[4] British Museum, *Add. MSS.*, 30870, F 135, 151.

correspondence with even the least reputable of English supporters of their cause.

Encouragement from English supporters poured from many sources. There was much support for the idea that the war was a civil war, not merely between two widely separated territorial units of the British Empire, but between two schools of English thinking. For all support from the British side American Patriots were deeply grateful. A cheap edition of Priestly's 'Observations on Civil Liberty and the Justice and Policy of the War with America,' which sold up to sixty thousand copies, so pleased Americans that Congress later invited that 'Patriot Saint and Sage' to settle in America.[1] Dr. Price's pamphlet exposing the British Government's lack of means to quell the rebellion, gave aid and comfort to the colonists, and the Continental Congress invited him to become an American citizen and to direct their troubled finances.[2] Other pamphlets appeared in London, dedicated to the American Congress 'nobly struggling under oppression for the sacred rights of mankind.'[3] A lord bishop denounced the Government's measures as arbitrary, without moderation, and hoped Heaven might take part against the execution of a plan big with mischief and impiety.[4] Brochures went the rounds in England intimating that the King might be 'a

[1] Kent, *The English Radicals*, 81–82.

[2] *Archives des Affaires Étrangères, Angleterre*, 515, no. 31; Wharton, *Diplomatic Correspondence*, II, 60, 61, 474, 756; L. Stephens, *English Thought in the Eighteenth Century*, II, 257.

[3] *A Defence of the Resolution*, etc. (W.L.C.L.).

[4] *A Complaint*, etc. (London, 1775), 28.

greater rebel and traitor to the realm than any individual could be against him.'[1] Many articles in the London press hailed with exultation the rumored Patriot victories at Lexington, Concord, and Bunker Hill. Some went so far as to praise 'American heroism' and denounce the English soldiers as poltroons, villains, scoundrels, and murderers. Late in June, 1775, London societies were subscribing funds for the relief of the widows and orphans of men who at Lexington and Concord 'had preferred death to slavery.'[2] The Government found it well to be on the alert to intercept 'treasonable correspondence' with American 'rebels.' Every ship bound for America was held up and searched, and the letters read for this purpose. Lists of suspected captains were sent to the naval commanders.[3]

The City of London, from the first, and, indeed, throughout the war, showed its dislike of the ministerial cause. To Dr. Price, for his famous pamphlet in America's behalf, the City sent, in a gold box, worth fifty pounds, a citizen's right. The Mayor of London opposed the use in that city of the 'press warrants' so necessary for the filling of the ranks of the King's army.[4] Day after day the Corporation

[1] *A Defence of the Resolution* (1775), (W.L.C.L.), 93, 95.

[2] *Archives des Affaires Étrangères, Angleterre*, 510, no. 128; Force, *American Archives* (4th Series), II, 921; *Public Advertizer* (London), June 17, 1775; Hinkhouse, *The Preliminaries of the American Revolution* . . . 186, 188, 192–93. One of the advertisements which spoke of the 'American Subjects . . . murdered by the king's troops' was declared by the Attorney-General, Wedderburn, to be a 'seditious libel,' and he was ordered to prosecute the offenders. P.R.O., *State Papers, Domestic, George III*, 11.

[3] *Colonial Office*, 250, pp. 221, 222, 248, 249, 250, 268, 291.

[4] *Correspondence of King George III*, III, 405.

Jonathan Boucher, who knew his Virginia well, did not hesitate to assert that one cause — not the least — of the American revolt was the immense debt owed by the colonists to the merchants of the British isles. Nothing is so impossible of proof as the motives of men, but Boucher was not unreasonable in assuming that some men at least were not unwilling to cancel their burdensome debts by the resort to war.[1] But whatever may be true of American motives, it is quite likely that British creditors found their hearts where their treasure was, and hoped for peace.

So worried were the British merchants that William Knox, an Under-Secretary of State, who had written pamphlets which Burke thought worthy of a reply, was inspired to print a brochure entitled, 'The Interest of the Merchants.'[2] Knox sought to persuade the merchants that their American debtors reasoned as follows: We are prevented by an Act of Parliament from entailing our estates to the prejudice of our English creditors. We now owe them about four millions, and if this Act were out of the way, we could make all our families rich by buying lands instead of paying our English creditors, thus rising on the ruins of England. Therefore, Knox insinuated, they resolved to deny Parliament's authority, and actually ask British merchants to

[1] J. Boucher, *View*, xi. See Harrell, *Loyalism in Virginia*, 26–29.

[2] William Knox, *The Interest of the Merchants* (1775), 18–23. Knox came to the rescue of the Government repeatedly from 1765 on. In 1765, he wrote *The Claim of the Colonists to an Exemption*; in 1768, *The Present State of the Nation*; in 1769, *The Controversy Between Great Britain and her Colonies*; in 1774, *The Present State of the Nation.*

help bend Parliament to the colonial will.[1] Indeed, he asserted, the Virginia Legislature attempted to make Virginia lands and negro slaves freehold and not liable to payment of book debts, so that a planter might buy with English credit lands and negroes which his children might inherit without paying a shilling to the English merchant with whose money he bought them.[2] Having thus tried to make their fortunes out of British capital, Knox added, they are brazen enough to expect British merchants to pay all the taxes for the liquidation of a debt contracted in defense of America during the Seven Years' War, and for a military force to protect what only Americans enjoy.[3] One-sided as the argument was, it sufficed, no doubt, to embitter the minds of many merchants and to reconcile them to the war, deadly as it was to the hope of collecting American debts. Others, however, clung to the idea of peace as their only salvation.[4]

Many British merchants were, doubtless, hard hit. John Wesley, founder of Methodism, and itinerant preacher during these troubled times, going

[1] Knox, *The Interest of the Merchants*, 23; Russel, *Review of American Colonial Legislation*, 125–36; Harrell, *Loyalism in Virginia*, 18–29.

[2] Knox, *The Interest of the Merchants*, 18; Schlesinger, *Colonial Merchants*, 36–38.

[3] Knox, *The Interest of the Merchants*, 22.

[4] The West India planters and merchants had taken alarm early because of Congress's Association, and had begged Parliament to go slow, to remember the seven million pounds sterling invested in the West Indies. *Petition by West India Planters* (1775) (W.L.C.L.). A fine review of the economic conditions in the West Indies as a result of American disturbances may be found in R. Glover, *The Evidence Delivered on the Petition Presented by the West India Planters and Merchants to the House of Commons* (London, 1775) (W.L.C.L.).

into every part of England, wrote to Lord Dartmouth that he found trade exceedingly decayed except in three or four manufacturing towns. He told of going to dinner with a merchant, and, before he left, the bailiffs took possession of the house. He had thought this merchant rich, and, indeed, he *was* so, but the American war had ruined him. Trade was so bad, Wesley averred, that thousands of people were quite unemployed; some he knew to have perished for want of bread; others he had seen creeping up and down like walking shadows. People were generally dissatisfied, and the King himself the object of their anger, contempt, and malice. Exasperated almost to madness, cured of love and reverence for the King, they were, he believed, ripe for rebellion and wished 'to imbrue their hands in his blood.'[1]

The masses were doubtless torn by conflicting emotions. Actual military engagements in America affected the national and military pride of the people. After all, being in, they must bear it that the opposer might beware of them. They were sorry, but it was too late to turn back. Besides, one must 'support the Government,' preserve 'our dominions.' Moreover, the loss of American commerce was not yet generally felt. Contemporaneous European troubles kept up a brisk trade, as did also the very supplying of the army and navy, which likewise gave employment to many. Shipping was busy in transport service; contractors foresaw a

[1] Hist. MSS. Com., *Fifteenth Report*, pts. I and II, 220; *Wesley's Journal* (Curnoch ed.), VIII, 325–28.

golden harvest, and war profiteers of all sorts were counting their gains. The merchants, sneered Burke, 'began to snuff the cadaverous *haut goût* of lucrative war.' The Government found few of the needed supplies on hand, and prices rising at an alarming rate.[1] Few had the imagination to look ahead to the days when all the immense public debt rolling up would have to be paid by the toil and misery of the masses.

Camden was, therefore, in the main right as to the common people and the merchants, and also as to the landed interests.[2] The votes of country squires, of manorial lords, of the great country magnates in Parliament were simply a registration of the opinions of their class, already expressed, indeed, in the approving petitions which had poured in upon George III and Lord North.

Romney's 'Beaumont family' in the National Gallery shows us the elegance of this English aristocracy. We behold there a soldier son in his red tailed coat, his hair in a queue down his back, a light vest and knee trousers, silk stockings, silver-buckled shoes, cane in hand. In the group is another son with powdered hair, reddish brown tailed coat, golden brown trousers, vest and light stockings. Still another is in green coat and black trousers. All have faces that have never felt a want, nor experi-

[1] *Annual Register*, XIX, 38–39; Hist. MSS. Com., *Am. MSS.*, I, 59, 64. A big contractor speaks of workmen 'universally engaged in combinations and all the licentiousness arising from a superabundance of employment.'

[2] Hinkhouse, *The Preliminaries of the American Revolution . . . in English Press*, 202–03.

enced a sorrow, easy, graceful, sure. Few works of art reveal more clearly the spirit of an age that is gone.

Class interests alone determined the views of such men. To protect one's political and social privileges, to keep up one's monopoly, to hunt cynically for sinecures and places of profit was the common pursuit of those who dominated the English political life. For them the world was as God made it, and not theirs was the work of reform. The landed gentry spent little time worrying about the unfortunate masses, but lived rather 'like the gods, careless of mankind.' The rich were resigned to their riches; the poor ought to take poverty in a like spirit. Generations were yet to pass across the English stage before a triumphant democracy was to make the chief business of Parliament an effort to relieve the miseries of the masses. Throughout the eighteenth century the rich middle class ruled; the poor obeyed. One third of the nineteenth century was to pass before the spirit of democracy was to brood over the English political deeps and make them pregnant.

This stubborn middle class and high-born minority, entrenched in Parliament, was fated to rule England for fifty years to come. It was led by arrogant men, proudly sensitive, selfishly exclusive, sure as a Stuart of their divine right to rule; more concerned about agricultural and commercial profits than about any duty to pass laws for the relief of the lower classes. The English aristocracy was quite pleased to pose as 'a benefactor to distressed indigence' or as a 'liberal encourager of public institutions,' such as new bells for the parish church; but it yielded gracelessly to any efforts to give political power to the people that they might be their own benefactors and supporters of public institutions.[1] The brutality with which the English poor were treated under the eighteenth-century laws of the realm was due to lack of imagination, and no more of that rare spiritual gift was used in dealing with English colonists three thousand miles oversea. No serious efforts were made in London to do away with poverty, dirt, overcrowding; why expect greater care about the rights of man in the American wilderness? All Europe was still ruled for the good of the aristocrat, and even England's political leadership had not advanced beyond that stage.

No British constitutional development had changed the convictions of the ruling class. One could not expect Englishmen to act contrary to the dictates of their own natures, and, indeed, to that of most upper-class Europeans of that time. There was a scriptural advice as to the moving of mountains, but no guidance for shifting the ideas of an English country gentleman, firm in the conviction of the superiority of the British Constitution. Century-old conventions ruled, and all new thought was viewed with suspicion, even with fear; age alone furnished firm foundations for political ideas; new theories and dreams of a better order of things were viewed askance in good society.

Aided by the famous canvases of the day, we may

[1] Hist. MSS. Com., *Report, Lothian*, 293–94.

picture the Prince of Wales and his gay companions with their frilled shirts, high, loose coat-collars, bushy heads of hair, which they shook sadly as they thought of the ungrateful American subjects, filled with pernicious doctrines — republicanism being the worst. As they looked about upon the elegant forms and proud faces of their aristocratic companions, they were sure that the world was theirs, and could only be well ordered by their guidance. They thought, and so thought most English squires, that if the British Constitution could not remedy a political evil in the American provinces, then that evil must be beyond human cure.

Not even Burke or Pitt would listen patiently to proposals to revise the 'ark of the covenant,' the finished product of centuries of human wisdom. On that hung all the law and the prophets. And it was the same with the accepted economic theories and the habits of colonial government. As well destroy the Pyramids of the Pharaohs as the Mercantile System or the accepted manner of governing colonies. The waters of the constitutional stream seemed to have been impounded, as far as colonial government was concerned, and lay in a backwater, which was rising daily and threatening overflow, revolution. It was this fact which killed all hope that any really conciliatory move would be made by the ministerial group firmly in power when rebellious America challenged the British Government at Lexington, Concord, and Bunker Hill.

CHAPTER IX

THE CLASH OF PAMPHLETEERS AND STATESMEN

Few things are more certain in the history of the American Revolution than that England as well as America was a house divided against itself. As one reads the official correspondence of the British Government, one is constantly impressed with the fact that two rival forces are opposing each other in high places in England — one favoring the King and his policy of coercion; one convinced of the righteousness of the American cause, or at least of the folly of fighting the colonists, and making every effort to aid them.[1] Some of the best-known figures in England took up the King's cause.

Of these, John Wesley, with his immense influence among the people, was very significant. There is not much mystery about his support of George III, for he and his father and brother were staunch Tories. He was a high churchman, bred to belief in submission and non-resistance, a natural champion of order and the royal person. The King, who believed in the Bible, feared God, and loved the Queen, had shown favor to Methodists. One of his Ministers, Lord Dartmouth, was a leader in the evangelical movement stirring England in that day, and saw no antithesis between a coronet and prayer. The court of George III was clean, and his conduct worthy of

[1] P.R.O., *Colonial Office*, 5–250.

an Englishman, a Christian, and a King, and Wesley felt the urge of a patriot to put out the flame which he saw everywhere rage against the King. Wesley was already on record against democracy, holding that God was the source of power, not the people, who therefore had no right to choose their own rulers. The type of government he devised to rule his Methodist societies proved him wary of the troubled waters of democracy. He opined that no government under Heaven was so despotic as a republican. 'Republics shew no mercy,' he dogmatized.[1] He believed in divine right and felt called to defend it, in spite of a real sympathy with some of the American demands, doubting even whether any man could defend the measures taken by the Ministry against the colonists. Finally, he seems to have been quite captivated by the arguments of his friend Dr. Johnson in 'Taxation no Tyranny.' This so changed his views that Wesley wrote his famous pamphlet, 'A Calm Address to our American Colonies.'

Forty thousand copies were sold within three weeks and one hundred thousand before it lost its vogue. A Government subsidized edition was peddled out at all the church doors in London. At once a 'hurricane of abuse' broke on Wesley's head. He was, wrote the Christ-like author of the 'Rock of Ages,' a fox in clerical robes, a 'low and puny tadpole of divinity.' Toplady 'tarred and feathered' the 'old fox' by showing with the deadly parallel

[1] Wesley, *A Calm Address to Our American Colonies*, 17, quoted in *A Letter to the Rev. John Wesley*, etc. (W.L.C.L.), 7.

column that Wesley had merely taken the arguments of that 'whale in politics,' Dr. Johnson.[1] Wesley sought, said critics, lawn sleeves and a mitre, but he deserved a hempen neckcloth. Accused of having one eye on a pension, and the other on heaven, he replied, that not to get money, nor to please any, high or low, not even for royal favors beyond civil and religious privileges, had he written his pamphlet.[2] Indeed, while he argued that Parliament had the power to tax, that the colonists did tax themselves in the same sense that nine tenths of the English did, and had as much liberty,[3] and that it was only just for the colonies to reimburse England for their defense, he was writing personal letters to Lord North and Lord Dartmouth, asserting that Americans were asking no more than their legal rights; that they were fighting for their wives, children and liberty, and could not be subdued by soldiers who fought only for pay. Was it common sense, he asked, to use force against them?[4] Taking all these facts into view, Wesley seems to have been sincere in saying that he stepped out of his apostolic chair only with the hope of putting out the flame

[1] *An Old Fox Tarred and Feathered* (W.L.C.L.).

[2] He accepted fifty pounds from George III, to be used for charity. *Wesley's Journal* (Curnoch, ed.), VI, 67, 82.

[3] Americans have the same rights as Englishmen so far as they can exercise them, reasoned Wesley. If Americans were electors when they left England, they deprived themselves of the power to exercise that right when they came to America. If *non*-electors, then they never had any privilege except to be governed by just laws. By abandoning right in one legislature, they did not acquire right to constitute another. *A Calm Address*, 8.

[4] *Wesley's Journal* (Curnoch, ed.), VIII, 325.

which was raging over all the land.[1] 'Let us not bite and devour one another,' he pleaded with the Americans. He urged them to put away their sins, the real ground of all calamities, which could not be removed until they feared God and honored the King.[2]

It was quite true that Wesley had used Dr. Johnson's arguments, but England's literary hero was rather pleased than otherwise, writing pompously that he was encouraged to continue to lecture as long as Plato stayed. In his famous pamphlet, 'Taxation no Tyranny,' he displayed with genius all the narrow, surly, prejudiced views of the country squires whose influence dominated Parliament. As was his custom, he made his little fishes talk like whales, and rolled along his periods like ocean billows. The Americans, he wrote, had robbed their creditors by fraud, had obeyed no law they could violate, and imparted no good which they could withhold; they bellowed as patriots, blustered as soldiers, domineered as legislators. Why, he was wont to sneer, do we hear 'the loudest yelps for liberty among the drivers of negroes?'[3] He roared against their 'delirious dreams of Republican fanaticism,' their political ideas, 'abortions of folly,' born only to scream and perish.[4] He who would not give half a

[1] The above treatment of Wesley's part in the American Revolution is based largely upon W. Sweet's article in the *Methodist Review* (1917).

[2] *Calm Address* (revised ed.), 18.

[3] *Boswell's Johnson* (Hill, ed.), III, 201.

[4] *Taxation no Tyranny* (4th ed.), 1–5, 80, 88. His hatred of republicanism came out even in his *Lives of the Poets* (Hill, ed.), I, 157, where he wrote that Milton's republicanism was 'founded in an envious

guinea 'to live under one government rather than under another' was sure to have little patience with men who demanded a free government. Though Johnson was democrat enough to say that, 'about the things on which the public thinks long, it commonly attains to think right,' he was a bitter enemy of that principle in America. He scolded at prejudice who was himself most prejudiced. The most he granted his opponents was 'honest stupidity,' and he overwhelmed them by the roars which so frightened his Boswell.

Answering Burke and the American addresses to Great Britain at the same time, he called their arguments 'too foolish for buffoonery, too wild for madness.' He reviewed with sneers and guffaws the arguments in favor of the Americans, calling their defenders, 'zealots of anarchy,' 'libertines of policy.' With ponderous erudition he traced from the Huns and Vandals to John Smith the processes of colonization, and flouted the sentiment about Americans who fled from tyranny to rocks and deserts, only to be 'plundered by harpies of taxation.' They were, he jeered, only asked to pay the cost of their own safety, and he belittled their contributions to the French and Indian War, 'excited by their outcries, continued for their protection.'[1]

He ridiculed the idea of their determining themselves how much they would pay for the defense of the Empire. Particularly absurd he found the idea

hatred of greatness and a sullen desire of independence.' Milton, he said, hated monarchs and prelates, 'all whom he was required to obey.'

[1] *Taxation no Tyranny* (4th ed.), 88.

of a violation of the British Constitution by taxing the colonists. 'We do not like taxes, therefore we will not be taxed,' was all their logic came to. Told they had not been taxed before the late controversies, he snapped back: 'Very well, the longer they have been spared, the better they can pay.'[1] To put down their asserted rights under the charters he used the current reasoning that colonial governments were mere corporations to be revoked at Parliament's will, not being more than vestries of a large parish, and asked triumphantly 'if America can make a legislature, then why can they not make a king?' With witty quips and sophistries he set at nought their complaints about governors and judges. Johnson's opinion became the 'law of nature'; he would make no concession of need of change; whatever was, was right. He upheld the thesis that in sovereignty there were no gradations; that Parliament could not be *half* sovereign, and being wholly so, could do as it chose. English superiority, American obedience, was Johnson's battle-cry.[2] English power, English honor were the important matters, and he ranted most at those Englishmen who had not virtue enough to love England more than justice to America.[3] He laughed to scorn those who appealed first to 'the oppressed and pitiful condition' of the Americans, and then tried to inspire fear of their greatness and opulence. All he would grant was that three millions of Whigs, who 'multiplied with the fecundity of their own rattlesnakes,' would

[1] *Taxation no Tyranny* (4th ed.), 62, 72, 73.

[2] *Ibid.*, 89. [3] *Ibid.*, 3.

soon become too powerful for restraint and could not be subdued too soon. 'Bend obstinacy,' he cried, 'before it becomes more obdurate.' He rejected all forbearance, all pleas to show love for the colonists — a sort of Mahatma Gandhi 'soul force' programme, which was to bring Americans to the feet of their sovereign.[1] In conversation, he made poor Boswell, who sympathized with the Americans, very unhappy by his bluster about burning and destroying those 'rascals, robbers, pirates.' He was willing, he fumed, 'to love all mankind except an American,'[2] but his crony, Joshua Reynolds, said the truth was that Johnson believed every foreigner a fool till proved to the contrary; that he hated the Scotch, the French, the Dutch, and had contempt for all other Europeans.[3] The only mercy that Johnson would show the Americans was to send so large a military force as to scare them, thus subduing them by terror rather than violence.[4] Yet he swore that had he been the Prime Minister at the time of the Stamp Act, he would have sent a ship of war and leveled one of America's principal cities to the ground.[5] On the whole, he justified the prediction that the King's friends would find in him a lamb, and the King's enemies a lion.

All this churlishness and malevolence recoiled

[1] *Taxation no Tyranny* (4th ed.), 88.

[2] *Boswell's Johnson* (Hill, ed.), III, 221, 290. (This was in 1778.) Tinker, *Boswell, Letters*, II, 273.

[3] *Boswell's Johnson* (Hill, ed.), IV, 15.

[4] *Taxation no Tyranny* (4th ed.), 79–80.

[5] *Yale Review*, October, 1924, p. 96. (Reported by William White, First Bishop of Pennsylvania.)

upon the famous author. Englishmen were warned to beware of the Johnsons and the Wesleys, who would persuade them that they were born slaves. Wilkes dubbed Johnson 'the pensioned advocate of despotism,' for it was rumored that his emolument from the King had been increased two hundred pounds. A rival pamphleteer expected to see 'the philosophical doctor lolling in his carriage-and-four with an income equal to the revenue of a good bishopric.'[1] Another moralized that of all tyrants bigotry was the most despotic, and Johnson, with his 'monkish, cell-bred mind and sordid spirit,' was its victim.[2] The poet Cowper, still further incensed by the 'industrious cruelty' with which Johnson, in his 'Lives of the Poets,' belabored Milton, 'the acrimonious and surly republican,' cried out, 'Oh! I could thrash his old jacket until I made his pension jingle in his pocket.'[3]

But Johnson was only one of the many literary men bound by golden chains to the throne, for McPherson, author of 'Ossian,' received a secret pension of five hundred pounds, and wrote for his royal master 'The Right of Great Britain Asserted,' which enjoyed ten editions, and was also translated into French.[4] Many other pamphleteers there were, among whom William Knox and Ambrose Serle

[1] *Boswell's Johnson* (Hill, ed.), III, 79, note; *Plain English*, 17 (W.L.C.L.); *A Constitutional Answer to the Rev. Mr. John Wesley* (1775), 9. (W.L.C.L.)

[2] *A Defence of the Resolution*, 16. (W.L.C.L.)

[3] British Museum, *Add. MSS.*, 24154, F 18.

[4] B. Saunders, *McPherson*, 274. He wrote also a *Short History of the Opposition During the last Session* (1779), of which there were eight editions.

shone in the defense of the policy of George III. Serle proved to his own satisfaction that the Americans were against liberty, that all their conduct tended only to tyranny and slavery.[1]

This was the general political atmosphere in England, when, faced with the rising tide of rebellion in America, both North and his Opposition brought before Parliament plans for reconciliation. North's resolution (February 20, 1775) 'amazed all' and made the Treasury benches 'seem to totter,' because many thought it marked a change in ministerial and royal policy, but it was at best a specious plan, leaving trade laws unrepealed in America, grievances unredressed. Parliament, first pledging itself not to part with any of its sovereign authority over the colonies, promised not to levy any tax on any colony which would make a satisfactory arrangement with Parliament to pay its part of imperial expenses. The proceeds of duties laid for the necessary regulation of imperial commerce should go to the colony's credit.[2] Though an opponent thought 'fiscal supremacy' was thereby 'waived if not given up,' Franklin called the resolution 'the language of a highwayman.'[3] Burke averred that, instead of a standing revenue, it assured a perpetual quarrel. George III, obsessed with the idea of 'submission,'

[1] A. Serle, *The Americans Against Liberty* (ed. 1775). This famous Calvinistic writer accompanied the British army to America in 1776, and for two years controlled the press in New York.

[2] Macdonald, *Doc. Source Book*, 171; *Correspondence of George III with Lord North* (Donne, ed.), I, 232–33.

[3] Force, *American Archives* (4th Series), I, 1600; Franklin, *Letters and Works* (Smyth, ed.), VI, 314.

'highly approved' of the resolution, assuming it 'put an end to Congress.'[1] The Continental Congress, in its 'Declaration of the Causes of Taking up Arms,' found it an insidious effort to divide the provinces, to set up a 'perpetual auction of taxations,' colony bidding against colony.[2]

Though enemies spoke of the ministerial phalanx as 'broken, disordered,' North's 'symbol of peace' was passed, 274 to 88, and sent to the colonial governors. Tryon, Royal Governor of New York, believed oceans of blood would be spilled before America would accept.[3] In his opinion no one colony had the power, even if it had the wish, to meet the terms of North's resolution. Passed as it was in the midst of coercive measures, stopping the trade and fisheries of New England, it was rendered less likely to succeed, and the attempt to ignore the Continental Congress, so 'terrifying to the King,' who actually wished to arrest and imprison all abettors of it, doomed the conciliatory measures to failure. Yet doubtless the mere proposal of it was useful to the Ministry, because in some minds it acquitted the administration of the charge of wantonly pushing matters to extremity with the Americans, of giving them no alternative but war.[4]

The French Minister in London thought Lord North was influenced by a superior will which he

[1] *Correspondence of George III with Lord North*, I, 231.

[2] July 6, 1775. Macdonald, *Doc. Source Book*, 180.

[3] Becker, *Political Parties in the Province of New York*, 239–42; *Sparks MSS.*, no. 43, III, 223–24.

[4] *An Address to the People of Great Britain* (Bristol, 1776), 15–16.

must obey, cost what it might, and so went blindly on.[1] Indeed, Lord North had his virtues, a homely good sense, and, as Gibbon says, an incomparable felicity of temper. No assault could reach that, though, as Fox found, it could bring his tears. He had the politician's art calmly to repeat solemn commonplaces until he carried conviction. Though familiar with corruption, he also understood how to win without a bribe. He was indolent, of unwieldy bulk, awkward, ugly in feature, with bulging eyes, a mouth that gaped like a buffoon, anything but dignified, and a favorite sport with the caricaturists.[2] If like the toad he concealed a precious jewel in his head, the wit and humor which delighted his colleagues, it did not endear him to those opposed to his stern measures. Even his friends had to overcome a natural aversion to his harsh and unmusical voice, the agent of his spiritual charms.[3] With him to avoid defeat was to win a victory, and he was disingenuous to either end. He read aright the weakness of the governing classes, and the policy of maintaining the legislative supremacy of Parliament was the appeal with which he won support. He refused to see anything but sovereignty on one side, independence on the other. As an enemy said, 'Lucifer himself could not make out his plan, for there was only the confused notion that it was improper to recede.'[4] With the appeal 'the nation and its

[1] *Archives des Affaires Étrangères, Angleterre,* 515, no. 31.

[2] Not even the engraver's art could conceal North's ugliness. See J. Burke's engraving of N. Dance's portrait.

[3] Winstanley, *William Pitt,* 322–23.

[4] *Plain English* (*to the King*), 16. (W.L.C.L.)

honor,' North won popular support up to 1778. It was this success that made him seem to deserve M. de Castries' sarcastic query whether Lord North was made a Knight of the Garter because he had lost America.[1]

North's opponents, too, had their plans for conciliation. A month before North's effort, Chatham, his gout not having put in a veto, limped into the House of Lords with Benjamin Franklin on his arm, and moved the recall of Gage. Proud 'to see men, not afraid of God, afraid of me,' he thundered his defense of his motion, 'knocked at the Minister's door to wake him.'[2] With the old magnetic power, 'the something that was Pitt,' he pleaded with the Lords to repeal America's fears and her resentments, that they might hope for her love and gratitude.[3] He had himself advanced to greater sympathy since his speech of the preceding May.[4] Where he had once asked only leniency, he now demanded justice. Having before even urged a larger military force, he now asked recall of all the troops. Having once suggested an apology from Massachusetts, he now defended her action.[5] There was no method, no order of ideas, digressions without number, but, as Camelford declared, he took his hearers in rapid flight to a region that looked down upon argument. But Chat-

[1] *Correspondence of George III with Lord North*, I, 223.

[2] *Correspondence of William Pitt*, etc., IV, 371, 376.

[3] *Ibid.*, 383.

[4] Indeed, it had grown ever since the Stamp Act. There was a strong suspicion that Pitt, himself, had penned the Declaratory Act at that time. J. Macpherson, *The Rights . . .*, 50.

[5] *Correspondence of William Pitt*, 377–84.

ham was no logician, troubled by inconsistency, for his political ideas were emotional convictions. It was not logic which carried his speeches, but soul and grace, exquisite sensibility, a style of conscious superiority, and a voice which at its best 'swelled into the fullness of a great organ.' Even his critics compared him with Pericles and with Cicero.[1] But all the effort of such genius was in vain against the finest body of 'brute votes' in Europe, and George III, 'with infinite satisfaction,' saw the rejection of Chatham's motion.[2] He could never forgive his 'abandoned' conduct, his 'specious words and malevolence.' He came to wish for the time when Chatham would be 'totally unable to appear on the public stage.'[3]

But that 'trumpet of sedition' would not desist. Seeing the fate of Old England at stake as well as that of the New; convinced that England would be no more if the colonies resisted; and holding a noble ideal of imperial unity of which the links would be loyalty and love, the worn-out invalid pressed on to one more effort. He called Franklin to Hayes to see his plan. Two days later, all the world was agape while his own carriage stood at the American's door. Finally, Franklin was again at Hayes for four hours, and Chatham, 'so full and diffuse,' so hard to interrupt, that they got hardly halfway through. Then on February 1, 1775, he faced the House of Lords

[1] Hist. MSS. Com., *Buckingham*, xiv (9), 299.

[2] *Correspondence of George III with Lord North* (Donne, ed.), i, 223–25.

[3] *Correspondence of King George III* (Fortesque, ed.), iii, 242, 449.

with his plan — not a logical, properly drawn bill, such as a Grenville or a Townshend would have offered, but, nevertheless, a practical document that might have been 'an everlasting monument of clemency and magnanimity' could it have been administered by its sympathetic and imaginative author.

In Chatham's view he was offering a new Magna Charta, a decree of policy for the future relations between England and America. He first insisted upon recognition of the supremacy of Parliament in the Empire; but that was doubtless to save the pride of England, and because Chatham was statesman enough to know that without that stipulation no British Government could stand a day. That 'the guardian navy of the whole British people' might be upheld, he insisted also upon Parliament's right to make navigation and trade laws for 'the whole dominion.' A hostile critic may make much of the futility of stating such principles in the existing state of the American mind, but there follows the stroke of genius, the uncanny sensing that America had become 'a mighty continental nation' of which the voice was Congress. He finds a way of getting an American revenue,[1] not from jangling provincial legislatures, but by using the very machine devised by the rebellious Americans, the Congress at Philadelphia. This body, so terrifying to George III and Lord North, was to fix the quotas of a 'perpetual revenue' to be borne by each province. An Ameri-

[1] W. L. Grant, *The Colonial Policy of Chatham*, in Bulletin, Queen's University, no. 1, October, 1911, pp. 6–9.

can Congress was to vote American money.[1] It was the British-American legislature which Galloway had already suggested in Congress, where it was rejected by a single vote, and destined to become the solution for British imperial problems in the distant future. Finally, there was to be a repeal of all the laws and ordinances offensive to America, and the list of them had been prepared by no less a person than Benjamin Franklin, who stood there at the bar of the House, denounced by the Earl of Sandwich as the bitterest, most mischievous enemy England had ever known, praised by Chatham as an honor 'not to the English nation only, but to human nature.' This proposed 'most so solemn national accord' was voted down 61 to 32, and no one is wise enough to say whether it might have averted impending calamities. Jefferson approved; Franklin saw in it a 'foundation of a lasting good agreement'; but it was scouted by American extremists like Samuel Adams. Chatham's political ideals were not just those of Americans, but his radical fervor pleased them, and he had the broad, imaginative sympathy to tolerate them. They knew him not unwilling to assault the 'rotten parts' of the British Constitution, and they knew he could not tolerate 'the bloated spiders of corruption.'

One other friend of America made an effort at conciliation before the fatal clash on Lexington Green.[2] Edmund Burke rose in that long, narrow,

[1] For a slightly different view see R. G. Adams, *The Political Ideas of the American Revolution*, 28.

[2] E. Burke, *Works* (ed. 1871), II. (*Speech on Conciliation with America*, March 22, 1775.)

galleried room, the House of Commons, and addressed the stolid country squires on those five tiers of benches, in words that were to be immortal, aimed not at a point of law, but at restoring tranquillity. His nasal twang, his Irish brogue, too rapid in its flow, his awkward gestures, were a poor vehicle for his truly noble eloquence, abounding in the 'immense excursions of his genius.'[1] A friend tells of 'repeated flashes of wit like the forked glare of lightning in a thunder storm under the line,' and says that Burke's opponent 'shrivelled under it like a blooming tree after a hurricane.'[2] Members, on this occasion, strolled in and out, indifferent to the beautiful stirring imagery, the high flights, the fervid sentiment. They little understood him when he begged them not to break the colonial spirit, the spirit that had made America, not to consume its strength, because it was British strength they would consume.[3] Burke wished as little as any man 'to impair the smallest particle' of Parliament's supreme authority, but he pointed out that even despotism was obliged to truck and huckster; that the Sultan got such obedience as he could, governed with a loose reign that he might govern at all. In all extensive and detached empires, it was an eternal law, he cried, that 'whatever is got by acts of abso-

[1] Madam D'Arblay (*Diary*, II, 146) looked upon Burke with more favor. 'He is tall, his figure is noble, his air commanding, his address graceful; his voice is clear, penetrating, sonorous and powerful; his language is copious, various, and eloquent; his manners are attractive, his conversation is delightful.'

[2] Hist. MSS. Com., *Fourteenth Report, Rutland MSS.*, III, 11.

[3] Burke, *Works*, II, 119.

lute power, ill obeyed because odious, or by contracts ill kept because constrained, will be narrow, feeble, uncertain and precarious.' For all service, whether of revenue, trade, or empire, Burke would trust to America's interest in the British Constitution, whose spirit, 'infused through the mighty mass, pervades, feeds, unites, invigorates, vivifies every part of the empire even down to the minutest member.'[1] The practical parts of Burke's plan, embodied in thirteen resolutions, did not go beyond setting up the old order of things and admitted no need of change in the British Constitution. Yet there was a noble sympathy with the colonists, wholly incomprehensible to 'the profane herd of those vulgar and mechanical politicians,' the little minds, which Burke found to go so ill with great empire. They rejected his plan with an insolent and overwhelming vote. The Lord North forces were not yet ready 'to let the ape and tiger die.'

The difference between North's conciliatory gesture and that of his opponents was that he offered the olive branch with one hand and brandished the sword with the other, while they discovered in every motion peace and reconciliation. North could see no hope for the future of the Empire save in submission by America. Chatham and Burke and their adherents believed the Americans were fighting for English liberty as well as their own. Whatever loss of liberty might result in America, England would suffer also in time.[2] America was 'the last asylum' of

[1] Burke's *Speech on Conciliation* (Bemant, ed.), paragraphs 44, 119, 134, 137.

[2] Albemarle, *Memoirs of Rockingham*, II, 276; (Dawes), *A Letter to*

persecuted Liberty, her defenders held, and should the fury of her enemies prevail, that 'bright goddess' must fly off from the face of the earth, and 'leave not a trace behind.'[1] Should the Ministry succeed in picking American pockets, they would not forbear to pick those of Englishmen.[2] Even Frederick the Great prophesied that.[3] Camden pleaded that English ancestors had paid great enough price to make their children free. 'We must not let this precious heritage escape our hands.'[4] Indeed, it was a common theme of America's defenders, that her cause was England's cause; that Washington and Greene were fighting for England as for themselves. 'Happy Britons,' cried one, 'if they shall owe the revival of their liberty to the success of their American brethren.'[5] Against the 'croakers of calamity' Dr. Johnson wrote, ridiculing the idea that a 'rill from the American Pactolus' would be used to purchase the remains of English liberty;[6] and when Alderman Lee ventured the opinion, 'Poor old England is lost,' Johnson parried with, 'Sir, it is not so much to be lamented that Old

Lord Chatham, etc., 22; *Correspondence of the Earl of Cornwallis*, III, 360; Walpole, *Letters* (Toynbee edition), VI, 409; *Chatham Correspondence*, IV, 333.

[1] Fonblanque, *Burgoyne*, 167.

[2] C. Macaulay, *An Address to the People of England*, 25.

[3] Circourt, III, 121.

[4] *Archives des Affaires Étrangères, Angleterre*, 515, no. 21 (March 14, 1776).

[5] Hinkhouse, *The Preliminaries of the American Revolution* . . ., 193–94.

[6] *Boswell's Johnson* (Hill, ed.), III, 201; *Taxation no Tyranny* (4th ed.), 64–66.

England is lost as that the Scotch have found it!'[1] This failure to take a dire situation seriously was not peculiar to Dr. Johnson, but prevailed with the country squires for whom he was Sir Oracle.

Although Englishmen were the inventors of political liberty on the scale of the great nation-state, even as Greece was the inventor of like liberty on the scale of the little city-state, yet they were for the moment falling behind their own colonists in the race for the goal of human freedom. There were Englishmen who saw their country slipping back, and who lamented it. The Bishop of St. Asaph, at whose country seat Franklin had long been welcome, wrote: 'I look upon North America as the only great nursery of free men now left upon the face of the earth. We have seen the liberties of Poland and Sweden swept away, in the course of one year, by treachery and usurpation. The free towns in Germany are like so many dying sparks, that go out one after another and which must all be soon extinguished under the destructive greatness of their neighbors. Holland is little more than a great trading company, with luxurious manners and an exhausted revenue; with little strength and less spirit. Switzerland alone is free and happy within the narrow enclosure of its rocks and valleys.' 'As to England,' he confessed sadly, 'I should say she has a sickly countenance, but I trust she has a strong constitution.'[2]

It was a like faith in America's righteous prin-

[1] *Boswell's Johnson* (Hill, ed.), III, 78.

[2] Force, *American Archives* (4th Series), I, 103.

ciples that led most of the finest spirits in England to lean to her side. It was not, as opponents said, the hopes and delusions of a discontented party, nor the minority's enjoyment of the applause of a mob,[1] that made Adam Smith unwilling to violate the sacred rights of mankind and advise 'letting the erring sisters go in peace.' He preferred faithful, affectionate, and generous allies to turbulent and factious subjects. America friendly would be a source of commercial gain to England; America conquered, and therefore alienated, would be a drain on English strength, a menace to British peace. For like reasons, Coke of Norfolk was ready to 'clog the wheels of government,' rather than to follow the King and Lord North. The first commoner of the kingdom, wealthy enough to dispense with place, patronage, royal favor, or popular approbation, he opposed the American war in spite of the frowns of the court, and became most obnoxious to George III, one of those whom the King classed as 'wicked and desperate persons.'[2] And so Lord Effingham, believing that colonial liberties formed the best security for their fidelity and obedience, resigned his command in the army rather than to serve against the Americans.[3] The Earl of Coventry begged the House of Lords to give up delusive schemes of

[1] *An Appeal to the Unprejudiced* (Oxford, 1776), 6, 42.

[2] Stirling, *Coke of Norfolk*, 99, 103, 104.

[3] *Annual Register*, XIX, 42. Chatham's son also resigned from the army until, in 1778, the war was turned also against France. Could Lord Effingham's refusal to serve in America have been due to his resentment of his treatment by the King a year earlier? See *Correspondence of King George III*, III, 107.

dominion, thoughts of fleets and armies. 'If you look at the map of the globe,' he urged, 'and view Great Britain and North America, and compare the extent of both; if you consider the soil, the harbours, the rivers, climate, and increasing population of the latter, nothing but the most obstinate blindness and partiality can prevail on any man to entertain a serious opinion that such a country will continue under subjection to this.' [1] If the Ministry persisted in thinking so, it would 'like the base Indian throw away a pearl inestimable.' [2] But the friends of America only cried in the wilderness. They were compared to the lame at the pool of Bethesda, longing for the troubling of the waters, and were urged to pack up their seditious principles, retire to America, lead 'the honorable Congress,' and ride upon the rising storm.[3]

One last plea with which the friends of America sought to turn the North Ministry from its purpose was that, whether victorious or vanquished in the struggle, it would have exhausted its treasury, sacrificed its finest troops, ruined or lost one of the richest parts of its empire.[4] Statisticians had long been figuring how many gallant Englishmen would fall — one hundred thousand at least — if the war lasted only three years, and that the expense would exceed ten million pounds sterling.[5] They showed

[1] Hansard, *Parliamentary History of England*, XVIII, 1200.

[2] *Plain English (to the King)*, 16.

[3] *An Address to the People of Great Britain* (Bristol, 1776), 20.

[4] *Archives des Affaires Étrangères, Angleterre*, 515, no. 21; Report of Camden's speech, March 14, 1776.

[5] *Pennsylvania Evening Post,* November 16, 1775 (quoting London sources).

that in the year following the battle of Lexington stocks had fallen six per cent, causing a loss on the national debt of seven million pounds.[1] That debt was already (1775) £135,943,050, on which the Government had to pay each year £4,440,821.[2] Why heap still another mountainous Pelion on this Ossa of debt? And even this would not insure dominion.

But America's English friends might have saved their statistics and their sentimental appeals; for the ministerial mind was fixed, as was that of its supporters. North's friends evaded the issues, refused to defend Parliament's policy; merely dodged the many and good blows of the Opposition. Parliament seemed as afraid 'of entering into the question of American grievances or of its own rights,' said a friend of America, 'as a zealous Catholic is afraid of examining the foundation of the power of the Church.'[3] Instead they talked of 'ingrates,' revolting against benefactors, refusing taxation, 'the best attribute of sovereignty,' thus leaving only the shadow. Lord Lyttelton asked what their ancestors would say from the depths of the tomb if Parliament was robbed of supremacy by 'unhappy rebels.' Their cold ashes would redden if America were lost ingloriously, not on the field of honor.[4] They might as well let Congress be legislature for the Empire,

[1] *Boston Gazette*, August 19, 1776 (quoting London sources).

[2] Chalmers, *Estimate*, etc. (1786), 136.

[3] *Remarks on the Principal Acts of the Thirteenth Parliament* (Lind, 1775), 486. (Lord Mansfield's copy of this pamphlet in W.L.C.L.)

[4] *Archives des Affaires Étrangères, Angleterre*, 515, no. 4.

cried General Burgoyne, as to fail to make valid the laws of Parliament in America.[1] With such slogans North's party pressed on to war. After the news of Lexington and Concord began to arrive in London, George III hardened his heart, assuring himself over and over that he was only doing his duty and had no wish to retract. We must show the 'rebellious Americans,' he wrote, 'that the English Lion when rouzed has not only his wonted resolution but has added the swiftness of the Race Horse.' By the end of the year 'haste' and 'hurry' and 'vigilance' were the most used words in his vocabulary.[2] After the news of Lexington arrived, there were two meetings of the cabinet at Lord North's house. The Ministers agreed at last to what Gage had long urged, an augmentation of the army at Boston. Exert every force! Down rebellion! was the determination. The added troops were to come from any place but England — from Ireland, from the Highlands of Scotland, from Gibraltar and Minorca, from Canada, and especially from foreign countries, perhaps Russia and Germany. At first it was thought that these reënforcements might be ready by the following spring, but by the end of August Lord North wrote the King that it would be much later before adequate forces could be sent. 'The cause of Great Britain' was not yet 'sufficiently popular.' To block up and intercept the American 'contraband trade,' a number of frigates were to be sent to Admiral Graves, and the Admiralty was to prepare

[1] *The Address of the People of Great Britain* (1775), 65.

[2] *Correspondence of King George III*, III, 235, 331.

adequate transport ships as soon as possible.[1] The slogan of the Ministry from this time on was that 'manly force is the only cure for avowed rebellion.' Lord Rochford was rather relieved that 'The Rubicon is passed.' Lord North thought the war now grown 'to such a height' that it must be treated as a 'foreign war.'[2]

Harsh measures like those which kings and proud governments had meted out to rebels from time

[1] P.R.O., *State Papers, Domestic, George III*, II, 88/15*a*, 88/15*b*. The cabinet met June 15 and June 21, 1775. There were present the Lord Chancellor, Lord President, Lord Suffolk, Lord Rochford, Lord Sandwich, Lord Dartmouth, Lord North. At the first meeting they agreed, '1st. to recruit the Regiments in America by draughts from the marching Regiments in Great Britain and Ireland to augment their Establishments. 2nd., To augment the establishment of marines to 70 men per company and to apply to the Government in Ireland for recruiting them there. 3rd. To write to General Carleton and if legal to direct him in case he sees no objection to raise as many Canadians, not exceeding 2000, as he sees proper to act as light infantry in concert with the King's troops. 4th. To raise if it can be speedily done, a body of Highlanders. 5th. That the proper steps to be taken to inquire into the practicability or propriety of procuring a body of two or three thousand foreign troops. . . . That an additional number of frigates be put into commission to be sent to Admiral Graves in order to enable him the more effectively to carry into execution the act of Parliament in the middle and southern Colonies. That directions be given to the admiralty to procure without loss of time such a number of transports as may be necessary.'

At the second meeting they agreed: 'To direct General Carleton immediately to raise 2000 Canadians if he sees no objections as provincials to be employed as light infantry under the command of General Gage. That the Royal Regiment of Highlanders be augmented to 1000 men and sent to America and that the regiment in Ireland be augmented to replace the Royal Highlanders. That three Regiments be sent from Gibraltar and three from Minorca to join the troops in America and that His Majesty be requested to replace the said regiment by troops of the Electorate of Hanover in British pay. That the regiment now in America and those which shall join them from Gibraltar and Minorca be augmented to a larger establishment.' *Correspondence of King George III*, III, 240.

[2] *Correspondence of King George III*, III, 214, 234.

immemorial followed one upon another. There was no unusual bitterness or uncharity, just the old stern justice, measured out with conscious rectitude, and much self-righteousness. Even if the Ministry had been gifted with the genius to catch the vision of a distant future, when pride in sovereignty would cease, when no people should be governed save by their own consent, it would still have lacked such supreme qualities of leadership as must have been shown to convince its British constituency that it was wise to act on such untried principles. And, after all, a cynic might ask, was Lord North's purpose different from that of Abraham Lincoln several generations later?

In August, 1775, the King issued a proclamation against traitorous correspondence with rebellious Americans. In September, Richard Penn, bearing a conciliatory petition of Congress to the King, was told that there would be 'no answer.' To receive it would, forsooth, recognize Congress. The King's Speech, read to Parliament on October 26, accused Congress of aiming at independence, and declared the Crown's determination to reduce rebellion by arms. At the same time the Duke of Grafton, who had previously urged conciliation, resigned, went into the Opposition, and was succeeded by Lord Dartmouth. The latter's place was then filled by Lord George Germain, who was violent against Americans, and who thenceforth directed from London the military operations in America.

During the debate on the King's Speech (October, 1775), Rockingham pressed some vague measures of conciliation. Grafton urged the repeal of all offensive acts since 1763. Charles James Fox, a new political genius — and an evil one for Lord North — praised the spirit of the Americans, and arraigned the Ministry with a stormy eloquence. This young man, of the noblest lineage, an erstwhile supporter of Lord North, and one who, having once scorned popular right, had already, at the age of twenty-six, come over to the cause of liberty, or, as King George saw it, had 'so thoroughly cast off every principle of common honour and honesty that he must become as contemptible as he is odious.'[1] A born actor, eager, warm-hearted, he became a master of debate, a leader of the Opposition to Lord North. So feared was he that the King urged North when Fox was abroad to get as much done in Parliament as possible — when it would not be interrupted by 'noisy declamations.'[2] He was everything that would have shocked the Puritanical New-Englanders whose cause he embraced, a fop, extravagant, dissolute, ever gaming, losing fabulous sums at reckless play, and again 'elbow deep in gold.' He lost eleven thousand pounds in twenty-two hours before one of his famous speeches in Parliament. Having started a faro bank, which throve prodigiously, he appeared in new clothes, 'clean and smug as a gentleman,' but in a few days Jews sold him up for debts.[3] It was his amazing vigor, mental and physical, that singled him out among men. It was said that he was so foolishly admired by his friends as

[1] *Correspondence of King George III*, III, 69. [2] *Ibid.*, 402.
[3] Hist. Mss. Com., XV, no. 5, pp. XXI, XXVI.

to have become almost frenzied with vanity. His strong build, bright eyes, high color, black hair, seemed to defy every dissipation to impair them. He did, early, become fat, his voice was poor, his gesticulations ungraceful, but his wit, his perfect mental clarity, his abounding good-humor, and his power to win the affections even of his political enemies, soon placed him in the front rank of America's English friends.

In spite of Fox, the King's Address was carried. In the middle of November, Burke again brought in a bill for composing the imperial troubles, which the House of Commons rejected.[1] Then North offered a bill forbidding all trade and intercourse with America, and providing that all colonial goods taken at sea should be forfeited.[2] Even this measure, which easily passed, was given a thin coating of sugar, for the Crown was empowered to appoint commissioners, who were to go with the armed forces to America and there inquire into grievances, receive into the King's peace such districts or colonies as might return to obedience. To act in this capacity the Crown appointed (April, 1776) Admiral Richard Lord Howe, about to take the British fleet into American waters, and his brother, General Howe, who was to command the British army. One fear the King had — that the Howes were too friendly to America, and would concede too much.[3] Who can

[1] The vote was 210 to 105.

[2] *Statutes at Large*, XXXI, 135; *Parliamentary History*, 1028–1106; *Parliamentary Register*, III, 231–87.

[3] *Correspondence of George III with Lord North* (April 13, 1776), II, 18.

tell but that in his first fear King George was right, as the story of their activities may seem to indicate? With the olive branch in one hand and the sword in the other, the brothers set forth to induce the colonies, in the words of the King's Speech (May 23, 1776), to 'return to their duty.'

CHAPTER X

THE SOUTH WAXES REBELLIOUS

While King George was worrying lest his peace commissioners should concede too much to his rebellious subjects, they were moving with varying speed in different sections of the thirteen colonies toward total estrangement and independence. Though many reasons have been ventured to explain why New England, and the States south of Maryland, were ready to take the final step before the Middle States were of that mind, it must never be forgotten that the sections which moved most rapidly had felt in one form or another the embittering effect of actual war. Nothing so heated the blood as shedding it, and before the fateful July 4, when America threw down the gauntlet to Great Britain, the only section which had not seen open warfare with the King's forces was that of the middle colonies. They, as John Adams wrote, had 'never tasted the bitter cup.'

New England's struggle has been told; the South had not long to wait before feeling the iron hand of a stern ruler seeking to quell rebellion. The British Government imagined the Carolinas swarming with Loyalists who would rally around the King's banner wherever it might be unfurled. The King and his Ministers had every reason, however, to believe the prophecies of Loyalist aid, since letter after letter from Governor Martin and others assured them solemnly that only a little help was needed to bring about a complete overthrow of the 'infatuated rebels.'[1]

It is true that there were some Scottish Highlanders in the up country, adjacent to South Carolina, who had good reasons for being loyal to the King. Close to them and farther west, however, were some Scotch-Irish frontiersmen who were just as hot on the other side. In Mecklenburg County, the leaders of these radical Patriots, in a meeting at Charlotte, May 31, 1775, passed a resolution declaring null and void all civil and military commissions granted by the Crown. It also declared the 'constitution' of the colony suspended, and arranged to carry on their own affairs until 'laws' should be provided by the 'Congress.' There is a local tradition of a Mecklenburg Declaration of Independence eleven days earlier than this, but scholars reject it as mythical.[2] Had such a 'Declaration' been made, it would have been inept, premature, and with no effect on the country as a whole. It would have been much like Wendell Phillips's threat, in his abolition fanaticism, to *secede* from the State of Massachusetts. The authentic resolutions of May 31 are surely radical enough to suit the most fastidious patriot.

But whatever the facts were as to strongholds of British friends, the Government moved too late. The

[1] *Correspondence of King George III*, III, 266, 270, 271; *Colonial Records of North Carolina. Clinton Papers* (W.L.C.L.), Campbell to Dartmouth, July 19, 1775.

[2] Hoyt, *Mecklenburg Declaration*, 22; Ashe, *North Carolina*, I, 437; *American Historical Review*, XI, 548–58; XIII, 16–43, 394–97.

Ministry, like Austria, 'just behind with an army or an idea,' managed early in the war, as often later, to miss the one opportunity which might have put the South under British control. While yet an army was mewed up in Boston, troops, under temporary charge of Cornwallis,[1] were sent in a fleet commanded by Sir Peter Parker from Ireland to Cape Fear,[2] to attempt a precarious union with the loyal Scottish Highlanders who would come down from the uplands of North Carolina.[3] So badly had Martin, the royal governor, synchronized the rising of the Highlanders under Donald McDonald [4] with the coming of the army from Ireland that the Scots arrived near Wilmington weeks before the King's army arrived off Cape Fear to support them. Moreover, bad weather delayed the transport of arma-

[1] *Correspondence of King George III*, III, 271. The plan fairly complete by October 15, 1775, Cornwallis solicited this subordinate command of Lord George Germain. *Ibid.*, 295.

[2] The delays experienced by Parker are well described by Lord Sandwich. *Ibid.*, 328–30.

[3] These Highlanders held their lands direct from the Crown, and disliked the lowland-dominated North Carolina Legislature which neglected them. The expedition was vaguely planned as early as July 26, 1775, as the minutes of a Cabinet meeting show. (*State Papers, Domestic, George III*, 11, 88/15c.) Little was done, however, until the Earl of Dartmouth resigned November 10, 1775, and Lord George Germain received the seals on the same day. (*Colonial Office*, 5–250, p. 281.) Then, on December 6, 1775, the expedition to Charleston was planned at Whitehall. Germain gave orders, and five regiments from Cork sent in a fleet commanded by Sir Peter Parker. (*Colonial Office*, 5–250, p. 295.) In order that the 'Friends of Government' might be armed (especially those in North Carolina, ten thousand stand of arms and ammunition were sent to Howe. (*Ibid.*, 250; *Correspondence of King George III*, III, 259, 260, 266.)

[4] The British Ministers were, perhaps, to be blamed, for they had promised their troops in January, and they began to arrive only in April, after three months at sea.

ment for that army so that the Patriots were again justified in giving Providence the credit for their salvation.[1] As a result some sixteen hundred Loyalists were met and overwhelmingly defeated, February 27, 1776, at Moore's Creek Bridge, near Wilmington, by Colonel Moore in command of Patriot forces.[2] As Concord and Lexington stirred the hearts of New-Englanders, so Moore's Creek Bridge stirred the South.

When, six weeks later, Sir Henry Clinton, detached from the army at Boston, reached the rendezvous off Wilmington where he was to meet the army with which he was to conquer the South, he realized the folly of attempting a march up into North Carolina, lacking the expected aid. Thereupon he ordered his transports with two thousand men to sail on to Charleston.[3] There, in conjunction with Sir Peter Parker with eight frigates, he hoped to win a victory before the time when he was explicitly ordered to join Howe at New York.

Charleston was little protected from sea attack except by sandy shoals and Sullivan's Island, whereon was a redoubt of sound and spongy pal-

[1] E. E. Curtis, *The British Army . . .*, 127.

[2] S. A. Ashe, *History of North Carolina*, 498–505; *Colonial Records of North Carolina*, x, 441–45, 482–93.

The Patriot contingents actually in the fight were under the Colonels Caswell and Lillington. Cornwallis with twenty companies, two artillery ships and four victuallers (and hoping 'the rest of the fleet not far behind') was still three hundred and seventy leagues from Cape Fear seven weeks *after* this battle took place! *Germain Papers*, Cornwallis to Germain, April 18, 1776.

[3] This attack on Charleston had been planned December 6, 1775, at Whitehall, and directions given by Lord George Germain. P.R.O., *Colonial Office*, 5–250, p. 295.

metto logs, called Fort Moultrie, in honor of its resourceful defender. After long delays, every hour of which was precious to the defenders of Charleston,[1] Clinton's army was landed upon an island close to the north of Sullivan's Island, and Sir Peter Parker prepared to bombard Fort Moultrie from the south. Ten days before the actual attack on June 28, 1776, Clinton ascertained that the shallow waters which separated his mosquito-tormented army from Sullivan's Island were unfordable, being seven feet deep even at low tide. He notified Parker, who acknowledged his letter, that his army would be unable to aid the fleet, as had been planned, unless enough boats were furnished to carry his troops across the dividing waters.[2] A few days later, Parker went ahead, notwithstanding, bombarded the fort, which military science — at least that of General Charles Lee — said was untenable, and withdrew after ten hours with the loss of a ship and two hundred men killed or wounded. Moultrie's loss was inconsiderable; the greatest Southern seaport was saved for the time being. Clinton hung about for three weeks hoping that Providence would do what he had failed to do, and then betook his fleet and army northward where greater glory awaited him on Long Island.

While the Carolinas were anticipating and successfully resisting attack by the British armed forces, Virginia's political temper was being raised

[1] Congress was aware as early as January 1, 1776, that this attack was planned. *Journals of . . . Congress* (Ford, ed.), IV, 15.

[2] *Clinton Papers* (W.L.C.L.), Clinton to Parker, June 28, 1776, July 12. 1776; Parker to Clinton, June 20, 1776, December 21, 1776.

to a blood heat by internecine war, and a maddening conflict with Governor Dunmore. The events which led to this strife are a significant part of the war for Independence. It will be necessary to review some of the pre-war history which explains Virginia's forwardness for Independence.

Until the near approach of the Revolution made radical measures inevitable the conservative and the extreme factions in Virginia had been almost one in their opposition to the British Government. The gulf between them began to open when, to express indignation over the Boston Port Bill, Patrick Henry and Thomas Jefferson got a fast-day resolution through the House of Burgesses.[1] A fast day was not Virginian in character, but the Assembly trod in the footsteps of the Long Parliament. Its action showed Virginia's sympathy with Boston on June 1, when the hateful bill would go into effect. Governor Dunmore in wrath sent the Assembly home, but it merely went from the State House to the Apollo Room of the local tavern. There it adopted an association meant to bulldoze England with a boycott on all trade in or out, asked for local county committees to enforce it, and directed the counties to elect members to a convention to meet August 1, 1774.[2] That August meeting marks the beginning of the Revolution in Virginia.

The county elections returned mainly the old burgesses, for the choice was not large, and was, in the older counties, pretty well determined by cus-

[1] Jefferson, *Works* (Memorial ed.), I, 9.

[2] Van Tyne, *Causes of the War . . .*, 427.

tom. A Virginia county was a little, narrow, self-sufficient world in itself, where a few fairly well-educated and experienced public men led opinion. It was bound together in the east, by family ties, a stratified society, where wealth and social position were important, and some ability, because of the rivalry between families. Below this aristocracy were the small farmers, who in eastern Virginia crowded about the customary speakers on the court-house green. Led by a few cheering and swearing gentlemen, who fanned the flame of rebellion, the admiring rustics roared their liberty songs over tavern tables and toasted their village Hampdens with ale. Even balls and parties in those spirit-stirring days became patriotic meetings. As a result, Jonathan Boucher dryly commented, 'Everybody seemed to be on fire, either with rum or patriotism or both.' [1]

In this election old wine went into new bottles. The old dominating class wrought the change, and so there was no social convulsion. The time-honored constitution of Virginia died a painless death. When the old burgesses came to the new convention, they resolved upon an even more extreme embargo on all English commerce, and left it to be enforced by county committees whose members were merely the former county justices of the peace,[2] or former vestrymen — the old local leaders for the most part, and most efficient.

The Convention then elected members to the Con-

[1] *Reminiscences of an American Loyalist* (Boucher, ed.), 109.

[2] Force, *American Archives* (4th Series), I, 1061.

tinental Congress, wherein Richard Henry Lee soon proposed the plan of an association in all the colonies [1] — a non-importation and non-exportation device, meant to dismay the British merchants, as it did, but failing to affright the British Government, still dominated by the great landholders.

This Continental Association was enforced in Virginia, as had been the Provincial one, by local committees, untrammeled at first by central authority, yet working smoothly and with little violence. The shutters went up in the county courts, for their justices were busy on committees, 'setting and pricing goods, imprinting books,' managing everything, as Tories said, with a 'bullying conduct.' The committee members were respecters of law, tried and trusted men, the 'gentlemen' who had always led the body of the people, chosen as of yore by the freeholders assembled at the court-house. Being gentry, they could use ostracism, an important weapon, to coerce the backward, and loyalism was soon quite out of fashion.

If Virginia sentiment was, on the surface, mainly Patriot, it was because the Association was so assiduously enforced by committees of country gentlemen that Loyalists and neutrals hardly dared to wear their hearts upon their sleeves. The committeemen were chiefly planters, and not the traders who were 'asked to be melancholy spectators' of their own destruction. The committee was not only

[1] Of this delegation Randolph Bland, Pendleton, and Benjamin Harrison were conservatives; Washington, Henry, Jefferson, and R. H. Lee, radical.

judge and jury, but executioner as well. Under a jealous eye, men must walk a straight and narrow path. One sinner who merely wrote that the common people showed no enthusiasm for roasting Lord North in effigy was denounced as a 'wicked enemy of America.' Critics of the Revolution, drinkers of tea, and men 'intemperate of speech,' were given over to public wrath as 'monsters of ingratitude.' Drunkenness alone, a palliation for every crime in that time and place, could excuse a man for 'treason,' the ugly name by which violations of the Association were deprecated. Though a ruling passion in Virginia was horse-racing and card-playing, the committees enforced the Association injunctions against gambling. Even the prohibition of 'feasting bounteously' was insisted upon, and that this puritanical meddling with private affairs was endured is a measure of the state of public emotion. Committees broke open all letters to British officials, and examined the merchants' books for traces of illegal trade, or of increase of prices, a crime jealously watched. The merchants, who had long endured being looked down upon by the planters, now felt 'lashed with a rod of iron,' a 'red-hot one fresh from the infernal forge of tyranny,' glad to fly to 'any corner on the face of the earth.' By such methods the tidewater planters, who had started the committee system, led the colony into revolution, which they dreaded.

While the county committees were keeping the countryside 'one hundred per cent American,' the Virginia leaders in the Convention broke into two factions — one for nothing more rash than a trade boycott, one for revolution and an appeal to the 'God of Hosts.' Patrick Henry, who thought he could hear chains clanking 'on the plains of Boston,' was for defense measures. His resolution to that end, hateful to the 'Tories,' but backed by Washington, Jefferson, and Lee, carried, 65 to 60, in spite of Bland, Pendleton, and Benjamin Harrison, who would go slowly, and who were not ready to hear the King called a tyrant, a fool, and a puppet. The conservatives did not mind sitting in an illegal assembly, but they halted before unlawful war measures against England. Though Henry got a radical committee to carry out the purpose of the resolution, the slower group retarded action, so that, while the courts closed and the militia drilled, Dunmore sat in his palace unmolested.[1]

But Henry was quite right that the next gale that should sweep from the North would bring to their ears 'the clash of resounding arms.' Lexington and Concord, April 19, 1775, ruined the conservative programme. After that news the two factions got along after a fashion. Conservatives helped the radicals crush open Toryism; radicals yielded to the conservatives in the matter of keeping hands off Dunmore, the legal 'head of the state.' The Governor was thought 'timid,' but he suddenly seized the colony's powder store and put it on a British ship, offering a lame excuse about a threatened 'slave uprising.'[2] Anger blazed everywhere, and

[1] I am indebted to H. J. Eckenrode, *The Revolution in Virginia*, for much of the matter in these pages.

[2] Hist. MSS. Com., *Report, Dartmouth MSS.*, II, 294.

Patrick Henry, with an ever-growing mob of armed men, marched on the capital, whereupon Dunmore offered pay for the powder, which Henry accepted. The fiery patriot seemed checkmated, but, doubtless, he realized that the conservatives were still 'lying supinely on their backs and hugging the delusive phantom of hope.' Dunmore, weak, unstable, oscillating between faintness of heart and defiance of the lightning, issued a proclamation branding Henry, the idol of the hour, as an outlaw. When this was ignored, Dunmore called the Assembly, to which came, June 1, 1775, the members of the revolutionary Convention, only to approve the Convention's measures, reject Lord North's conciliatory measures, and express their disgust with Dunmore.[1] Even Bland talked of hanging him. Then, as feeling rose, bands of long-frocked riflemen, 'shirtmen,' from the Uplands reached Williamsburg, and Dunmore, realizing the advantages of a floating 'Palace,' fled on board the Fowey at Yorktown.

After protesting, as an Assembly, the members, acting as the Convention, took the rôle of legislature and executive. Yet so great was the love of England, so deep-rooted Virginia's constitutional principles and respect for legal methods, that the conservatives tried to get the Governor to agree to a substitute to act as Governor. Upon his refusal, such efforts ceased, but, nevertheless, during the fall, revolution almost stood still, for the conservatives elected Pendleton chairman of a Committee of Safety, and succeeded in delaying local hostilities, 'crying peace,' as Henry

[1] See H. J. Eckenrode, *The Revolution in Virginia*, 53–54.

said, 'when there was no peace.' Pendleton, though risen from obscurity, had become, with prosperity, the defender of the ruling class, a buttress of the crumbling social order. His person fine, his manners elegant, he was suspicious of democracy, and put his faith in government by gentlemen. To him Dunmore was sacred.

Though the Convention had long been, in fact, Dunmore's open enemy, it was only the inevitable struggle for Norfolk, 'infamous nest of Tories,' that forced their hands. For that town of six thousand inhabitants war meant trade ruin, and Dunmore's presence and protection made open loyalty possible. He had gathered there a motley company of British regulars and sailors, Scotch clerks, and some runaway and kidnaped negroes, almost ignorant of the use of arms. The latter had been seized by the British sloop of war, Otter, which raided plantations for slaves and provisions. When its tender got aground one day and was burned, trouble began. Ruined business in town had lessened zeal for the colonial cause, yet the mob there sometimes attacked insolent British sailors, and when, in September, Dunmore's marines raided the propaganda press, carrying off both it and the printers, resentment increased. The people of that region were in a sad plight. None could travel without a pass from a Patriot committee, nor get outside intelligence except by their consent. 'All newspapers are stopped, none are allowed to be given to the public,' wrote a traveler.[1] Bad news especially was not allowed to

[1] *Journal of N. Cresswell,* 170. This was just as true a year earlier.

travel. On the other hand, Dunmore used every means to make the Virginians join the loyal cause, luring the lower classes, coercing the upper. The tension reached its height in the middle of November, 1775, and hostilities began.

It was Dunmore who opened the war and forced the Committee of Safety, the Convention's executive, to attack. Though companies of 'minute-men' had existed for months, the Convention passed an ordinance, July, 1775, authorizing two regiments of regulars and companies of riflemen.[1] The Convention also gave financial support by a tax levy, and an issue of paper money to the amount of £350,000.[2] A month later the direction of these forces was put into the hands of the Committee of Safety, not a legal executive, but one born of necessity. Of this body Pendleton became chairman, sure to stave off war as long as possible. Powerful at first, his influence waned as the war went on. Four radicals on this committee pressed for war; the seven conservatives hung fire.[3] All were men of means and social position, and had immense power. They conducted correspondence with other colonies, directed troops, supervised local committees, giving them guidance and listening to their complaints and appeals. Though mild at first in dealing with loyalism, their moderation was lost

[1] Hening, *Statutes at Large*, IX, 9.

[2] *Ibid.*, 65–68. The Virginia paper money was good at first, but gradually sank until in 1782 one gold dollar would buy a thousand paper ones.

[3] Jefferson, Washington, Henry, and R. H. Lee, who would have reënforced the radicals, were in Congress or on military duty.

as the war advanced, especially toward the Loyalists about Norfolk, who robbed Patriot plantations of plate and money, burned some houses and dragged a few Patriots away captive. Such conduct was driving the reluctant committee on toward war, when Dunmore, with a small, well-drilled British force, attacked a Patriot body near Great Bridge, and, having won, let loose his 'black rascals' on the helpless inhabitants of a near-by hamlet. He then declared martial law, erected the King's banner, exhorting every one to rally to it or become a traitor, and forced all to wear the British badge of red on their breasts. Hoping for a servile insurrection, he proclaimed freedom to all slaves and indented servants of 'rebels,' though some of the slaves were mere savages, ignorant even of English speech. Rumor made this far worse than it really was. 'The flame runs like wildfire through the slaves,' wrote one who thought that 'Hell itself could not have vomitted anything more black.' He imagined the slaves in their 'nocturnal revels' thinking now of their liberty rather than of music and dancing.[1] That was, of course, absurd, but many believed it, and were enraged, accordingly.

Could the British Government have then spared Dunmore a regiment from Boston, where many regiments were doing nothing, a Tory party might have been created in Virginia and the royal cause saved.[2]

[1] *Letters on the American Revolution* (Willard, ed.), 233.

[2] Indeed, in July of 1775, Pownall ordered three thousand stands of arms, with three hundred rounds of powder and ball for each musket, sent to Virginia, but, if they ever arrived, it was too late. P.R.O., *Colonial Office*, 5–250.

But the Governor, a weak and ordinary man, lacked forces adequate to make a success of his fitful bursts of courage. These passionate actions lost him all influence. Denounced as 'that ignoramous negro-thief,' [1] he was universally detested, and none scrupled to make war on him. All his follies, moreover, were laid to the British Government.

The Committee of Safety now became recognized by all. When it prepared to attack Dunmore, Patrick Henry, who had hurried back from Philadelphia bent on military fame, was eager to command the Virginia troops. He was colonel of the First Regiment and ranking officer. But Pendleton blocked the popular orator's quest for martial glory, sharing Washington's doubts as to Henry's military fitness. Henry retired to civil life, and Colonel William Woodford marched toward Norfolk with seven hundred men to save the southeastern counties from civil war. On December 9, he took the fort at Great Bridge, defended by a force of some five hundred, of which only two hundred were British regulars. Reënforced by two hundred men from North Carolina, Woodford then seized Norfolk, forcing Dunmore to take on shipboard his mob of Loyalists and slaves, who there suffered greatly from bad food and ill quarters.[2]

Then Dunmore committed the crowning folly, opening fire on the town and landing marines to apply the torch to the houses. Again he stupidly played into American hands, for Norfolk would

[1] *New England Chronicle*, May 30, 1776.

[2] Force, *American Archives* (4th Series), IV, 223–28.

always be useful to the British as a base of operations, would always be at the mercy of their fleet, while Virginians would hesitate wantonly to destroy it. Here was their opportunity. Woodford's soldiers seized the chance for plunder, burned more houses, twenty times as many as the British, and sacked the town for two days — with due attention to the rum shops — before Woodford stopped them.[1] The British had burned only the water-front, while the Virginians made a heap of ruins of the whole town. The colonists were pleased, yet all the odium was cast on Dunmore and the British Government. Another great reason for Independence was found, and loyalism in Virginia was crushed. Dunmore added fuel to American hate for a time by raids along the shore, but two days after the Declaration of Independence, which he had done so much to hasten, his ships slipped cable and put out to sea.[2]

Not only had the conservative faction, by this episode, lost the power to prevent war on the constitutional head of the state, but they also lost control of the revolutionary forces which were attacking the very existence of the 'rule of gentlemen.' Nearly

[1] H. J. Eckenrode, *The Revolution in Virginia*, 86–89. Virginia State Commissioners later reported that Dunmore burned thirty-two houses, November 20, 1775, nineteen, January 1, 1776, while the Virginia soldiers destroyed eight hundred and sixty-three houses, and the Convention ordered four hundred and sixteen more destroyed later. What actually happened was pretty accurately described at the time by the Ministry in reply to the Opposition. See French report of debates in the House of Lords, *Archives des Affaires Étrangères, Angleterre*, 515, no. 4.

[2] The whole chapter is based on Eckenrode, *The Revolution in Virginia*, and Lingley, *The Transition in Virginia*, but the sources have been checked and some new material added.

all denizens of the uplands, the back-country of Virginia, were not content with seaboard rule. They complained of lack of proportional representation, and of a capital city located too far to the east.[1] To the aid of this naturally democratic community came the small farmers, the poor of eastern Virginia, who were fired, early in 1775, with the idea that the revolution meant not only opposition to Great Britain, but antagonism to the established order of Virginia society. These men usually had food enough, but were housed in hovels, their education neglected, and many were sunk in brutal dissipations. Their leaders now began to broadcast French ideas of equality, and there came to them a hope to rise, to get a greater share in their own government. The planter class, on the contrary, had been little touched by eighteenth-century liberal thought. They were untroubled by any ideas of bettering society. English thoughts and English institutions still prevailed among them. They frowned on dissenters and democrats. One of them, Landon Carter, opposed 'British oppression,' but was fearful, too, of 'internal oppressions and commotions.'[2] As the revolution drifted toward Independence, the question rose as to the nature of the political institutions under a new order. Thereupon, religious dissenters, social reformers, political idealists, all clamored for 'rights,' and thus the rights of America became merged into the rights of man. The planter class had begun agi-

[1] Van Tyne, *Causes of the War of Independence*, 149; Lingley, *The Transition in Virginia*, 18–20.

[2] *William and Mary Quarterly*, XVIII, 43, 44.

tation against the British Government without a thought of Independence, and when that loomed before them they hoped to stop there; but the democratic faction, well led by Henry and Jefferson, began the lasting struggle for power, for equal right and a democratic state.

In resisting this new movement the 'gentlemen' let 'I dare not' wait upon 'I would,' because of the danger of being classed as 'Tories.' Loyalism was sternly repressed by the revolutionary Convention. It is only a superficial view that British sympathy hardly existed in Virginia — alone of all the colonies. There was 'a large latent opposition to rebellion,' but the British Government, perhaps unavoidably, allowed it to be crushed. The Scotch merchants especially of the seaboard towns were converted to loyalism by the trade laws. These men were generally the factors of the tobacco lords in Glasgow, who are pictured clad in scarlet coats, cocked hats, and powdered wigs, bearing gold-headed canes, and caring about as much for American liberties as did their immortal critic, Dr. Johnson. These factors were hard hit when ordered to cease supplying British ships and to send no provision, out of Virginia. Their protest was only rebuked, and there began their detachment from the colonial cause. From rebuke, ostracism, and mob menace, the persecution advanced, by May of 1776, to a point where, as public temper hardened under stress of war, the Convention resolved to imprison open Loyalists, and in some cases to confiscate their estates.

Imprisonment in that day was worse than unpleasant. The ill-smelling jail at Williamsburg was badly ventilated, overcrowded, the negro quarters filthy. The diet was not bad, reported a critical commission, but the inmates complained of it bitterly.[1] Those not in robust health suffered what was called 'putrid fever.' Still there was little unnecessary cruelty. As Patriot irritation grew and property rights became less carefully guarded, men were ruined, estates forfeited. Most of the trading class and some planters went into exile. The spirit of the Patriots was tyrannical, but rarely cruel. When a 'test oath' was demanded, refusal was met by a seizure of arms and ammunition. No Tories were put to death even by the mob, and there was not much use of tar and feathers. The Loyalists were never given a chance to concentrate, and few open enemies were left in Virginia after the spring of 1776. To avoid courting a fate of this kind, the aristocratic planter, though opposed to the democratic side of the revolutionary movement, bridled his tongue and watched his step.

It was through the events and trials here recounted that Virginia changed the dominant political sentiment in less than a year from a solemn declaration, August 1, 1775, 'before God and the world,' of true allegiance to its 'lawful and righteous King,' to that solemn resolve of its Convention (May 15, 1776), that its delegates in Congress be instructed to declare the United Colonies 'free and independent states.' The New England States were

[1] Eckenrode, *The Revolution in Virginia*, 154–55.

ready for Independence, but wisely left the proposal to other sections. The laggards were the five middle colonies, of which Pennsylvania and New York were the chief, and we shall turn first to the story of the Quaker colony's slow inspiration of the spirit of Independence.

CHAPTER XI

CONSERVATIVE AND RADICAL DISTURB THE PEACE OF THE QUAKER STATE

In Pennsylvania, as in Virginia and the colonies to the South, the progress toward an independence of Great Britain was accompanied by an advance toward more liberal political institutions. Pennsylvania moved more slowly toward the destined end, because it did not feel the spur of actual war within its borders, and because of political conditions which must be examined in some detail to be understood.

It is an open question whether Pennsylvanian or Carolinian history best illustrates that struggle, growing with the growth of the quarrel with England, between the colonial aristocracy of the seaboard and the back-country peoples, reënforced by the middle and lower classes of the Atlantic cities. The socially elect of the seaboard were not hard to distinguish.[1] Wealth, aristocratic family connections, a social flair and means to maintain it, all helped to place one in the right 'set,' 'the quality,' as they said in the South. A colonial 'gentleman' must walk in the shoes of the English gentry, have his ancestors in oil on the parlor walls, employ a London tailor and hatter, be in the governor's council, or have his friends and relatives there. On the outer edge of this class of 'gentry' were men with some social or business claim on the 'elect,' climbing upward as fast as their talents permitted; constituting the rank and

[1] Van Tyne, *Causes of the War of Independence*, 425.

file of the colonial aristocracy. Such people ruled American politics until the turmoil of the Revolution gave them their first setback.

Confronting this group on the colonial stage, especially in Pennsylvania and the South, were the small farmers, German and Scotch-Irish of the back country, woodsmen, in the earlier generation, clad in homespun, made quick-witted and shifty by the dangers of their life. There was nothing to keep this society fixed in the cake of custom. Traditions and ancestors were forgotten. The Westerner, like Charles Surface, would have been inclined to sell his ancestors to the highest bidder. It was easy to rise in the world, if one had courage to push into the wilds; so that there was economic quality. Few would be servants, all were individualistic, jealous of political control by others. Linked with this frontier class in political interests were the artisans of the seaboard cities, the debtors and the voteless men, led often by young lawyers with a gift for stump-speaking. Between these classes and the aristocrats was waged a political conflict, set agoing during the French and Indian wars because of seaboard indifference to frontier dangers, and waxing hotter each year until the outbreak of the Revolution. It was the genesis of an age-long struggle between East and West, the voter and the voteless, rich and poor, privilege and the interests of the common man.

The natural antagonism between the seaboard and the frontier existed all the way from New England to Georgia. In the eyes of westerners the merchant rulers of the seaboard town were little better than swindlers, while the eastern aristocrats looked upon their western neighbors as a 'pack of savages.'[1] Idle, propertyless, talkative, and passionate; impatient of restraint, legal, moral, or religious; grumblers against taxes, rulers, and schoolmasters — these were seaboard epithets and adjectives which described the pioneers for fifty years after the Revolutionary period.[2] The pioneer retorted against the 'corrupt and effete East,' the land of money-changers and slave-owning aristocrats, complained of land laws made for the eastern rich man, a money system hard on debtors, of inadequate representation, and a system of justice devised to give power to men who would crook the knee to kings, men of showy lives and arrogant manners, who scorned and exploited the rural west.

In Pennsylvania there was perhaps as democratic a society as America possessed, but dominated by a Quaker minority entrenched in the Provincial Assembly. Yet even the Quaker embraced principles as democratic as those of his Presbyterian neighbor, for all of their religious experience was built on contract and God-given rights, while a spiritual aristocracy, selected by God, dwarfed all other distinctions. Moreover, their common political teachers were Buchanan, Harrington, Milton, and Sidney, and both Calvinist and Quaker accepted Penn's dictum that 'any government is free to the people

[1] Charles Biddle, *Autobiography*, 142; Shearer, *Political and Constitutional History of Pennsylvania*.

[2] President Dwight's *Travels*, quoted by F. J. Turner, *The Frontier in American History*, 251.

under it, where the laws rule and the people are a party to the laws.'[1] The prevailing religious toleration, too, led to a respect for the opinions of others, one of the foundation stones of democracy. Finally, the variety of people, Dutch, English, German, Scotch-Irish, and Welsh, compelled a tolerant spirit working to the same end.

When in the early eighteenth century the Scotch-Irish began that great migration to America, and particularly to Pennsylvania, which was to people that province, the Great Valley, and the western counties of Virginia and the Carolinas, they came with more faith in the rights of man, political and religious, than in the British Government. As for 'genuine Hibernians,' wrote Graydon, 'it was enough for them to know that England was the antagonist' to sweeten any fight, and all expected to tussle for any right they would enjoy.[2] Indeed, Lord North was convinced that even in Ireland the Presbyterians were 'almost to a man favourers of the American Cause.'[3] In Pennsylvania their first contention, as it happened, was with the Quaker Government and the Penns, whose legal rights in the western lands they ignored almost as much as those of the Indians. To the latter they were 'very rough,' seizing their lands on the principle that it was 'against the laws of God that so much land should remain idle while Christians wanted to labor on it.'[4]

[1] Lincoln, *Revolutionary Movement in Pennsylvania*, 8, 9, 13.
[2] Watson's *Annals*, II, 260.
[3] *Correspondence of King George III*, III, 530.
[4] Lincoln, *Revolutionary Movement in Pennsylvania*, 33.

As to legal title from the Penns or the Quaker Government, they set that at nought almost as contemptuously, and by 1726, it was estimated that one hundred thousand persons were settled in Pennsylvania with no proper title. In more than one sense they threatened to make themselves proprietors of the province. A year before the battle of Lexington, they made one third of the total population of the colony, though by no means represented in that proportion in the governing assembly.[1]

Dwelling in the western counties, as well as the eastern, were the Germans, who came to Pennsylvania attracted by the Quaker principles of peace and religious toleration. Their chief desire was to be let alone, for they were suspicious of all governments, after faring badly at the hands of both German and British rulers. Though never active allies of the Quakers, they acquiesced in their appropriation of political power, and joined their opposition to the Penn family.[2] Where they clashed with the Quaker was mainly in the west, exposed to Indians and French. Against these dangers the Quaker-dominated assembly refused aid. The Germans, lacking leaders and capacity for organization, seemed helpless, but the Quakers failed to realize their faculty for fight and forgot that the Scotch-Irish neighbors in the west would furnish leaders. The Scotch-Irish taught them also to evade

[1] Lincoln, *The Revolutionary Movement in Pennsylvania*, 34, 35.

[2] *Ibid.*, 23, 24. The quarrel with the Penns was mainly over the right of the Assembly to tax proprietary lands for public purposes.

taxes to the Penns, and to the land companies, just as 'baneful and oppressive.'[1]

On the eve of the Revolution there was a difference between east and west as to the relations between Quaker and German. Among the rich Germans in or about Philadelphia there was a strong conservative party as late as 1775, and at that time the wealthier members were admitted into that social aristocracy which controlled Pennsylvania politics. Though the poorer Germans favored the other side, the Mennonites of Lancaster County and Germantown, with scruples against bearing arms, were bound to the Quaker faction by that religious tie. Thus the German and Quaker alliance had in the east political, social, and religious foundations. In the western counties the Germans, jealous of Quaker rivals in the fur trade, angered by neglect, fearful of taxes, rejected the leadership of the rich Germans of the east, and, leagued with the Scotch-Irish, finally dominated the German group in Pennsylvania. They showed an 'amazing spirit,' coming out finally against both King and Quaker-ridden Assembly, and in the famous Convention of 1776 resisting all halfway measures. Thus in the strategic contest for German votes between the Quaker politician on the Delaware and the Scotch-Irish politician on the Susquehanna, the latter won the final victory and carried Pennsylvania for Independence.[2]

Yet, curiously enough, the struggle for independ-

[1] Lincoln, *Revolutionary Movement in Pennsylvania*, 24–26.
[2] *Ibid.*, 15–16, 27–33, 38–39.

ence of England, fought to its end by westerners and the lower classes of the eastern cities, was upheld at the beginning by the wealthy and 'respectable' classes in Pennsylvania. The Quaker rulers of that colony had long been opposed to outside political control, either by the proprietors, governors sent by them, or by the British Ministry. Individual initiative and communal independence were fundamental principles with Friends, and as the rule of Pennsylvania by instructions from England would mean the end of local self-government, the Quakers fought it, and their struggle with the Penns during seventy years for self-rule was a buckling on of armor — though they would have disliked the figure — for the fight with England. But reaction in Philadelphia and in the west against Quaker abuse of power resulted in a revolution in colonial politics as well as a rebellion against England. Many reasons which led the colonists to seek freedom from England led Scotch-Irish and Germans in the Susquehanna Valley to seek freedom from rule by eastern Quakers. There was no racial bond between the Quakers in the east and the Scotch-Irish of the west, and as the trade of the west tended to follow the path of the Susquehanna to Baltimore, there was not even a commercial bond. Allied with the westerners were the Philadelphia mechanics and artisans and shopkeepers, the discontented middle and lower classes, who had as little chance in elections to get on a ticket as 'a Jew or a Turk.' As the hostility to Quaker domination grew, there became popular 'leveling principles,' anarchy 'hallowed by the phrases of Equality and the Rights of Man.'[1] The rival factions exchanged epithets. The aristocratic Graydon worried about the 'canaille'; another noted 'turbulence and malignancy' in the people. One of the gentry even heard 'the vermin begin to croak.' In the other camp lawyers were denounced as 'aristocrats who let out their tongues and talents for hire,' and the respectable Thomas Wharton was sneered at as 'the Marquis of Barrataria.' A growing demand for a 'full suffrage' brought about the overthrow of Quaker government more than Quaker coldness to military resistance.[2] Quaker power went down before the discontented classes of Philadelphia allied with the disgruntled Scotch-Irish and Germans of the west, than whom no people in America were more democratic. Both welcomed the national movement for Independence because under its cover they could revolutionize their colonial political conditions. To resist this endeavor, the Quaker aristocrats of Pennsylvania's eastern counties leagued with England against the western uprising, resisting the Revolution because American Independence meant Quaker political subordination.[3] It is safe to say that as long as the outcome of the war was in doubt, the majority of Pennsylvania's citizens were open or secret friends of the royal cause, led by the socially elect, especially the Quakers.

The story of the Quaker political downfall so clearly exposes the methods by which the demo-

[1] Lincoln, *Revolutionary Movement in Pennsylvania*, 14–16, 38, 39, 77, 79, 80.

[2] *Ibid.*, 80, 86, 91.

[3] *Ibid.*, 14, 54.

cratic forces rose to power that it is an essential chapter of the history of the Revolution. In reply to Boston's appeal for help there gathered, May 20, 1774, in the City Tavern of Philadelphia, a famous mass meeting, summoned by the radical leaders Mifflin, Reed, and Thomson. In the addresses there was warmth and fire and pathos. Charles Thomson declaimed until he fainted, but came to and went at it again. The result was a victory of the popular party over the Quakers who clamored against 'violence,' and disapproved the resolve of the citizens to stand by Boston.[1] The message sent to Boston by a committee chosen at the mass meeting was not wholly consoling, but the great thing, as Samuel Adams in far-off Massachusetts clearly saw, was that the people, assembled in a mass meeting, had spoken without waiting for their legislature to act. Moreover, their committee was empowered to call future meetings. Legality was unhorsed and Revolution was astride.[2]

On June 1, the day the Boston Port Bill was to go into effect, Philadelphia shops closed, church bells tolled, and the text of the Presbyterian pastor was: 'In every province whithersoever the King's commandment and decree came, there was a great mourning.' But Pennsylvania's sympathy was not limited to church bells and sermons. The radical forces compelled a calling of the Assembly to choose delegates to the Continental Congress. In order to

[1] Stille, *John Dickinson,* Appendix II, 105; Watson, *Annals,* II, 325–26; W. B. Reed, *Life of Joseph Reed,* I, 65.

[2] Lincoln, *Revolutionary Movement in Pennsylvania,* 164–66.

show the Assembly what the people wanted, county committees were elected, who were to choose members to a provincial convention, which met in advance of the Assembly and dictated its conduct. Radical leaders from Philadelphia toured the western counties to ascertain the ideas held by the Germans. They found that the frontier people heartily endorsed the idea of a provincial convention where they would have proportional representation as they did not have in the Assembly. The Assembly met, July 18, 1774, obeyed to the letter the will of the Convention, yielding rather than to lose its position of authority. The only sign of its real will was the instruction to the delegates in Congress not to be 'indecent or disrespectful to the Mother State,' and to seek 'Reconciliation and Harmony.' The noteworthy fact was that the Convention, an organization on a popular basis, had laid down the law to the legal representative body of the province. From that time on the city and county committees were the true rulers of Pennsylvania, revolutionary Jehus driving the slow coach of the legal assembly.[1]

So great, however, was the inertia, so strong the old political machine, that the success of the popular movement was long in doubt. True, the Assembly did confirm all the measures of the Continental Congress when it adjourned, but it was plain that the moderate Assembly members meant to support the radicals only in resolutions. The only class in Philadelphia eager to fight was that which had long thought itself ill-treated by the Assembly. Not

[1] Lincoln, *Revolutionary Movement in Pennsylvania,* 178-81.

until April 25 was the Assembly pushed farther, when, on news from Lexington, eight thousand people gathered at the State House in Philadelphia, and resolved to defend themselves with arms. When Committees of Correspondence thereupon took charge of military affairs, the Assembly, remembering the eight thousand citizens, advanced another laggard step and granted the money of which Bellona is ever avid. Every yielding to the insurgents' demands hastened the Assembly on its road to ruin. By the middle of May, 1775, it counted for nought.[1] The real executive also was by that time the Committee of Safety, a small oligarchy, bent to the will of Benjamin Franklin. The real legislative power was an unwieldy city committee of sixty-seven members, acting for both city and colony, which (June, 1775), ordered the Assembly to raise a military force to be directed by a Committee of Safety and Defense. The Conservative Assembly meekly obeyed. Having formerly allowed itself to be driven by popular meetings, step by step into rebellion, it now cringed to a dictatorship by military forces.[2] Thus it was that late in 1775 and through 1776 the Revolution in Pennsylvania became harmonious with the national movement.

But there were yet a few steps to the brink. In September the Committee of Safety began to press the Assembly for laws to compel all to aid in the defense of the colony. The militia, 'Associators,' as they were called, cried out against the business

[1] Lincoln, *Revolutionary Movement in Pennsylvania,* 192–209.

[2] *Ibid.,* 210–14.

and other advantages reaped by those whose time was not consumed in training. 'Compulsory service' was the slogan. Counter-agitation by Quakers was overwhelmed by a campaign in which even the non-combatant sects, the Mennonites and German Baptists, joined, offering to pay if they did not fight. Acting on this idea the Assembly yielded and enacted the requested laws. When, however, it was urged, November, 1775, to steer a course toward the haven of Independence, the Assembly adjourned to February, 1776. Thereupon the helm slipped from its hands, and committees chose the course, ever more radical and more violent.

Thus here as elsewhere, the Revolution fell, as it progressed, into the hands of men holding more and more radical and sweeping theories, less and less restrained by tradition and the old order of things. These men knew what they wanted and they had the dash, the will, and the temerity to take a leap in the dark. In Pennsylvania, as in Virginia and some other colonies, the Revolution fell into quite other hands than those that set it going. Besides a superiority in numbers there was an ardor and enthusiasm in the friends of Congress which was generally wanting in the supporters of the King's Government. This was not a new thing in the world, for even Thucydides found boldness and energy more important to the success of revolutions than intelligence or other qualities. 'A few that are stiff,' wrote Bacon, 'do tire out a greater number that are more moderate.'

Suffrage limitations alone had kept Philadelphia conservative and controlled by the well-to-do.

Though the people were now urged to 'reject all timorous, fearful and dastardly spirits' in choosing new Assemblymen, the election in April, 1776, governed, in Philadelphia, by the old suffrage rules, convinced the masses that under the old Assembly there would be no real change in provincial politics.[1]

The masses, therefore, now put their hopes entirely in committees and a revolutionary Convention. This impulse was strengthened by the appearance of Thomas Paine's 'Common Sense,' which subordinated the constitutional arguments and appealed to the mob sense. Government by a convention, newly chosen by the people, and on a popular basis, found favor with the western peoples of Pennsylvania. A Convention, elected so that the westerners would have a just representation, would give them the political control. The city masses and the west now (May, 1776) became pitted against the eastern conservatives for and against a convention of delegates from the counties, a body representing the minds of 'the people,' sure to be radical and sure to become the real ruler of Pennsylvania.[2]

At this point the Continental Congress, now fully in the saddle, and riding rapidly toward Independence, gave great aid to the Pennsylvania radicals. Members of Congress who were eager for a resolution of Independence saw that achievement bound up with getting a change of the control of Pennsyl-

[1] Lincoln, *Revolutionary Movement in Pennsylvania*, 218–34. One radical assemblyman had won in Philadelphia, but though the Whig candidates were generally successful in the west, such was the apportionment that the conservatives still controlled the Assembly.

[2] *Ibid.*, 235, 245.

vania's government. Congress is, wrote R. H. Lee, 'heavily clogged with instructions from these shamefully interested Proprietary people.'[1] To secure a change from conservatives to radical hands, John Adams pressed through the famous resolution of May 15, which amounted to inviting the people of the colonies to disregard their old colonial governments. Sitting as Congress did in the very capital of Pennsylvania, this resolution had profound effect. Though influential men like Dickinson, Wilson, and Robert Morris favored the retention of the old colonial charter, and therefore the government under it, Franklin, Rush, and McKean were opposed. The latter group prevailed because the people refused to be ruled longer by an Assembly, which a majority disliked, and which yielded reforms only under threats. A great agitation arose against 'aristocrats,' and a demand for the recognition of the 'wearers of leather aprons.' Five days after Adams's portentous resolution, seven thousand of the good people of Philadelphia, perhaps a quarter of its inhabitants, gathered in the State House yard, choosing a radical, Roberdeau, as chairman. The meeting resolved that the Assembly, the present government, was not competent to rule, for it was elected by adherents of the King, while many 'worthy inhabitants' were excluded from the franchise. When the Assembly met, two days later, it was confronted with a petition asking for a new constitution and government, and a withdrawal of its instructions to the delegates in Congress against voting for Independence. But

[1] *Letters of . . . Continental Congress* (Burnett, ed.), I, 429.

the gods were making the Assembly mad. After yielding, showing fear of the mob as it had in the past, it had only to resist to invite destruction. Moreover, economic forces worked for the radicals. Non-importation led to scarcity of goods, scarcity, to a rise in prices, and that, to dissatisfaction with the Assembly which was blamed for taking no action against the monopolists, 'emissaries of North, Howe, and Dunmore.'[1] Hard on the heels of this discontent came the inspiring example of the other colonies favoring Independence. Still the Assembly could only dally and sleep on it. Independence was being bitterly debated in Congress, Pennsylvania's leaders resisting. On June 8, its delegates voted five to two against the resolution of Independence. Under compulsion only did the Assembly then change its position, though, perhaps, most of its constituents in the eastern counties did not change at all. On July 2, however, Pennsylvania's delegates voted three to two in favor of Independence.[2]

Only drastic action had wrought this change. The City Committee invited a provincial Conference at Philadelphia, and this revolutionary body of one hundred and eight members, expressing only the popular will, met June 18, and assumed control of the colony.[3] It dealt sledgehammer blows to the old order, denounced the legal assembly, approved Congress's resolution of May 15, summoned a

[1] Lincoln, *Revolutionary Movement in Pennsylvania*, 258.

[2] J. Dickinson and Robert Morris absented themselves for this end.

[3] Meanwhile the Whig delegates bolted the Assembly, which, left without a quorum, adjourned.

Provincial Convention to form a new government, liberalized the franchise, endorsed a new oath of allegiance, in which the name of George III was missing, and adjourned. Conservatives like Wilson and Morris begged the Assembly to save itself even now. Offer a new constitution, they urged, which, though made by conservative and experienced hands, would recognize the change of provincial sentiment.[1] But the die-hards refused to see that the world was moving. On July 4, when Congress declared Independence, Morris and Dickinson had stayed away from the Congress Hall, with the result that a bare majority of Pennsylvania's vote was cast in favor of the momentous decision. As a result of this action in Pennsylvania's own State House, all the advantage of the political situation passed into the hands of the radicals.

[1] Lincoln, *Revolutionary Movement in Pennsylvania*, 258–73.

CHAPTER XII

NEW YORK CONTRACTS THE FEVER OF REVOLT

ANOTHER of the reluctant central colonies was New York. The state of affairs in New York City was such that, even if that port were not the strategical center of the thirteen colonies, there was every reason for the British Government to expect to find champions in that quarter, and therefore to select it as a center of military operations. The historical facts which account for this British hope depict so well in miniature the general trend of political events in all the colonies that they are worthy a close examination.

As far back as January of 1775, the New York Assembly, still the legal governing body, was so dominated by loyal sentiment that it expressed disapproval of the First Continental Congress and refused to appoint deputies to a second.[1] The loyal churchman, Samuel Seabury, asked whether decrees passed in Philadelphia by enthusiastic republicans, 'horrid combination of seditious men,' were to bind the people of New York in a state of slavery,[2] and the answer of the majority of the Assembly seemed to be in the negative. Instead, they sent, on their own motion, a petition to King George, a memorial to the Lords, a remonstrance to the Commons,[3] an

[1] C. L. Becker, *Political Parties in . . . New York*, 177.

[2] Seabury, *An Alarm to the Legislature*, 4–8. (January 17, 1775.)

[3] *American Archives* (4th Series), I, 1313, 1316, 1318.

packet.[1] Since he had been a kind of hostage against attack by royal men-of-war, many now took flight from the city. Members of the Provincial Congress who thought they were sick were only in a funk, as their excuses of 'slow fever, reluctance to food,' and 'want of sleep' pretty plainly indicated. Nor was it an idle fear, for British officers actually had orders to fire on the house of Isaac Sears, a radical ringleader, and to beat it down. The Provincial Congress itself had been more in fear of the royal ships than of the Continental Congress, and with the attendance daily falling, it called in desperation for a new election in November.[2] It must be borne in mind that all this time an American army, led by a general chosen by Congress, was besieging Boston, and that the battle of Bunker Hill had been fought.

The Provincial fall election took place in the midst of a strong Loyalist reaction, and a steady radical drift toward Independence. Not only was there a declining hope of reconciliation, but there was the cumulative economic effect of the Continental Association, rather strictly enforced now for a year. A country actually preparing for war was thereby deliberately depriving itself of the sinews of war under the delusion that it was punishing its enemy.[3] In New York the local Congress seemed

[1] C. L. Becker, *Political Parties in . . . New York*, 222–25. Tryon had been warned as early as August 22, 1775, that he and any other royal officers in any of the colonies were to be seized as hostages to be held for the 'redemption' of such Provincial officers as might be taken by the King's troops. *Clinton Papers* (W.L.C.L.), *Private Intelligence to Tryon.*

[2] C. L. Becker, *Political Parties . . .*, 226–27.

[3] *Letters of . . . Continental Congress* (Burnett, ed.), I, 437. There

to stand for a policy of economic decay and starvation, for hundreds of families in the city saw the wolf at their door. Imports from England had almost ceased, and in New York as elsewhere it was clear that there must be either advance or retreat, either open ports and a Declaration of Independence, or submission to George III.[1] The conviction of this dreadful alternative drove all out-and-out conservatives to oppose the new Provincial Congress. Only a reign of terror forced even a fraction of the counties (nine out of fourteen) to choose delegates at all. The conduct of Queens County was so opposed to Whig purposes that the Continental Congress sent Colonel Heard with twelve hundred men from New Jersey to disarm six hundred Loyalists and carry off nineteen prisoners. When the smoke of the battle at the polls had cleared away, it was found that seven or eight Loyalists had not been returned, and though three of them were, the radicals thought the new body better than the old.[2]

With representatives from only nine out of fourteen counties, the Congress met (December 6), after three weeks of waiting for a quorum. Following a session of sixteen days with an average attendance

could be no better answer to those who sneer at Congress's professions of loyalty for six months after Lexington, while they were actually making war. Had they meant *war for Independence*, common sense dictated giving every facility to trade which gave the sinews of war.

[1] Macpherson's *Annals of Commerce*, III, 564–85. British imports fell from £2,687,000 to £213,000. There had been clandestine trade allowed by Congress in order to get arms.

[2] C. L. Becker, *Political Parties in . . . New York*, 228–33, 245; *Canadian Archives* (1912), *Correspondence and Journal of Bishop Inglis*, 215.

of twenty-seven out of the seventy-four elected, it turned over its whole power to a Committee of Safety with twelve members, seven being a quorum. American belief in representative government was hardly demonstrated by a body reduced from a hundred apportioned representatives, to seventy-four chosen, to twenty-seven who met and committed their power to twelve, of whom seven might rule the province.[1] No wonder the committee was denounced by the Loyalists as a 'lawless power,' which issued citations, sat in judgment, and inflicted pains 'in the teeth of all law.' In the midst of revolution, however, men cannot be particular about forms; they must use any means which their followers will accept. Even this revolutionary committee had to be scourged to its duties by threats that if they failed the province must accept military government by the Continental Congress. It was, indeed, an amazing state of affairs that, while Boston was being besieged and troops being raised in every colony, the hostile ship Asia still got its supplies from Long Island and New York, and supplied arms to loyal citizens of Queens County.[2]

Such vigorous action as was taken was the work of a mob under Isaac Sears, who gathered a hundred kindred spirits (November, 1775), seized the bold

[1] Becker, *Political Parties ... in New York*, 232–35. The whole Congress did meet again in February and March, 1776, only to turn its power over to a second Committee which ruled until a third Congress met in May, 1776. Even the Committee of Safety had great difficulty in getting a quorum. *Ibid.*, 235.

[2] *Ibid.*, 236–38. The Provincial Congress finally voted to cease all relations with Queens County but refused to use arms to coerce them. *Letters of ... Continental Congress* (Burnett, ed.), I, 295.

pamphleteer, Samuel Seabury, hustled him to a prison in Connecticut, and then wrecked the press of James Rivington, loyal printer, and threw his type into the river.[1] Here again, democracy, in a state of revolution, ignored one of its favorite traditions, 'liberty of the press.'

The Loyalists despaired at last of any good coming out of the Provincial Congress, and Governor Tryon, from his place of exile, now the good ship Duchess of Gordon, tried in vain to convene a new loyal Assembly (February, 1776). It was too late, for, under orders from the Continental Congress, Colonel Heard, of the Continental Army, had disarmed some six hundred Loyalists in Queens County, and under like orders General Schuyler with three thousand men had forced the Loyalist leader in Tryon County, Sir John Johnson, to surrender all his arms and military stores, and to swear, with all his Scotch followers, a firm neutrality.[2] Moreover, General Charles Lee had arrived with orders from Washington to get New York City in a state of defense. Lee's coming had a curious effect in the city. He was 'hourly expected,' wrote an officer, 'as if from Heaven, with a legion of flaming swordsmen.'[3]

Nothing better reveals the provincialism of the Americans of that day than their naïve acceptance of this strange creature as a sort of 'Guardian

[1] Becker, *Revolutionary Parties . . . in New York*, 245–46.

[2] *Journals of Continental Congress* (Ford, ed.), IV, 27; A. C. Flick, *Loyalism in New York*, 86–87; Mass. Hist. Soc., *Proceedings*, vol. 60, p. 101.

[3] Greene, *Life of Nathanael Greene*, I, 232.

Angel.'[1] He was not the first nor the last of favorite American humbugs. Richard Henry Lee apparently brought that wolf into the Patriot fold, introducing him to Samuel Adams as a 'most true and worthy friend to the rights of human nature in general, and a warm spirited foe to American oppression.'[2] Indeed, nobody could talk more glibly about 'the liberties of our country,' the 'fate of posterity,' and the 'rights of mankind,' than Lee. He affected great knowledge of the world, and had it, perhaps, for he had been a soldier at eleven years, had been aide-de-camp to the Polish King, commander of some Cossacks, had chatted with Frederick the Great, and fought the Turks. Having survived freezing in the Balkans and an earthquake in Constantinople, he could talk of 'disastrous chances' and 'hairbreadth escapes.'

He had first come to America while serving under Braddock in the British army. Later, under Sir William Johnson in the Indian service, his adopted Mohawk brothers had dubbed him 'boiling water.' After a period of adventure in Europe, he returned to America, in 1773, just in time to pose as a military expert before the Continental Congress. Resigning his half-pay in the British army, he went over to the American cause.[3] He had only made a virtue of necessity, for King George had already ordered him struck off the half-pay list.[4] Soon his tall, lank, thin

[1] *Correspondence of J. Jay*, I, 82.

[2] *R. H. Lee Letters* (Ballagh, ed.), I, 110, 181, 194, 256.

[3] *Essex Gazette*, July 6, 1775.

[4] P.R.O., *Colonial Office*, 5–250, pp. 227–34. Lord Dartmouth knew as early as July 28, 1775, that Lee was 'very active in aiding and abetting the unnatural rebellion.'

form was striding about the American camps, an object of great awe. He had a British officer's contempt for the Patriot soldier, at whom he 'flung and cursed and swore,' threatening to have the riflemen fire on them. 'Men, I do not know what to call you,' he raved. 'You are the worst of creatures.' [1] Like a character in fiction he was a man 'that thunders, lightens, opens graves and roars.' There was in all he said or wrote a freakishness which was a deceptive imitation of genius.[2] An English acquaintance labeled him 'that heterogeneous substance called General Lee.' [3] Mercy Warren, though awed by him, described him to Samuel Adams as 'plain in his person to a degree of ugliness; careless even to impoliteness; his garb ordinary; his voice rough, his manners rather morose; yet sensible, learned, judicious and penetrating.' [4] Lee's unbridled tongue and boundless insolence was borne rather than admired because he was thought indispensable.

Lee's mission to New York was regarded there as an interference with the affairs of a province, and some, who were most vociferous for this doctrine, premonitory of anti-federalism in days to come, were the very radicals who all along had urged Continental union for the purpose of resistance! Exigencies of war, however, gave the whip hand to

[1] Conn. Hist. Soc., *Collection*, VII, 129; Lossing, *Pictorial Field Book of the Revolution*, 224, note 1.

[2] Indeed, his letters have a good deal of literary distinction. New York Hist. Soc., *Collections* (1871–74).

[3] Hist. MSS. Com., *Report*, XIV, pt. 9, p. 307.

[4] James Warren was of about the same opinion. *Warren-Adams Letters*, I, 69, *note*.

advocates of union, and forced the consent of the Committee of Safety. On February 4, 1776, as General Clinton sailed south on his ill-fated expedition to Cape Fear and Charleston, Charles Lee arrived in New York with a bodyguard of riflemen, and grew frantic, as only he could, when he tried in vain to get the Committee of Safety to cut off intercourse with British ships. All that either he or his successor, or even a committee from the Continental Congress, could get was 'more careful restriction,' [1] until Washington, in April, sent one of his scathing letters. If America is at peace, he wrote, why are ports blockaded, property destroyed, citizens made captive? If at war, his imagination was 'not fertile enough' to conceive why intercourse was continued with the enemy. Then the Committee acted, trade was stopped, the British fleet dropped below the Narrows, and mere forms of amity ceased.

Step by step with the American change had come one on the British part. Though Lord North had got commissioners appointed who were to make certain overtures to the colonies, he had also, November, 1775, further restrained American trade, thus cheerfully giving aid to non-intercourse, the coercive policy against England, to the dismay of the Continental Congress. Reconciliation had failed. As North said, the time had come to prosecute war as against any enemy. The Congress at Philadelphia also gained more conviction. About the middle of March, 1776, it recommended the disarming of Loyalists every-

[1] Becker, *Political Parties in . . . New York,* 242–49; Mass. Hist. Soc., *Proceedings,* vol. 60, p. 101.

where, and the forcible suppression of all who spoke against the Congress.[1] A little later, it advised throwing open all American ports to the world. Non-intercourse had failed, and all economic argument pointed to Independence. Pamphleteers began to urge Independence as a remedy for ruined commerce.

All these changes were taking place in the general colonial policy, when, in April, 1776, there took place in New York the election of a third Provincial Congress. Already the Loyalists had been driven from the arena of politics to that of war. But there was now division in the ranks of the Revolutionists. Some were for Independence at once, some favored delay. One group wished it declared by the Provincial, one by the Continental Congress. If there were to be new State Governments, the conservatives would have the power in the hands of an oligarchy, made up of men like John Jay, James Duane, and the Livingstons; but the radicals wished it broadly democratic. Electors were warned against men reputed mainly for their noise and bustle, and urged to seek men of sound judgment, who knew the science of government. They seemed, in New York City, to heed this advice, for in the main the conservative ticket was elected.[2] In the counties, the Loyalists having withdrawn, there was no contest, but there, too, the conservatives seem to have been victorious. The Congress met, no longer troubled as

[1] Becker, *Political Parties . . . in New York*, 249–52; Flick, *Loyalism in New York*, 65–66.

[2] Becker, *Political Parties in . . . New York*, 256–60. Thirteen counties elected one hundred and one delegates, and these furnished an average attendance of twenty-eight.

to a quorum, nor obliged to resort to a Committee of Safety.

The new Congress met problems at once which tested its character. Civil war had begun in New York. There was no longer delay about stopping trade with the royal ships. The resolution of the Continental Congress (March 17), urging disarmament of the Loyalists, had been neglected until the meeting of this third Provincial Congress, but at once a committee on 'intestine enemies' was chosen, and went earnestly to work, making elaborate examinations and coming to discriminating and moderate decisions. The Loyalists, expecting Howe, with forty thousand men, were alert and active, but now some were paroled, some jailed, some exiled to Connecticut. Early in June, the mob, tired of this slow, judicious method, hunted out the 'Tories' and used the rougher processes of rail and tar-bucket. They had 'some grand Tory rides,' and soon scarcely a Loyalist face was to be seen in the city. The Provincial Congress was then forced to more summary military methods. After a conspiracy to capture General Washington, and the hanging of one of his guards for complicity, feeling ran high, and there was little mercy for 'Tories.'[1] Washington even complained that the 'abandoned and profligate' part of his army spread 'ruin and terror' wherever they went by 'rapine and plunder.'

In the matter of Independence and new government, however, the new Provincial Congress was not

[1] Becker, *Political Parties in . . . New York*, 264–65; *Writings of Washington* (Ford, ed.), IV, 188.

so easily accelerated. Many of its members were men who would say to the tides of revolution: Thus far shalt thou go and no farther. When the Continental Congress (May 10) advised new governments where no legal ones existed, and five days later added the assertion that every kind of royal authority ought to be suppressed, the conservative nature of the New York Congress was revealed. If the Philadelphia advice be obeyed, there was but a step to Independence. The radicals urged that the New York delegates in Philadelphia be instructed to vote for Independence. Duane, a conservative, would wait a bit. John Jay, bold yet cautious, stood between these factions. The question also arose whether new delegates, fresh from the people, or members of the conservative Provincial Congress should construct the new government. Those who had property at stake wished the latter method as more likely to preserve the old forms of government, but Gouverneur Morris urged new delegates. His faction argued that 'rich and designing men' had crept into Congress. Such men would take no chances in their country's cause, and would subject their fellow citizens, if not to British tyranny, then 'to a tyranny of oppression among themselves not much better.' Here was a new voice in American politics, the common man, fearful of the propertied classes, no longer acquiescent in the rule of the well-born. The 'oligarchs' in the Provincial Congress kept control of both questions, Independence and the making of the new government. By first arguing that the matter of Independence be left to the decision of the Continental Congress with its larger view of the whole situation, and then later, when 'that august body' did take up the question, resolving that it was inexpedient to ask 'the will of the people,' the New York Congress managed to keep that province from having any part in the famous resolution of July 2, 1776.

John Adams expressed the wrath of the radicals. 'What is the reason that New York is still asleep or dead in politics and war?' Could nothing 'inspire it with one generous sentiment? Are the people destitute of reason or virtue?' He forgot that the cautious politicians of that province were faced by an armed foe, hedged in by domestic enemies. They were not for monarchy nor yet for democracy in any extreme form, and whatever was done as to Independence, they would have done by colony, not by Congress. New elections were taking place, the questions of Independence and new governments being involved. A week after the Continental Congress resolved upon American Independence, the new and fourth Provincial Congress of New York met and declared Independence.[1] The door of reconciliation was closed. Hereafter, parties would divide on new issues, questions as to the breadth of franchise, and as to the nature of New York's relation to the other States. As will appear when we resume the account of military events, this decision of the faction dominant in New York to support the cause of Independence, and to crush all opposition, was taken none too soon.

[1] Becker, *Political Parties in . . . New York*, 266–74.

CHAPTER XIII

HOWE'S NEW LAURELS FADE AT TRENTON

When General Howe sailed, March 17, 1776, with one hundred and seventy ships, ingloriously out of Boston Bay, bound for that 'cursed, cold, wintry place,' Halifax, it was not hard to guess where the British army would next appear. Washington had already taken measures to fortify and hold New York, and now redoubled his efforts. But for the ill-fated expedition to Canada, he might have had sufficient arms and fairly well-drilled troops enough for the purpose. But the munitions and troops lost at Quebec, and vainly sent to that region for some five months after the manifest failure of that expedition, left Washington short of supplies, and dependent upon poorly drilled militia, hastily called from the neighboring states in quotas never fulfilled. On the other hand, the Canadian expedition caused General Howe to delay until June the transfer of troops from Halifax to New York. Montgomery, therefore, did not die in vain, nor was Arnold's heroism wasted when he led through the forest of Maine that march beset with incredible hardships, and fell wounded as he strove to take the heights at Quebec. Artillery sent for the defense of Canada had to be reshipped to New York, and thus delayed until August the attack on Long Island. Is it not at least probable that if New York had been captured before July of 1776, a resolution of Independence could not have been carried at that time in the Continental Congress? And if not at that time, what great and fateful changes in the sequence of events might have altered the outcome of this revolutionary struggle? Such speculations are not history, but they offer alluring intellectual diversions.

Early in August, Sir William Howe began the landing, from the fleet commanded by his brother, Admiral Lord Howe, of an army which by mid-August numbered at least thirty-four thousand men.[1] Onlookers gazed with awe on a pageant such as America had never seen before — five hundred dark hulls, forests of masts, a network of spars and ropes, and a gay display of flying pennants. There were ships of the line with frowning sides, three tiers of guns and high forecastles; there were graceful frigates, alert and speedy. Finally, there were tenders and galleys to land the thousands of men from the unwieldy transports. Moreover, quite unknown to those who marveled at this vast armada, General Howe had with him such a military chest as no commander in the history of the world had ever carried beyond the seas. Just before sailing, Lord North had sent Howe £840,776, hoping it would nearly suffice for the rest of the campaign, and urging him to watch it with great care.[2]

[1] R. Beatson, *Memoirs*. Germain wrote Howe on May 3, 1776, that he was sending 3500 Highlanders, 8200 Hessians, sailing next day, 1090 Guards, and 4000 more Hessians to follow soon. Clinton, with the Southern expedition, was to let nothing prevent his juncture with Howe in time to attack New York. *Germain Papers, Military Despatched* (W.L.C.L.).

[2] Hist. MSS. Com., *Am. MSS.*, I, 47.

New York, though not in size the first of American cities,[1] was the obvious place to strike a blow to crush rebellion. The King's ships could control the bay, and the city was the natural military base from which to seize the line of the Hudson. When a sea-power, like that of Great Britain, dominated the ocean lines of communication, British armies had only to hold the Hudson, and New England would become an isolated province, entirely surrounded by hostile lands and seas. Moreover, it was by way of the Hudson that British armies from Canada would naturally come, by paths already traversed by Montgomery, to unite with British armies stationed at New York. Upon that city, therefore, converged the greater part of the greatest fleet and army which Englishmen had ever sent across the seas, greater than Wellington commanded nearly forty years later, when he confronted at Waterloo the still mighty genius of the art of making war, Napoleon Bonaparte.

To meet the British armada and invading host, Washington, perhaps against all his convictions, undertook to fortify every assailable point around New York.[2] General Lee, an experienced soldier,

[1] General Robertson caused the inhabitants to be counted after the city was captured, and he found eleven thousand persons. P.R.O., *State Papers, Domestic, Military*, 19, no. 10, pp. 74–75.

[2] *American Historical Review*, I, 651. C. F. Adams says it never occurred to Washington that his problem was insoluble, but the mere absence of letters to that effect does not prove this. For political reasons, Washington must try to defend New York, and he would hardly complain of his fate. Yet it may be that his inexperience made him hope in vain. Washington made other mistakes at first, but he learned with experience.

declared there was no possibility of defense against an enemy in command of the sea, and Washington probably agreed with him, though he had no choice but to lead the forlorn hope.[1] He knew intuitively that to give up New York without a struggle would be an almost fatal blow to American morale. Redoubts were built at wisely chosen points, and equipped with nondescript guns from the Bahamas, from Boston and Ticonderoga, and from gun foundries which Congress conjured up everywhere. Behind Brooklyn Heights fortifications, 'well planned but ill executed,' were prepared, lest the enemy land on Long Island, seize the heights, and thus command both East River and New York City. Rather amateurish efforts were made to obstruct rivers and channels by sinking hulks and even fastening a twenty-one-hundred-foot chain across the Hudson.[2] These and cunningly devised fireships all failed, when the British arrived, for they soon sent the Phœnix and the Rose, favored by a brisk breeze and flowing tide, past shore batteries and all attempted barriers, to points on the Hudson, where they menaced the American rear.

To meet the British army and to man all the redoubts Washington had, perhaps, twenty-one thousand men fit to fight. But these men were scattered along the New Jersey shore, above Harlem River, on Long Island, and on Governor's Island. The parts of this dispersed army had no means of communica-

[1] *Lee Papers*, July and August, 1776.

[2] Force, *American Archives* (5th Series), I, 125, 620, 762, 766, 790, 886, 935; *Writings of Washington* (Ford, ed.), IV, 242, 292, 293.

tion save the waters which might at any hour be dominated by the British fleet.[1] Many of the seasoned troops had been sent to Canada, and Washington was left with an army a large part of which was made up of new recruits and of raw militia from the near-by provinces, so poorly trained that some fled at the first fire. New Jersey was the assembling-place for levies from that province, Pennsylvania, Delaware, and Maryland. New England militia gathered on Manhattan Island or on Long Island. The commander never knew what part of a Provincial quota would actually appear: a half, a fifth, a tenth, any fraction might arrive with an equipment as uncertain as the numbers.[2] As Washington looked at these raw recruits, he must have had a stout heart, indeed, not to flee to the back country and live in a wigwam, as he expressed a desire to do, rather than attempt the defense of New York.

Sometimes a hundred British sail were seen coming up the Narrows in a single day. At last, by mid-August, four hundred transports, fifty-two sail of the line, and some twenty-seven smaller craft had appeared off New York, terrifying evidence of the might of the British Empire.[3] All this fleet, with the martial host it brought to conquer rebellion, was equipped far better than American armies were ever to be during the best days of the struggle now begun. Its big guns far outclassed the American pieces, its

[1] Force, *American Archives* (5th Series), I, 834–35.
[2] *Ibid.*, 819.
[3] *Letters from America* (trans. Pettengill), 176.

soldiers were better clothed, often better fed, and its discipline, taking British and Hessian soldiers together, much superior.

There were three methods that Howe might choose for attack. First, he might make a direct assault on the city; second, he might — after the Phœnix and the Rose had shown the way — land troops above the city, on the Hudson, attack in the rear, and thus cut off any retreat. A third plan, the one chosen, was to seize Long Island, and from Brooklyn Heights dominate East River and New York itself.[1] Howe had disembarked and assembled his troops during July and early August on Staten Island, and on August 22, landed on Long Island, eight miles from the American lines, 14,700 seasoned men, professional soldiers, later increased to 20,000, whom he encamped from the Narrows to Flatland.[2] There had been bad weather since August 16, and on the 21st there was a severe storm, but the British were not Chinese and could make war in the rain. If the roads were bad for the British, so they were for the Americans.

To meet just this mode of attack, General Greene had for four months been constructing redoubts to make an entrenched camp behind Brooklyn Heights,[3] and mastering the facts about every road and path by which it might be approached. At the moment when all this knowledge was most needed, Greene fell ill and was nigh unto death when the British

[1] Long Island Hist. Soc., *Memoirs*, II, 330, Doc. 79.

[2] *Kemble's Journal*, in N.Y. Hist. Soc. *Collections* (1883), I, 84; Long Island Hist. Soc., *Memoirs*, II, Doc. 24; III, Docs. 9, 37.

[3] From Gowanus Bay to Wallabout Bay.

attack was about to begin.[1] Sullivan and then Putnam were ordered to take up the task, but with no time to master the facts as to the terrain. The obvious passes through the wooded heights by the Narrows road and by Flatbush and Bedford Pass were guarded, and Washington drained his lines on Manhattan to strengthen these points as soon as the British plan was clear. But there was a way by which all this advanced line of defense might be turned on the American left, and Howe, a master of his craft, chose just that approach.[2] Sending Grant and de Heister, with a little over half of the British forces on Long Island to feign a frontal attack along the coast road and at the passes where they were expected, Howe sent the rest, about ten thousand men, under Clinton, Cornwallis, and Percy, by a night march north and east to the unguarded Jamaica Pass, thence to turn directly west and strike the American lines in their rear. The turning movement, guided by Long Island Tories, was perfectly executed, timed as if by a clock, and on the morning of August 27, while the Americans under Lord Stirling and General Sullivan were resisting desperately the British and Hessians in their front, they found themselves attacked from the rear. Those who were able escaped to their entrenched camp, but Stirling and Sullivan and about ninety officers were captured, with about one thousand of the rank and file.[3]

[1] Greene, *Life of Greene*, I, 205–07.

[2] C. F. Adams, 'Battle of Long Island,' in *American Historical Review*, I, 650.

[3] Howe was in personal command. Long Island Hist. Soc., *Memoirs*, III, Docs., 2, 5, 20, 21; H. P. Johnston, *Campaign of 1776*. (Long

The news of this victory was hurried off to London, and Lord Germain was quite lyric in his praise. He remembered the courage and spirit of Howe's youth. Now, Germain wrote, he united 'to the fire of youth all the wisdom and conduct of the most experienced commander.' The King had made him a Knight Companion of the Bath. Later, when Howe failed repeatedly to gather the fruits of victory, the War Minister wished his panegyrics had been less precipitate.[1]

Howe had nearly twenty thousand men, fatigued from marching and fighting, but eager for assault upon the nine thousand Americans now penned in the entrenched forts. Perhaps, with Bunker Hill in mind, he decided on taking the camp by siege, and thus lost an opportunity to add to humiliating defeat the capture of half of Washington's army, possibly the complete overthrow of the American cause.[2] Howe's delay and a strong northeast wind, which kept the British fleet from entering East River,[3] made possible the retreat upon which Washington at once decided, and which he directed for

Island Hist. Soc., *Memoirs*, III, 202–06.) Howe had 63 killed, 283 wounded, 31 missing. *Ibid.*, 34, 189.

[1] *Germain Papers, Military Despatched*, Germain to Howe, October 18, 1776; *State Papers, Domestic, George III*, 11.

[2] General Montresor testified before the House of Commons (1779) that the abattis before the American lines was very perfect, that reconnoitering parties could not (during the night) have got where they could see that the enemy had gone. P.R.O., *State Papers, Military*, 18, pp. 12–19.

[3] Nevertheless, the timidity of the British naval commanders in this affair is not easily explained. The presence of the fleet was hardly felt, although the things it might have done constituted the greatest menace Washington faced.

forty-eight hours without closing his eyes, and hardly dismounting from his horse.[1] For thirteen hours of a dark night and foggy morning, amid torrents of rain at first, and a gale in which only Marblehead sailors under Colonel John Glover could have handled the motley collection of boats, the army, its wounded, and most of its stores were ferried to Manhattan Island. And this was accomplished, although the fear was such that 'those in the rear were mounting on the shoulders and clambering over the heads of those before them,' as an eye-witness declares.

Putnam wrote of this unhoped salvation, that Howe was either a friend of America or no general. Indeed, it was said in England that the Howes were mere tools of the Opposition; that they had no heart in shedding American blood.[2] Others made dark hints of North's diplomatic efforts, and of secret instructions to the Howes quite opposite to their public orders. Those who liked their criticism spiced with scandal talked of a 'wanton with a velvet brow,' a 'favorite Sultana' who lost three hundred guineas in a night at cards, and who came on from Boston with General Howe. This 'Boston lady,' whose husband, it was said, held several places bringing him in six thousand pounds a year,[3] lost Sir

[1] Force, *American Archives* (5th Series), I, 1230, 1244, 1246; also in *Writings of Washington* (Ford, ed.), IV, 374.

[2] If General Sullivan can be believed, there was much truth in this assertion. 'It was a great pity so brave a nation should be cutting one another to pieces,' said Howe. *Correspondence of J. Jay* (Johnston, ed.), I, 84.

[3] *The Detail and Conduct of the American War* (3d ed.), 17.

William the honor, the laurels, and the glory he might have won. In the battle of Long Island, Howe had shown the hand of a master, perfect attention to the details of his strategy, the choice of the flanking attack, the resort to the Indian style of fighting, using trees, stone fences, and the single file in the flanking march, a great improvement over the customary European formation. Women, wine, and the card-table, however, seemed to have unnerved this pleasure-loving Anthony, leaving him unequal to the emergency, when it was well to listen to Nelson's dictum that no victory was won as long as there was anything left to capture which might be captured.[1] To lose nine thousand men who were to be had for the taking was enough to break the reputation of one greater than Sir William Howe.

Nor was Washington to come off free of criticism. Only luck and a dilatory enemy saved him from his almost fatal errors in both strategy and tactics, in this his first experience in chief command of active fighting in the field. With little genius, and not much natural aptitude for war, it was courage, noble character, the gift of inspiring confidence, and the ability to learn by experience which were, before the war's end, to place him in the forefront among the leaders of men, safe and competent as a commander-in-chief.[2] Even in the midst of his worst errors, his greatness, his magnanimity surmounts everything.

[1] H. Belcher, *First American Civil War,* II, 156; Moore, *Diary of the Revolution,* 668.

[2] *American Historical Review,* I, 665; C. F. Adams's article on the battle of Long Island.

Moreover, few military chieftains have ever worked in the midst of more disheartening conditions. The Continental Congress gave him impossible tasks to perform with utterly inadequate means. Congress *resolved* to raise regiments, *resolved* to make cannon, *resolved* to make and import muskets, powder, and clothing, but, confessed a member, 'it is a melancholy fact that near half of our men, cannon, muskets, powder, clothes,' are to be found nowhere but on paper.[1] As a result, Washington appeared to have everything he wanted, but in reality had only a small part. He must, moreover, beg men for his army in part from Congress; in part from Provincial Governments or local committees.[2] In return, he got orders from both, often conflicting, and at times against his own judgment. Every province which the enemy could possibly invade demanded protection. However desirable it might be to concentrate, the demands of New Jersey, Pennsylvania, Connecticut, and New York for protection forced the wide dispersion of troops at Perth Amboy, on Manhattan, on Long Island, and in the Hudson Highlands, so that the several units were separated by waters over which Washington had no control. The penalty of ignoring these local outcries was that the inhabitants would turn Tory and go over to the British. If troops were not so disposed that the men thought they were fighting for their own province, the temperature of their zeal was often greatly lowered. In spite of the greatest tact in these

[1] *Letters of . . . Continental Congress* (Burnet, ed.), I, 455.

[2] Force, *American Archives* (5th Series), I, 371, 449, 450, 736, 819.

matters, Washington was fairly maddened by the discontent, desertion, and disobedience with which he had to contend.

Because his army and his staff were still in the making, his intelligence service was poor, coöperation bad among his subordinate officers. The marksmanship of those using his pitiful collection of artillery was wretched. There was not enough powder to spare for practice. On Long Island the Americans had six field pieces to the British forty, of better make and caliber. No attempt was made to meet Howe when he landed on the island because there were no portable cannon to take there. Instead of the Patriot army, therefore, a thousand loyal farmers and landowners cordially greeted Howe as he landed, and some of them acted as guides in the famous turning movement. No such service was proffered Washington, and he lacked the necessary cavalry to keep him informed, because Congress regarded them 'as expensive troops and of little use.' [1] Thus Washington, begging men, now of Congress, now of a Committee of Safety, forced to be attentive to the commands of both, getting only fractions of the men promised, and those half-trained and ready 'to fly from their shadows,' his best general sick unto death, his staff arrangements faulty, was obliged to meet an enemy greatly superior in numbers, discipline, and equipment, supreme over all the waters which divided his meager force.

[1] *Letters of . . . Continental Congress* (Burnett, ed.), I, 314, 443, 448. C. F. Adams criticizes Washington for not using cavalry, but he could not ignore Congress. *American Historical Review*, I, 667–68. See Washington, *Writings* (Ford, ed.), IV, 217.

He attempted what he never had a chance to carry out successfully, and, if luck or a 'special Providence' saved him from his own and others' follies, nobody ever better deserved his good fortune than the man fated to be 'the father of his country.'

The Brooklyn Heights lost, British ships passing up and down East River as well as the Hudson, the waters of the Sound fully in Howe's control, he had only to choose the hour when he would cross and drive Washington off Manhattan, or pen him up and force surrender. The American militia, 'dismayed, intractable,' were running off 'almost by regiments, by half ones, and by companies at a time.'[1] Greene was for evacuating and burning New York to prevent its becoming a headquarters for the British army. John Jay, a property-owner there, agreed with him. Congress, safely deliberating in Independence Hall, vetoed the idea, having 'no doubt of being able to recover it.'[2] The military advantage would have been great, but the idea was repugnant then, and the common opinion of mankind is against such conduct to-day. Nevertheless, it was fired, just after the British entered, and over a fourth of the city was burned. Howe and Washington and Germain were all honestly enraged over it, the latter urging that every effort be made to discover 'the infatuated wretches.'[3] It certainly was not of British origin,

[1] *Writings of Washington* (Ford, ed.), IV, 379.

[2] Force, *American Archives* (5th Series), II, 182; Jay, *Life of Jay*, I, 89; Reed, *Life of Reed*, I, 235; *Journals of the Continental Congress* (Ford, ed.), V, 733. The British held it until November, 1783.

[3] *Germain Papers, Military Despatched*, Germain to Howe, November 6, 1776; Force, *American Archives* (5th Series), II, 462, 463, 466, 524, 548.

for they needed every house in what was to be their chief military port for seven years.

Fearing an attack across the Harlem, Washington moved half his force to Kingsbridge, but with the remainder clung to New York until Howe, after two weeks' delay, landed at Kip's Bay, drove the American troops into a panic and a rout which Washington failed to stop even with sword and pistol and a terrible exhibition of rage. 'Disgraceful and dastardly conduct' Washington called this running away without firing a shot.[1] By nightfall the fragment of his flying army stood on the heights above Harlem, having lost 'a prodigious deal of baggage.'[2]

The British had now possessed themselves of New York City. King George, pleased by the news, hoped that the 'deluded and unhappy multitude' would now return to 'a just and constitutional subordination,' and that he might soon stop the effusion of the blood of his subjects.[3] The French Ambassador in London thought everybody there drunk with joy. You can scarcely believe, he wrote, how all classes begin to fulminate against all the powers in the world, even menacing France. Their delirium shows how easily the nation goes blind and wild.[4] Ver-

[1] *Writings of Washington* (Ford, ed.), IV, 407, 408. F. L. Humphreys, *Life and Times of David Humphreys*, I, 67.

[2] His losses were 17 officers and 350 men. There is nothing but contemporary gossip, repeated by Thacher, Gordon, and Ramsay, to support the story of Mrs. Murray, with her cakes and ale, holding Tryon at luncheon, while Putnam with 3500 men slipped by on the road along Hudson River.

[3] *Correspondence of King George III*, III, 402; Hansard, *Parliamentary History*, XIX, 354–58.

[4] *Archives des Affaires Étrangères, Angleterre*, 519, no. 123.

gennes, in a note to Louis XVI, took the curious view that this capture rendered the situation less alarming for France. 'The English with a post in America for their winter quarters seem less to be feared than when wandering about over the sea not knowing where to take refuge. We risk nothing if we let them engage themselves ever more in a war where even the advantages which they flaunt are in reality losses.'[1] It was well for the American cause that the French mind could use such rose-colored logic about so obvious a disaster.

The next day (September 16), after the panic and rout at Kip's Bay, the same troops, so lately panic-stricken by surprise, drove British and Hessians, in the battle of Harlem Heights, a mile on an open, level field, and retired in good order at Washington's command.[2] It was at this juncture that Nathan Hale, a young man of intelligence, character, and high sense of responsibility, undertook the repugnant and hateful office of a spy. The exigencies of his country demanded this peculiar service, and he reasoned that it became honorable by being necessary. Too frank and too open for deceit and evasion, he was detected and captured. Since he confessed, Howe ordered his execution without trial, and he died with the noble regret that he had but one life to lose for his country. This brave deed, common enough in the annals of mankind, and oft-repeated

[1] *Archives des Affaires Étrangères, Mémoire et document, France,* 1897, F 70. Yet Deane in Paris thought that the French, ready to sign a treaty of alliance, hung back when they learned of the taking of New York. *Deane Papers,* N.Y. Hist. Soc., *Collections,* I, 395.

[2] H. P. Johnston, *Battle of Harlem Heights* (ed. 1897).

in any great war, became through the hero's personal charm, his social position, and an element of chance, symbolic of all noble actions of that kind, and therefore surrounded with a sentimental glamour.[1]

Morale was restored, briefly at least, by the results at Harlem Heights; Howe was checked and made no further offensive move for a month. Critics talked of dinners and card-parties with Briseis in New York in that interval, but Howe explained, three years later, to Germain and to a sullen House of Commons that he was moving in a country 'difficult to be known,' a country of quagmires, morasses, and bush-covered land, 'devious and dangerous places.'[2] Doubtless, Westchester was not so well kept as an English countryside.

Washington meanwhile improved Fort Washington, hoping in vain that it, with Fort Lee on the Jersey side, would stop British ships passing up the Hudson. When Howe threatened to sever the American communications with New England by landing on the shore of the Sound at Throg's Neck and then at Pell's Point, Washington moved thirteen thousand men to White Plains, where the British, in slightly larger numbers, attacked (October 28), taking Chatterton Hill, a key position.[3] Howe was

[1] H. P. Johnston, *Nathan Hale* (1914 ed.). Ten books, sixteen poems, and twenty-six magazine articles commemorate Hale and his act.

[2] *Germain Papers* (W.L.C.L.), April 22, 1779.

[3] Howe was criticized for not following up this victory, but Lord Cornwallis testified to the House of Commons, later, that the defeat of the corps on the enemy's right made that impossible. P.R.O., *State Papers, Domestic*, no. 18, pp. 8–9.

bitterly criticized that he did not at once assault and destroy Washington's army. He granted it might have meant victory, but 'I never wished to put anything to hazard where I could hope for an advantage on more equal terms.' Pressed in the House of Commons, he took refuge in 'political reasons for not explaining why that attack did not take place.' [1] Reënforced to twenty thousand men, Howe was about to attack Washington's main position when the latter withdrew to the heights of North Castle. Defeated in the maneuver to get in the American rear, Howe succeeded, nevertheless, in getting some sixty-five hundred men, between the troops about Forts Washington and Lee, and the main army under Washington in the Highlands. That spelled disaster for the American army.

Howe concentrated thirteen thousand men, British and Hessian, about Fort Washington, stormed the outworks, November 16, and forced Colonel McGaw, the officer left in charge, to surrender over twenty-eight hundred men, and all ammunition and stores.[2] Congress, Washington, Greene, and the grinding necessities of the general political situation have to share the blame for the loss. Congress was stern in its instructions that the fort was not to be abandoned. Greene asked for orders, and Washington left him to his own discretion. When British

[1] *Germain Papers* (W.L.C.L.), Heads of speech, April 2, 1779.

[2] Force, *American Archives* (5th Series), III, 1058, 1059. There were taken at Forts Washington and Lee 146 pieces of artillery, 2800 small arms, 400,000 musket cartridges — a terrible loss to an army already fighting half-equipped. Howe lost 78 killed, 374 wounded, while the Americans had 59 killed, 96 wounded.

ships passed easily up the Hudson, Washington wavered, thought it not prudent to try to hold the fort, called a council, which decided against evacuation. He and Greene visited the fort, just before investment, and withdrew only barely in time. Washington said frankly later that the whole thing caused 'warfare in his mind, hesitation, and ended in loss of garrison.' Again he had been urged to do the impossible, again he tried. It was Greene who made the final wrong decision.

Cornwallis crossed at Yonkers with the purpose of taking Fort Lee, but Greene, leaving great quantities of stores, and 'the very pots boiling on the fire,' drew off his garrison during the night, and joined Washington who had crossed with the main army at Hackensack.

Then began the famous retreat across the Jerseys. Howe, with some display of energy, might have annihilated Washington's little, shattered, half-clad remnant of an army, but again he displayed that aversion to complete military victory which marked his whole career in America.[1] He intimated later that he understood such to be the wish of the Ministers; that if they wished severity they might have said so. His orders, he grumbled, should have been clear, 'not whispers across the Atlantic,' so 'ambiguously expressed that they might always be explained away.'[2]

[1] Yet Cornwallis, an able general, testified before the House of Commons that he could recall 'no instance when Howe had omitted to seize an opportunity to attack the enemy when there was a reasonable prospect of success.' P.R.O., *State Papers, Domestic*, 18, pp. 10, 26.

[2] *Germain Papers, America* (W.L.C.L.), April 2, 1779.

The command of the Hudson, at least, was then and there his for the taking, and later Burgoyne was to lose an army in the effort to remedy this neglected opportunity. The pursuit of Washington by Howe across New Jersey was leisurely but inexorable.[1] If Howe took pains never actually to seize his prey, and if he seemed to halt to give his hard-pressed quarry time to breathe, he at least kept up a relentless pressure, aggressive and rapid, indeed, in the last days, until Washington and his army stood on the Pennsylvania side of the Delaware, worn out, but feeling safe because all the river craft was carefully assembled on that bank of the river. Washington's rear guard embarked to cross the river at Trenton, December 8, just as the British advance guard entered the town.[2]

Howe had calculated, said a critic, with the greatest accuracy the exact time necessary for his enemy to make his escape. The American army had been on the brink of total annihilation, attaining by flight but one good military end, that of tempting its pursuer to leave too tenuous lines of communication with the base at New York.[3] Howe had placed

[1] Howe was severely criticized later for sending off two thousand men to take Newport, Rhode Island, just at the time when that number of men would have enabled him to destroy Washington's fleeing army. P.R.O., *State Papers, Military*, 19, no. 10, pp. 105–11.

[2] Washington, *Writings* (Ford, ed.), v, 71; Force, *American Archives* (5th Series), III, 1187. There were many solid reasons against crossing, Cornwallis declared before Parliament. Though he had taken every measure to have boats secured for the purpose, none were to be had. P.R.O., *State Papers, Domestic*, 18, pp. 11, 16.

[3] Cornwallis always defended the tenuous lines because of the necessity of protecting the New Jersey Loyalists. *Ibid.* Howe reasoned likewise. *Germain Papers, America*, April 2, 1779. Clinton,

troops in a train of camps eighty miles in length, over an area intersected by streams and ponds, a rash step, as John Adams shrewdly judged. Howe defended his leaving unduly long lines by urging the need of protecting the Loyalists.[1] Moreover, all he required was a frozen river, and he might have pushed on to Philadelphia, 'the Rebel capitol,' twenty miles beyond his outposts at Bordentown. Indeed, late in November, he decided to do that.[2] General Robertson calculated that in eight or nine days a pontoon bridge might have been built across the Delaware. He reflected that 'Cæsar's bridge over the Rhine cost him but ten days.' It was difficult, yes, with an enemy on the other side, but the Rhine, the Rhone, the Danube, he recalled, had been passed in that manner. Cannon would help greatly.[3] But classical example had no effect on Howe, and he gave up the idea, though the Continental Congress had fled to Baltimore, expecting nothing less.

The British general seemed to have had glory enough for one year. He went into winter quarters, graciously granted Cornwallis a leave of absence, applied to Lord George Germain for ten thousand men with which to complete the conquest of America, and settled down to virtuous enjoyment of his

however, criticized the stringing of cantonments along. *Clinton Papers, History*, 75.

[1] Howe's *Narrative* (1780), 7, 8; Force, *American Archives* (5th Series), III, 1317. Yet he admitted to Clinton that it was a mistake. *Clinton Papers*, July 6, 1777.

[2] Force, *American Archives* (5th Series), III, 925, 926, 1315, 1317.

[3] P.R.O., *State Papers, Domestic, Military*, 19, no. 10, pp. 79–83.

laurels and his ladies. The Lord, it was said, had sent a Delilah to sheer away the strength of the British Samson.[1] He must have his pleasures, wrote a critic, though everything went to wreck in the Jerseys.

On the British outposts at Trenton were stationed, as a mark of polite recognition of the German allies, three regiments of Hessians under Colonel Rall, hero of many wars and especially proud that under the Russian General Orloff he had fought the Turks.[3] After the ease with which he had seen victories won over the Americans, whom he had watched on the run for some four months, he had for them only an amused contempt. Ordered to construct redoubts, he expressed a complacent reliance on bayonets. Since he spoke no English, he got, through an interpreter, such intelligence as came through Tory spies. Finally, he was too fond of bowls of punch.[4]

Washington resolved, by an encounter with such an enemy, to retrieve his fallen fortunes. Fate, which had been most unkind to him for months past, now smiled again. General Charles Lee, disobedient and disloyal, had withheld several thousand troops

[1] Professional soldiers of that age were always against the hardships of winter campaigns, and were in no hurry to end war which meant life in a garrison — or half-pay. Moreover, Howe disliked the North policy toward America, and his very orders kept his mind wavering between the sword and the olive branch.

[2] *The Detail and Conduct of the American War* (3d ed.), 17.

[3] General Clinton, always critical of Howe, defended leaving the Hessians at Trenton. They 'behaved finely at Fort Washington.' *Clinton Papers, History* (W.L.C.L.), 75.

[4] The best and most detailed account of Trenton is in W. S. Stryker, *The Battles of Trenton and Princeton*, 1–237.

for weeks in spite of Washington's repeated commands, talking vaguely of attacking Howe's rear, reconquering the Jerseys, 'startling' the enemy by revealing his presence, and intimating all the time that 'a certain great man was damnably deficient.' [1] Now he was providentially captured at Baskingridge by a British detachment; and his forces, commanded by Sullivan, became available to reënforce the remnant of an army under Washington. He must do something before this army should melt away, as was threatened when the terms of many men would expire at the approaching New Year. Neighboring States had done what they could to augment his army, but it was not much.[2] The inhabitants of each locality were chiefly intent on protecting their own property.

Congress had solemnly passed a resolution permitting their military chief to recross the Delaware, and he saw an opportunity, by making just that venture, to reanimate and save the cause with the six thousand men briefly available.[3] He ordered his army to cross the river in three divisions, each with a duty assigned, bearing on the capture of Rall's Hessians, camped in the hundred houses which made up the village of Trenton. Only the northern division, two hundred and forty strong, crossing eight miles above Trenton, under Washington,

[1] Force, *American Archives* (5th Series), III, 1072, 1122, 1138, 1201.

[2] *Ibid.*, 1092, 1094, 1103, 1122, 1124.

[3] A return of Washington's whole force, December 22, 1776, may be found in Force, *American Archives* (5th Series), III, 1401. There were 8 brigades, 37 regiments, 593 commissioned officers, 729 noncommissioned, 4707 privates fit for duty.

Greene, and Sullivan, overcame the difficulties of the floating ice and darkness, and marched through rain and sleet, as severe a night as Thomas Rodney ever saw, upon the Hessian outposts near the town.[1]

Though warned, Rall had taken no precautions, counting on the weather, the ice, and the disordered army of his enemy.[2] Moreover, Washington's whole conduct was quite un-European. When told as he neared the town that much of the powder was wet, he replied, 'Use the bayonet, penetrate into the town.' Sleeping secure from the storm, the Hessians were taken utterly by surprise, confused 'as when the last trump shall sound,' when the trumpets and bugles warned. 'It rained, hailed, and snowed and was a violent storm,' wrote Greene to his wife. 'The storm of nature and the storm of the town exhibited a scene that filled the mind during the action with passion easier conceived than described.'[3] Cannon and howitzers were placed at each end of the streets, but most of the work was done with pikes and bayonets, and in forty-five minutes Trenton was lost and won. Rall with one regiment sought escape by the Princeton road, but Greene covered it with artillery, and when the Hessian leader tried to reënter the town, a rain of lead from windows and doors met him, and he fell mortally wounded, saved,

[1] Ten days before, Washington had written Congress that most of his men were 'so thinly clad as to be unfit for service.' Washington, *Writings* (Ford, ed.), v, 103.

[2] Cornwallis put all the blame on Colonel Rall's 'negligence and imprudence.' The Hessian troops, he declared, were 'brave and well-trained.' P.R.O., *State Papers, Domestic*, no. 18, p. 14.

[3] *Greene's Letters* (W.L.C.L.), December 30, 1776.

however, from the great wrath of the Landgrave of Hesse-Cassel. 'The action lasted,' wrote Greene, 'about three fourths of an hour. We killed, wounded, and took prisoners of the enemy between eleven and twelve hundred. Our troops behaved with great spirit.'[1] A thousand men surrendered, and were hurried across the Delaware, and on to Philadelphia, to be miserably paraded for the edification and encouragement of the citizens of the Quaker City.[2]

The effect was great, wrote an English traveler in Virginia in bitter chagrin. 'Now the scale is turned and Washington's name is extolled to the clouds, Alexander, Pompey and Hannibal were but pigmy generals in comparison with the magnanimous Washington. . . . It is the Dam'd Hessians that has caused this, curse the scoundrel that first thought of sending them here!'[3] Indeed, in polite society in London this reversal became known as 'the late unhappy defeat of the Hessians.'[4]

Germain, wise after the event, wrote Howe that the 'rebels' must, of course, 'appear contemptible in the eyes of a soldier,' yet they must not be held *too* cheap. Though 'too pusilanimous to face real soldiers' in the field, they may attack in the dark, and Germain hoped British officers would never think so meanly of their enemies as to permit themselves to be off their guard. Sorry that the brilliancy of Howe's successes was tarnished even 'in the

[1] *Greene's Letters* (W.L.C.L.), December 30, 1776.

[2] Seventeen Hessians were killed, and seventy-eight wounded.

[3] N. Cresswell, *Journal*, 181.

[4] Hist. MSS. Com., *Report*, Lothian, 300.

least' by this disagreeable occurrence, Germain closed with the fear that it might elate the enemy.[1] A little later, learning that Howe's troops got little rest from the Americans, Germain showing his customary incapacity for drawing logical conclusions from a statement of facts, flattered himself that 'these winter efforts of the Rebels are rather the effects of despair than of courage,' and were really symptoms of weakness.[2] The King, who spelled rebels with two *ll*s, offered the pious wish that though *now* elated they would soon fall into their former dejection.[3] America was less doleful about it.

Congress had fled to Baltimore just before this happy change. In that 'dirty, boggy hole' which 'beggared all description,' the members came together on horseback, because their carriages mired except when 'the weather paved the streets.' The day after Washington's victory, they did in desperation what Greene in a dramatic and eloquent letter had urged upon them a week before. They granted the Commander-in-Chief many of the powers of a dictator, assured by Greene that 'there never was a man that might be more safely trusted,' that there could be 'no evil nor danger,' and that it would be folly to wait the deliberative counsels of a legislature, when a day's, nay, an hour's delay, might mean destruction.[4]

[1] *Germain Papers, Military Despatched* (W.L.C.L.), March 3, 1777.

[2] *Ibid.*, April, 19. [3] *Correspondence of King George III*, III, 421.

[4] *Continental Congress Papers* (*Greene Letters*), (Library of Congress), December 21, 1776. *Letters of . . . Continental Congress* (Burnett, ed.), II, 196, 198–99. *Journals of Continental Congress* (Ford, ed.), December 27, 1776.

One of the greatest handicaps, indeed, from which Washington had suffered had been Congressional interference. The prevailing political theory put great faith in the rule of the many, and when Congress had chosen Washington, it jealously limited his powers lest he become a dictator. To themselves, with their petty jealousies and varying views, they assigned the supreme direction. The Commander-in-Chief, given full power to do as he thought best, must 'obey instantly' all orders from those 'sixty gentlemen.'[1] Often he had two masters, Congress and the State Governments. At times they quarreled with each other, and Washington was uncertain which to obey. They countermanded each other's orders and his own, even entering into ruinous rivalry in the matter of the bounties which they offered to recruits.[2] There was discord intense over the choice of the higher officers, and the Commander pleaded in vain for a decision. Vacancies in lower offices he could fill until the Provincial will was known, but the results were bad, and Washington cried out in vain against the folly.[3] Charles Lee thought Washington 'much to blame for not menacing them with resignation unless they refrained from unhinging the army by their absurd interference.'[4] Congress sent him French officers, unable to talk or comprehend English, whose appointment aroused

[1] *Writings of Washington* (Ford, ed.), II, 476–81.

[2] *Ibid.*, V, 141–43.

[3] *Ibid.*, IV, 469. *Letters of . . . Continental Congress* (Burnett, ed.), I, 210, 211, 214. Only in the desperate days of late December, 1776, did Congress yield. *Ibid.*, II, 196, 198, 202.

[4] *Lee Papers*, II, 261–62.

the ire of American officers, and Washington, in despair, was left to settle the troubles as best he could. He actually had to plead with Congress to inform him of the dispositions they made of troops, and the orders they gave to officers, since ignorance of these involved him in difficulties.[1] They went so far as to discharge troops of which he had need, and they ordered him to do futile things like building fire-rafts on the Hudson quite against his better judgment. Only in the hysteria of flight did they finally give him full power, which they partly withdrew when they felt safe again. But they had lost a bit of their self-assurance, and talked thereafter of not wishing to 'counteract the judgment of your Excellency.'

[1] *Writings of Washington* (Ford, ed.), v, 356; *Journals of Congress* (Ford, ed.), v, 520, 591, 596.

CHAPTER XIV

VICTORY AT PRINCETON, AND THE MORALE OF BOTH ARMIES

CORNWALLIS, on leave, and about to sail, was hurriedly sent to the rescue of the remaining Hessian troops. Washington, reënforced, rested his men, who had been forty consecutive hours under arms in sleet and snow, and then recrossed to the Jersey shore. There he faced larger forces, and might have been routed had the British attacked at once instead of waiting until morning. While Cornwallis was fooled by a well-imitated camp life, replenished bivouac fires, and digging of trenches by candlelight, Washington passed the enemy's flank and rear, marching on toward Princeton to seize the British stores at New Brunswick beyond. Near the college town the Patriot army came upon several regiments on the way to aid Cornwallis. The British, astonished, 'as if an army had dropped perpendicularly upon them,' fought with a signal exhibition of bravery, but were defeated with serious loss — three or four hundred being taken prisoners. British troops now advanced from Trenton, 'in a most infernal sweat,' as Knox wrote, 'running, puffing, blowing and swearing at being so outwitted.' Washington's troops being utterly worn out, having been without 'rest, rum or provisions for two days and nights,' he gave up the stores at New Brunswick, and pushed on to the Highlands of central New Jersey, where he constituted such a menace that Howe thought best to recall all his forces within easy distance of New York. New Jersey was thus regained, and the British were left with no possession in America except the region about New York, and Newport, Rhode Island, seized by the fleet early in December. Greene could write home: 'This is an important period to America, big with great events. God only knows what will be the issue of this campaign; but everything wears much better prospect than they have for some weeks past.'[1]

An unsympathetic Englishman, overtaken by war, records the effect in Virginia. 'The minds of the people are much altered. A few days ago they had given up the cause for lost . . . now they are all liberty mad again.' Where recruiting parties could get nobody a week before, 'now the men are coming in by companies. Confound the turncoat scoundrels.'[2] The moral effect of Howe's campaign was lost, and most of his work had to be done over again. General Knox devoutly thanked 'the great Governor of the Universe for producing this turn in our affairs.' In later years a Patriot thought that 'thus God turned the battle to the gate and gave a finishing to the foundation of the American Republic.'[3] Never was an inspiring event more needed to restore the morale of a desperate army.

An examination of the morale of the Revolutionary army during 1776 will convince one how near

[1] *Greene Letters* (W.L.C.L.), December 30, 1776.

[2] *The Journal of N. Cresswell,* 179–80.

[3] Thornton, *Pulpit of the Revolution,* 444.

to wreck was the Patriot cause in this crisis. Patriotism of the kind shown in the Civil War, nearly a century later, or of that even higher variety manifested in the Great War (1917–18), was very rare. The 'Spirit of '76' meant in the main enthusiasm for Independence, loyalty to a great commander, hate of George III, but not love of country, of a great ideal, of a cause worth more than life itself. Washington rose to that, as did a few others who had the nobility and the vision, but in the masses loyalty to county, province, or section was the ruling motive. Throughout the future of American history, from that day to this, the grander sentiment was to grow. Patriotism was not a plant, like that obedient to the magic of an Indian juggler, to spring at once into full bloom. Accept that fact, and remember that much of the worst that must be recorded about the American army applies to the militia rather than to the regular Continental troops, and one may accept the truth with less revulsion.

The morale of the army in the early months of 1776, compared at least with that after the Long Island defeat, was good. 'The summer soldier and the sunshine patriot' did so well then that Washington worried rather over the small numbers in his army than over the spirit.[1] 'Ardent zeal for the service,' eagerness for immediate action, work of fortification 'going on with spirit' were common tributes in those times.[2] Yet even in those golden

[1] Washington, *Writings* (Ford, ed.), IV, 202; Force, *American Archives* (5th Series), I, 835, 849, 1120.

[2] *Ibid.*, 935, 1030, 1083, 1144.

days there were reports of amazing 'supineness and indolence' prevailing in some brigades,[1] of jealousy and lack of discipline, and, finally, a serious amount of sickness, real or feigned, which left whole regiments useless. Many of the surgeons, 'very great rascals,' as Washington wrote, received 'bribes to certify indispositions.' Officers, wrote Hooper, 'stimulated their men to desertion' to find an excuse to follow them. A company of over four hundred cavalry, when asked to serve as foot soldiers, refused and went home.[2] Men tormented Washington with stories of plowing to do, corn to hoe, hay to get in, and he found that regiments of Connecticut farmers had actually enlisted under the promise that they would be allowed to return to work as soon as possible. He was asked even to detach Continental troops to help the farmers take in their crops. Men begging to go because of sick families to care for were enough, wrote Washington, 'to make a man's heart ache.'[3] They showed him proofs that their families were 'neglected, starving, freezing.' There was wholesale desertion by the Pennsylvania 'Associators' of the army in New Jersey, and all John Adams could say in defense of New England was that the soldiers of the Middle States were 'as clamorous and impatient of discipline and as mutinous as ours, and more so.'[4]

[1] Washington, *Writings* (Ford, ed.), IV, 202; Force, *American Archives* (5th Series), I, 372, 800.

[2] *Ibid.*, 192, 371, 414; *North Carolina Colonial Records*, X, 818.

[3] Force, *American Archives* (5th Series), I, 172, 198, 337, 375, 936–37; *Letters of E. Huntington*, 78.

[4] *Ibid.*, I, 750, 885, 908; (4th Series), IV, 272.

Bad as were these conditions, they were pleasant compared with those which followed the defeat on Long Island. Clouds of gloom descended upon all. The morale of the army never recovered during the rest of the year. From then on, defeat, hardships, longing for home, expiration of terms did their deadly work.[1] Clinton saw only ruin for the army if desertion continued as he saw it in September. Washington, helpless, saw thirty to forty soldiers leaving at a time, and feared the cause would be lost if the tide could not be stemmed.[2]

The Northern army under Schuyler, 'wretched remains,' demoralized by its harrowing defeat in Canada, could do little else but fight the ravages of smallpox.[3] Charles Lee, it is true, was reporting his army in good spirits, but there was little truth in him, and his motive for a favorable report was that he might inspire more confidence than Washington.[4] Moreover, the depression was worst among Washington's troops because they were suffering most. At Fort Washington, Greene saw 'only confusion, disorder, dispiritedness,' and he declared that those lost at Fort Lee were 'rascals that skulked out of the way for fear of fighting.'[5] Not only was there loss and defeat and the horror of bloody combat to inexperienced men, but cold weather brought on the

[1] Force, *American Archives* (5th Series), I, 337; II, 498, 1299; (4th Series), IV, 272; Washington, *Writings* (Ford, ed.), IV, 439.

[2] *Ibid.*, I, 338; II, 498, 1299; IV, 272; Washington, *Writings* (Ford, ed.), IV, 439.

[3] *Ibid.*, I, 190, 232, 261, 375–76, 697, 1073, 1166, 1199; II, 479, 480; III, 1589.

[4] *Ibid.*, III, 542, 857, 1121.

[5] *Ibid.*, 1071.

'terrible disorder of homesickness,' which grew as the winter wore on. Men seemed to have no thought but of going home, and when they went they usually 'stole' their arms and equipment.[1]

The very orders of general officers reproved the army for shameful want of 'spirit, alertness, and industry.'[2] In November the roads from White Plains were 'crowded with deserters.' Men left when their time was out, 'though their eternal salvation was to be forfeited.' Cicero could not persuade them to tarry. The Niagara Falls would as soon kindle a fire as would their patriotism, wrote one who knew them well.[3] They would not reënlist, nor, even in the hour of danger, stay a few days to save the cause. Greene declared that in the whole retreat of one hundred miles, the army was not joined by over one hundred men. Washington reported 'no augmentation,' but rather loss by sickness. On December 24, Washington reported that a mere fraction of Gates's army had reënlisted and none of Lee's.[4] Terms were expiring, States delayed recruiting, the militia hung back, and Washington found his army melting away in the face of an advancing enemy, who perfectly understood his weakness.[5] Even those who remained were disobedient

[1] Force, *American Archives* (5th Series), I, 1217; III, 859, 899, 1301–02, 1400; Washington, *Writings* (Ford, ed.), V, 192. Congress took stern measures to stop the stealing of arms by soldiers leaving the army. *Journals of Congress* (Ford, ed.), V, 758.

[2] Force, *American Archives* (5th Series), III, 528.

[3] *Ibid.*, III, 484, 920, 1107; *Letters Written by Ebeneezer Huntington*, 53.

[4] *Ibid.*, III, 1400, 1071. Washington, *Writings* (Ford, ed.), V, 100.

[5] *Ibid.*, III, 547, 766, 1326.

beyond belief, even refusing to work on fortifications for their own protection. In the general orders Washington pleaded in vain against the straggling from camp, the useless firing of guns, the failure to prepare food for the coming march; and he declared he might 'almost as well attempt to remove Mount Atlas' as try to stop the plundering of the inhabitants during the retreat through the Jerseys.[1] In this matter, he declared, the American troops were more formidable to the farmers than were the enemy.

The reason for all this was not far to seek. There was in the 'embattled farmers' every latent possibility for the best of soldiers, but very few of them were developed. Washington always doubted whether short-term, ill-trained American soldiers could be counted on against professional soldiers in the open field, and the Long Island battle confirmed him in his unbelief. Though many of them were convinced that they were 'fighting the Lord's battles' and were 'ready for any infliction,' yet when they were 'fed with promises,' 'clothed with filthy rags,' and had lain for forty hours in the rain on the rain-soaked ground, even the fires of patriotism died out.[2] Under such conditions even better-trained soldiers might have failed; but raw recruits, militia with only a few weeks' drill under incompetent officers, fled before regulars as they always have since the begin-

[1] Force, *American Archives* (5th Series), I, 1128, 1140, 1248, 1249; II, 446–47, 498, 994, 1310, 1311; III, 544, 787, 1061; J. Adams, *Works* (Ford, ed.), III, 83; *Journals of Continental Congress* (Ford, ed.), V, 784, 808, 842–44; Washington, *Writings* (Ford, ed.), IV, 448.

[2] *Letters of E. Huntington*, 30, 37, 88.

ning of time. Washington put it to Congress in a nutshell. Men who never heard the din of war, dragged from their tender scenes of domestic life are timid and 'fly from their own shadows.' Sudden change in manner of living brings on sickness. Men used to unbounded freedom and no control cannot brook discipline. To change that, he wrote, is not the work of a day, a month, or even a year, and therefore short-term enlistments were death to any hope of an efficient army.[1] Nothing was wanted, said Greene, except 'officers and discipline . . . to make the American troops equal to any in the world.'[2] But good officers and discipline were just what they did not have. The soldiers, wrote Washington, when deepest in the Slough of Despond, 'never had officers, except in a few instances, worth the bread they eat.'[3] Some regimental officers, driven by scant pay to 'low and dirty arts,' were dishonest, filched from the public, and actually encouraged misbehavior in their men, even leading plundering expeditions, and refusing to restore stolen goods. The only excuse Washington could offer for them was that their pay did not enable them to 'support the character of gentlemen,' so they stole from the public to augment their 'allowances.'[4]

Ideas of democracy in some States, especially New

[1] Washington, *Writings* (Ford, ed.), IV, 443–45.

[2] Force, *American Archives* (5th Series), III, 1072.

[3] *Ibid.*, II, 496, 868; Washington, *Writings* (Ford, ed.), IV, 459. General Greene agreed with him. Greene, *Life of Greene*, II, 428.

[4] Washington, *Writings* (Ford, ed.), IV, 441, 447, 449, 487; Force, *American Archives* (5th Series), III, 1073–74, 1400; I, 502, 676; II, 498–501; *Journals of Continental Congress* (Ford, ed.), V, 844; *Orderly Book*, 23–31.

England, placed officers and men on the same footing, and led to the election of the officers by the men, and agreements wherein the officers promised to pool their wages with those of the men, share and share alike. The lowest arts of the demagogue were employed to court election. Soldiers even declared that they were not bound to obey officers whom they had not chosen, would not enlist, indeed, until they knew who was to be their colonel, major, or captain. The officers worried Washington with complaints of favoritism in the appointments by Congress and the States, resented having to act as factors for their men, and clamored against the inadequate pay in paper money which daily slid down the steep Avernus of depreciation.[1]

After Congress, urged by Washington, amended the Articles of War, and provided adequate punishment for officers who were guilty of disobedience, cowardice, fraud, stealing, or destroying ammunition and public stores, exciting mutiny or sedition, going in search of plunder or embezzling the stores captured from the enemy, signing false certificates, excusing the absence of fellow officers or men [2] — sins often reported by Washington in the past — he was urged by a virtuous member of Congress not to 'bate' the officers 'an ace' in the future, nor allow them 'to cheat or to mess with their men, to skulk in battle or to sneak in Quarters,' but make them do

[1] Force, *American Archives* (5th Series), I, 196, 628, 1122; II, 157, 495, 496; III, 510, 1498; *Journal of Continental Congress* (Ford, ed.), V, 856; Greene, *Life of Greene*, II, 422–26; *Letters of E. Huntington*, 32–39; Washington, *Writings* (Ford, ed.), IV, 58, 62, 209.

[2] *Journals of Continental Congress* (Ford, ed.), III, 331–34.

their duty and look and act like gentlemen.[1] Yet even devoted and competent officers would have had a giant's task to inspire courage in men half-armed, ill-supplied with tents, blankets, clothing, even common salt, and listening to the ghastly talks of a hospital service badly organized, dishonestly administered, ill-supplied, and of camps where thousands of sick went uncared for, amid scenes of suffering and death.[2] The pay offered nurses was so poor that none could be hired, and yet at times one fourth to one third of the army was down, unfit for duty.[3]

So black is the story of the hospital service in the Revolution that one can tolerate it only by bearing in mind the extraordinary conditions during the war, and how primitive was the medical science of that day. In the summer of 1775, Congress met an emergency by choosing Benjamin Church, director of the army hospital service, with surgeons, apothecaries, and mates.[4] When, three months later, the new director was accused of treason, Dr. John Morgan, of Philadelphia, succeeded, and was in turn dismissed.[5] As the war spread and troops augmented, Congress provided one surgeon and five mates for

[1] *Letters of . . . Continental Congress* (Burnett, ed.), I, 253–54.

[2] Force, *American Archives* (4th Series), VI, 1069; (5th Series), I, 38, 39, 950, 991, 608, 207, 232, 1051; II, 841–42, 1242; III, 575, 588, 591, 831, 832, 1242, 1358; I, 898, 1114; II, 497; III, 463, 1259, 1031, 1246.

[3] *Ibid.*, I, 507, 639; II, 327–30, 449–52, 607. *Continental Congress Papers* (L.C.), *Greene Papers*, October 20, 1776; Washington, *Writings* (Ford, ed.), IV, 334, 374, 457; Heath, *Memoirs*, 61; *Journals of Continental Congress* (Ford, ed.), V, 842; VI, 858.

[4] *Journals of Continental Congress* (Ford, ed.), II, 210, 211.

[5] *Ibid.*, III, 294; VII, 24. Thacher, *Military Journal*, 31. *Journals of Continental Congress* (Ford, ed.), V, 568; VII, 161–64, 232–57.

each one thousand men, and enlarged this, early in 1777, to an organized hierarchy with a Medical Committee, a Director-General, deputy director-generals, surgeons, and on down to the clerks who kept accounts.[1] Hospitals and a surgeon-general for each army, records, visits, inspections, all the wearisome devices for getting efficiency, proved in vain, and a large number of sick, scattered up and down the countryside, were left to die while two learned doctors quarreled over jurisdiction.[2]

Washington begged Congress for reforms that would spare his eyes and ears the looks and complaints of men perishing for want of proper care.[3] Still the directors of regular and of regimental hospitals quarreled over stores and equipment, until General Greene ironically wrote that it seemed to him immaterial 'whether a man die in the General or the Regimental hospital.' Men sick in the care of regimental surgeons, he declared, were in a wretched situation, and nothing struck 'a greater damp' upon the spirits of well men than the miserable condition of the sick, a spectacle shocking to human feelings, and sure to hamper the recruiting of a new army. Soldiers were heard solemnly to swear never to serve again unless there was a better supply of medicines.[4] Hundreds were dying daily from a 'shameful,' even

[1] *Journals of Continental Congress,* (Ford, ed.).

[2] *Ibid.*, v, 673; Force, *American Archives* (5th Series), I, 346; III, 463, 493, 618, 1591, 837.

[3] Washington, *Writings* (Ford, ed.), v, 204.

[4] *Continental Congress Papers, Greene Letters* (Library of Congress), October 10, 1776, December 16, 1776; Force, *American Archives* (5th Series), II, 574, 973, 974; Washington, *Writings* (Ford, ed.), v, 240.

'inhuman' neglect, because the general hospital could take care of only half the sick, and the regimental hospitals had no medicines nor supplies beyond the rations of a common soldier.[1] Complaints were rife that regimental surgeons abused their trust and embezzled the public stores, but, cried Greene, such losses were trifling compared with what the army suffered from want of supplies withheld so that they might not be stolen.[2]

By a cunning device of weekly returns, and a clockwork routine for removing the sick, regardless of weather or the patients' condition, Congress stopped the duplication of rations, but the soldiers died.[3] Washington had the good sense to propose doing away with rival jurisdictions, and giving the Director-General power to send surgeons and stores wherever needed.[4]

The Director never seemed to have surgeons enough, and men died for want of medical aid which came too late.[5] Indeed, there was a great lack of men trained in medical science, and many amateur surgeons must have done more harm than good.[6] A board of examiners put candidates through four hours' grill on anatomy, physiology, surgery, and

[1] Force, *American Archives* (5th Series), II, 1099, 1100.

[2] *Greene Letters, supra,* October 10, 1776, December 16, 1776.

[3] *Journals of Continental Congress* (Ford, ed.), V, 569. Washington, *Writings* (Ford, ed.), VI, 340; VII, 312.

[4] Washington, *Writings*, VII, 311; IV, 48.

[5] Force, *American Archives* (5th Series), I, 651; II, 602. General Wadsworth complained of having only one surgeon's mate for five regiments. (*Ibid.*, II, 995.) Heath had five thousand men with no general hospital and no surgeon. (*Ibid.*, III, 769.)

[6] *Ibid.*, III, 1259.

medicine, which James Thacher admits put them in a sweat, but incompetents managed to leap this hurdle until Dr. Shippen declared that more brave Americans fell a sacrifice to the neglect and iniquity in the medical department than by the sword of the enemy.[1] Young boys, ignorant and hired at half-pay, often cared for the sick. This and the want of fidelity in the doctors had, wrote a Congressman, slain ten soldiers to the enemy one.[2] Surgeon Waldo wished the 'cursed tongue' of one of his colleagues might be 'pulled out' for obtaining a furlough by lying and thus bringing scandal to New England surgeons. Yet, incompetent and unscrupulous as they were at times, one must have the grace to remember that the pay ranged only from four dollars a day for the Director-General to two dollars a month for nurses,[3] a stipend which was increased later only to make up for the tremendous depreciation of Continental money.[4] The surgeon's pay was so 'paltry and trifling' that Washington did not expect that a 'gentleman' with the 'least medical abilities or skill' could accept it, but a wise Congressman reasoned that if pay was low 'none but persons of the best ability would be employed.' [5]

[1] It was doubtless worse than this, for in the Seven Years' War, 1512 in the British army were killed in action, while 134,000 died of diseases and wounds. In our day science has so changed this ratio that in the Russo-Japanese War only one out of four died from *natural*, not *war* causes.

[2] Thacher, *Journals of the American War*, 113; *Letters of . . . Continental Congress* (Burnett, ed.), II, 188; Force, *American Archives* (5th Series), III, 1259.

[3] *Journals of Continental Congress* (Ford, ed.), II, 210, 211.

[4] Force, *American Archives* (5th Series), III, 1298; II, 1393.

[5] Washington, *Writings* (Ford, ed.), V, 287–88; *Letters of . . . Continental Congress* (Burnett, ed.), II, 321, note.

Moreover, the surgeon worked at times in hospitals shocking to humanity, a 'house of carnage,' as Wayne wrote of the one at Ticonderoga — no medicines, no beds or even straw to lie on, and no coverings.[1] When blankets and clothes were lacking, Congress made the brilliant suggestion of stoves as a substitute. As a result, some soldiers went to a hospital, not because they were sick, but to keep warm.[2]

As to shelter, a 'hospital' might mean anything from a thin tent to an erstwhile church. Usually the quarters were cramped, and men were herded together in barracks, hastily built huts, barns, outhouses, or, at best, taverns, college buildings, courthouses, or fine old mansions, surrounded by gardens and orchards.[3] Horrible sights might be seen in the worst. One witness, who entered the hospital at Ticonderoga, found one man lying dead at the door, and, just inside, two more dead, with two living men lying between them.[4]

The worst of all, of course, were the smallpox hospitals, or detention camps where men were being inoculated against that dread disease — 'ten times more terrible than Britons, Canadians and Indians

[1] Force, *American Archives* (5th Series), III, 1031, 1358, 1478. Gates had the same impression, I, 649.

[2] *Journals of Continental Congress* (Ford, ed.), IX, 941; Beveridge, *John Marshall*, I, 86.

[3] Force, *American Archives* (4th Series), V, 113, 416; VI, 608, 1573; III, 1074; (5th Series), II, 1099; III, 322, 361, 1060, 1071, 1568, 1579; *Pennsylvania Archives* (2d Series), I, 630; Thacher, *Military Journal*, 33, 112, 132–33; Greene, *Life of Greene*, II, 44; *New Jersey Archives*, (2d Series), II, 436–37; *Pennsylvania Magazine*, XXIII, 35, 210; *Journals of Continental Congress* (Ford, ed.), XII, 1174.

[4] *Ibid.* (5th Series), III, 1358.

together.'[1] At times it seemed as if the whole army, the clothes, the blankets, the air, the very ground men walked on, was infected with the foul malady. Some preferred to desert and face death before the firing squad rather than risk the disease or the inoculation to attain immunity.[2]

As to medicines to be found in these wretched places, where at times more than a fourth of the army was confined, there was 'no emetic, nor cathartic, nor mercurial or antimonial remedy, no opiate or elixir tincture, nor even any capital medicine,' wrote one desperate physician. The finding of a chest of lint for wounds was reported as if it were a chest of gold.[3] At Fishkill, in the winter of 1776, one hundred men were unfit for duty because there was no sulphur to cure them of the itch. The armies in the South could never get enough 'Peruvian bark' to fight the deadly malaria.[4] Even the allowance of soap was so small that Washington attributed much of the disease in the army to dirtiness.[5] Many 'putrid diseases' were ascribed by him to the large quantities of animal food 'untempered by vegetables, or vinegar or any kind of drink but water'; and this in the midst of a rich farming country, and in a land that never even dreamed of an Eighteenth Amendment.[6]

[1] Force, *American Archives* (4th Series), VI, 1083.
[2] *Ibid.* (5th Series), I, 651.
[3] *Ibid.* (5th Series), II, 445, 574, 1272; (4th Series), V, 263.
[4] *Ibid.*, II, 1363; (5th Series), I, 1266.
[5] Washington, *Writings* (Ford, ed.), V, 496.
[6] *Ibid.*, V, 495

Congress and Committees of Safety made great efforts to correct these evils, even to impressing medicines and surgeons' instruments, but with little success, though they ranged the wide world for such supplies, even as far as Cadiz, Holland, and especially the West Indies.[1] France was one of the most important sources of supplies. An invoice from Hortalez and Company listed the drugs — alum, gum arabic, myrrh, tartar, Peruvian bark, calomel, benzoin, sulphur, gum camphor, aloes, and rhubarb — while lancets, amputating instruments, syringes, and hooked needles were sent in large numbers.[2] The need of instruments, especially, was great, for, in 1776, there were recorded only six sets of amputating instruments, twenty-one cases of packet instruments, twelve cases of crooked needles, twenty-four tourniquets, and three pairs of forceps for the wants of twenty-one regiments.[3] Operations were often not much better than 'butcheries' at the best, and the ways of treating wounds and fractures must have been painful in extreme.[4] Yet Surgeon Waldo wrote with some pride of their advance over the home

[1] Force, *American Archives* (5th Series), III, 257, 1592; (4th Series), IV, 1026; V, 115, 382; *Journals of . . . Continental Congress* (Ford, ed.), III, 250; V, 570; VII, 34, 91, 140, 232; XI, 446; *State Records of North Carolina*, XIV, 436, 452; *Pennsylvania Colonial Records*, X, 292; Henry, *Life of Henry*, I, 475; *Maryland Archives*, XVI, 235–36.

[2] *Archives des Affaires Étrangères, États-Unis*, III, 128, 261–72. The home-produced medicines were made from ginseng, snakeroot, bloodroot (for cleansing sores), and horseweed, pennyroyal, horehound and purple bindweed. See Schoepf, *Travels in Confederation*, I, 236, 272, 288, 319, 321; II, 116.

[3] *Pennsylvania Colonial Records*, X, 604; *Journals of Continental Congress* (Ford, ed.), V, 568.

[4] Mass. Hist. Soc., *Proceedings* (2d Series), IX, 88; Middlebrook, *Maritime Connecticut during the Revolution*, I, 238, 239.

methods of old women and 'Doctor Bolus Linctus.' 'We gave them mutton and grogg, and a capital medicine once in a while to start the disease from its foundation at once,' he wrote. 'We avoid Piddling Pills, Powders, Bolus Linctus — Cordials . . . whose powers are only rendered important by causing the patient to vomit up his money instead of his disease.' [1]

It was little wonder that the outlook was black, indeed, for men lying ill of the various camp disorders, the very prevalent scurvy, jaundice, bilious attacks, dysentery, sore throat, grippe, and an appalling amount of rheumatism! It fully explains the dark pessimism of Surgeon Waldo's diary: 'I am prodigious sick and cannot get anything comfortable — what in the name of Providence can I do with a fit of Sickness in this place where nothing appears pleasing to the Sickn'd Eye and Nauseating Stomach, . . . I cannot eat Beef if I starve — for my stomach positively refuses such Company. . . . I am Sick — discontented — and out of humour. Poor food — Hard lodging — Cold Weather — fatigue — Nasty Cloaths — nasty Cookery — Vomit half my time — Smoak'd out of my senses — the Devil's in't — I can't Endure it — Why are we sent here to starve and freeze — What sweet Filicities have I left at home; a charming Wife — Pretty Children — Good beds — good food — good Cookery — all agreeable — all harmonious. Here, all Confusion — smoke, Cold — hunger and filthyness — A pox on my bad luck. Here comes a bowl of beef soup — full

[1] *Historical Magazine*, v, 133.

of burnt leaves and dirt, sickish enough to make a hector spue — Away with it Boys — I'll live like a Cameleon upon Air.'[1]

Particularly maddening to the soldiers was the neglect of the army by the non-combatants at home. Major Huntington, as he thought of it, 'flew into a fearful passion,' and was ashamed that he was born in America. 'You hold your purse-strings as though you would damn the world,' he wrote home.[2] In a rich farming country the soldiers were craving fresh meat and vegetables, and even flour was short. They were asked to dig trenches without spades, and build barracks without nails. Add to all this the poor pay, uncertain and irregular, at times six months in arrears, the commander borrowing on his personal credit to make even belated payments, and one may better comprehend the soldiers' state of mind.[3] In spite of all, exaltation might have come with victory, but, instead, there had been a year of almost constant defeat, failure in Canada, giving up of Crown Point, loss of Long Island and Manhattan, and the wretched retreat across the Jerseys. No wonder that Washington feared the cause would be lost.

Yet, while one must recount the story of the malingerer, the deserter, the coward, and even the traitor, one must recall also the conditions which made them — the first absence from home, the insufficient pay, the incredible hardships, the doubtful, almost hopeless cause, the competent enemy,

[1] Surgeon Waldo, Diary, in *American Historical Magazine*, v, 131.

[2] E. Huntington, *Letters*, 88.

[3] Force, *American Archives* (5th Series), I, 232, 1051; III, 465, 1514, 575; II, 1274; Washington, *Writings* (Ford, ed.), IV, 387.

better trained and equipped, and stark defeat which took away the heart finally even of heroes. Then there is the memory of those who did patiently endure to the end; of Nathan Hale who cheerfully gave his life doing a spy's hateful duty; of Lord Stirling's troops, including Colonel Smallwood's Maryland brigade, who in the Long Island battle gallantly stood their ground until resistance was hopeless, and of the small band who did endure with Washington the terrible retreat, and displayed the courage which took them back across the Delaware to the brilliant victories at Trenton and Princeton. During the campaign about New York and the retreat across the Jerseys, Americans learned for the first time the inevitable evils of war.[1] Whig and Tory had to learn that hungry and rapacious soldiers would not be particular about a citizen's politics; that the indispensable discipline imposed by war falls with impartial severity on friend and foe. Joyful Loyalists welcomed the royal forces when they disembarked on Staten Island. They took oaths of allegiance, enlisted in the loyal militia, welcomed the British officers to their homes, and afforded supplies for the invading army, but when their cattle and sheep were gone, and their means of serving the British vanished, consideration ceased, discipline no longer restrained the soldiery, and a spy declared that the people were ready to poison any British representative.[2]

[1] Except so far as in colonial wars with the French the frontiers had suffered during the Indian raids.

[2] Force, *American Archives* (5th Series), I, 106, 122, 174, 199, 692, 1110; *Letters from America* (Pettengill, trans.), 177.

The treatment of the inhabitants of Long Island by the opposing armies is another tale. In early summer, when only the American army was encamped there, and real war conditions did not yet exist, only the most active Tories suffered. Thefts of poultry, watermelons, corn, and greens were rebuked in Greene's orders, and those who harried the internal enemies burned a house now and then, but the prudent and the double-faced suffered little.[1] With the coming of the British, however, and the contrary pull of two hostile armies, evil days fell upon nearly all. A Hessian described it as a beautiful island, a multitude of meadows, tilled fields, fruit-trees of every kind, from which the 'rebels' had fled carrying off many things. They had been rich, had lived too well, and grew haughty, wrote a mercenary, reciting the lesson his masters taught him. As he looked upon luxuriant grain and hemp fields, beautiful orchards, barns crammed full of farmers' wealth, he pitied these victims 'of the intrigues and personal envy of a few demagogues.'[2] After the battle of Long Island, fear or true loyalty hastened many to renew their fealty to George III. Some were cited for valor in the British service during the fight; others merely accepted pardons or took oaths of allegiance, while loudly disclaiming any past favors to American arms. The most sincere enlisted in the victorious British army.[3] Queens County and

[1] Force, *American Archives* (5th Series), I, 896, 899, 911.

[2] *Letters from America* (Pettengill, trans.), 177.

[3] Washington, *Writings* (Ford, ed.), IV, 275, 281, 467; Force, *American Archives* (5th Series), I, 494, 789, 1211; II, 1159–63; III, 1404; Long Island Hist. Soc., *Memoirs*, III, Docs. 96–98.

some towns revoked all orders lately issued on authority of the Continental Congress.[1] Inhabitants who still evinced any rebellious spirit were disarmed and their property seized, and Howe threatened all those who refused supplies for his army that he would send troops to lay waste their farms.[2] He needed horses, wagons, and drivers in great numbers. Cattle, wood, forage, fresh provisions were in great demand from the island farmers, and they were so intimidated that they dared not sell elsewhere than in the New York market. All of their wheat, oats, rye, barley, and corn, as well as their flocks of sheep, must be brought to the commissaries of the British army, which they must also serve with their boats, mills, and barns. Loyalists and patriots alike were forced to sell until it hurt, and their families were left in actual want.[3] As army officers hardened their hearts toward the non-combatants, the rank and file paid less heed to regulations against plundering, and stole not only food and drink, but even horses for their own delectation. General Robertson, when he first landed on Long Island, saw a land rich with farm stock, poultry, and cattle, but later he saw nothing alive.[4] The sufferings of the Long-Islanders reached their height when, in the race for the control of the island food supplies, Pa-

[1] Force, *American Archives* (5th Series), II, 1046, 1164, 1219–20.

[2] *Ibid.*, I, 1211–12; II, 504–06, 565, 825, 1186.

[3] *Ibid.*, II, 189, 505–64, 825, 1024, 1029, 1186, 1042; III, 608, 674, 825.

[4] Long Island Hist. Soc., *Memoirs*, III, Doc. 97; Force, *American Archives* (5th Series), I, 1261, 1547; P.R.O., *State Papers, Domestic*, no. 19, pp. 30, 31.

triot authorities sought to remove or drive into waste and hidden places the cattle and sheep in the eastern parts to save them from the enemy which steadily extended its power toward that region. Troops from Connecticut disarmed and confined the known Loyalists, ferried many Patriot families, with movable property, across the Sound, and then drove cattle, fourteen hundred head in a single day, into hiding, firing the grain fields, dismantling the mills, and leaving misery and want in their wake.[1] Inertia, apathy, unwillingness to coöperate, a preference for British gold to Continental paper, marked the conduct of the majority; but there was no behavior that would deliver them from the sorrows of war. Not only was there the tug of opposing armies, but actual civil war between Whigs and Tories. During Washington's occupation of New York, and all through the trying days of the abandonment of Long Island and Manhattan, he was seriously weakened by having to employ his scanty forces to restrain the British sympathizers. When he deployed his forces to keep in check the disaffected, as he withdrew up the Hudson and across it, he learned to his dismay that his troops sacked and destroyed houses, stole the clothing of women, the window-draperies, and even pier mirrors, quite regardless of the political faith of those who were plundered. To stop this even courts-martial proved futile.[2] When

[1] Force, *American Archives* (5th Series), I, 145, 164, 621, 887, 896, 899, 1279, 1143, 1393, 1414, 1451, 1484–89, 1537, 1543, 1548, 1557; II, 170, 282, 296, 441, 623, 711, 975, 1088; III, 551.

[2] *Public Papers of George Clinton*, I, 262; Long Island Hist. Soc., *Memoirs*, III, Doc. 98; Washington, *Writings* (Ford, ed.), IV, 424,

the British overran the same region, they too pillaged and made no distinction between Loyalist and rebel. The Hessians here first showed their bright eminence in the art of plundering, carrying off everything from feather-beds to copper kettles and kitchen clocks.[1] Throughout America the Patriot's imagination was fired and his soul embittered by the recital of these wrongs. An English observer declared it was hard to conceive the amount of plunder collected by the Hessians, and that they took good care to have it guarded as their proper baggage.[2] Added to the ravages of the two armies was the gleaning by irregulars, 'skinners,' as they were called, who pretended attachment to either army, stole what they could, and provided against further depredations by razing or burning the remnants.

During the retreat through New Jersey the improved discipline of those who remained steadfast, the more stringent Articles of War, and perhaps even the very hurry of the march, lessened but did not eliminate the outrages of Washington's army.[3] Its numbers were dwindling because the terms of enlist-

448, 449; v, 2; Force, *American Archives* (5th Series), I, 1560, 1563; II, 197, 244, 413, 414, 448, 499, 1120, 1241; III, 333–36, 345, 544, 711, 1171, 1366, 1433, 1516.

[1] Force, *American Archives* (5th Series), I, 442, 452, 545, 728, 729, 1552; II, 948, 996; I, 1490; III, 789, 1123, 1379, 557, 559. *Public Papers of George Clinton*, I, 287, 463–65.

[2] *Remembrancer*, v, 83. General Robertson testified that Washington, after Trenton, restored twenty-one wagonloads which he took from the Hessians. P.R.O., *State Papers, Domestic*, 19, no. 9, pp. 30–31.

[3] Force, *American Archives* (5th Series), II, 1093, 1368; *Public Papers of G. Clinton*, I, 524; *New Jersey Archives* (2d Series), I, 257; Washington, *Writings* (Ford, ed.), IV, 139.

ment of over twenty-five hundred men expired on December 1, and large numbers left for home without waiting to confront the enemy not two hours' march away.[1] No aid came from the New Jersey militia nor the civilians, due to the peaceful inclination of the Quakers, and a prevailing fear of the British army.[2] Its success seemed certain, and opposition to it looked like self-destruction. Farmers fought against removal or destruction of their stock and provisions by the retreating Patriot army, because the prospect of selling for British gold was bright before them.[3] When the British came, the Jersey farmers took Howe's pardons, furnished him supplies and intelligence, and some even enlisted in his army; but when the invaders settled down on the country, increasing daily their demands for food, horses, and wagons, and when plundering and violence, especially by the Hessians, spread terror everywhere, hatred of them grew apace. This was nourished by propaganda published by state and county committees which made the imaginary terrors greater than the real.[4]

When all this was reënforced by Washington's victories at Trenton and Princeton, courage came again, a hostile spirit confronted Howe, and men

[1] Washington, *Writings* (Sparks, ed.), IV, 199.

[2] Force, *American Archives* (5th Series), I, 322, 812, 1447; III, 1186, 1278, 1292, 1302, 1342, 1344.

[3] *Ibid.*, II, 430–37; III, 629, 830, 831; Reed, *Life of James Reed*, I, 292.

[4] *Ibid.*, *American Archives* (5th Series), III, 1123, 1245, 1291, 1399; Stryker, *Trenton and Princeton*, 26, 367, 475; *New Jersey Archives* (2d Series), I, 242, 246, 274; *Clinton Papers*, I, 496; *Journals of the Continental Congress* (Ford, ed.), VII, 276–79, Report of Committee on Atrocities.

once cowed by his prowess burned his pardons and enlisted with the American forces. The evils of the occupation of New Jersey had been increased by the Hessian brutalities, occasioned in part by the promises made them at home by recruiting officers that they would be allowed to plunder at will in America, and even that they would be given land in the conquered provinces.[1] They had been eager to get into the Jerseys as a sort of Promised Land, and the British propaganda was also intended to make them regard the Americans as ungrateful rascals, rebellious against an indulgent king, so that they considered the country as an object of vengeance, which they ravaged 'at a high rate,' until it was said the Americans trembled at the very name of Hessian.[2] Nothing happened in the Jerseys to be compared to the atrocities suffered in territory occupied by hostile armies in Europe in that age. Neither American nor British officers condoned such marauding as took place, but were simply unable to enforce obedience. The Americans were at their worst in southern New York, the British in the Jerseys.

[1] General Robertson testified to this promise. P.R.O., *State Papers, Domestic*, 19, no. 9, pp. 30–31.

[2] *Remembrancer*, v, 83.

CHAPTER XV

THE FORCES OF UNION AND DISUNION

THE story of the progress toward a spirit of independence in certain representative sections of the thirteen colonies helps us to understand the advance of their delegates in the Continental Congress toward a resolution and a declaration that they would no more be subjects of the British King. Even after individual colonies had ceased to feel the tug of affection for England and loyalty to King George, there were still obstacles to any united action equal to the task of successful war against the British Government. How Congress met the measures of the North Ministry, how it overcame disunion forces within, what these were, and how some of them vanished before the logic of events will be the next object of inquiry.

Our review of political conditions in England during 1775 and the early months of 1776 showed the improbability of any real spirit of conciliation emerging there. The American state of mind during that period was no more favorable. The Ministry, in late August of 1775, could talk only of America misled by dangerous and ill-designing men, forgetful of allegiance, guilty of disorderly acts, obstructing lawful commerce, oppressing loyal subjects, and proceeding at last to open rebellion, and the levying of war against the King.[1] Congress at the same time

[1] Proclamation of Rebellion, in Force, *American Archives* (4th Series), III, 240, 241.

could only sigh like a furnace over the series of Parliament's acts, altering Massachusetts' form of government, extending the boundaries of Quebec and the jurisdiction of Admiralty courts, laying violent hands on the right of trial by jury, quartering soldiers on the colonies in times of peace, interdicting trade, and finally sending fleets and armies to begin cruel hostilities which culminated in 'butchery' and the burning of Charlestown.[1]

Already Congress had published (July 6, 1775) its 'Declaration of the Causes and Necessity of Taking up Arms,' which assured their 'fellow subjects' in England that they had no ambitious designs of separating from Great Britain, but that they would die like freemen rather than live like slaves, and that not only their own resources but 'foreign assistance' would be invoked before they would surrender that freedom received from gallant ancestors.[2] In spite of a concluding prayer to the 'Judge and Ruler of the Universe' to relieve the Empire from the calamities of civil war, it was clear that only such terms as the North Ministry would never grant held the least prospect of reconciliation.

The drift, therefore, from July of 1775 on to the fateful July of 1776 was steadily toward a full resolve to attain Independence. Never were the times so out of joint. If from England or from America there came a gesture of conciliation, the news of it arrived on the other side of the Atlantic

[1] *Journals of Continental Congress* (Ford, ed.), II, 224, July 31, 1775; Report on Lord North's Conciliatory Resolutions.

[2] *Ibid.*, II, 128, July 6, 1775.

just as some deplorable event incited new wrath, which, though hot, was not at all suited to turning swords into plowshares. An example was the petition to the King,[1] which an indulgent Congress permitted John Dickinson to draw up in a spirit of humility and submission disgusting to John Adams, who, unable to feel such scruples, called it a 'measure of imbecility.'[2] The petition made no claim, no mention of right, Dickinson admitted, but would, therefore, if rejected, make all the more firm for the impending contest the minds of all moderate Americans. This address to the Throne was about to be presented in London by Richard Penn on August 23, when, on that very day, the King's Proclamation of Rebellion was issued. Presentation was then delayed until September 1, when Penn was refused audience with the King, spurned with contempt from the foot of the throne, as America interpreted it. From that day, wrote Dickinson, 'not a syllable,' to his recollection, 'was ever uttered in favor of reconciliation with Great Britain.' That news, arriving in America at about the same time as the tidings that the King's American subjects were proclaimed rebels, had a profound effect.

America and England had reached the stage of calling names. 'You are rebels!' cried England. 'You are tyrants!' retorted America.[3] Considering that the colonists were rebels at that time by all the canons of correct diction, it is amazing how bitterly

[1] Agreed to July 5, but not engrossed and signed until July 8, 1775. *Journals of Continental Congress* (Ford, ed.).

[2] *Letters of . . . Continental Congress* (Burnett, ed.), I, 130, 157–59.

[3] *A Letter to those Ladies . . .* (W.L.C.L.), 6.

they resented the use of the word. It seemed to put a halter around their necks. 'A sure way to make rebels is to declare people such while innocent,' cried a clergyman who was blind to the rebellion all about him.[1] The colonists particularly objected to being called rebels by a 'King, supported by an abandoned ministry, and a venal set of prostituted Lords and Commons.'[2] In their eyes tyrants were treating as rebels people who did not suffer tyranny patiently enough, and small colonial executives were denouncing as rebels men who were simply demanding justice.[3] There was no sympathy in the America of 1776 with Martin Luther's famous opinion that whosoever could should 'smite, strangle, and stab [rebels] secretly or publicly, and should remember that there is nothing more poisonous, pernicious and devilish than a rebellious man.'[4]

Yet bitter and implacable as was the American spirit, still greater evils were to be suffered before real unity of action among the discordant provinces could be attained. Though, in Joseph Galloway, the wish was father to the thought, yet he did not much overstate, in his 'Candid Examination,' the colonial lack of unity. In respect to each other he thought them 'so many perfect and independent societies, different in forms of government, products of soil and views of commerce, entertaining high prejudices against and jealousies of each other.' Their different

[1] Force, *American Archives* (4th Series), III, 3, 9.

[2] *Essex Gazette*, no. 361, June 29, 1775.

[3] *Correspondence of Condorcet and Turgot*, 226.

[4] Robinson, *Readings in European History*, II, 107.

religious tempers and private interests conspired to create such diversity of inclinations, and judgments, and conduct, that he believed they would never be able to unite to avoid any general mischief, or to promote any general good. Whigs, too, were ready to despair of unity for the same reasons.[1]

Great physiographic facts, brought into being ages before the Mayflower's journey, had destined the early European settlements to be for generations self-centered, individualistic, and disunited.[2] The drowned rivers, the tangled, pathless forests, transportation in a rude stage of development, the vast extent of the American territory, and statesmen who saw fit by navigation laws to reënact the law of God, had prevented even the efforts of the British Government to unite its American territory under one government.

Observers from abroad, French statesmen, drew conclusions, half right, half wrong, from these conditions. They saw Americans brought together from every corner of Europe, made up of all religions, all languages, and scattered over great areas of the continent with little more attachment for each other than for England. Indeed, did not England count on this disunion of races, this commingling of nations as a means of conserving her colonies? A Massachusetts governor had thought bitterly that

[1] Joseph Galloway, *Candid Examination*, etc., 44, 45. Franklin agreed with him. *Works* (Sparks, ed.), IV, 41–42. Dummer, Keath, Pownall, and Shirley all bore like testimony. Dummer, *Defence of the Charters* (London, ed. 1765), 72–73; Pownall, *Administration of the Colonies* (ed. 1768), 63; *Letters of . . . Continental Congress* (Burnett, ed.), II, 48.

[2] Van Tyne, *Causes of the War of Independence*, 74.

it would be well for England and the colonies 'if every province was a distinct island.'[1] French spies noted that divine service in New York was carried on in English, French, German, and in 'a Dutch patois.'[2] Travelers noted many traditions of ill-feeling between the land of Winthrop, Bradford, Cotton Mather, and Roger Williams, where the stock was almost pure English, and the more cosmopolitan neighboring province peopled with Patroons, Palatines, and Knickerbocker families. The Swedes of Delaware and the Dutch of New York had quarreled in their earlier days. The mixed peoples, German, English, Welsh, and Scotch-Irish, of Pennsylvania, had not lived on the best of terms with the more purely English populations of Maryland and Virginia. Perhaps never in the verified history of the world had people from so many nations gathered in one land. Nor in colonial days had assimilation so far advanced as to make them all Americans, unaware of heterogeneous traditions, varying faiths.

Sectarian differences, too, promoted provincial intolerance. The Pennsylvania Quakers had good reason to hate the Massachusetts Congregationalists, whom they never failed to twit on the seventeenth-century hangings, and of their 'cruel and bloody practices against the Dear Servants of the Lord.'[3] Catholic Maryland was a thorn in the side

[1] Hosmer, *Thomas Hutchinson*, 221.

[2] Durand to Choiseul, *Archives des Affaires Étrangères, Correspondance Politique, Angleterre*, 474, F 273.

[3] Channing, *History of the United States*, II, 68–69; Livingston, *The Livingstons of Livingston Manor*, 200; Francis Howgill, *The Popish Inquisition*, etc. (ed. 1659), (title page).

of Episcopalian Virginia. The New York members of the Dutch Reformed Church had only sneers for the non-militant Quakers of Pennsylvania, while the aristocratic Episcopalians of colonial New York were bitter against 'John Presbyter' of New Hampshire, and the 'Puritan mobility' of Massachusetts. A Pennsylvania Friend feared 'a combination between Massachusetts Presbyterians and Virginia Churchmen to persecute if not exterminate the poor Quakers,' and efforts were made to rouse Pennsylvanians against the Continental Congress by declaring it was ruled by New England, which aimed at a national church, dominated by Presbyterians.[1]

Resulting from all these sources of provincial jealousy, there were bitter controversies between neighboring colonies, local vanities, sour judgments of fellow members of the Empire. Virginia taxed tobacco imported from Carolina, Pennsylvania the products of every adjacent colony. Little Rhode Island quarreled with 'Indigo Connecticut' over the exact location of their boundary line, while the latter had a like dispute with Massachusetts.[2] 'Papist Maryland' disputed long and bitterly with Pennsylvania that boundary line finally determined by Mason and Dixon — common surveyors, whose names seem thereby to have become immortal.[3] New York carried through the Revolution a running fight for its claims to what became Vermont. Dela-

[1] Lincoln, *Revolutionary Movement in Pennsylvania*, 192, 229.

[2] *Dartmouth MSS.* (W.L.C.L.), I, p. 3 (of Massachusetts Bay documents).

[3] Galloway, *Examination*, etc., 47.

ware was not too small to have a big quarrel with the great Quaker colony, which ended only when the 'Lower Counties' became independent. The rival claims of Connecticut and Pennsylvania in the Wyoming Valley were long a bar to friendly union. Virginia and Pennsylvania clashed in their western claims.[1] Onlookers thought they hated even Old England less than they did one another.[2]

No wonder the English pamphleteer Joshua Gee could not imagine the colonies uniting, and that Josiah Tucker, the eminent economist, wrote: 'The mutual antipathies and clashing interests of the Americans, their difference of governments, habitudes and manners indicate that they will have no centre of union and no common interest. They never can be united into one compact empire under any species of government whatever; a disunited people till the end of time, suspicious and distrustful of each other, they will be divided and subdivided into little commonwealths or principalities according to natural boundaries, by great bays of the sea and by vast rivers, lakes and ridges of mountains.'[3] Indeed, that was a common European opinion, and French statesmen were at last induced to aid America because they believed each province would become a separate republic; have no other relation

[1] *Letters of . . . Continental Congress* (Burnett, ed.), 206, 421. An amusing statement of conflicting economic interests of the several colonies is in Schlesinger, *The Colonial Merchants*, 24.

[2] Jared Ingersoll, in N.H. Hist. Soc., *Papers*, IX, 446; *Letters of . . . Continental Congress* (Burnett, ed.), I, 173, 186, 229, 279, 281, 320, 398, 421.

[3] C. F. Adams, *Studies Military and Diplomatic*, 218; Joshua Gee, *Trade and Navigation of Great Britain* (4th ed.), 103–04.

with each other than that of a political confederation.[1]

Even after the colonies began war, each wished to control its own troops. The commanders at Bunker Hill were 'the wolf-slayer,' Israel Putnam, for Connecticut; the 'blacksmith,' Nathanael Greene, for Rhode Island; John Stark for New Hampshire; the 'old church-warden,' Artemas Ward, for Massachusetts; and even Ethan Allen was commissioned by Connecticut rather than the Continental Congress whose common authority with the Great Jehovah he had bombastically claimed. Indeed, even after the strain of war drove Congress to form a Continental army, the members from rival States 'scuffled over appointments of general officers,' seeking office for men from the home colony quite regardless of their talents. To get a man from his own State, a member of Congress would nominate officers, wrote Washington, not 'fit to be shoe-blacks.'[2] Nor would the troops of one colony tolerate an officer from another. 'Connecticut wants no Massachusetts man in their corps,' wrote Washington; 'Massachusetts thinks there is no necessity for a Rhode-Islander to be introduced among them'; and so on until the Commander-in-Chief was quite beside himself with vexation. He vainly wished that he might banish 'every idea of local attachments.' But it seemed impossible, wrote Gen-

[1] Vergennes, *Reflections*.

[2] Washington, *Writings* (Ford, ed.), v, 40. There was objection to the troops of one State entering the territory of another except by permission of the latter State. *Letters of . . . Continental Congress*, Burnett, ed.), I, 339.

eral Greene, 'to unhinge the prejudices' that people had for their own provinces, and Washington at last gave up trying to 'reason away the prejudices of a whole army.' [1]

More revealing still of the strength of this particularism was that the very Loyalists who fled for protection from different colonies to the British army in New York City had there their special organizations, their special taverns, rendezvous for Pennsylvanians, Marylanders, or Georgians. In these haunts they schemed to get better concessions for their fellow colonists than for others, seeking for them better official positions, and endeavoring to convince the British Government that their particular colony had suffered most at Whig hands and therefore deserved most consideration.[2] While risking all for the cause of empire, many Loyalists were particularistic, interested first of all in their home province.

The bitterness of the provincial prejudices was amazing. Lewis Morris, of New York, provided in his will, 1760, that his son Gouverneur Morris be never sent to Connecticut, lest he imbibe in his youth 'that low craft and cunning so incident to the people of that country,' which no art could disguise, although 'many of them under the sanctified garb of religion have endeavored to impose themselves on the world as honest men.' [3] 'Party animosity be-

[1] *Letters of . . . Continental Congress* (Burnett, ed.), I, 137, 234, 255–56; II, 54–55; Washington, *Writings* (Ford, ed.), III, 208, 249; *Greene Papers* (W.L.C.L.), Greene to Ward, October 16, 1775.

[2] Van Tyne, *Loyalists in American Revolution*, 244–45.

[3] Channing, *History of the United States*, III, 468.

tween the Eastern States and the Inhabitants of New York,' Laurens wrote Lafayette, 'is almost co-existent' with their settlement, disputes being carried to such extremes 'as seem to threaten a dissolution of all friendships.' Yet men called this spirit 'the sinews of Liberty.' [1]

Schoepf, a German traveler, found Virginians near the close of the war complacent with the superiority of their State over all other States.[2] 'Who in America,' he reports one as saying, 'would dare count himself the equal of the noble Virginian? The poor New-Englander who gains his bread by the sweat of his brow? Or the Pennsylvanian who drudges like a Negro and takes butter and cheese to market? or the North Carolina pitch boiler? or the South Carolinian with his ever-lasting rice? Above all these stands the Gentleman of Virginia, for he alone has the finest horses, the finest dogs, the most negroes, the most land, speaks the best English, makes the most elegant bow, has the easy grace of the man of the world, and is a baron on his estates.' This 'baron' had great scorn of the 'Yankee pedlar' and trader, though a planter was quite as engrossed in selling tobacco as the trader his 'Yankee notions.' The traveler in Virginia reported that the talk, most of the time, was of the great advantage which the State of Virginia had over all other States in the world, and 'the nation of Virginia over all other nations.' [3]

Jonathan Boucher, of Virginia, found Philadelphia

[1] *Letters of . . . Continental Congress* (Burnett, ed.), III, 29.

[2] Schoepf, *Travels*, II, 92. [3] *Ibid.*, 91.

'flat and level.' Everything about it had for him 'a Quakerly or rather a Republican aspect.' Yet the universal topic of conversation was 'the superiority of Philadelphia over every other spot of the globe.' 'All their geese are swans,' he wrote, and they are 'ever trumpeting their own praise.' Lovell, a New England Congressman, blamed Pennsylvanians for Howe's successes in their State (1777). 'If he had been among Yankee stone walls,' not seventy of his men would have gotten from his ships with whole skins. The only hope, thought Lovell, was in the North.[1] Yet the Virginian, Washington, found the 'Yankees,' on first acquaintance, 'an exceedingly dirty and nasty people,' who might fight well enough, but that their officers were the 'most indifferent kind of people' he ever saw.[2]

This mutual jealousy gave rise to suspicions, fear for the safety of one's colony, bugbears which seem merely absurd to-day. Samuel Adams, during the siege of Boston, took alarm for the independence of his State from her sister States. Though perhaps necessary just then, he did not like the Continental army being kept so long within Massachusetts, for 'history affords abundant instances of established armies making themselves the masters of those countries, which they were designed to protect.'[3] While he and John Adams suffered this nervous solicitude about military aid from other colonies,

[1] Library of Congress (Force trans.), *Gates*, II, October 5, 1777.

[2] Letter of Washington to Lund Washington in Emmet Collection, *Magazine of American History*, XIX, 163; Washington, *Writings* (Ford, ed.), III, 97, 98, 101.

[3] Samuel Adams, *Writings*, III, 230 (October 29, 1775).

the Southern statesmen were harrowing up their souls with 'a secret fear, jealousy, that New England would soon be full of veteran soldiers and conceive designs unfavorable to the rest of the colonies.'[1] 'People here,' wrote a delegate from Philadelphia, think of us New England men 'as a set of Goths and Vandals who may one day overrun these southern climes.'[2]

In the early days of the warfare with the forces of the King, there was bitter jealousy between colonies because of the different gait at which they were advancing. General Greene complained, October 23, 1775, that, while some were at loggerheads with the British, others were merely sparring, others again in perfect tranquillity. While at Boston, he wrote, we are entirely depopulating the islands, removing all the stock in order to cut off Howe's source of fresh provisions; at New York, Philadelphia, and many other parts of America, the King's ships are supplied with everything they need, and the enemy lives in the midst of peace and plenty. How, he asked, can any one claim we are one people with a common enemy? Could the other colonies conceive of the distress and wretchedness in New England's seaport towns, it would kindle a blaze of indignation through all America against England's 'Commissioned Pirates and Licensed Robbers.'[3] Greene's lament was

[1] *Letters of . . . Continental Congress* (Burnett, ed.), I, 153. There was a great jealousy of a New England army under a New England general. *Ibid.*, 130. *Greene Papers* (W.L.C.L.), Greene to Ward, October 16, 1775.

[2] N.H. Hist. Soc., *Papers*, IX, 446; J. Boucher, *Reminiscences* . . . 132–33, 134.

[3] *Greene Papers* (W.L.C.L.), Greene to Ward, October 23, 1775.

a common one, always loudest from those actually suffering the ills of war, and often heard without emotion by those enjoying a period of peace.

Nor were State jealousies the only menace to unity, for the several sections understood each other as little. In New England, that 'chosen company of men,' picked out, as they piously believed, 'by a strange contrivance of God' to be the sifted wheat for planting an ideal commonwealth, hardly realized that they had done much of the sifting themselves by their bigoted opposition to the immigration of men with a different faith. Harshness of climate, barrenness of soil, a commerce offering only ordinary gains, and following lines of trade to the West Indies, Europe, and Canada, helped also to keep out the stranger and to isolate them from the other colonies.[1] For these reasons the people of New England were, as John Adams complacently wrote, 'of purer English blood, less mixed with Scotch, Irish, Dutch, French, Swedish, etc. than any other,' and, he went on ruminating, 'descended from Englishmen who left Europe in purer times than the present.' And, he explained, this was the reason why they were 'less tainted with corruption' than those they left behind, and why their institutions for the support of religion, morals, and decency excelled others. Leaving aside the debatable purity and excellence, New England's geographical and racial unity had produced dissimilar interests, habits, manners, morals, and speech almost sufficient to form a distinct nation.[2] If God had not provided in

[1] Morse, *Federalist Party in Massachusetts*, 5, 6, 7.

[2] *Letters of . . . Continental Congress* (Burnett, ed.), I, 259.

it 'a refuge for many' whom He meant to 'save out of the general calamities,' at least He had created 'a dissimilitude in character' enough to cause John Adams to dread the consequences,[1] and to make many expect the formation of at least two republics in America.[2] Jonathan Boucher pleaded with the Southern deputies in Congress to keep out of a 'mad Republic of mad Independents,' where in a few years all the Southern colonies would be seized upon by the more enterprising and restless fellow colonists of the North.[3]

Northern and Southern delegates in Congress clashed repeatedly on the subject of slavery and on the use of negroes in the war.[4] They pulled and tugged to get the location of Congress farther North or farther South.[5] The 'flour colonies' were jealous of the 'rice colonies' whenever the issue of commercial restriction arose. The rival members descended to personal abuse as they tried to fix the blame upon one section or the other for the failure of a campaign.[6] Epithets flew back and forth between the sections. The Southern party sneered at the 'Yankee,' and the New-Englanders retorted with 'Buckskin.' Jonathan Boucher, of Virginia, would as soon expect to see the greatest contrarieties in

[1] *Letters of ... Continental Congress* (Burnett, ed.), I, 260.

[2] *Ibid.*, 125. [3] J. Boucher, *Reminiscences ...*, 132–33.

[4] *Letters of ... Continental Congress* (Burnett, ed.), I, 207.

[5] *Ibid.*, 113.

[6] *Ibid.*, 85–87, II, 46. Pennsylvanians and Marylanders complained that their soldiers were uselessly sacrificed at Fort Washington because New-Englanders wanted an untenable position held. Graydon, *Memoirs*, 185.

Nature to meet in harmony and the wolf and the lamb to feed together, as Virginians to form a cordial union with the saints of New England.[1] John Adams complained that his section had to contend daily with 'the monarchical superstitions and aristocratical domination of nine other colonies.' 'The Southerners,' he found, imbibed with their mothers' milk 'higher notions of themselves' and ideas of a distinction between themselves and 'common people.'[2] Before the war was half over, Samuel Adams was reported as finding it clearer every day that the 'two empires,' Eastern and Southern, must eventually separate.[3] Vergennes hoped for several confederacies in America, not one.[4] Even after the war was over, the North and the South argued for generations as to whether Samuel Adams or Patrick Henry should have the honorable reputation of being the instigator of the Revolution.

Both the provincial and sectional jealousies stood out plain as a pikestaff in Congress. Adams saw at its first meeting 'the art and address of ambassadors from a dozen belligerent powers of Europe.'[5] So little acquaintance had the delegates from various sections with each other that they could not spell nor pick up correctly by ear the members' names. Duché became Dushay, Dutche, or Durkee, and

[1] Thacher, *Military Journal*, 16; J. Boucher, *Reminiscences . . .*, 134.

[2] *Letters of . . . Continental Congress* (Burnett, ed.), I, 260. Southerners thought the pay of privates too high, that of officers too low. *Ibid.*, 259.

[3] *Canadian Archives*, 29B, 1912, p. 185 (Gerard to Vergennes).

[4] Doniol, *La Participation . . .*, III, 561; Circourt, III, 283–84.

[5] J. Adams, *Works*, II, 391.

Rutledge got into John Adams's diary as Lutridge.[1] Adams found few virtues in Southern members, and he thought Harrison of Virginia 'an indolent, luxurious, heavy gentleman,' 'another Sir John Falstaff' of whose 'vices or follies' he took no notice, for policy's sake, though Harrison's conversation was 'disgusting to every man of delicacy or decorum.'[2] John Dickinson and John Adams were at times not on speaking or bowing terms. Once, when passing near enough to touch elbows, Dickinson haughtily refused to speak or to lift his hat. From the first Adams did not like his 'hair, gait or action'[3] — 'a piddling Genius' he described him.

With provincial, sectional, and personal relations so strained, great care was taken to stir up no subject of unusually controversial character. Congress had to agree early to keep quiet upon all ecclesiastical disputes, to keep out of sight 'those points about which mankind will ever differ.'[4] Indeed, after all hope of burying the hatchet with England was gone, and when war was on, Hewes, of North Carolina, confessed to his friend Johnson that there was little unity in council, little reason and argument, nor even decency and respect in debate, but rather jealousy, ill-natured remarks, recriminations, and soured tempers.[5]

When, therefore, in the summer of 1775, John Adams pitied fifty or sixty men who had 'a constitu-

[1] S. Deane's *Letters* (N.Y. Hist Soc., *Collection*), I, 48; *Letters of . . . Continental Congress* (Burnett, ed.), I, 15, 75.

[2] *Ibid.*, 368, 394. [3] *Ibid.*, 176, 195, 198. [4] *Ibid.*, 155.

[5] *Journals of Continental Congress* (Ford, ed.), IV, 222 (March 21, 1776).

tion to form for a great empire . . . a country of 1500 miles in extent to fortify, millions to arm and train, a naval power to begin, an extensive commerce to regulate . . . Indians to negotiate with, a standing army of 27,000 men to raise, pay, victual and officer,' he only half summed up the reasons for sympathy.[1] Congress, with none of the divinity which doth hedge about a king, had to act in all these matters through States whose rulers were in the midst of a nightmare of liberty, and whose people were dominated by individualistic traditions beyond the understanding of our present generation.

With all these forces and passions driving the colonies apart, what did bring them at last into a union which, as Franklin said with sarcasm, even the Six Nations of ignorant savages had accomplished earlier?[2] The answer is not simple. With all their differences, they did have common political institutions. The early colonial differences in forms of government had faded out. During years of struggle between royal executives and popular assemblies, the governor and his council were gradually shorn of their powers. The Southern type of government thereupon grew more like that of New England. Furthermore, the English language came to dominate, and newspapers, set up in the larger cities, carrying the news from colony to colony, and giving them common thoughts to think, took away isolation, softened prejudice. Better roads also bound the colonies together and created a new

[1] *Familiar Letters of J. Adams*, 85 (July 24, 1775).

[2] Franklin, *Writings* (Smyth, ed.), IV, 41, 70–71.

sense of solidarity. Occasional common efforts in repelling the Indian and French attacks, especially in the last French wars, had made clear the value of unity.

In the early months of the war, newspapers urged unity, pointing out that the Greek states fell before Philip of Macedon, because they contended for freedom separately; that for the same reason the states of Spain were subdued by the Carthaginians.[1] Plans of colonial union had long been in the leaders' minds.[2] Common political theories had caused the majority of colonists from New Hampshire to Georgia to view with like repugnance the British attempts at Colonial regulation. Perhaps the greatest force of all was the distance of the colonies from Europe and their manifest common destiny. Pride in America and intuitions of its manifest destiny were ruling passions in the American breast. Most of the 'heroes of '76,' and many of their contemporaries, not so heroic, would have agreed with Duché, the chaplain of Congress, that America was 'a vineyard planted by the Lord's right hand,' that He 'cast out the heathen and planted it.' They had come to this 'continent teeming with all the bounties of existence,' believing 'a garden of Eden' was before them, a 'desolate wilderness' behind, and that the first colonists had brought with them 'the charter of temporal freedom and the records of eternal truth.'[3]

[1] *Boston Evening Post,* July 4, 1774.

[2] *American Political Science Review,* August, 1914. (Article on Franklin's plans, by L. K. Matthews.)

[3] Duché, *The American Vine,* 17, 18. (Sermon, Philadephia, 1775.) Duché later became a Loyalist.

Such was America's faith and its vision. By such forces particularism was in part overcome, and 'thirteen clocks were made to strike together — a perfection of mechanism which no artist,' declared John Adams, 'had ever before effected.' [1]

Moreover, there were the thousand minor things, like the threads that bound Gulliver, no one of them significant by itself, but in the aggregate strong potential ties presaging future union. Throughout the eighteenth century there was a steady increase of intercolonial trade. Rice was shipped to the North; flour and iron were sent back in payment. New England took its breadstuffs from the Middle States, and in return sent rum, molasses, cattle, wool, and shoes. The raw materials of one colony were manufactured in another.[2] Growing business led to more correspondence, and under Benjamin Franklin's administration of the post-office the service improved, knitting the colonies ever closer.[3] Professional classes, lawyers, doctors, found ever-increasing occasions for exchanging letters. Scientific men did likewise, and so great was the correspondence among astronomers about the transit of Venus (1769) that its observation became a real coöperative scientific enterprise. Bartram, the botanist, traveled and observed in nearly every colony, and numbered his friends in them all. Business coöperation grew; men of different colonies

[1] J. Adams, *Works*, x, 283.

[2] M. Kraus, *Intercolonial Aspects of American Culture on the Eve of the Revolution*, 25–28, 32.

[3] W. E. Rich, *History of United States Post Office*, 29–35.

became common owners of ships, and united in speculations in Western lands as in the Indiana and the Vandalia Companies.[1] Planters corresponded with others in neighboring provinces as to all agricultural problems — another link in making intercolonial interests.

Fraternal societies spread their membership from colony to colony.[2] The 'Marine Society,' to aid ship captains in hard luck, was found in every port, and traveling Masons found groups of 'brothers' in distant cities. The Society of the Sons of Saint George and the Adherents of Saint Patrick were intercolonial groups which sought to preserve the racial bonds of the Old World. Abolition societies and other humanitarian unions cut across provincial lines. The alumni of the better institutions of learning, scattered widely throughout the English colonies, were united in college allegiance, ready to renew the ties of undergraduate days.[3]

For the meetings of all these groups, the ubiquitous taverns and clubs, centers of social life, were the focal points. There was no drouthy Amendment to keep an honest citizen from drinking stoutly, the readiest way for a wayfarer to recommend himself. The newspapers, on file from distant provinces, helped the formation of common views. Indeed, the growth of the press multiplying books as well as newspapers was a great force for union. Some gazettes went out to every colony, and school

[1] M. Kraus, *Intercolonial Aspects of American Culture on the Eve of the Revolution*, 33.

[2] *Ibid.*, 55. [3] *Ibid.*, 112–20.

books, like the universal New England Primer, standardized culture by purveying a common mental food.[1] Even the sports brought people together from distant points. The 'sport of kings,' especially, brought famous race-horses and their owners across colonial boundaries — a Narragansett pacer, perhaps, meeting a blooded horse from the Old Dominion.[2] The sale of lottery tickets, to build a college, a road, a church steeple, extended far beyond colonial lines. All this intercourse grew with the century, and counted when the need came for union.

Even the family ties among leaders in the several provinces had an influence. Intermarriage between the New York De Lanceys and the Pennsylvania Allens, the Lawrences and the Morrises, the Apthorps and the Hazards, became ties of blood and spirit.[3] Such spiritual tendrils grew even in England where would-be American lawyers from all parts of America met in the London Inns of Court. So, too, in Edinburgh, nursery of American medicine, congregated medical students from the trans-Atlantic colonies. When they returned, they formed societies for the dissemination of medical knowledge and intercolonial organizations against the ravages of smallpox and 'the sore throat distemper,' diphtheria. Such associations sought to curb the quack with his 'Imperial Golden Drops' and his 'pokeweed cure' for cancer. In spite of them the charlatan's medicines like 'tar-water' were famed from

[1] M. Kraus, *Intercolonial Aspects of American Culture on the Eve of the Revolution*, 48, 91–103.

[2] *Ibid.*, 54. [3] *Ibid.*, 42–43.

New Hampshire to Georgia.[1] There were, also, continental societies for encouragement of pure science, of which the American Philosophical Society was the first. Finally lecturers in that field passed from colony to colony.

The antagonism of certain religious sects has been indicated, but that was offset in part by the intercolonial activities of some churches, while religious books aided this welding process. Interprovincial efforts to strengthen the Anglican Church were met by the Presbyterians forming a Synod uniting distant congregations. The traveling Quaker found hospitality among his brethren anywhere in America.[2] The Great Awakening sent a common religious thrill through all the colonies, and though it separated the 'New Lights' from the 'Old Lights,' the intercolonial influence was unifying. With the widespread sentiment of solidarity grew toleration and religious liberty.[3] Bringing to fruition all these minor tendencies were the congresses, at Albany, 1754, the Stamp Act Congress, 1765, the Continental Congress, 1774. Members of each successive gathering found old acquaintances, and advanced — slowly enough, as we know — to better understandings.

Then there was the logic of events, the acts of the British Government, the reaction in Congress, the untoward things that happened in various colonies. Day by day the colonists nursed their wrath to keep

[1] M. Kraus, *Intercolonial Aspects of American Culture on the Eve of the Revolution*, 154, 161.

[2] *Ibid.*, 65, 73, 85. [3] *Ibid.*, 89.

it warm. The newspapers exploited every new 'outrage,' as it seemed in their eyes, when sloops, smuggling ammunition to the needy Patriot armies, were run down and sunk by British cruisers.[1] Indeed, all of King George's ships, seeking to suppress rebellion by raiding American commerce, became 'pirates' in the public press. 'That infamous old piratical scoundrel, John Goodrich,' whose ten-gun sloop was most successful in that work, aroused with each new capture new and more intense feeling. The American ships which contended with 'the cowardly scoundrels' were manned by 'our brave men' or 'brave little companies,' and their successes were always 'the will of God.'[2] Thus, as a Loyalist wrote, there was 'an abundance of political puffs and lies told to amuse the public.'[3] Whether in good faith or with the aim of encouraging the Americans, there were circulated many fabrications, rumors, and exaggerated reports. It was bruited about that Lord North had fled for his life to France, that Wilkes, Burke, Arthur Lee, heading an armed multitude in London, had destroyed Parliament House. British soldiers in Boston were led to believe that there was a New England army of one hundred thousand men. Writers of letters saw ten men in buckram where there was only one in Lincoln green.

Besides this often unconscious propaganda by the newspapers or writers of letters, the Conti-

[1] *Boston Gazette*, April 22, 1776.
[2] *New England Chronicle*, May 23, 1776.
[3] *Journal of N. Cresswell*, 173.

nental Congress was not blind to the value of spurring on public feeling. Propaganda and clever political management in the hands of masters like Patrick Henry and Samuel Adams had exercised no mean part in bringing the colonies to the verge of rebellion, and Congress early appointed a committee to collect 'a Narrative of the Violences and Depradations, the Rapine and Plunder,' fortified with evidence and affidavits as to the number and value of buildings destroyed, vessels seized, cattle and sheep plundered, a 'true story,' which should not omit the 'Butcheries' or 'robberies' or 'Piracies' of the enemy.[1] It was proposed to win over the Hessians with resolutions of Congress, translated into German and floated over the water into the hands of their sentinels. A little tobacco would increase the allurement of the bait.[2]

Another method of propaganda was used when Congress sent two 'Ministers of the Gospel' to the western parts of North Carolina to combat hostility to 'Patriot' measures.[3] Congress set fast and thanks-

[1] *Letters of . . . Continental Congress* (Burnett, ed.), I, 235, 237, 238. It was for the information of all the colonies, and 'Friends in England, in all Europe, and all posterity.' The members of the committee were John Adams, Wythe, and Deane. There were no results, because, doubtless, Congress was too busy with other pressing matters. John Adams was on ninety committees; *Journals of the Continental Congress* (Ford, ed.), VII, 276–79.

[2] *Letters of . . . Continental Congress* (Burnett, ed.), II, 59, 63.

[3] *Letters of . . . Continental Congress* (Burnett, ed.), I, 300. Congress sometimes forgot the history even of recent times, for on the committee sent to the uplands of North Carolina to urge them to join the Patriot cause were Richard Caswell, who had commanded the troops at Alamance, M. Moore, who had judged several of the Regulators guilty of treason, and condemned them to death, and the Reverend Patillo, who had preached against their cause. The upland Scots

giving days, not alone as acts of piety, but as aids to propaganda when sedition might flow from the pulpit and the clergy might assure their people that God would 'sweep away the ministerial tools.' General election day, 'Boston Massacre' day, and militia mustering day served the same purpose. The clergy did much recruiting, finding a good text in the words, 'Cursed be he that keepeth back his sword from blood.' They urged their people not to 'sink in slavery' to the English, 'more cruel than sea monsters toward their young.'[1]

Sometimes the Congress ordered matters favorable to their cause to be published in the papers, and, to aid propaganda with the French of Canada, the expenses of a French printer were ordered paid to remove his 'family and types' to Montreal, there to set up a 'free press.'[2] Congress recommended, January 2, 1776, to all colonial assemblies and conventions to distribute liberally among the people the proceedings of Congress, the speeches in Parliament of the great supporters of the American cause, and all other pamphlets and papers as tended to elucidate the merits of the Patriot stand.[3] This exhortation was carried out largely through the agency of newspapers.

Newspapers did not suffice, and from committees,

could not forget these things. See *North Carolina Colonial Records*, x, 266.

[1] A. M. Baldwin, *The New England Clergy and the American Revolution*, 122–26.

[2] *Letters of . . . Continental Congress* (Burnett, ed.), I, 340, 365. See Bates, *Fighting the Revolution with Printer's Ink*, in New Haven Col. Hist. Soc., *Papers*, IX, 149–50.

[3] *Journals of Congress* (Ford, ed.), IV, 19.

provincial congresses, and conventions came broadsides denouncing the 'enemies of the rights of mankind,' containing poems and sermons on the 'barbarous Redcoats.' Songs about the 'British butchers' were spread in this way. Men were exhorted to collect all proper evidence of the 'depredations committed by the ministerial army.' Other broadsides pleaded with men to come forth and defend 'their wives, their little ones, and their liberties' against the 'unrelenting tyrants of Britain,' who were 'spreading the calamities of fire, sword and famine through the land.' Printers furnished blanks which volunteers could subscribe, urged the militia to be ready, and exhorted them to provide firearms, shirts, coats, blankets, every need of a soldier. Sometimes the inflaming posters were anachronistic, and charged men to bring their helmets, bucklers, and their spears. Legislatures issued broadsides, inciting all Patriots to detect and defeat 'all conspiracies against the liberties of America,' and to confine in the jails all the 'notoriously disaffected,' where they could not partake 'in the exalted privileges of freemen.'

The clergy were implored to meet with their people and pray to God for success,[1] and they replied with a fervor that produced 'wonderful success,' thundering and lightning every sabbath.[2] One at least preached with a gun in his pulpit and a powder-horn suspended about his neck. They harangued

[1] Massachusetts Broadsides, Mass. Hist. Soc., *Collections*, 1775, *passim*. Also collection of broadsides in William L. Clements Library.

[2] *Familiar Letters of J. Adams*, 65, 76, 90.

especially against the Anglican doctrine of non-resistance, the 'courtly doctrine of passive obedience.' To accept it was 'high treason against God.' Disobedience to Congress was the real sin. Fighting England for liberty and independence was likened to the fight against flesh and sin, which was expected even of those 'redeemed by the blood of Christ.'[1] The pulpit was then a direct and effectual way of reaching the masses, and the dissenting clergy had a great part in arousing the 'fierce spirit of liberty' which made men ready to fight.

In all this work of arousing the spirit of revolt the British officers played into the hands of the Patriot leaders, furnishing new 'causes of increasing enmity, and new reasons for wishing an eternal separation.'[2] Besides the actual battles of Lexington, Concord, and Bunker Hill, into which the British military forces were driven by the logic of events, were the accidents, as in the burning of Charlestown or the excesses, as when Captain Mowatt burned, October 18, 1775, one hundred and fifty houses, churches, and public buildings at Falmouth, a defenseless town. Such a wanton act would stir the embers of any revolutionary spirit, and within a week the printers were flooding the countryside with broadsides, blowing the deed in every eye. It mattered not whether the British Government approved; its agents had done what could not be recalled.[3]

[1] *American Historical Review*, XIX, 57–58. (Van Tyne article.)

[2] Franklin to Quincy. *Letters of . . . Continental Congress* (Burnett, ed.), I, 422.

[3] He had exceeded his instructions and was reprimanded by the British Government. Yet Lord George Germain wrote, 'I am to sup-

It became 'a flaming argument' for Independence.

Lord Dunmore was provocative and ineffective in Virginia; Governor Martin the same in North Carolina. Everywhere George III's agents were adding fuel to the conflagration his own stern sense of duty had enkindled. His own proclamation against 'traiterous correspondence' with rebellious subjects, and later the bill forbidding all trade and intercourse with America, and the news of his efforts to hire 'barbarous Russians' and 'cruel Germans' to fight his own people — all these natural and logical efforts to quell rebellion were of the greatest service to the radicals in and out of Congress. All of their most extravagant charges seemed proved up to the hilt.

pose Admiral Graves had good reasons for the step he took . . . and that he did not proceed to that extremity without an absolute refusal [of the town] to comply with those requisitions' in his orders from the Admiralty. See *Germain Papers, Military Despatched,* January 5, 1776.

CHAPTER XVI

THE SPIRIT OF INDEPENDENCE MARCHES ON

MEANWHILE, there had been loosed, January, 1776, a pamphlet which pierced 'a hundred thousand hearts,' aiding immensely the work of conversion. Thomas Paine's pamphlet, 'Common Sense,' did 'wonders, and worked miracles, made Tories Whigs and washed Blackamores white.'[1] Everybody read it, even the Germans for whom a translation was issued within two weeks. A hundred thousand copies were soon passing from hand to hand, the printer getting all the profits and Paine obliged to buy the few copies he gave to his friends. Some denounced it as 'artful, insidious, and pernicious' addressed to the passions of the mob.[2] 'One of the vilest things that was ever published to the world,' an English traveler declared it, full of lies, calumnies, and treason — republican and subversive of kingly government.[3] Even John Adams, glad of any help in his Independence campaign, found its phrases 'suitable for an immigrant from Newgate.' It had much weight with the masses, he granted, but vanity compelled him to add that there was not a fact nor a reason for Independence in it but had been urged in Congress for nine months before — by

[1] *Pennsylvania Evening Post*, February 13, 1776.

[2] *The True Interest of America* . . . (J. Humphreys, printer), p. v.

[3] *Journal of N. Cresswell*, 136.

John Adams, of course.[1] Landon Carter, of Virginia, a cautious patriot, always wondered 'at the prodigious, rash Praise' given to that 'most nonsensical of all Pamphlets, "Common Sense."' It was 'just sentiment,' and popular only 'because of the latent desire of many to be as arbitrary as possible.'[2] Hewes, of North Carolina, found it a 'curiosity,' while George Washington accepted it as 'sound doctrine,' 'unanswerable reasoning.'[3]

In England the literary exquisite, Horace Walpole, wrote Paine down 'another corsair,' his style 'so coarse that you would think that he means to degrade the language as much as the government.'[4] Doubtless it was shallow, scurrilous in parts, rude in its plans for new governments, but it was clear, rapid, living, full of specious phrases which made a superficial reader catch his breath with sudden conviction. Paine knew how to elaborate proof of what a deeper man would assume not to need proving. 'Common Sense,' in spite of rhetoric which offends good taste, and logic which is often puerile, did compel the reason and carry conviction. It was Franklin who had induced Paine to come to America, and he surpassed his patron in the art of swaying the human mind. Men have held that his pamphlet was as effective in uniting Americans for Independence as Foxe's 'Book of Martyrs' was in knitting Englishmen together to repel a Spanish invasion.

[1] *Letters of . . . Continental Congress* (Burnett, ed.), I, 345. J. Adams, *Works*, II, 509.

[2] *William and Mary College Quarterly*, XVIII, 43, 44, XVI, 152.

[3] Washington, *Writings* (Ford, ed.), III, 396.

[4] Walpole, *Letters* (Toynbee, ed.), XIV, 405.

With Paine 'right was forever on the scaffold,' wrong 'forever on the throne.' Whether as grocer, Grub Street poet, usher, or excise officer, he was always fighting the battles of the victims of superstition, or of despotic power, of the slave, even of a king if he were persecuted as was Louis XVI. Though he displeased Danton by trying to make revolutions with rosewater, yet during his life he numbered among his friends or companions Goldsmith, Jefferson, Robespierre, Marat, and Danton himself, while men like Washington, Franklin, Fulton, Vergennes, Sieyès, Lafayette, Burke, and Erskine took a warm interest in him at one time or another during his eventful life.

On Paine's arrival in America (1775), it took him only a few months to penetrate the American mind and to perceive what prejudices restrained many from the idea of an independent America. In 'Common Sense' he struck directly and without apology at the sanctity of kingship, the reverence for the British Constitution, and the glories of imperialism. On these ruins he erected a monument to colonial vanity, appealing to the already nascent idea of American manifest destiny.

As to the King, Paine quickly saw that many colonists, though discontented with British rule, had a pious conviction of the monarch's divine right. To them the Bible was the word of God, and in it they read, 'Curse not the king, no, not in thy thought.' Preachers who defended the Crown reminded them that the King's wrath is 'as the roaring of a lion,' his favor 'as the dew upon the grass.' A simple creed, easier to comprehend than arguments in support of democracy, was to say, 'I am bound by God's law to honor the King.' [1] The quibble that an oppressive ruler was a tyrant, and not a king, was unconvincing, for that went little beyond the old Sanskrit law book which said three thousand years before, 'The king who is virtuous is a part of the Gods. He who is otherwise is part of the demons.' [2] Samuel Langdon (1775), in an election sermon, met divine right squarely with counter-quotations from the Scriptures, but he preserved the dignity of a preacher and his words went little farther than his congregation. [3]

Until very recent years, moreover, the King had held a warm place in American hearts. Even Franklin seemed to agree with the mood of Horace Walpole when he admitted

> ''tis the sweetest of earthly things,
> To live with princes and to talk with kings.' [4]

For he joyfully wrote his son (1772) that the King 'has lately been heard to speak of me with great regard,' and George III at that time was in his mind the 'best of kings,' a 'wise and good prince.' Indeed, even after the Revolution he was a bit vain that he had literally 'stood before kings' — five of them —

[1] Charles Lee wrote, nevertheless, that passive obedience was nonsense; that only a head that had begun to 'itch for a mitre' would believe in it. Most Americans, he declared, believed it was silly to regard as rebellion the Civil War that brought Charles I to book. *Strictures on a Pamphlet*, etc. (1774).

[2] Lord Ronaldshay, *India, A Bird's-Eye View*, 137.

[3] *American Historical Review*, XIX, 62, 63.

[4] H. Walpole, *Letters* (Toynbee, ed.), XI, 186.

and even dined with one. He urged his friends (1770) to 'hold fast our loyalty to our King, who has the best disposition toward us.' [1] Later, he began to suspect that the measures adverse to colonial interests were 'very much the King's own,' but Henry Laurens thought the King 'under bad councillors.' Warren, also, preferred to believe that 'The royal ear, far distant from this western world, has been assaulted by the tongue of slander, and, villains, traitorous alike to King and country, have prevailed upon a gracious prince to clothe his countenance with wrath.' [2] Henry Laurens, even as he was signing the Association, agreeing to bear arms against the King's forces, still thought him 'misinformed, ill-advised' by the 'machinations of a few wicked men,' and had no wish to 'remove him from his throne, the crown from his head or the sceptre from his hand.' [3] Even on the floor of Independence Hall, Duché, the chaplain of Congress, prayed (July 7, 1775) for 'our dread sovereign Lord, King George,' and asked Heaven to remove all who 'seek to change his government into oppression.' It was an 'envious cloud of false witnesses' that surrounded his throne and intercepted 'the sunshine of his favor.' The 'God of the armies of Heaven' was implored to teach George III that his highest temporal glory must consist in preserving a free people their undoubted birth-right.' [4] Against all such 'nonsense,' as Paine

[1] W. C. Bruce, *B. Franklin*, 165.
[2] Niles, *Principles and Acts* (ed. 1876), 113, March 5, 1775.
[3] Wallace, *H. Laurens*, 173, 208, 209.
[4] Duché (sermon, 1775), *The Duty of Standing Fast*, etc., I, ii, 17.

thought it, and the 'divine right' idea, with its consequent 'submission doctrine' — which kept many good souls out of the rebel ranks — 'Common Sense' leveled its arrows.

Kingship, Paine wrote, is 'the most prosperous invention the devil ever set on foot for the promotion of idolatry.' Monarchy and hereditary succession, he declared, had laid the world in blood and ashes. Indeed, he wrote, with a cunning appeal to Puritan bigotry, 'Monarchy is the Popery of Government.' Only by means of history 'stuffed with fables' had the hereditary right of kings been 'crammed down the throats of the vulgar.' Original sin and hereditary succession were parallels. William the Conqueror, 'a French bastard,' landing in England with 'an armed banditti,' was a very proper ancestor for the 'hardened, sullen tempered Pharaoh of England.' A king was usually only the 'principal ruffian of some restless gang,' and one honest man was worth 'all the crowned ruffians' of all time. 'Where is the King of America?' 'He reigns above, and does not make havoc of mankind like the Royal Brute of Great Britain. The law is king; there ought to be no other.'[1]

It was the vigor and directness of Paine's attack that got the results, for kingship had been attacked before by English radicals. Milton had mourned that Englishmen should 'fall back, or rather creep back . . . to their once abjured and detested thraldom of kingship,' and he asked, 'Where is this Goodly Tower of a Commonwealth, which the

[1] T. Paine, *Common Sense, passim.*

English boasted they would build to overshadow Kings?'[1] It was a far cry from this back to Francis Bacon's 'A king is a mortal God on earth, unto whom the living God hath lent his name.'

As early as 1750, American writers, like Jonathan Mayhew, had begun to discuss kingship as if the whole question of its rightful existence was a problematical one.[2] Perhaps no American was predisposed to accept the dictum that kings were 'as absolute as Adam over his creatures.' Their very charters caused them to favor Locke's idea that kings had a compact with their people. All ideas, indeed, that would rescue them from their political troubles adhered to the colonial mind, while the opposing ideas glided off. Not content with a rule of kings and priests, they took up easily a philosophy which limited their power or threw it off altogether.

By December 1, 1774, a Whig ventured to write in 'Rivington's Gazette' that a good king was a miracle, that the history of them was 'nothing but the history of the folly and depravity of human nature.' Six months later the 'Essex Gazette, was republishing in large type the London 'Crisis' — burned by the common hangman there — which asserted that 'all kings have a divine right to be devils,' as was shown by George III 'tearing up the constitution by the roots.'[3] About that time Charles Lee asserted that ninety-nine out of every hundred Americans thought of Charles I as an 'execrable tyrant,' meeting no harder fate than he de-

[1] Masson, *Life of Milton*, v, 647. [2] J. Mayhew, *Sermon*, 1750.
[3] *Essex Gazette*, May 18, June 6, June 19, 1775.

served, and that his two sons ought to have met the same end.[1] The conviction grew, therefore, that 'as the rivers hasten to mingle their waters with the sea so monarchies lose themselves in despotic power.'[2] Nevertheless, as late as March 23, 1776, R. H. Lee failed to get an admission, in a resolution of Congress, that the King, not the Ministry, was the author of America's misery.[3]

After Paine's pamphlet the tide turned powerfully against kingship. Not the King, but the people were 'the Lord's anointed.' Subjects could claim as intimate relations with God as could kings. There was no solemn conclave to hush the rising spirit of freedom, with the dictum, 'Kings derive not their power from the people but from God.' Representatives in the Massachusetts Provincial Council were instructed that George III was 'the worst of tyrants'; that loyalty to him 'is now *treason* to our country.' Pennsylvania and Maryland freed their governments 'from that worst of plagues the King's Evil.'[4] By June 26, 1776, George had become 'a full-blooded Nero.'[5] He was shortly a 'brutish tyrant,' a 'frantic potentate in breeches,' as unfitted to rule 'as Phaeton to drive the chariot of the sun.'[6] Cain, Nimrod, Ahab, Judas, Herod, Attila, and the Duke of Alva were soon the only prototypes used in describing George III, who, perhaps, possessed

[1] Charles Lee, *Strictures on a Pamphlet*, etc.
[2] . . . *Taxation no Tyranny . . . refuted* (1775).
[3] *Letters of . . . Congress* (Burnett, ed.), I, 404.
[4] *New England Chronicle*, June 20, 1776, May 30, 1776.
[5] *Connecticut Journal*, June 26, 1776.
[6] Moore, *Diary*, I, 436, 453.

their characteristics least of any contemporary monarch. Paine, and the rising tide of war feeling, had overwhelmed kingship in colonial Whig minds.

'Common Sense' attacked the venerated British Constitution with the same slashing weapons. It was good enough for the 'dark and slavish times' for which it was erected. As for its lauded checks and balances — nonsense! The House of Commons is merely a clog on the King, not a check. The British governmental contrivance merely slows up tyranny, but it comes at last. The British locked the door against absolute monarchy, and then like fools gave the King the key. The matter is only befogged. The Constitution is so complex that the nation may suffer for years without being able to discover where the fault lies. In absolute monarchy one knows at least *who* makes the people suffer. It is the Constitution of the English people, not the constitution of government which prevents oppression equal to that of the Turks. Paine was destitute enough of property and radical enough to think any government, 'like dress, the badge of lost innocence.' Government, any government in fact, was a 'necessary evil.' There was less worship of the British Constitution among the American masses, at least, after they or their leaders had read Paine's pamphlet.

There remained still another 'delusion,' as Paine thought it, which held men back from secession. Pride in the glory of the British Empire, the belief that America was protected by British power; even a sense of gratitude to the 'parent' country made many hum and haw and boggle. As to the Empire, united America and England, defying the world, Paine asked virtuously if it was not better to have commerce and friendship with the world? Was it not better for America to have Peace and Plenty sit smiling on her brow? British protection was a delusion. But for England's quarrels with France and Spain, America would not have needed protection. England would have defended Turkey for the same motives as she defended her colonies. Indeed, colonial trade was actually injured by the connection, because if England got into war the trade of America was ruined by the fact of her being part of the Empire. As to the colonists' duty to the parent country — nonsense! Europe, not England, was the parent country of America.

Finally Paine appealed to American vanity. He carried their imaginations forward to that time when the new continent would be the glory of the earth. The Old World was overrun with oppression; America must prepare an asylum for mankind. The 'sun never shone on a cause of greater worth'; all posterity to the end of time was virtually involved. And, if their pride in America did not make them desire Independence, he would remind them of their wrongs. Saying that he did not exhibit horror for the purpose of provoking revenge, he went on to array every *wrong*, real or fancied, which America had suffered — their prayers rejected with disdain, men and women driven from home, cities burned, throats cut, fathers and brothers killed, even the Indians and negroes stirred up against them. Only one conclusion could be drawn. 'The blood of the slain, the weeping voice of nature cries, 'tis time to part.'

A beautifully written copy of this pamphlet was made by some one and sent to the French Government in whose archives, among the *Mémoires et Documents*, it lies to-day.[1] Was it read, as it might have been, by Louis XVI, and if so what did he think as he read Paine's tribute to kings, whose palaces were 'built on the ruins of the bowers of Paradise'?[2]

Paine's arguments were chiefly valuable as food for the masses. The deeper minds, the more conscientious characters, had passed through a much more protracted period of conversion. For them there had been the tedious evolution of America's political theory, the growth of an American conception of the proper constitutional relation of the colonies to Parliament and to the King. When that reached a stage where American leaders of political thought would acknowledge no other connection with England than that they had a common king, the political bond would easily break. There would then remain only to reach the conviction that the King was tyrannical, and guilty of all the ills which war had brought upon the colonies. The story of the political theory, though it repeats some facts already told, is necessary at this point, in order that

[1] *Archives des Affaires Étrangères, France,* 463, F 161–81.

[2] Yet consistency had nothing to do with the decisions of the French Government. While France was entering into an alliance with the liberty-loving Americans, the French court was ordering Raynal's *Histoire Philosophique* to be burned and the author banished from France. J. Droz, *Histoire du Règne de Louis XVI* (Paris, 1858), 200.

the success of the Independence campaign may be fully comprehended. It takes us back for the moment to 1764.

The Sugar Act had raised in colonial minds questions to which they had given little thought. Assemblies had long been pitted against governors, but the rights of Assemblies in respect to Parliament was a question little mooted heretofore. 'The gentle current of tranquillity' that had so long 'run with peace through all the British states' seemed 'suddenly turned out of its true course into unusual and winding channels.'[1] The nature of the British Constitution became suddenly a matter of great moment.[2] Discovering that the colonies had interests distinct from those of England, colonial statesmen began to ask whether Parliament, whose members understood only the wants of the realm, should be at the same time party and judge of the interest of remote parts of the Empire. James Otis made some cogent comments upon that question, but when in 1765 violent means had rendered void an Act of Parliament, the responsible managers of colonial politics sought justification in a theory of the Constitution which would prove the Stamp Act unrighteous, beyond the powers of Parliament. This was done by assuming that an eighteenth-century principle of the Constitution was an ancient tradition of British liberty. No Englishman, the colonists declared, could be legally taxed except by his

[1] S. Hopkins, *Rights of Colonists Examined*, 22.

[2] The three stages in the constitutional controversy are ably stated in R. G. Adams, *Political Ideas of American Revolution*, 69–85. Also in Carl Becker, *Declaration of Independence*, chap. III.

consent through his representatives, and American British subjects, not having representatives at Westminster, could not be taxed by the Parliament there. When told that they were virtually represented, they rejected the idea. Their only real representation was in their colonial legislatures. 'There was not that intimate and inseparable relation between the electors of Great Britain and the inhabitants of the colonies which must inevitably involve both in the same taxation.' Acts oppressive and injurious to Americans in an extreme degree might become popular in England.[1] But, the colonists hastened to say, we do not wish to have representatives in Parliament, overwhelmed by numbers as we should be. That representation would but justify taxation without in any way preventing it. No, we can allow taxation only by our own colonial legislatures. Yet Parliament had for generations laid trade duties. Was its customary action to be denied? Well! no; Parliament might lay 'external' taxes, but 'internal' never! The Stamp Act Congress implied such a distinction, and this was the stage at which colonial argument had arrived when the Act was repealed.

Two years later, they were taken at their word by that brilliant trifler, Charles Townshend. He gave America its 'external' taxes, though he held that any such distinction from 'internal' taxes was 'perfect nonsense.' With the new taxes came 'commissioners' and troops to back them. Customs duties were actually collected, and a new retreat for stra-

[1] Daniel Dulany. *Consideration on the Propriety* . . . (1765), 1–10.

tegic reasons became imperative. If the truth must be told, American leaders now declared, Parliament could not constitutionally take the money out of their pockets by any kind of tax whatever. At once they were asked, 'Why had they for a hundred years permitted Parliament to lay duties through laws regulating trade?' John Dickinson, the Philadelphia lawyer, was equal even to that dialectic emergency. It was all a matter of the intention of Parliament. Did they pass such laws to collect revenues or to regulate trade?[1] The Townshend Act clearly 'intended' revenues. But might not later laws be more difficult to determine? Dickinson hoped that Americans, 'to their latest existence,' would never want understanding sufficient to discover the intentions of those who ruled over them. They alone, like all states, have the right 'of judging when their privileges are invaded.' But the colonists discovered taxation was not the only way of invading their privileges. In 1768, their assemblies were commanded in the king's name to rescind and disapprove of the Massachusetts Circular Letter.

Again, a New York Assembly was suspended by royal order, and the fear arose that all colonial self-government might in time be abolished. To meet that danger a new step was needed in building up the colonial theory of the British Constitution. The respective jurisdictions of Parliament and colonial legislatures must be stated. There must be less talk about the rights of British subjects and more emphasis placed on the rights of the colonists under

[1] John Dickinson, *Letters from a Farmer* (1768), Letter II.

'the law of God and nature.' Were they to be any more dependent on Great Britain than 'one free people could be on another'? Could they not be 'subordinate,' without being 'subject'? Their favorite political thinkers told them that the British Constitution was 'fixed,' founded on 'the immutable laws of nature.' There were many legislatures in the Empire, all limited by the British Constitution. Though, in the Empire, Parliament had some sort of supreme, superintending authority which no colonial Assembly could pretend, yet Parliament was bound to respect the 'natural right' of Americans to dispose of their own property or to enjoy any other essential natural right. Was Parliament or were colonial legislatures to determine what were 'essential natural rights'? There was the rub.

The pragmatic Benjamin Franklin cut that Gordian knot. Parliament has a power to make all laws for us, he said, or it has a power to make no laws for us. 'I think the arguments for the latter more numerous and weighty, than those of the former.' He was tired of such expressions as 'the supreme authority of Parliament' or 'the subordinacy of our Assemblies to the Parliament.' The truth was the parts of the Empire had equal rights and liberties, and were united only in having a common king.[1] All Parliamentary legislation had been pure usurpation. The colonial charters all proved that. James Wilson came to the same conclusions and added that Parliament's jurisdiction was limited by what was consistent with 'the principles of

[1] *Writings of B. Franklin* (Smyth, ed.), v, 115, 260.

liberty and with the happiness of the colonies.' The 'Commons of Great Britain have no dominion over their equals and fellow subjects in America.'[1] 'All men are by nature equal and free. No one has a right to any authority over another without his consent; all lawful government is founded on the consent of those subject to it.' That is the ultimate end of all government, and Parliament could not go beyond it. Natural Law, the British Constitution, and the decisions of British courts — all, Wilson declared, proved the colonies to be dependent on Great Britain only so far as they were loyal to its King.

But this advanced thinking was only in the minds of a few intellectuals until, in 1773, Parliament granted to the East India Company an intolerable monopoly in American markets. American resentment reached a climax when tea belonging to the India Company was spoiled in Boston Harbor. To punish Boston, the 'Intolerable Acts' were passed by Parliament and the representatives of the enraged colonists met in Philadelphia, September 5, 1774, only to find that they were of many minds. In order to get the approval of all to a proposed Declaration of Rights, they used phrases which would satisfy those who stressed natural law and also those who would build the foundation of their rights on their own idea of the British Constitution, or, perhaps, on colonial charters. In one of these three ways they were entitled to 'life, liberty, and property.' Their ancestors enjoyed them in England:

[1] James Wilson, *Works* (ed. 1804), III, 237–38.

by emigration they had not been forfeited. As to Parliament's power to regulate trade, the Declaration admitted the fact, avoided a denial of the right, but implied that hereafter, at least, both fact and right were matters needing colonial assent, yielded to-day, but perhaps denied to-morrow. Though a many-minded Congress could agree on nothing more candid, Drayton, of South Carolina, could go directly to the point. 'Any taxation or legislation by the British Parliament over America without her consent is no better than mere tyranny.' [1] It was but another step to Independence, an act morally and legally sanctioned by the theory that the British Empire was a confederation of free states united under a common king with whom the people of each state had originally contracted and from whom any group of people if badly treated was free to secede.

It was due to this theory that in the Declaration of Independence the Parliament with which the colonists had quarreled for a dozen years was never mentioned. Parliament had nothing to do with them. They had their own legislatures which, with the King, had done their political business. They mentioned neither Parliament nor the rights of British subjects, because they were appealing to the rights of man for justification. Once on a time these colonial people had of their own free will joined the British Empire, but their right had been violated and they would withdraw, as they entered, voluntarily. It was this political theory which prevailed

[1] R. W. Gibbes, *Doc. Hist.*, 29.

in Congress when the state of affairs in the colonies made possible final moves toward Independence. To this the Americans had progressed since their first denial of Parliament's right to tax. No wonder they were stigmatized as 'Proteus-like, perpetually changing their ground.' 'Had an angel descended from Heaven,' cried an English pamphleteer, 'with terms of accommodation, which offered less than independence, they would have driven him back with hostile scorn.'[1]

As a result of Paine's pamphlet, added to all the chance events, like the impolitic actions of the British Ministry or its agents, the organized propaganda of radical leaders, and the many personal motives and tendencies which enter into a determination of all great human dramas, the course of Congress in the early months of 1776 began to move inexorably toward Independence. The formal instructions which the members originally bore with them to the Quaker State House empowered them merely to 'restore harmony,' to accommodate or redress the 'unhappy differences' with Great Britain, to get a repeal of the offensive acts. Three delegations were to preserve and defend American rights and liberties, one to reëstablish them, one merely to advance the best good of the colonies, while three were bound by no special injunctions.[2]

Some delegations got new orders as time went on; others took a chance and ventured beyond the

[1] John Lind, *An Answer to the Declaration* . . . (1776), 117.

[2] Only Maryland and North Carolina at first, and Georgia and New Jersey later, specifically bound the State to abide by the resolutions of Congress. (Maryland forty-three times out of sixty-three refused.)

depths prescribed, but on the whole they were 'obsequious to the reins of the States,' with no will of their own, only representatives in 'a diplomatic assembly,' as John Adams said. On all important committees one member from each State was thought necessary. Yet uncertain as was its authority, lacking any formal grant of jurisdiction or power to govern, Congress was soon carried by the tide of the revolutionary sea on which it was afloat to the utmost bounds of sovereign power. An army, a navy, a treasury arose like magic palaces as Congress rubbed the political lamp. Yet all depended on a state of mind. If the people in the several provinces cooled, if the spirit of exaltation died, the magic creations would pass away, vanish in a night. It was not at all as English Tories imagined that a small junto in Congress had terrified the nation and with knife at the breast compelled it to arm.[1] The arch-Tory, Samuel Seabury, exaggerated, too, when he said that Congress breathed 'not a word of peace and reconciliation,' not even a soothing expression, but rather 'threw all into confusion,' 'reviled and trampled' on the authority of Parliament, and 'made the breach a thousand times more irreparable' than it was before.[2] Congress dared go no farther than its supporters dared, perhaps never quite so far, and there was talk of reconciliation up to the very last. It did, however, direct and unify the action of the rebellious-minded people of thirteen States, which was more than the British Government ever did, or,

[1] *Archives des Affaires Étrangères, Angleterre,* 515, no. 4.

[2] S. Seabury, *The Congress Canvassed,* 5–6.

perhaps, ever had a chance of doing, with the numerous Loyalists to be found in every province.

Carried on the flood of radical feeling, the Continental Congress, mouthpiece of the Patriot party in all the colonies, advanced far enough, January 2 and March 14, 1776, to advise the States to disarm the Loyalists, and thus 'restrain the wicked practices of these men.' At the last date the arms were to be furnished to those who were fighting America's battles. The first disarming resolution provided that the army was to assist.[1] The committee records showed a rich variety of arms, a 'morning' sword, a halbert hanger, a silver-hilted sword, a cutlass, a paunch belt and canteen, a pair of double-barreled pistols, a small blunderbuss, a cartouche-belt, and a pair of holster pistols. Although each was forced to swear that all firearms, sidearms, powder and lead were given up, it was rumored that some gave up their poor arms and concealed the good ones. Some, it was said, were audacious enough to fire their muskets in pure bravado. Not long after the last resolution, Congress urged the inhabitants of the thirteen colonies to fit out privateers, who could prey on British trade, and show King George what they thought of his proclamation closing American ports.[2] On April 6, they opened the ports of America

[1] James Wilson had proposed this in Congress as early as January 1, 1776. *Letters of . . . Continental Congress*, I, 293, and next day it was voted. *Journals of Congress* (Ford, ed.), IV, 20. January 3 orders were given to Colonel Heard to enforce this resolution in Queens County, New York. *Ibid.*, 27; *Letters of . . . Continental Congress* (Burnett, ed.), I, 293, 297, 300, 388, 392. Van Tyne, *Loyalists*, 123–26.

[2] *Journals of Congress* (Ford, ed.), March 23, April 3, 1776; *Letters of . . . Continental Congress* (Burnett, ed.), I, 386, 395. Shipowners had petitioned for letters of marque. *Ibid.*, I, 371, 384.

to all countries not British.[1] Although Independence was, John Adams sneered, 'a Hobgoblin of so frightful mien, that it would throw a delicate Person into Fits to look it in the face,' yet, he hinted, be patient, what signifies a word? There would soon be independence enough.[2]

New instructions were daily coming in, giving more and more power to the delegates. Congress not only received these new impulses toward Independence, but it used its own powers to induce them.[3] Members made journeys to wavering Assemblies and fired them with eloquent appeals. Even the Continental army was ordered to lend aid to local committees fearful of being overwhelmed by local majorities. After John Adams had for some time been able only now and then to 'snatch a transient glance at the promised land,' and after 'millions of curses' had been poured out upon him for his efforts to prevent people being lulled with 'idle hopes of reconciliation,' his faction secured the famous resolution of May 10, 1776. The several Assemblies were recommended, since they had no adequate government, to adopt one best suited to the happiness and safety of their constituents. Five days later, the significance of this resolution was made unmistakable, when, after much heat and debate, by a vote of 6 to 4, a preamble was attached reciting some crimes of His Britannic Majesty and

[1] *Journals of Congress* (Ford, ed.), April 6, 1776. This had been proposed repeatedly before. *Letters of . . . Continental Congress* (Burnett, ed.), I, 174, 191, 290, 338, 355, 409, 415.

[2] *Letters of . . . Continental Congress* (Burnett, ed.), I, 406, 424.

[3] *Ibid.*, I, 424.

his Lords and Commons, and asserting that all oaths to support the King's Government were against reason and conscience. The exercise, therefore, of authority by that government was totally suppressed. Its place should be taken by a government under the authority of the people of the several colonies.[1] This 'most important resolution ever taken in America,' as Adams wrote, 'cut the Gordian knot.' A 'machine for fabrication of independence' his enemy branded it, but Adams admitted with a smile that it was that monster itself.[2]

There must yet be, however, a formal resolution and declaration of it. A thousand atomic forces were driving Congress toward the great decision; many others were flying in the opposite direction. The resultant force in nearly all parts of the country was toward Independence. One body hammered another until Congress itself felt the shock, started, perhaps, in some far-off back country where the conservative interests of commerce exercised least restraint. The Committee of Safety in Cumberland County (April 22, 1776), instructed its delegates to the Virginia Convention to declare for Independence, to adjure any allegiance to his 'Britannick Majesty, and bid him a good Night forever.' [3] Other counties being like-minded, the Virginia Convention, on May 15, 1776, authorized instructions to its

[1] *Letters of . . . Continental Congress* (Burnett, ed.), I, 358, 454. The Maryland legislature refused to go so far. Force, *American Archives* (4th Series), V, 1589. Maryland still had hopes of a reconciliation.

[2] *Letters of . . . Continental Congress* (Burnett, ed.), I, 445, 446.

[3] H. R. McIlwaine, *Proclamation of the Committee of Safety of Cumberland . . . Counties*, 35.

delegates in Congress to propose a resolution declaring the United colonies free and independent States.

Obedient to that mandate, Richard Henry Lee moved, June 7, 1776, that the connection of the colonies with Great Britain was dissolved. John Adams, who for weeks had seen 'horror, terror and detestation' marked on the faces of some members when he 'laid open' such ideas, was on his feet in an instant to second the motion, but he was over-sanguine and found great opposition which it took weeks to vanquish. Over two weeks earlier, this 'Atlas of Independence' wrote exultingly to his friend James Warren, 'Every Post and every Day rolls in upon Us, Independence like a Torrent'; but he was too optimistic when he asserted that the four colonies to the south were perfectly agreed with the four to the north. There was hesitation at least in South Carolina and Georgia. The five colonies in the middle were not so ripe, he granted, and he was quite right when he said that 'eccentric' Maryland was 'sometimes so hot, sometimes so cold; now so high, then so low.' At least he was joyful to see Congress 'now daily passing Resolutions, which I most earnestly pressed for against Wind and Tide Twelve Months ago'; and it was meat and drink to him to have Dickinson, the 'bell-wether of the aristocratical flock,' confessing 'the falsehood of all his Prophecies, and the Truth of mine.'[1]

[1] *Works of J. Adams,* II, 407–08; *Warren-Adams Letters,* I, 249. Maryland resolved against the resolutions of May 10 and 15, but later joined for Independence. *Letters of . . . Continental Congress,* I, 464. Edward Rutledge was opposed on June 7 to Lee's motion. *Ibid.,* 476.

CHAPTER XVII

THE DECLARATION OF INDEPENDENCE IN AMERICA AND IN ENGLAND

AFTER the vote on Richard Henry Lee's motion was put off for three weeks, John Adams wrote, 'Objects of the most stupendous magnitude, and measures in which the lives and liberties of millions yet unborn are intimately interested, are now before us.' If he could once get them completed, he would think that he had answered the end of his creation and would sing his *nunc dimittis*, return to his 'farm, family, ride circuits, plead law, or judge causes, just which you please.' To attain this end he 'put in the busiest month' he ever saw.[1] Many were yet 'feeding on the dainty food of reconciliation.' Even after Parliament's prohibitory act, December 22, 1775, after the bloody days at Lexington and Bunker Hill, after George III 'spurned' their petitions, many members of Congress clung to the hope of reconciliation. Pride in the Empire, their empire as well as Lord North's, the tradition of grandeur not second even to Rome, pride in English history, and a sense of security within the Empire held many back from a last step toward Independence.

For three weeks after June 7, Lee's resolution for Independence seemed but an apple of discord. Committees had been appointed (June 12) to draw

[1] *Letters of . . . Continental Congress*, I, 478; Abigail Adams, *Familiar Letters*, 177, 188.

up a draft of articles of confederation and prepare a plan of treaties, but still the formal decision for Independence was staved off. On the morning of July 1, the war of words reached its height in 'the greatest debate of all.' John Dickinson, polite and candid, but with all his eloquence, brought together everything that had been said against a resolution of Independence at that time. There was no reporter present, but the letters and diaries of those who held like views reveal the main points.[1] It was an improper time, Dickinson argued. Public honor was engaged to await terms of peace about to be offered by the British commissioners. America, with no fleet or alliance with a naval power, was too defenseless. The protection of her trade was essential to success in war. It was a blind, precipitate measure to throw off her connection with Great Britain and give herself up to the arms of France. That court, 'famous for intrigues and deceptions,' would exact much severer terms for her aid, if America seceded first and sought alliance later. 'A man must have the impudence of a New-Englander,' wrote Rutledge, to propose a treaty with France in the present disjointed state of the provinces. They must adjust their own disputes over boundaries and much else, before being 'lugged into independence.' The continent would be torn to pieces over intestine

[1] Carter Braxton, James Reed, James Wilson, John Jay, Robert Livingston, Edward Rutledge, and Duane agreed in a greater or less degree. *Letters of . . . Continental Congress*, I, 420, 421, 431, 476. James Wilson finally voted for Independence. R. Morris continued to avow his disapproval three months later. *Letters of . . . Continental Congress* (Burnett, ed.), II, 135–36.

wars and convulsions. A grand continental league must be made first. A resolution of Independence would only cause dissensions, when it was union that was wanted. Finally, it would unite the people of England against the colonies — a strong objection to those, like John Jay, who would fight only America's enemies there.[1]

There was sense and reason in all this if we forget the outcome as we know it. All was dark and misty before them. Only high moral courage led Dickinson to risk sinking from leader to martyr as a result of this stand. Already the Adamses had ceased to call him the 'illustrious Farmer,' the 'penman of the Revolution,' and were whispering about that he was 'timid, apathetic,' deficient in energy. Not even flattery or the convivial glass as a 'conversational aperient' had been able to turn him from his love of as ettled order of things. Loving liberty, he also loved peace. In passing judgment, remember that, though a Quaker, he and McKean were the only members of Congress who actually took up arms in defense of Independence. When it was decided upon, in spite of his opposition, Dickinson regarded that determination as the voice of his country with which he resolved to stand or fall.[2]

John Adams, 'Atlas of Independence,' 'by merit raised to that bad eminence,' was urged to reply.

[1] *Letters of . . . Continental Congress;* also Stillé, *Life and Times of John Dickinson,* I, 192–204, 368–75; Lincoln, *Revolution in Pennsylvania,* 206–07, 225. Jay's idea was an interesting precedent for the idea sponsored by President Wilson during the Great War that we should fight only the German Government, not the German people. *Letters of . . . Continental Congress* (Burnett, ed.), I, 386, 395.

[2] Stillé, *Life and Times of J. Dickinson,* I, 204.

Wishing for the talents and eloquence of the orators of Greece or Rome, sure they would have supplicated Minerva and Mercury, he summed up what he had said twenty times before.[1] He had no patience with waiting longer for terms of reconciliation. As to trade, declare Independence, he urged, and foreigners will exert themselves to supply us with what we want. Privateers will swarm and supply our needs. Independence will not leave us at the mercy of France, for 'foreign powers already know that we are as obnoxious to the British court as we can be.' Once we have Independence, the colonies will hesitate no longer to complete their governments. They will pass test laws, make Toryism a crime, stop sedition, and treason in the press, and slanders on public men. Governments will get a new vigor, and encourage the manufacture of saltpeter, sulphur, powder, arms, cannon, and mortars, inspiriting military operations by sea and land. Instead of uniting the people of England against us, a Declaration of Independence will raise such a storm as will obstruct the war, throw the kingdom into confusion. 'Make the tree good and the fruit will be good.' [2]

On the third day of July, John Adams wrote his wife, 'Yesterday the greatest question was decided which ever was debated in America, and a greater perhaps, never was nor will be decided among men.' Soon, he assured her, there would be a Declaration

[1] It is from Adams's letters and diary that we can reconstruct his probable speech. *Letters of . . . Continental Congress* (Burnett, ed.), I, 501–02, 522–24.

[2] Adams, *Familiar Letters*, 192–93.

'setting forth the causes which have impelled us to this mighty resolution, and the reasons which will justify it in the sight of God and Man.' He believed that July 2 would be 'celebrated by succeeding generations as the great anniversary festival.' It ought to be 'solemnized with pomp and parade, with shows, games, sports, guns, bells, bonfires, and illuminations, from one end of this continent to the other, from this time forward, forevermore.' [1]

Because of the prevailing jealousy of one-man power, Congress left all of its tasks to committees, and the drafting of the Declaration of Independence was no exception. John Adams, who says he was on ninety committees, was not spared from this. Franklin, Sherman, and R. R. Livingston were there, too, but the first draft was wisely left to Thomas Jefferson.[2] Changes and corrections by Adams and Franklin altered this draft slightly, before it came before Congress.[3] There it suffered more changes, but was finally adopted in such a way that Congress as well as Jefferson must bear such criticisms as a 'candid world' has made of its 'facts' and its philosophy.

Loyalists in America, Lord North adherents in

[1] *Letters of . . . Continental Congress* (Burnett, ed.), I, 526. He says there was not one dissenting colony, but the New York delegates were not given permission to approve until its convention acted favorably on July 9.

[2] The committee was appointed June 11, 1776, and it reported its draft June 28. See interesting details in C. Becker, *Declaration of Independence*, chap. IV. See also Hazelton and Fridenwald on the Declaration. Jefferson had combined in the draft his previously written preamble to the Virginia Constitution, Mason's theory of liberty found in that instrument and R. H. Lee's resolution of Independence. J. C. Fitzpatrick, *The Spirit of the Revolution*, 5, 7.

[3] Franklin seems to have made eleven changes. *Ibid.*, 11–14.

England, historians and publicists ever since have assailed the Declaration from all angles. Some have attacked its style, but if its literary merit alone would not, to use the phrase of Sir Thomas Browne, make it a work 'too hard for the teeth of time,' its connection with a tremendous crisis in the life of one of the greatest of modern nations has secured its fame. It cannot perish, to resume the phrase of Sir Thomas, 'but in the general flames, when all things shall confess their ashes.' The solemn tone of the opening paragraphs, the firm conviction of the charges against the King, the catching accents, the something that was Jefferson at his best, can never lose interest for mankind.[1]

As to the philosophy, it was, said Jefferson, just the common sense of the whole matter; 'no more,' to quote Condorcet, 'than the naïve expression of what common sense should teach all men.' [2] Both were quite unaware that many men in their own times and of a later generation, might regard the political ideas as fallacies which no man of sense would accept. Loyalists, indeed, on that glorious Fourth of July, and for many years after, declared that Jefferson and his friends had 'outdone the utmost extravagance of all former fanatics.' Lind wrote, as to natural rights, that 'The German Anabaptists indeed went so far as to speak of the right of enjoying life as a right inalienable.' They held that even a magistrate could not righteously deprive

[1] See Becker, *Declaration of Independence* (chap. v), for his charming chapter on 'The Literary Qualities of the Declaration.'

[2] *Œuvres de Condorcet,* VIII, 18.

a man of life, but Congress went farther and added the right to enjoy liberty and to pursue happiness. Were penal laws, then, contrary to the law of God? Could thieves not be restrained from theft, murderers from murder, rebels from rebellion?[1] What nonsense! Thomas Hutchinson wanted to know how the Southern delegates justified the depriving more than one hundred thousand Africans of their right to liberty and the pursuit of happiness, if these rights were so inalienable?[2] Congress, however, found these logical hurdles easy enough to leap, and, by appealing to the common man's conception of good and bad, easily proved that life, liberty, and the pursuit of happiness were in accord with Nature and God's will.

Nor could Loyalists abide the idea that all men were created free and equal. True, Henry VIII, more celebrated for the plurality of his matrimonial ventures than for his passion for liberty, had freed two slaves with the words, 'Whereas God created all men free,' and a Roman jurist fifteen hundred years before Jefferson expressed the idea that all men are created equal. The idea was old enough not to have been so shocking to Loyalists, but Jonathan Boucher was provoked to argue quaintly that 'a musical instrument composed of chords, keys or pipes all perfectly equal in size and power, might as well be expected to produce harmony as a society composed of members all perfectly equal to be productive of order and peace.'[3]

[1] John Lind, *Answer to . . .*, 121–22.

[2] T. Hutchinson, *Strictures . . .*, 9.

[3] J. Boucher, *A View . . . American Revolution* (ed. 1779).

An English opponent of the Declaration asked wherein are all men created equal? 'Is it size, strength, understanding . . . figure . . . or situation of life? Every plowman knows they are not created equal in any of these.' No two men in the whole world are created equal. Anyway, what of it? Is that any reason Americans should turn rebels, because the English are their fellow creatures? [1]

Nevertheless, when such ideas appeared in the Declaration of Independence, the Whigs of America greeted them with approval. These ideas were strung along the intellectual highways of mankind from early ages. Protagoras, Plato, Aristotle, Cicero, had dreamed them; [2] Hooker, Sidney, Locke, had preached them seriously to their generation. Men had died for them in Cromwell's time. Jefferson and his followers have been accused of borrowing the philosophy of natural rights from the English of the seventeenth century, but the truth is that they inherited it. 'Jefferson copied Locke and Locke quoted Hooker.' [3] Jefferson, reader of English books, member of a Congress steeped in the English political philosophy, could not have escaped the ideas found in the Declaration if he had tried.[4] Josiah Quincy revealed the prevailing convictions of American leaders when, having willed to his son the works

[1] *London Chronicle*, September 10, 1776.

[2] American Historical Association, *Report*, I, 67–81; James Sullivan, *The Antecedents of the Declaration*; Becker, *Declaration of Independence*, chap. II.

[3] Becker, *Declaration of Independence*, 79; *Magazine of American History*, XII, 46–56.

[4] See Jefferson, *Writings* (Ford, ed.), IX, 71, 481; X, 376, for his recommendation of Sidney, Locke, and Priestley.

of Sidney and Locke, he invoked the spirit of liberty to rest upon him.

The American mind seemed to have an affinity for the writings of Locke; it was unable to resist them. His arguments were not always clear; many a colonial mind could not have followed them; but his conclusions fitted colonial needs perfectly. Americans, indeed, had an aversion to opposing ideas. American souls, as those of the Levelers, cried out 'for natural rights derived from Adam and right reason.'[1] The 'sentiment of the day' was that human reason had discovered some natural rights, and these should rule in any state and test its right to live. Becker points out that all through the seventeenth and eighteenth centuries mystery was disappearing from the physical world, and men could easily ask why should it not from the world of political thought. If the laws of light and gravitation could be found out by man, why not those which gave or took away power from a king.[2] Nature, the eighteenth-century God, had yielded to the inquiring mind of man much knowledge of the physical laws; surely it was necessary only to seek the laws of man's conduct in political society and one would find.

Locke had begun this inquiry and the eighteenth-century Americans had great faith in his results. Men, largely by the use of their natural faculties, 'could ascertain natural laws — even in the political world.' It was true that George III might read the book of Nature differently from Samuel Adams, but in America at least there were more of Adams's way

[1] Becker, *Declaration of Independence*, 34. [2] *Ibid.*, 41.

of thinking. Only an adherent of King George could write sneeringly: 'Our ears have been wearied with repetition of "Natural Equality, of inherent Rights, of original Contracts and delegated Power. Ideas: which tho' they boast a contemplative Locke, or a visionary Rousseau for their support, may, generally speaking, be said to have existence only in the heads of such vain Philosophers."' It is too late 'for the reasonable part of mankind to be imposed on.' One might 'as well swallow a poison potion because the name of Boerhave is on the prescription.'[1]

For the revolution-bound American it was not in Moses that one would find 'what God had said to Rousseau,' but in the laws of Nature. If that was merely consulting one's idea of what was right and what was wrong, at least it required less toil than poring over dusty records, and after all it led to the pleasant result of believing what one wished to believe. We claim our rights, wrote Dickinson, not from parchments and seals, but 'from a higher source, from the King of kings and the Lord of all the earth.' The conviction that political right was the law of God made it take a pleasing precedence over human law — laws made in Parliament — and if it were presumptuous to hold that the mind of the Infinite and the mind of man were one and the same, even that was not beyond an Adams and many other eighteenth-century thinkers.

But philosophy alone would not justify rebellion to an onlooking world. Congress must list the 'injuries and usurptions." The first Continental

[1] *An Address to the People of Great Britain* (Bristol, 1776), 5, 6.

Congress had begun to enumerate these grievances in its Declaration and Resolves,[1] and the second Congress, nine months later, added more complaints to explain the indignation of a 'virtuous, loyal and affectionate people,' and the causes of their taking up arms.[2] To that point they had disavowed all design of separation from Great Britain, but in May and June of 1776 the 'train of abuses' became too long to be endured. Towns and provinces published lists of government 'crimes,'[3] and finally, summing up all the former charges, Jefferson, in the Declaration, added a few more 'facts.'[4] A candid world must understand that Congress would not overturn a government for 'light and transient causes'; since their theory of their place in the Empire had come at last to be that King George, a common king, was the only bond which united them with England, this monarch must be shown to be aiming at absolute tyranny. The colonies were pictured entreating and petitioning the King after each cruel blow, and he, 'unfit to rule a free people,' multiplying his evil acts, until at last it came to be a question of submitting to slavery or severing the

[1] *Journals of . . . Continental Congress* (Ford, ed.), I, 63–64.

[2] Force, *American Archives* (4th Series), II, 1867–69.

[3] *New England Chronicle*, May 30, 1776 (Boston town meeting list). *Statutes at Large of Virginia* (Hening, ed., 1821), IX, 109–10 (Virginia Bill of Rights and Constitution). In a broadside, June 18, 1776, Governor Trumbull arraigned George III for many of the crimes later listed in the Declaration.

[4] He had already prepared a list of twenty-three charges for use in the Virginia Constitution, and for use in the Declaration he added three new indictments, and expanded the sixth of the Virginia Preamble in the eighth, ninth, and tenth of the Declaration. J. C. Fitzpatrick, *Spirit of the Revolution*, 5–6.

bonds. To make the list of tyrannous acts more impressive, the acts of George III, 'for suppressing a most unnatural, unprovoked rebellion,' were assigned as the causes of the rebellion.[1] When loyal Englishmen read in the Declaration that George III had transported armies of mercenaries, plundered seas, impressed Americans, ravaged coasts, burned towns, destroyed lives, they snorted in wrath. What else could a conscientious monarch do with rebellious subjects?

'Having disclaimed their allegiance to the Sovereign,' sneered Macpherson, 'disobeyed the acts of the Legislature, destroyed the property, and insulted the persons of the servants of the State, assumed the functions of sovereignty, and rushed into actual rebellion; they complain of a want of moderation in Government, for exerting the power vested in it by the Constitution, for restoring tranquillity, enforcing legal submission to the laws of the state, and for protecting the injured and punishing the guilty.'[2] If the poetic Macpherson had lacked a pension, and had been for some months in violent rebellion, he would better have understood Jefferson's sincere belief in the truth of his charges. The actors in the great Revolutionary drama could not also look coolly down upon it and judge the causes as future ages would do. A calm investigation to-day of each charge against the King leaves that worthy man with a much whiter record than his American subjects granted him.[3]

[1] Thomas Hutchinson, *Strictures* . . . 28.

[2] J. Macpherson, *The Rights of Great Britain Asserted*, 48–49, 64.

[3] Becker, *Declaration of Independence*, 24; Friedenwald, *Declaration of Independence*, chaps. x, xi.

Except as to the King's efforts to overthrow rebellion, the major charges in the Declaration might just as truthfully have been made against William and Mary or any English sovereign thereafter as against George III. Even the exercises of his 'prerogatives' had not lain more heavily on them than in previous reigns. The King had duties to perform, and he acted naturally, in the light of the past conduct of mankind, not according to moral and political standards of an age to come. Jefferson and his fellow revolutionists did not, on the other hand, regard it as part of their work to recite any mistaken steps of their own. They were trying to convince a candid world that all the blame rested on 'the tyrant' George III. Since the 'divine right' theory made rebellion immoral, they tried to destroy the divinity. They denied rebellion, or at least tried to make it look attractive and the natural sequence of the conduct of their King. They would not even accept Diderot's charitable epigram that 'happily tyrants are more stupid than they are wicked.'

America had at last done what men of vision had long said she would eventually do. Literary men, Sir Thomas Browne and Horace Walpole; politicians and political writers, Sir William Yonge and James Harrington; economists, Sir Josiah Child and Charles Davenant; philosophers, Emanuel Kant and David Hume; and envious statesmen like Choiseul, Turgot, and the Count de Vergennes — were all gloomy or rejoicing prophets of an independent America. The Lords of Trade had feared it three generations before it happened. Governors, from the earliest to Thomas Hutchinson, had foretold it.[1] Travelers, such as Eddis and Kalm, were sure that Independence was the inevitable end.[2] The colonists themselves from 1754 on were playing with the idea.[3]

Sir Thomas Browne (1684) foresaw America 'well peopled, civilized, and divided into kingdoms,' and then they would admit no subjection to England. The Board of Trade (1701) wrote that the American thirst for Independence was notorious. Horace Walpole had many visions about America, and fancied he saw 'twenty empires and republics forming upon vast scales over all that continent . . . too mighty to be kept in subjection to half a dozen exhausted nations in Europe.'[4] Peter Kalm (1748) almost exactly guessed the time it would take the colonies 'to form a state by themselves, entirely independent.'[5] Eddis was certain they could not, after they became populous, be retained as British subjects.[6] Englishmen were full of forebodings. Sir Thomas Sutton (1774) warned the House of Commons that all colonial actions 'conveyed a spirit and wish for independence.' 'If you ask an American who is his master, he will tell you he has none, nor any

[1] Root, *Pennsylvania and Great Britain*, 391–92; A. Brown, *Genesis*, I, 63; Hutchinson, *History of Massachusetts* (1772). *Journal des Savants* (Mars–Avril, 1881).

[2] Eddis, *Letters*, August 30, October 1, 1769; Peter Kalm, *Travels into North America*, I, 263–65.

[3] Becker, *Political Parties in New York*, 44, 49, 59; J. Adams, *Works*, I, 23.

[4] Walpole, *Letters* (Toynbee, ed.), VII, 378 (1770).

[5] Peter Kalm, *Travels*, I, 262–65 (thirty to fifty years, he said).

[6] Eddis, *Letters*, 16.

governor, but Jesus Christ.' Total independence was their only thought.[1] Mansfield reminded the Lords of Charles Davenant's prediction that America only awaited sufficient strength before forming herself into a separate and independent state.[2] The Earl of Camden augured the same end.[3] A pamphlet, 'Plain English' (1775), said it was absurd to expect so immense a country to continue in subjection to 'such a spot' as England. Already too powerful to manage it would soon form a vast independent empire. Look into human nature, into the temper of mankind; that was the book to inform one that the Americans were a hardy people who would never brook an everlasting subjection.[4]

One wonders at times whether the reiteration of the accusation of the desire for independence was not a factor in creating that desire, as the witches suggested murder to Macbeth. Certain it is that from 1772 the expressions of the idea grow in volume to July 2, 1776, the fateful day when Congress made its decision. By April, 1774, Hooper, of North Carolina, thought the colonies 'fast striding toward independence,' building 'an empire on the ruins of Great Britain.'[5] The press was filled with talk of a 'separate state,' an 'American Magna Charta,' a 'Runnymede in America,' and at last a 'declaration of independence.' Yet there had been conflicts at Lexington, Concord, and Bunker Hill before any

[1] Force, *American Archives* (4th Series), I, 77.

[2] Hansard, *Debates*, XVIII, 956.

[3] Mass. Hist. Soc., *Proceedings*, vol. 50, p. 448.

[4] *Plain English* (1775), 12.

[5] *Life of Iredell*, I, 197.

considerable number of Americans talked seriously of seceding from the Empire. George Washington, crossing the Potomac on his way to the Second Continental Congress, met his old friend Boucher, who warned him, with a Loyalist's fervor, that he was on his way to 'civil war' and a Declaration of Independence. The noble character, who in one short month was to be chosen the American leader in that 'civil war,' replied with perfect sincerity: 'If you ever hear of my joining in any such measures you may set me down for everything wicked.' 'So dangerous it is to make one false step,' moralized Boucher, as he wrote this down in his memoirs.[1]

Men came to the meeting of the Second Continental Congress who went away Loyalists, while some, who stayed and accepted the Independence decision, missed by the narrowest margin going to the Loyalist side. Anthony Wayne, whose fighting spirit will not be questioned, declared publicly, September 25, 1775, for himself and his militia company, their 'abhorrence even of an idea so pernicious in its nature' as Independence.[2] Reading the letters and documents of the year preceding July 2, 1776, we see the idea grow slowly, then swiftly, and finally bear down and silence all opposition. At first it was a timid suggestion, in July of 1775; a definite query in the autumn, but answered in the negative; insistent during the winter, but meeting emphatic

[1] *Reminiscences of an American Loyalist* (Boucher, ed.), 109.

[2] Sharpless, *Quakers in the Revolution*, 117. John Jay, James Wilson, John Dickinson, Robert Morris were probably opposed to Independence in January, 1776.

noes; assertive in the spring, and denial fainter; but during May and June growing apace.[1]

Having resolved on Independence, the Congress debated the plan of a Declaration which Jefferson, for a committee of five, had drafted, using the matter he had already written for the preamble of Virginia's Constitution.[2] Its only purpose was to justify to the world the secession from the British Empire. After Jefferson had been made to writhe a little under the acrimonious criticisms, the revised Declaration was adopted, July 4, 1776, by a vote of twelve states. The members did not sign that day, did not, until July 19, even order the rough draft engrossed — though copies were printed on the night of the fourth to send out to the army and to State Assemblies. August 2, all present signed, while others added their signatures from time to time for months, but no names were made public until late in December of 1776.[3]

The scenes when Congress voted the resolution and later the Declaration, and when the members signed, were sights to be seen only once and never to be forgotten. One member, in a state of exaltation,

[1] *Letters of . . . Continental Congress* (Burnett, ed.), I, XXI.

[2] For interesting details see J. C. Fitzpatrick, *The Spirit of the Revolution*, 1–23; C. Becker, *Declaration of Independence*, 135–244; Friedenwald, *Declaration of Independence*, 120–23. The Declaration was probably regarded as a mere piece of routine work. J. C. Fitzpatrick, *The Spirit of the Revolution*, 15. It actually seems to have been forgotten for fifty years.

[3] J. C. Fitzpatrick, *TheSpirit of the Revolution*, 26. Some who were not delegates in Congress on July 4, but were elected later, signed when they entered Congress. See *Documents and Records of New Hampshire*, VIII, 203.

wrote on July 4, that he was 'among a Consistary of Kings,' which would be the greatest assembly on earth, if it could make good that declaration.[1] As Macaulay wrote of the vote on the Reform Bill, 'It was like seeing Cæsar stabbed in the Senate House, or seeing Oliver taking the mace from the table.' The members of Congress 'might be exalted on a high gallows,' reflected one, and Ellery was curious to see how they all looked 'as they signed what might be their death warrant.'[2] There had been no effort 'to envelope the light in a cloud,' and thus, like Beccaria, defend the cause of humanity without being a martyr. No startling spectacle of clanking chains had frightened them into any concealment of thought. Fate had in store for them 'freedom or a halter,' wrote Abraham Clark. John Adams had experienced already one 'ugly reflection' about his own revolutionary activities. 'Brutus and Cassius were conquered and slain, Hampden died in the field, Sidney on the scaffold, Harrington in jail.' He found little comfort. 'Politics are an ordeal path among red hot plowshares.' Later in life, when he was told by Count Deodati that he would be hated and persecuted like all Republicans, Aristides, Phocion, Miltiades, and Scipio, he did not doubt it.[3]

That Congress had kept its finger on the public pulse — or at least on that of the Whigs — was proved by the reception of the news of the Declaration. From July 8, when John Adams complained

[1] *Letters of . . . Continental Congress* (Burnett, ed.), I, xxi.

[2] *Ibid.*, I, 528; Davol, *Two Men of Taunton*, 253.

[3] J. Adams, *Works*, IX, 339, 614.

of the bells ringing far into the night, until late August, Independence was proclaimed and greeted with acclamations at ever-increasing distances from the Philadelphia State House. One may see the wave widen daily, starting, July 8, in the Quaker City, from 'that awful stage in the State House yard,' reaching Princeton on the 9th, touching Virginia by the 10th, far into Massachusetts by the 16th, Newport on the 22d, and a grand celebration in Charleston on August 14th.[1] Newspapers published it everywhere; military officers proclaimed it to the militia companies and regiments of soldiers; heads of councils and Assemblies read it to vast concourses of people in the State House, from its balcony, or about the Liberty Pole.

At Princeton, Nassau Hall was illuminated. Crowds greeted the Declaration with 'three loud huzzas'; 'drums were beating, fifes playing, guns firing, bells ringing, cannon booming — always thirteen times — and there were bonfires with King George's coat of arms torn from the walls of the court-house or the governor's palace.' All other 'odious signatures of despotism' such as 'Lion and Crown,' 'Pestle and Mortar and Crown,' 'Heart and Crown,' which until then had 'disgraced' the fronts of taverns or apothecary shops, were torn down and cast into the fire. Effigies of the King were carried

[1] Moore, *Diary of the Revolution*, I, 269–70, July 8 and 9, 1776; *American Historical Review*, VI, 107; *American Gazette*, July 16, 1776; *New York Gazette*, July 15, August 12, 22; *Pennsylvania Evening Post*, August 1, 1776; *New England Chronicle*, July 25, August 2, 1776; *Pennsylvania Gazette*, August 7; *Letters of . . . Continental Congress* (Burnett, ed.), II, 1, 2, 8.

through the town to no small merriment of onlookers, and thrown in a fire with the sentiment, 'Thus may it fare with all tyrants.' This was followed by banquets, 'proper collations,' where the toasts were 'the downfall of tyrants,' 'the universal Prevalence of Civil and Religious Liberty.' At one banquet the sobriety of the feasters was tested by twenty-four toasts, one of which was: 'May the freedom and Independence of America endure until the sun grows dim with age and this earth returns to chaos.'[1] It was quite true, as a Loyalist wrote, 'No man may by speaking or writing contradict any part of this Declaration without being deemed an enemy to his country, and exposed to the rage and fury of the populace.'[2]

When Independence was proclaimed at Ticonderoga, 'Every face seemed to say, "Now we are a people! We have a name among the states of this world."'[3] The 'sublime manifesto' of the United States of America did not leap the Atlantic by swift mail steamers nor by aeroplane, cable, or radio, but was at last borne by the tardy sailing vessels to the attention of Europe. That 'all Europe applauded' it, as Mirabeau later declared, is doubtful. The aristocratic classes got from it only such pleasure as they derived from seeing England in trouble.

[1] Based on the above references and the following: *Independent Chronicle*, Boston, October 3, 1776; *Pennsylvania Evening Post*, August 15; *Newport Mercury*, J. H. Edmonds, *How Massachusetts Received the Declaration of Independence*, in American Antiquarian Society, *Proceedings* (1925), 248–49; *Essex Journal*, July 26; *New Hampshire Packet*, July 26.

[2] T. Hutchinson, *Strictures* . . . 32.

[3] *Pennsylvania Evening Post*, August 15, 1776.

Silas Deane thought it well received in France. Condorcet certainly welcomed this 'example of a great people.' He approved, too, 'the simple and sublime revelation of those rights so sacred and so long abandoned.' It was not enough that the 'rights of men' should be written in philosophers' books, nor merely in the hearts of virtuous men; better in the American Declaration, where ignorant and weak men could read them.[1] There the French people, hoping for a freer France, could read with joy the proclaimed realization of abstract political thought. Mere booklore was now to live in the acts of men. This was true for the French liberals, but in royal circles the list of wrongs must have been more satisfactory reading than the political philosophy. This American example, moreover, was very bad, indeed, for the subjects of His Most Christian Majesty. His government could hardly be said to derive its powers from the consent of the governed. Nevertheless, if he wished to assist in breaking 'that noble China vase,' the British Empire, he must grin and bear the political ideas which were to be its undoing.

In England, George III did not fancy the Declaration nor its philosophy, yet only recently he had knighted Blackstone for the writing of a book containing the same doctrine as to the origin and end of the state. Perhaps he had not read the book. When copies of the Declaration began to arrive in England,[2] the North Ministry employed James Macpherson,

[1] *Œuvres de Condorcet,* VIII, 11.

[2] The London newspapers were strangely silent on the subject of the Declaration of Independence for two or three weeks after they must have received the news of it.

author of the poems of Ossian, to write a popular reply. 'The Rights of Great Britain asserted against the Claims of America' went through many editions. As its success was greater than 'Taxation no Tyranny,' by Dr. Johnson, with whom Macpherson had just fought a great literary duel, the Scotch poet derived other satisfaction than his pension from King George.[1] The poet was as much of a bully as Johnson, and he fell upon Congress and its Declaration without mercy.[2] They 'adapt their reasonings to the weakness of the prejudiced,' he writes, 'and their facts to the credulity of the ignorant.' He would not spare America. 'The law of God and of Nature is on the side of an indulgent Parent, against an undutiful Child, and should necessary correction render him incapable of future offense, he has only his own obstinacy to blame.' [3] In those days it was the custom to correct undutiful children.

John Lind, another 'friend of Government,' examined and disputed every assertion of the Declaration. He undertook this reply rather than the King, he explained, because 'a sovereign cannot enter into altercation with revolted subjects.' The cause was that of British citizens, since 'His Majesty is insulted for supporting *our* interests.' [4] The theory of government contained in the Declaration 'put the axe at

[1] B. Saunders, *Life . . . of J. Macpherson*, 259.

[2] In *Rivington's Gazette*, November 17, 1781, appeared an amusing parody of the Declaration of Independence. It contained a long series of charges against the Continental Congress, such as those which the original Declaration made against George III.

[3] James Macpherson, *Rights of Great Britain* . . . 49, 80.

[4] John Lind, *An Answer to the Declaration of the American Congress*, 5.

the root of all government,' cried Lind. Indeed, 'The opinions of the modern Americans on Government, like those of their good ancestors on witchcraft, would be too ridiculous to deserve any notice, if like them, too, contemptible and extravagant as they be, they had not led to the most serious evils.' [1] Lord George Germain was so pleased with either this or Macpherson's pamphlet that he sent General Howe some five hundred copies for distribution among the British troops and the inhabitants of rebellious America.[2]

The effect of the Declaration in England was, perhaps, to strengthen the Ministry, because it split the Opposition. The Marquis of Rockingham, leading one faction, believed that the Americans meant what they said; that reconciliation was impossible and the 'erring sisters' should be left to go in peace. There was no great following for this view at first. The English friends of America followed in the main Burke and Pitt, who still believed reconciliation possible; that *liberty*, not *independence*, was the real quest of the colonists. In that belief they condemned the King's policy, and pressed on under the banner of reconciliation. The masses, insulted by the Declaration, embittered by the damage to trade, despising men who would secede from the Empire, listened to the glib ministerial promises — a brief war, costing little, and that paid later by American

[1] Lind, *Answer to the Declaration of Independence*, 119.

[2] *Germain Papers, Military Despatched*, November 6, 1776. Thomas Hutchinson, *Strictures upon the Declaration* . . . also took up the complaints clause by clause, answering many of them pretty well from his point of view. 'Exaggerated,' 'false and frivolous,' he thought it.

taxes. They supported the King, damning him meanwhile for getting the country into such a mess, but eager to win now the battle was on. Even the gentlest spirits, like Cowper, came to believe that America was emancipating herself from one master only to serve a score, and with laurels upon her brow, sigh for her former chains again.[1] As a result there were few to protest, when, with more and more regiments and with ever mightier armaments, the British Government pressed the preparations for a new campaign against its rebellious subjects.

[1] Cowper, *Letters*, I, 177.

CHAPTER XVIII

PLANS FOR GETTING A BRITISH ARMY FROM CANADA TO NEW YORK

THE British campaign of 1777 had much the same purpose as the original plan for the great campaign of 1776. Yet the decision of Howe to pursue Washington's army through the Jerseys, instead of going up the Hudson to join Carleton coming down from Canada by way of Lake Champlain, so changed the apparent objective in 1776 that the original aim has almost been forgotten.[1] Howe's whole campaign had been belated, it is true, and it was rather late in October when his decision to follow Washington's army southward drew him away from the proposed junction with Carleton coming down from Canada. But Carleton, too, was late, and largely due to the prodigious energy and daring of Benedict Arnold. Indeed, the greatest authority on the influence of sea-power on history declares that then and there Arnold saved the American Revolution.[2]

After the failure at Quebec, the stubborn little American army endured much, retreated, fought a final battle, June 8, 1776, at Three Rivers, and then fled, starving and ravaged by smallpox, back to Lake Champlain. Arnold, barely recovered from his wound at Quebec, was at Crown Point. Not without naval experience gained in the West India

[1] P.R.O., *Colonial Office*, 5–253, p. 214.

[2] Clowes, *Royal Navy*, III, 363, 368; A. T. Mahan, *The Major Operations* . . . 3, 4, 25.

trade, he set about building boats to delay, if not stop, the British advance southward by the Champlain waterway, the only route by which an army could traverse the wilderness. It must be accredited to that 'sluggard in war,' General Gates, that with no gentle methods he placed Arnold in charge of that work despite Congress itself.[1] Carleton, at St. John's, built a flotilla with an equal frantic haste and with prodigies of labor, but with far greater resources.[2]

Late in August, Arnold set sail from Crown Point with a 'wretched, motley crew,' the 'refuse of every regiment' of an army, wherein, as Gates wrote, 'the sick, the lame, the lazy' made an unreasonable proportion, and where 'more than one half that eat do not act.' There were seamen who never saw salt water, and there was 'not a spare oar in the fleet,' though 'the blowing season' was coming on. Early in September, Arnold begged for watch-coats and blankets for men 'extremely bare of clothing' and 'the season coming on severe.' He had not enough powder for practice firing, but trained his men in the exercise of guns.[3]

[1] Force, *American Archives* (4th Series), VI, 1107–08; *ibid.* (5th Series), I, 1186–87. Washington and Schuyler had already begun increasing the naval armament on the Lakes. *Journals of Continental Congress*, May 22, May 25, June 17, 1776. Washington, *Writings* (Ford, ed.), IV, 101.

[2] He had ordered materials and boats in sections and Germain had tried to get them from the Admiralty, but they never came. P.R.O., *Colonial Office*, Class 5–123, p. 69, January 15, 1776. Schuyler badly underestimated the British capacity to build a strong fleet. *Continental Congress Papers* (*Schuyler Letters*), 153, III, 307.

[3] *Cont. Cong. Papers* (*Schuyler Letters*), 153, II, 303–04, 372–73, 398–99, 439.

When at last, near Valcour Island, the rival forces met, Arnold had deliberately placed his small fleet in a little bay whence retreat seemed impossible. His one aim was to delay the British as much as possible, while the preservation of his force was secondary. The very building of the fleet, which forced Carleton to delay months in preparation of a rival naval armament, attained this end in a large part, and now Arnold recked not the loss of his own force so long as he delayed the British until the season should be too far advanced for Carleton to get his army through to Albany, and a junction with Howe.

Arnold's own account of the battle gives a vivid picture. On October 11, the attacking force destroyed a schooner and gondola, and seemed to have Arnold's fleet at its mercy, but that night, favored by a fog, the American fleet passed the British vessels entirely undiscovered and by daylight were quite out of sight. Stopping leaks, mending sails, and caring for the wounded, they pressed on until at Split Rock the pursuing enemy came alongside. A galley, the Washington, in a shattered condition, many men killed and wounded, struck to the enemy after a few broadsides. Arnold's galley, the Congress, fought on until the sails, rigging, and hull were shattered. He then ran her ashore in a small creek, ten miles from Crown Point, firing her and four attending gondolas, but saving the small arms. Escaping bands of savages who lurked in the woods, the crews all reached Crown Point. The American loss was eighty, the British forty men. Gates, writing of the ruin of the fleet, added: 'It has pleased Providence to preserve General Arnold. Few men ever met with so many hairbreadth escapes in so short a space of time.' [1] In a few days Carleton took Crown Point, but gave up the idea of an attack on Ticonderoga. Arnold had fought and would fight again in bigger battles, but never for bigger stakes. It was the American cause that was saved that day. Had Ticonderoga been taken and held that coming winter, Burgoyne's campaign of 1777, starting from that point, would have almost certainly succeeded.

Having regard to all the factors in the problem, even Solomon was not wise enough to say with confidence what Carleton should have done. He had driven the Americans out of Canada in a summer's campaign, and even Germain, awesome as he was to King George, could not prevent Sir Guy being made Knight Companion of the Most Honorable Order of the Bath.[2] Carleton's judgment about retiring from Crown Point to St. John's was based on long experience, which none of his critics had enjoyed. Ticonderoga, he reasoned, was too strong for a *coup de main*, and the season too late for a siege. The fort had been recently strengthened by the Polish engineer Kosciusko, and Carleton did not like its forbidding aspect. Even a victory he could not follow

[1] *Cont. Cong. Papers* (*Schuyler Letters*), 153, II, 453–55, 457. Arnold's letter is in Sparks, *Letters to Washington*, I, 545–46. The two best secondary accounts are in A. T. Mahan, *The Major Operations* . . . 13–26; C. O. Paullin, *The Navy of the American Revolution*, 75–78. Contemporary accounts are in Force, *American Archives* (5th Series), I, II, III.

[2] P.R.O., *State Papers, George III*, 11, no. 77; *Correspondence of King George with Lord North* (Donne, ed.), II, 4, November 17, 1776.

up, and winter would be on him before he could build barracks for the soldiers. If he would stay at Crown Point, he must employ 1100 men for six weeks on the fortifications, and meanwhile the army could not go into winter quarters. Besides, he could come back in the spring to that point without opposition, since the American fleet was destroyed.[1]

Burgoyne, trying to be loyal though critical, reported himself quite opposed to giving up Crown Point, holding that Ticonderoga might have been taken and Crown Point surely held, if Carleton had used his own good sense rather than the advice of 'dull, formal, methodical, fat engineers.'[2] Phillips, more bitterly critical, thought, as to Ticonderoga, that the 'whim of a drunken Indian,' Carleton's spy, prevailed. True, Gates was at Ticonderoga with 9000 men, but Phillips believed them in a panic, and that their 'ignorance renders stratagem and surprise so easy to succeed.' Every art of war, he wrote, should have been tried to frighten them out of Ticonderoga. Anyway, a corps with provisions should have been left to hold Crown Point for the winter.[3] The army,

[1] M. von Eelking, *Riedesel*, 65.

[2] Burgoyne to Clinton, *Clinton Papers* (W.L.C.L.), November 7, 1776; *Correspondence of King George III*, III, 405–06.

[3] Fonblanque, *Burgoyne*, 218–20. Baron Riedesel, of the German contingent, seems to have agreed with Carleton. M. Von Eelking, *Riedesel*, 65, 70–71 (November 10, 1776). Lieutenant-Colonel Christie, probably a tool of Germain's, was far more bitter in his criticism. He told of wasted time before deciding to build boats, of stores wildly dispersed, artillery carried back and forth without purpose, a commissariat 'intolerably' managed, foolish and useless fortifications, and the immoderate ambitions of a commander wholly unfit. Hist. Mss. Com., *Stopford-Sackville Papers*, II, 45–46. Christie was probably a rogue, and his tirade against Carleton is worth quoting only because it almost certainly affected the action of the King and Ger-

he declared, 'was distressed and hurt by the languor shown.' After all both Burgoyne and Phillips seem to have acquiesced in Carleton's decision when face to face with the actual situation.

In London the chimney-corner warriors, poring over maps with inked mountains and penciled woods, easily and valiantly criticized Carleton. In Paris, Beaumarchais, eager for American success, pointed out the false victory on 'Lake Ticonderoga,' and cried, after all the successes of Carleton, behold, how he returns to Quebec. 'La belle Campagne!'

In the American army, Schuyler, cruelly and unjustly blamed for the failure in Canada, victim of every calumny, 'barbarously traduced,' was supplanted, near the end of September, by Gates. He took command with the cheerful comment that the campaign and climate had so worn him down that the honor 'will be to me no more than the last blaze of the candle.' With characteristic unction he hoped nevertheless that he could 'serve mankind.' [1] Schuyler stood by until the danger had passed, though eager to return to Congress to defend his outraged reputation.[2] Arnold's reputation also was cruelly attacked. Both were blamed for what Congress had failed to do, though it in turn had ample excuse in the paucity of its means. As a result the

main in substituting Burgoyne for Carleton in the next campaign. See *Canadian Historical Review*, IX, 131–33, article by S. Morley Scott.

[1] *Cont. Cong. Papers* (*Schuyler Letters*), 153, II, 331, 345, 369–71, 393.

[2] *Cont. Cong. Papers* (*Schuyler Letters*), 153, II (letters of October 26, 1776, and May 26, 1777).

Northern army, distressed by every want, went through an appalling experience that winter which followed the Declaration of Independence. Samuel Wigglesworth declared it would make a heart of stone melt to hear the moans and see the distress of the sick and the dying, sometimes half a regiment down at a time.[1]

It was against this distraught army that Burgoyne's famous campaign of 1777 was launched. That general, who seemed doomed to be always present where there was British disaster — with Howe at Boston and with Carleton when he turned back from Ticonderoga — had hastened home before ice closed the St. Lawrence to write and talk himself back into favor with the King and Germain, which he had lost by being with Carleton.[2] Ambitious, but probably not malicious, Burgoyne succeeded in supplanting both Sir Guy Carleton and Sir Henry Clinton in command of an army which was to go from Canada to join Howe.[3] Though it was Burgoyne's elaborate 'Thoughts,' written late in February, 1777, which with modifications became the basis of the plan for the Northern campaign of that year, yet King George himself outlined the essentials of that plan as early as December 13, 1776 — at three minutes past five in the afternoon, as

[1] Force, *American Archives* (5th Series), II, 574.

[2] His 'Thoughts for Conducting the War' etc., February 28, 1777, are conveniently found in Nickerson, *The Turning Point of the Revolution*, 83–89. Carleton's very kindness to 'American Rebels' got him into trouble at home.

[3] *Correspondence of King George III*, III, 406–07. As late as February 24, 1777, the King proposed Clinton. *Ibid.*, 421, 427.

that precise monarch chose to fix the time.[1] Moreover, four days before Burgoyne set down these 'Thoughts,' his royal master had suggested Clinton for Canada and Burgoyne to join Howe.[2] Converted, no doubt, by the glib assurance of Burgoyne, the Cabinet on the very next day chose him to be 'employed in Canada.'[3] Germain would have retired Carleton altogether, but the King upheld the latter's right to govern and defend Canada, though willing to accept a more 'enterprising man' for the march through the wilderness.

The extent of the activity of George III in all his kingdom's affairs is amazing. His papers are full of varied memoranda in his own handwriting. He rivaled Homer in cataloguing all his ships, whose full names, with the kind and number of guns, he painfully wrote down. He even included the frames of the sloops to be sent to the heart of the wilds for use on Lake Champlain. The number of horses, blankets, and watch-coats were not beneath his princely notice. With his own royal hand he listed all his generals and officers, the name of each regiment, the Gibraltar forces and the Irish army in every detail. There were laborious plans for keeping poor officers out and good ones in.[4] He figured out just how many men were at Boston, and the names of every officer there. In the midst of this, and with royal scorn of good spelling and of the use of period and semicolon, he replied to endless requests for pensions, titles,

[1] *Correspondence of King George III*, III, 406–07. [2] *Ibid.*, 421.

[3] P.R.O., *State Papers, Domestic, George III*, no. 12.

[4] *Correspondence of King George III*, III, 305–27.

offices, archbishoprics, finding time to copy a letter from David Hume which must have shocked immensely his kingly orthodoxy. He never tired of solicitude for Lord North, prescribing 'abstinence and water' for his cold, and begging him to care for his health. The King's kindness extended even to good services for North's family and readiness to give him twenty thousand pounds to end his financial worries.[1] There was nothing lazy or heartless about George III. If naught came of his talk of extending the olive branch to his rebel subjects, it was because he followed a sturdy conscience, bred in the past and unillumined by an imagination which might have revealed new ways of ruling a distant part of the Empire.

If the Ministers made some mistakes in their military judgments, in the spring of 1777, there was reason enough in the sea of troubles that nearly overwhelmed them. The Opposition pestered them on every conceivable matter. Chatham, filling the avenues that led to the House, so that the Lords could get to their seats only with difficulty, proposed, in May, a cessation of hostilities in America.[2] 'We have tried for unconditional submission; try what can be gained by unconditional redress.' Lord North's brute votes triumphed against this motion, of course, but only after the Ministry had been sadly hammered by the Duke of Grafton, the Bishop of Peterborough, the Duke of Manchester, and Lord Camden. In the Commons there was a long debate

[1] *Correspondence of King George III*, III, nos. 2057–60.

[2] Hansard, *Parliamentary History*, XIX, 316–23.

and bitter attacks upon an effort to increase the Civil List, the eight hundred thousand pounds yearly which the nation gave and which the King spent at will, often to support his influence in Parliament. Moreover, the Ministry was charged with reckless expenditure of public money, with brazen corruption, with reckless grants of contracts to its friends.[1] It thus became the interest of many to prolong the war, declared the Earl of Shelburne. Indian nabobs, not content with the pillage of the East, now pillaged the West. All this, cried North's enemies, might mean opulence to his friends, but meant ruin to the public. On every occasion — the presentation of the budget, the proposed increase of the navy, even an address of thanks to the King — the waters of bitterness poured upon the Ministry. Amid all this, it possessed its soul, but not in peace.

As far as Burgoyne was concerned, there was no good reason in his past record for questioning his capacity. He had fought valiantly in Portugal, and was always brave, handsome, and adored by his men. He shared with every soldier the dangers and afflictions of a campaign.[2] During his seven years' exile in France — through sheer impecuniosity — he had picked up valuable military ideas which strengthened the British army. His first appointment to America, however, was questioned by a coolheaded, classical scholar, who thought him 'a desperate gamester to play so difficult a game.'[3] 'Men

[1] Hansard, *Parliamentary History*, XIX, 184.

[2] P.R.O., *State Papers, Domestic, Military*, 18, pp. 30, 42, 81.

[3] Hist. MSS. Com., *Report*, XIV (9), 306.

of broken fortunes,' he moralized, 'generally lose every good principle.' Indeed, Burgoyne did gamble — rather too successfully, Junius hinted — and his work as a playwright and an amateur actor might have suggested that his imagination was, perhaps, stronger than his judgment. Moreover, a man who had approved in Parliament of the idea of 'compassion united with bravery' in fighting the Americans, and who had confessed his anger disarmed by their 'dreams of liberty,' and who wished them convinced by persuasion rather than the sword, was hardly the messenger of vengeance that George III would wish to choose.[1]

The King might have recalled, too, that, soon after the news of Lexington startled England, Burgoyne had craved permission to go, as a member of Parliament, 'a friend of human nature,' into those American provinces, to which war had not extended, and to seek reconciliation. King George's good sense told him that Americans were yet 'too angry, too suspicious'; that Burgoyne would probably merely be seized as a valuable hostage.[2] Was this man of fashion, this amateur actor, asked his enemies, just the man on whom to rely when the 'fate of the British Empire' was at stake?

The plan which Burgoyne was sent to execute is not so simple as has always been supposed. Since to march an army down from Canada, and to get control of the Champlain-Hudson line, would

[1] Burgoyne's speech, February 20, 1775. Also Almon's *Debates*, IX, 152.

[2] Hist. MSS. Com., *Report*, X, Appendix VI, 9.

separate New England from the other colonies, and leave it to be conquered unaided by them, military experts have assumed that this was the aim of the British Government and its generals. In all the available correspondence as to the aim of the campaign, not a sentence makes any such proposal.[1] All the logic of the situation and military custom point to that as the object, but for this idea there is no contemporary document. Burgoyne's 'Thoughts' did offer the suggestion that, if troops were available out of the total British force to start from Rhode Island and meet the southward-marching army, that contingent might turn aside at Ticonderoga and come down the Connecticut River, conquering that valley and possibly all New England; but the King and Germain struck that out,[2] as well as another suggestion that the reënforcing army *might* be sent around to Howe by way of the St. Lawrence and the sea. Germain wanted Boston and Massachusetts to 'feel the distresses of the war' which their 'detestable principles' caused, and must have regretted that they could not thus be devastated.[3] The King greatly disliked the sea-transfer idea, because it would require leaving more troops in Canada and transferring fewer to Howe. An army coming south-

[1] *Clinton Papers, Germain Papers, Correspondence of King George III,* Hist. MSS. Com., *Stopford-Sackville Papers.* Channing (III, 250) suggests that he has noticed this, but does not emphasize the point.

[2] Notice that if this were done, there would be no conquering of the Hudson Valley and *isolating* New England, but rather Burgoyne's army, aided by troops from Rhode Island, would conquer it.

[3] Hist. MSS. Com., *Stopford-Sackville Papers,* II, 43. He pitied the other colonies, 'gradually seduced into rebellion by these Independents.'

ward by way of Lake Champlain and the Hudson would keep the reënforcing troops always between Canada and Washington's army. Burgoyne's plan, stripped by Germain and the King of the sea-transfer idea, and that of the New England invasion, had just one aim — to bring aid to Howe so that his army could go against the entire army of Washington. Of course, while doing that the invading army would have to engage part of Washington's army to the northward, and that would prevent its going against Howe.

Besides the main plan there were subordinate matters in which responsibility must be divided. Burgoyne originally asked 12,000 men, but in his 'Thoughts' seemed content with 8000. He had to be content with little over 7000 effectives.[1] He suggested a diversion by way of Lake Ontario, Oswego, and the Mohawk River under Lieutenant-Colonel St. Leger, for which in the end only 675 men were assigned. For his own and St. Leger's expedition, Burgoyne relied on a supplementary force made of Indians, Canadians, and Loyalists — all of which failed him signally when he needed them most.[2] Germain shared — indeed, always had — this delusion as to all the armies he directed in America. In spite of all of Carleton's efforts, sincere and devoted, in spite of his ill-treatment by the Ministry, he could not secure for Burgoyne the Indians and the Canadians called for in the plan.[3]

[1] Hist. MSS. Com., *Report, Stopford-Sackville Papers*, II, 62.

[2] *Ibid.* Burgoyne denied later that it was *his* plan. Indeed, it had been seriously changed by the Ministry.

[3] P.R.O., *State Papers, Domestic, Military*, 19, no. 7, pp. 27–30.

Burgoyne, full of the secrets of his plan, reached Quebec on May 6. He was mortified to find a paper handed about town describing the whole design of the campaign as if copied from Germain's orders.[1] Yet four months earlier General Schuyler had, from a spy serving in Canada, a forecast of every essential of the prospective campaign.[2] Indeed, there was no great mystery about it, and any experienced military man could have made a fairly accurate guess. For centuries, as Gates wrote Hancock, it had been the uniform plan of France and England for the conquest of America. Howe and Carleton had tried it only the previous year.[3]

Burgoyne found Carleton as helpful and devoted as a brother. A critic thought Carleton 'proud, austere, narrow-minded' and though environed by flatterers, and with the powers of a dictator, yet disappointed in all his views and ambitions.[4] After all, though he hated Germain, Carleton was a gentleman and loved his country. There was a serious shortage of transport, which Carleton, during a long winter, had done little to remedy. In spite of every effort the expedition was short of horses, not enough even for the train of artillery — some 138 guns, needed especially at Ticonderoga. For transportation beyond that point 500 little two-wheeled carts of green timber were hastily made up. Yet this inadequate transport was burdened with far too

[1] P.R.O., *State Papers, Domestic, Military*, 19, no. 7, pp. 30–31.

[2] *Cont. Cong. Papers* (*Schuyler Letters*), 153, III, 36–37, January 13, 1777.

[3] Library of Congress (*Force Trans.*), *Gates Letters*, I, April 29, 1777.

[4] Stevens, *Facsimiles*, no. 1571.

much baggage of the officers.[1] Burgoyne's orders, often repeated, were positive against this excess. A knapsack was enough, he said, for a devoted officer. A little tent and a valise was his advice to General Riedesel, whose soldiers were especially accused of not complying. In one case two barrels of madeira and two of rum were found in violation of the order.[2]

When Burgoyne's failure was being aired in Parliament two years later, it was asserted that 2000 women were with the army and fed from the rations of the soldiers. The Adjutant-General, under fire there, dodged the question as to how *many* women there were: 'I had not much leisure for attention to the ladies, and I know very little of their beauty or their numbers.' He insisted women were not an impediment, and were fed from the rations of the men they followed. He believed there was an order limiting their number to three for each company. He would have been sorry to have 2000 along![3] Burgoyne, the tongue of scandal whispered, was only interested in one.

Burgoyne's army gathered at St. John's, where,

[1] For the whole subject of land transport for the British army see E. E. Curtis, *The British Army in the American Revolution*, 134–47.

[2] P.R.O., *State Papers, Domestic, George III*, no. 19, pp. 4–6; P.R.O., *State Papers, Domestic, Military*, 19, no. 7, pp. 3–4, 10–13, 125; no. 18, p. 62; no. 5. The Adjutant-General, before the House of Commons two years later, said officers sometimes bought horses and wagons for carrying their own luggage. His memory was very defective as to the officers' obedience to the baggage order.

[3] P.R.O., *State Papers, Domestic, Military*, 19, no. 7, pp. 128–29, 134, 136. The military regulations of the time allowed 60 women and 12 servants to each regiment, wherein there were 677 men and officers. P.R.O., *Colonial Office*, Class 5, p. 123.

on June 15, its effectives numbered about 8000. Musicians, women, and servants brought the number perhaps close to 10,000.[1] The Canadian contingent was most disappointing — only 150 — and the Indian added only 400. When his army left St. John's to ascend the Richelieu to Lake Champlain, there entered the somber depths of the American forest a resplendent pageant, combining the resources of both America and Europe to make it so. As the great fleet pushed out into the lake, the Indian forces were first, in great birchbark canoes. Then came the British advance guard, followed by the flotilla which had beaten Arnold, and the bulk of the army, in row galleys, forming the rear. Into the still blue of the lake, and against the varied greens of the wooded shore, came a rainbow of color such as the wilds had seldom seen. There were, in the combined British and German troops, companies and regiments in blue coats, others in red or in green with cuffs of red. The breeches might be of yellow buff, or of white, or even the leather of the dismounted dragoons. In headdress there were little caps of black leather, plumed cocked hats, and the high hats of grenadiers — the British, of black bearskin, the German, faced with gleaming metal; and finally, there were the ever-present and incredible soldiers' queues. In footgear the most notable things were the high-spurred jackboots of the German dragoons, whose whole outfit was far too

[1] But of these the regulars, British and German, numbered only 6489. P.R.O., *State Papers, Domestic, Military,* 19, no. 7, pp. 20–23. All official returns on this campaign are confusing.

heavy for forest warfare. Finally, as if to clog the dragoon still further, he carried a broadsword with a three-pound scabbard. Swelling this riot of color were the varied regimental flags flaunting in the breeze.[1]

As this gorgeous and confident fleet bore down on Ticonderoga, what were the conditions in the American army there? During the fall, winter, and spring the command of the Northern army had passed like a shuttlecock from Schuyler to Gates,[2] back to Schuyler, again to Gates, and back to the unlucky Schuyler just in time to make him responsible for the fate of Ticonderoga. There were other factors, but the chief was the rivalry of New York and New England, of 'Yorker and Yankee.' Factions have rarely hated each other more cordially. When Gates, in 'Yorkers'' phrase, had 'poisoned the minds' of most Congressmen,[3] and maneuvered Schuyler out and himself in, he wrote Washington of his triumph, and gushed so much about his own integrity that he seemed to be in doubt about it.[4] Within two months he was complaining to a member of Congress how little help he could expect from Washington; that generals were like parsons, 'all for

[1] For the elements of this picture I have drawn on Nickerson, *The Turning Point of the Revolution*, 104–12. Had Germain left the selection of the troops to Carleton, familiar with forest warfare, the heavy dragoons would, perhaps, have been left in Quebec. P.R.O., *State Papers, Domestic, Military*, no. 18, pp. 23–25, 27.

[2] At least as far as concerned the Canadian army. *Letters of . . . Continental Congress* (Burnett, ed.), II, 3, 11, 48.

[3] *Ibid.*, 377, Library of Congress (*Force Trans.*), *Gates Letters*, I, Gates to Lovell, May 12.

[4] *Ibid.*, *Gates Letters*, I, March 26, 1777.

christening their own child first.'[1] Then suddenly Congress did Schuyler justice, restored his command,[2] and Gates posted off to Philadelphia, where 'discomposed, chagrined, angry,' he demanded an audience. Admitted to Independence Hall, he made, says a witness, a most 'unhappy figure.' Seated in an 'Easy Cavalier Posture in an Elbow Chair,' he took out of his pocket some scraps of paper containing a narrative of his 'Birth, Parentage, and Education, Life, Character, and Behavior.' His manner was 'ingracious,' void of all dignity; his delivery incoherent, broken with 'frequent chasms in which he was poring over his scattered Notes.' His 'Vanity, Folly, and Rudeness' were such, as he browbeat his 'mortal enemies,' the New York delegates, that at last Paca 'caught fire,' and moved his withdrawal, which was voted after a 'General Clamour.' Through all this scene New England members aligned themselves solidly against New Yorkers and their friends.[3]

For the time New York won; Schuyler took command. Reading this Dutch patrician's letters,[4] one finds him prudent, shrewd, logical, able to detect an enemy's ruse to deceive. He was fairly patient, but lacking in that serenity which Washington had, except in great crises. He was not easily discouraged, ready to take infinite pains to see that the Government was not cheated, and that all was done to

[1] Library of Congress, *Gates Letters*, I, May 25, 1777.

[2] *Journals of Continental Congress* (Ford, ed.), VII, 364.

[3] *Letters of . . . Continental Congress* (Burnett, ed.), II, 377, 382, 384, 385, 386.

[4] *Cont. Cong. Papers* (*Schuyler*), 153, III, *passim*.

secure success. He could be stern in ordering executions when plainly for the good of the service, but he was just, conscientious, and appreciative of work done by subordinates. Not a great soldier, he was a noble character and a true patriot, with no rivals but Washington and Greene.

The army he now commanded would have put black despair into the heart of a conventional European officer. Two months before the British arrived, Ticonderoga was manned with only 1900 men, sick and well, of whom one fourth were destitute of arms, using spears as a substitute, and numbers of them were barefoot.[1] Patching, mending, and making up everything they could lay hands upon, the troops at Peekskill were barely covered with tents, the old being too rotten to mend.[2] There was neither gun, cartridge-box, flint, nor ammunition at Bennington; there was no quartermaster or wagon-master; 'no mortal man' with power to pay expenses or get baggage and men forward.[3] Gates complained that many men were sent without provisions, as if the equipment for a soldier grew in the woods. He found that carters, bringing ordnance from Boston, left it wherever 'their villainy, laziness, or other reason suggested.' The army was short 2000 tents and 10,000 blankets.[4] Cannon and stores due at Ticonderoga were found at Albany. He pleaded in vain for cartridge paper, begging Congress to send old books if there was no regular paper. In trying to

[1] Library of Congress (*Force Trans.*), *Gates Letters*, I, April 25, 1777.
[2] *Ibid.*, May 3. [3] *Ibid.*, *Heath Letters*, April 25, 1777.
[4] *Ibid.*, *Gates Letters*, I, March 21, 1777.

get troops from New England, he found 'such an apathy as nothing but the cannon of the enemy will waken.'[1] If Gates found this difficulty, how much more Schuyler, under whom the New York militia would serve willingly, but who was an object of hate to all 'Yankees.'

One might easily think, on reading the complaining letters of any one general — Washington, Greene, Schuyler, Gates, Montgomery, or Lincoln — that this particular officer was a half-hearted grumbler, but when one finds the same story from every source, there is no escape from the conviction that the short-time, half-trained American soldier was but a broken reed, and that the utter lack of any trained and experienced military organization, fitted to maintain supplies and get them to the places where they were wanted, made the task of any American leader heavy beyond mortal shoulders to bear.

Gates, doubtless, did the best he could, but Schuyler could make little change before the British were upon Ticonderoga. An engineer, described by Wilkinson as a 'second-rate carpenter,' was pushing an 'unmeaning plan,' while men prayed for Kosciusko to come back 'for God's sake.'[2] So extensive were the works that Schuyler was alarmed at the smallness of the garrison, which was in fact quite

[1] Library of Congress, *Gates Letters*, I, April 22, 1777. As Washington wrote Quincy, they 'apprehend no danger until it stares them in the face.' March 24, 1776 (W.L.C.L.). It was due he thought to 'an unaccountable stupidity.' Washington, *Writings* (Ford, ed.), III, 87.

[2] Library of Congress (*Force Trans.*), *Gates Letters*, I, Wilkinson to Gates, May 31.

inadequate. The quartermaster's 'languor' in sending 'working cattle' and batteau repairs had left all in confusion. The naval force was not ready to meet the enemy, because the materials and the soldiers to do the work had not arrived. Ten days before the British reached Ticonderoga, beef and pork for sixty days, and flour for one hundred and twenty, reached camp, but the troops were miserably clad and armed, all ragged, many barefooted. Not a room was finished in the hospital. At the last moment there was sad disappointment as to militia that had not come up, beef that was rotten, and even the gifts for the Indians belated.[1] When the New England militia did come, late in July, they stayed four or five days, and then went off home, because the grain was ready to cut, and would be ruined by delay![2] The 2000 men, actually in the fort at the critical moment, was entirely too small a force to man the vast works.[3]

In late April and in May, 3000 stands of arms arrived at Portsmouth from France, 25,000 at Boston from the same source, together with several thousand pounds of powder, 15,000 suits of clothes and tents for 30,000 men.[4] This help from abroad

[1] *Cont. Cong. Letters* (*Schuyler Letters*), 153, III, 154, 155,176–208.

[2] *Ibid.*, 222, 226.

[3] *Ibid.* (*Heath Letters*), Washington to Heath, July 19. Washington says St. Clair had 2089 effectives and 900 militia. He wonders where 2830 Massachusetts militia, who marched, could have gone. The 900 militia stayed three days, says St. Clair, and 700 of his 2000 refused to stay another day because their terms had expired. Library of Congress (*Force Trans.*), *Gates Letters*, August 1, St. Clair to Gates.

[4] Library of Congress (*Force Trans.*), *Gates Letters*, I, April 25, May 25; (*Heath Letters*), April, 1777, Knox to Heath.

was about the only bright spot in a very dark picture.

Burgoyne landed his army at Crown Point and approached Ticonderoga with a good deal of unnecessary caution. Though Gates had been offered the command, he shrewdly gave way to Major-General St. Clair, a fine-mannered man of aristocratic lineage, who, as a British soldier, had fought at Quebec under Wolfe. St. Clair's position was very bad, as the British experts quickly saw. Burgoyne had only to seize Mount Defiance, towering above Ticonderoga, and that fort was at his mercy. A sagacious Indian thought that the great father of the sun must have created it of late, else why had it never been occupied before?[1] The American officers thought its sides too steep, but General Phillips refused to admit that a goat's climbing dexterity was superior to a man's, or that cannon could not be hauled where a man could go. When men and guns stood on its summit, St. Clair could do nothing but evacuate and beat a hasty retreat, saving what he could. At the 'whiff and the wind of the victor's sword' Ticonderoga fell, 'like Priam before Pyrrhus.'

King George, reminding one of King Valoroso in the 'Rose and the Ring,' rejoiced like a schoolboy that he had 'beat all the Americans,' and John Adams doubted whether Congress could ever defend a post 'until we shoot a general.'[2] Samuel Adams hinted darkly at treason, 'evident Marks of Deliberation and Design,' and Congress ordered both

[1] Stevens, *Facsimiles*, no. 1571, p. 10.
[2] *Familiar Letters*, p. 292.

Schuyler and St. Clair to appear before it, that the saddle might be laid on the right horse.[1] Many reasonable men saw that not generals, but lack of men, means, organization, made the evacuation of Ticonderoga inevitable in the face of such a force as Burgoyne's.[2] The one solid reason for removing Schuyler was the sectional spirit of New England which was keeping her militia from serving under the New York general. Besides, public opinion was aroused and somebody must be thrown to the lions.[3] Schuyler was in desperate straits and feared the enemy would get control of all that region, yet he would not despair or despond. After Ticonderoga, numbers of soldiers strolled home, lost their arms, and there was the greatest disorder and confusion in the retreat.[4] By the end of the month Schuyler had only 3000 Continental troops and 1300 militia — daily decreasing, 'not a man left from Connecticut.'

There was a 'shameful tardiness' in making the levies, and one third of the few sent to the front were 'boys, aged men, and negroes, who disgrace our arms.' One third of Schuyler's Continental troops were

[1] *Letters of . . . Continental Congress* (Burnett, ed.), II, 434–35.

[2] *Ibid.*, 415, 417, 424–26, 427, 428, 429, 433, 434.

[3] Schuyler declared, and doubtless truly, that he could easily have exculpated himself if he could have published his letters to Congress and Washington, but that would be against public interest, and he preferred calumny. The inquiry dragged on, and as late as December 29, 1777, he was begging for a chance to prove that he had done his whole duty. Not till February, 1778, was the court-martial ordered, and not convened until October 1. On December 3, 1778, the verdict was unanimous, 'not guilty.' *Cont. Cong. Papers* (*Schuyler Letters*), no. 153, III, 145, 228, 260–62.

[4] *Cont. Cong. Papers* (*Schuyler Letters*), no. 153, III, 222, 226, 228; Library of Congress (*Force Trans.*), *Heath Letters*, July 18, Heath to Schuyler.

negroes. 'Is it consistent,' he asked, 'with the sons of freedom to trust their all to be defended by slaves?' There were, moreover, desertion, great sickness due to too much fresh meat, losses in skirmishes, militia threatening to leave in a few days — in a word, 'alarming weakness.' To requests for reënforcements, Massachusetts made no reply, Connecticut only promised, and the militia that did appear took the field 'literally naked, without blankets, ill-armed,' and led by officers who 'would be a disgrace to the most contemptible troops.' Cashiering did no good, was no punishment, because they had 'no sense of honor.' Some would shed a luster on the best army that ever was, but others 'stood by and suffered the most scandalous depredations on the ruined and flying inhabitants.' [1]

With such an army Schuyler had made his stand, August 1, at Stillwater, where he fortified and awaited aid. Burgoyne's army, flushed with victory, was coming upon Schuyler's force; 'weak in numbers, dispirited, naked, in a manner, destitute of provisions, without camp equipage, with little ammunition and not a single piece of cannon.' [2] On August 10, Schuyler received the resolution of Congress putting Gates in his place. As Gates dallied about taking command, Schuyler was left until the news of Bennington arrived. It was then, of course, that the tide turned, and Gates got the credit for the better aspect of American affairs.

[1] Library of Congress (*Force Trans.*), *Heath Letters*, July 28; *Cont. Cong. Papers* (*Schuyler Letters*), no. 153, III, 230–36.

[2] *Letters to Washington* (Sparks, ed.), I, 394–95.

CHAPTER XIX

THE TRIUMPHANT BURGOYNE ENCOUNTERS A SETBACK

BURGOYNE, in possession of Ticonderoga, pressed the pursuit of St. Clair's army vigorously at first. Pursuing the Americans that fled by the Castleton road, Reidesel and Fraser learned at Hubbardton that there was still fight enough in the 'Yankee' soldiers. A dearly bought victory was won, and Seth Warner's troops fled to fight another day, but not until serious flaws were shown in the British and German fitness for forest warfare. Pursuit by the St. Anne route was even less successful, and Burgoyne's officers learned still more about fighting in the woods. Indeed, before the campaign was over, the Earl of Balcarras, one of Burgoyne's best officers, paid American soldiers the tribute, that they were 'never contemptible in the eye of a soldier.' At all times when he met 'the Rebels,' they fought with 'great courage and obstinacy.' They never defended their entrenchments after making them, but always marched out of them and attacked the British. Neither their attack nor resistance was to be despised.[1]

Except some 900 men, which Burgoyne had to leave for defense of Ticonderoga, his army was concentrated largely at Skenesboro. Carleton had

[1] P.R.O., *State Papers, Domestic, Military*, 18, no. 5, pp. 26, 39, 41, 43. The Earl of Harrington agreed.

refused men for the fort's defense, because of the minuteness of his orders from Germain. Yet Burgoyne could not 'leave the post in weakness' and the garrison was a heavy drain on the 'life-blood' of his force.[1] From July 9 to August 9, a precious month, Burgoyne delayed, spending twenty hours, as he had long before realized that a commander in America must do, thinking how to feed his army, to one as to how to fight it. His problem, after Ticonderoga, was to get from the Champlain waterway to the Hudson River waterway over the divide. For his army's march he had chosen the route by Skenesboro and St. Anne, instead of that by Lake George, which he had once praised, but he caused the provisions and ammunition to be carried by the Lake George route. Perhaps his choice for the army was determined by his long-cherished desire to worry New England with the fear that his troops turn that way. This would keep the 'Yankees' within their own borders.[2]

Having chosen to take his whole force forward, Burgoyne's difficulties multiplied. His previous troubles, 'remote situation of the troops, currents, winds, roads, want of materials for caulking the vessels, inactivity and desertion of the Canadian corvées,' began to look small.[3] In the first place, he had too much artillery along [4] — five or six guns to

[1] P.R.O., *State Papers, Domestic, Military,* 19, no. 7, pp. 79–83.

[2] P.R.O., *State Papers, Domestic, Military,* 19, no. 7, pp. 27–30, 43. He wrote urging the King not to worry, for in spite of this feint the army was actually going straight to Albany, as ordered.

[3] He summed these up on July 11, 1777. P.R.O., *State Papers, Domestic, Military,* 19, no. 7, p. 39.

[4] Robertson did not think so. *Ibid.,* pp. 77–78.

each thousand men — and in the meanest place in the world to carry it. The boats taken from Champlain to Lake George, and thence to the Hudson for the transportation of provisions, required ten or twelve oxen for each wheeled frame on which they were carried. The provision carts of green timber broke down. On the other route where the army moved, Schuyler got 1000 axemen busy as beavers felling trees. They were so chopped down as to interlock and jam together until these forest giants formed a barrier only penetrable by the Canadian axemen. Heavy rains had soaked the clay soil, swamps were at their worst, and forty bridges were needed at the swollen streams.[1] Moreover, there was sultry heat, mosquitoes and black flies to torment, and often not enough provision for two days ahead,[2] while the fleeing inhabitants drove off their cattle, burned their crops and destroyed food. The only thing in plenty was port and madeira for the British and German officers.

The British army, July 24, set in motion toward Fort Edward. Schuyler, knowing that he could leap his horse over its ramparts, did not wait, but retired with his 2000 men until, by August 12, new levies of militia swelled his numbers to 4400. To offset his unpopularity with New England men, Congress had sent him Arnold and Lincoln from that section, but rumors against Schuyler and St. Clair continued to lower the morale, and there was alarming desertion.[3]

[1] B. de Fonblanque, *Burgoyne*, 268–69.

[2] P.R.O., *State Papers, Domestic, Military*, 19, no. 7, pp. 44, 46.

[3] *Cont. Cong. Papers* (*Schuyler Letters*), 153, III, 234–46, 242–43.

When things were at their worst, all was changed by the battle of Bennington where the eastern militia, in Gates's exalted phrase, 'clipt the wings of Burgoyne's flying camp.'

Burgoyne was getting restive because the Tories he expected did not 'swarm.' Moreover, his army was threatened with hunger. There were rumors of vast stores at Bennington, not far from the German auxiliaries on his left flank. Why not seize them and 1300 horses to mount the heavy-footed German dragoons, who needed mounting, if ever dragoons did. The plan at last agreed upon with General Riedesel was to send Colonel Baum [1] — attended and advised by one Skene, a local Tory — with some 800 men on this alluring raid which would 'try the affection of the country.' [2] There was to be great caution, no risks, no plundering, no offense to the inhabitants, who were assumed to be largely Tories. The stress was on two things: first, get all the horses, oxen, carriages, food possible and give receipts; second, use every means to spread the idea that Baum's troops are merely the advance guard of the whole army, marching to Boston to meet British troops from Rhode Island.[3]

[1] P.R.O., *State Papers, Domestic, Military*, 19, no. 7, pp. 58–60. Fraser didn't like sending Germans, who 'are not a very active people,' but they were on the army's left and courtesy demanded it. *Ibid.* The Earl of Harrington said Riedesel asked to have Baum in charge, and that the latter was perfectly satisfied with the division given him. *Ibid.*, 18, no. 6, p. 9.

[2] Six hundred and fifty rank and file of which 170 were clumsy dragoons. There 374 Germans altogether; 300 Tories, Indians, and Canadians.

[3] P.R.O., *State Papers, Domestic, Military*, 19, no. 7, pp. 72–73. 'Use every principle of humanity' in getting these results, were the orders.

About a fortnight before the inception of this raid occurred the murder, by Burgoyne's marauding Indians, of a beautiful young woman, Jane McCrea. This inevitable outcome of the employment of Indians by the British was conjured up in Burke's ironical picture of the keeper of His Majesty's menagerie flinging open the dens of wild beasts, while exhorting the gentle lions, humane bears, tender-hearted hyenas, as Christians, not to hurt man, woman, or child.[1]

The question of the use of Indians arose both in Congress and in Parliament early in the war. Congress knew them and hesitated. They were cruel, unreliable, and expensive allies. Members of Parliament acted on reason, sentiment, or mere partisanship. Pownall, who perhaps knew more about it than any other member, declared that no war could be carried on in America wherein the Indians would not mix. 'Indian neutrality is dangerous, delusive nonsense,' he said. 'We must have them with or against us.'[2] Nevertheless, use against an invading army was one thing, while use in the settled territory of an enemy by an invading army was quite another. Ethan Allen, about to invade Canada, 1775, urged Indian warriors, 'join with me and my warriors and ambush the Regulars. . . . I will give you money,

[1] Chatham also railed against it, but the Earl of Hardwicke, Earl Gower, and Lord Lyttelton pointed out that Pitt had authorized the use of Indians in the Seven Years' war. Hist. MSS. Com., *Report, Dartmouth,* II, 447; Hansard, *Parliamentary History,* XIX, 495, 508. Chatham denied this. Hansard, *Parliamentary History,* XIX, 507, 509, 512. Denbigh, thereupon, called him 'the great Oracle with the short memory.' *Ibid.,* 511.

[2] Hansard, XIX, 702, 704.

blankets, tomahawks, knives, paint, and anything there is in the army, just like brothers.'[1] The Massachusetts Congress tried to enlist the Mohawk tribe and tempted the Stockbridge Indians, with 'a blanket and a yard of ribbon,' to whet their hatchets and 'with us defend our liberties and our lives.'[2] These facts coming to Lord Dartmouth's ears, he sent Dunmore the King's command to engage 'a body of Indians.'[3] Yet Congress, at that time, was doubtful of the value of Indian aid, and voted to seek such alliance only in case the British did so.[4] Peace and friendship Congress wished very much, and its agents at first merely urged the Indians to stay home and 'keep the hatchet buried deep.'[5]

The British Indian agent in the South, acting on the orders of Germain, succeeded, October, 1776, in getting the Creeks and Choctaws to make peace, and to join in an attack on the 'Rebels.' A large party of each met before Stuart's house. Both parties were highly painted and carried a white flag. Halting some three hundred yards apart, their chiefs sang the peace song and waved eagles' tails and swans' wings over their heads. Joining hands, they gave to Stuart two clubs painted red and laid

[1] Force, *American Archives* (4th Series), II, 714.

[2] *Ibid.*, I, 1350, II, 611; April 1, 1775. New York sought only neutrality, *Ibid.*, II, 1842. Congress to Kirkland, Belcher, *First American . . . War*, I, 164.

[3] *State Records of North Carolina*, X, 138b, August 2, 1775.

[4] *Journals of Continental Congress* (Ford, ed.), II, 123.

[5] *Ibid.*, II, 182. Washington approved this policy. Washington, *Writings* (Ford, ed.), III, 48.

down their arms, which Stuart agreed to bury very deep in the ground.[1]

Day by day Stuart reported to Germain the intrigues of 'Rebel' traders and pack horsemen to turn the Indians against the British Government.[2]

The arguments used by both sides to win over the Indians in council were simple enough. British agents told how the colonists had turned basely wicked and ungrateful, and were trying to drive the 'Great English Father' out of America. Only the King's troops kept the Americans from falling on the 'Red Children,' and killing them.[3] Agents of the colonists were just as eloquent upon deep-laid 'plots' of the British Ministry to take away 'our liberty and your liberty' and let us have 'nothing to eat, drink or wear but what they say we shall.' They will do the same to you, and if they will destroy us who are of the same blood, 'what can you Indians expect?' If they cut our throats, who will protect you?[4]

But far more potent with the Indians, were economic arguments, gifts of guns, powder, blankets, clothing, trinkets, and these the British had manufactured and furnished for years past. Americans, famished for these things themselves, could ill spare

[1] P.R.O., *Colonial Office*, 5–78, p. 30. Germain later congratulated Stuart on this peace. *Ibid.*, 125.

[2] P.R.O., *Colonial Office*, 5–78, pp. 30, 76, 77, 125. A Choctaw chief begged Stuart to stop the selling of rum before his people were wholly extirpated. He had lost over one thousand men in eighteen months from excessive drinking.

[3] *North Carolina Records*, x, 343.

[4] Force, *American Archives* (4th Series), I, 1347, 1350; II, 611, 612; III, 483.

them for the Indians.[1] Fairly blackmailed by threats from the Indians, Congress made every effort, but often in vain.[2] A great aid to Congress, handicapped in this way, was the Reverend Samuel Kirkland, who had great success in keeping the Indians friendly and neutral. News of victory was always useful, too, and a special messenger hastened to tell the Six Nations of the victory at Trenton.[3] Neither this, the dire threats of Congress, nor Gates's assurance to them that the friendly King of France was sending ships daily, with brass cannon, powder and arms for America, could keep the majority of these Nations from joining Burgoyne.[4]

Up to May 26, 1776, the chief effort of the States and of Congress was to keep the Indians neutral.[5] On the border the settlers were ever crying for help. The defenseless west of Georgia, Virginia, Pennsylvania, and New York was ravaged from the first, and Congress could do little, since it had no adequate force, and a weak military effort would merely provoke further attack. It was only when Canada was about to be wholly lost, May, 1776, that Congress reluctantly passed a resolution that

[1] *Archives Nationales*, K, 1364, F. 64; M. de Fleury to Duc de Broglie.

[2] *Journals of the Continental Congress* (Ford, ed.), II, 175; IV, 330; X, 105; Force, *American Archives* (4th Series), II, 611–12.

[3] *Journals of Continental Congress* (Ford, ed.), III, 351; *Cont. Cong. Papers* (*Schuyler Letters*), 153, III, 371.

[4] *Letters of . . . Continental Congress* (Burnett, ed.), II, 38; Library of Congress (*Force Trans.*), *Gates Letters*, May 7.

[5] Force, *American Archives* (4th Series), III, 792; IV, 908, 1482; *Journals of Continental Congress* (Ford, ed.), III, 351, 401; IV, 96–97, 191.

it was 'highly expedient to engage Indians in the service of the United Colonies.' Washington was empowered to employ two thousand in Canada. A bounty was to be paid for every officer and private of the King's army captured and delivered.[1] Washington tried to carry out these instructions, but a few Mickmack, St. John's, and Stockbridge Indians were all he enlisted. The losses in Canada made the Indians less friendly, and Schuyler found only the Oneidas ready to ally with America.[2] When, in September of 1777, the American army stood at bay, Schuyler induced three hundred Oneidas and Tuscaroras to accept the war belt. They were equipped, and joined Gates's army at once, in time to intercept Burgoyne's dispatches and take thirty prisoners.[3]

Both sides had employed Indians; therefore, when Burgoyne decided to use them in his campaign,[4] 'Gentleman Johnny,' as he was nicknamed, had supreme confidence in the value of palaver. After beginning his campaign with a pompous and menacing proclamation — which he never meant — wherein he talked of letting loose his thousands of Indians, as 'messengers of Justice and Wrath' to

[1] *Journals of Continental Congress* (Ford, ed.), IV, 394; V, 421; Force, *American Archives* (4th Series), VI, 742, 914, 992; (5th Series), I, 425.

[2] *Journals of Continental Congress* (Ford, ed.), V, 527; Force, *American Archives* (5th Series), I, 189, 856, 1223, 697, 676.

[3] *Cont. Cong. Papers* (*Schuyler Letters*), 153, III, 253. Yet Schuyler describes his house as 'daily crowded with Indians and I have nothing for them.' *Ibid.*, 27.

[4] See J. Lind, *Answer to Declaration of Independence*, 109, and R. H. Lee, *Letters*, I, 156, 160, for current opinion on this matter.

overwhelm his 'hardened enemies' with every horror, he roared just as ungently to his Indian allies. To these savages, 'heathen, tall, warlike, and enterprising, but wicked as satan,' he preached the laws of war.[1] 'Aged men, women, children and prisoners must be held sacred from the knife or hatchet.' Scalps, being the Indian 'badge of victory,' might be taken, but only from the dead, killed by their own fire. The Indians, hearing the voice of their 'great father beyond the lake,' promised, though 'tried and tempted by the Bostonians,' to sharpen their hatchets upon their affections, obey Burgoyne, and fight for King George. And thus Burke's 'tender-hearted hyenas' set out only to prove one of Burgoyne's greatest delusions.[2]

The murder of Jane McCrea was only one of many Indian atrocities, but that was an incident to touch every imagination. A beauty in her bridal dress, hastening to her lover, her murder, and then the scalp with the lustrous hair dangling from the belt of a savage — this was a picture to fire even a calculating Provincial. The New England militia now had the needed motive. Instead of being terrorized, they were maddened to resist. Rumor and propaganda played fast and loose with the facts, and, like Othello, men acted on what they believed for the moment, not on the truth. Gates wrote Washington that 'this polite Macaroni, Burgoyne,' paid ten dollars for each scalp taken, 'a stain on the honor of

[1] *Letters from America* (trans. by Pettengill), p. 82.

[2] See comments of Dú Roi in his *Journal*, *German-American Annals*, September, 1911, p. 164.

British arms,' and he rebuked that fine gentleman, 'soldier and scholar' for his baseness.[1] Gates, admitting that at first his army was 'quite panic-struck by the Indians,' hoped the bloody hatchet Burgoyne had so barbarously used might 'find its way into his own head.'[2] Arnold raged about the 'infernal savages, joined by a number of more savage and infernal Tories painted like furies' harassing and scalping 'our people.'[3] There was even talk of King George greedily counting the scalps sent in bales to him, and very accurate statistics as to the number of old men, boys, women, and girls from whom such trophies had been taken.[4] In England the King's enemies pictured him gnawing at the end of a human bone, while one of his red-skinned allies gnawed at the other.[5]

But nobody was more horrified by the bloody Jane McCrea affair than Burgoyne. He called the Indians to council, threatened the culprit with death and his officers dissuaded him only by forcing him to see that such an action would cause a total defection of the Indians, who might go over to the enemy or even endanger Canada if they returned there in wrath.[6] He insisted that no Indian party should go out without a British officer responsible

[1] Library of Congress (*Force Trans.*), *Gates Letters*, I, August 28, 1777; September 2, 1777.

[2] *Ibid.*, Gates to Washington, August 22.

[3] *Ibid.*, August 5, 1777.

[4] During the Great War an Irish Catholic bishop in Detroit published equally amazing statistics about King George to a gullible public.

[5] T. Wright, *Caricature History of the Georges*, 336.

[6] P.R.O., *State Papers, Domestic, Military*, 18, no. 6, pp. 5–6.

for them. When great discontent followed, Burgoyne declared he would rather lose every Indian than connive at their enormities. Many did leave, resenting the restraint on their cruelties and plunder.[1] Yet no amount of virtue could now rid Burgoyne of the consequences of employing savage allies. New England was up, and Burgoyne was to reap the whirlwind.

New England was nervous over having a British army hovering on its western border. New Hampshire was first to move. John Stark, who led its troops at Bunker Hill, had since become a Yankee Achilles, sulking over real wrongs from Congress. He was bitter against New York, would not serve Congress, but would fight for his native State. Financed by John Langdon's 'hard money,' household plate, and seventy hogsheads of Tobago rum, 'sold for what it would fetch,' Stark recruited a rustic army, even breaking the precious New England Sabbath to enlist 4000 of the men. This free lance, with an independent brigade of some 1500 officers and men, refused to coöperate with Lincoln — who was told to mind his own affairs[2] — and struck Baum's left rear at Bennington, August 16, winning a complete victory. Nor was that all, for, when the German leader learned that 1800 Americans were before him, he notified Burgoyne,[3]

[1] P.R.O., *State Papers, Domestic, Military*, 18, no. 6, pp. 7, 8, 9.

[2] *Cont. Cong. Papers* (*Schuyler Letters*), 153, II, 237. 'The untimely objections of General Stark are a new source of distress to us,' wrote Schuyler.

[3] P.R.O., *State Papers, Domestic, Military*, 18, no. 16, p. 11. Stark's army had increased to perhaps 2000 before the battle was fought.

who dispatched Colonel Breyman with over 600 men, and they, coming up too late, were also defeated by Stark and Colonel Warner with fresh troops.[1]

History offers few examples of such a victory of untrained militia, over regulars. It was won, moreover, in spite of mean-minded particularism. Stark succeeded in spite of a jealous spirit that spelled disaster. Luck that disgraced fiction was all with him, and the conditions favored the frontier warriors. Baum's troubles had begun at once. His Indians ran wild, looted and ravaged. They ruined every horse they met.[2] The countryside was not friendly, as Skene promised, and yet success rested on that. The 'Tories,' who at last appeared to be gathering, proved to be Stark's soldiers in shirt-sleeves, who thus got an initial advantage over the brave but rather stupid Baum. The Germans resented the American method of fighting; 'they lie like bacon hunters behind the trees, and slip from one tree to the other' was the complaint.[3] Indeed, they fought Indian fashion, 'behind stone walls' and never made one 'gallant or manly attempt' on their enemies. In a word, they did not walk up in the open, dressed in red coats, to be shot. The British, who might beat them in the 'plains of Europe,'

[1] Of Baum's 374 Germans, only 9 privates ever returned. Stark took 700 prisoners. Of Breyman's 642, there were 20 dead, 69 wounded, 142 missing. Stark and Warner lost 30 killed, 40 wounded. Library of Congress (*Force Trans.*), *Gates Letters*, I, Stark to Gates, August 22, 1777. Warner had been a tower of strength to Stark throughout.

[2] P.R.O., *State Papers, Domestic, Military*, 18, no. 7, pp. 66, 68.

[3] *Letters from America* (trans. by Pettengill), 80.

risked, therefore, being vanquished in the woods of America.

Stark declared that his army could not have behaved better if they had 'been Alexanders or Charleses of Sweden.' Though he had been at Bunker Hill and with Wolfe at Quebec, he thought it the hottest action he was ever in. Losing his bridle and his saddle during the clash of arms may have strengthened this conviction.[1] 'The whole country resounds with the fame of your victory,' wrote Gates.[2] The most serious consequences to Burgoyne were the reduction of his army by a thousand men, and the new flame in the hearts of the New England militia which brought them trooping to swell Gates's army. All this reduced the 'boasting stile' of the fluent author of proclamations, sneered Gates, and he began 'in some degree to think and talk like other men.'[3]

Meanwhile, Fate had dealt Burgoyne's plans another serious blow. It was about time that St. Leger, another hero of the Plains of Abraham, was due to appear in the Mohawk Valley to distract part of the American Army of the North. Three hundred miles, he was to come, by the St. Lawrence, Lake

[1] Hist. MSS. Com., *American MSS.*, I, 143; Library of Congress (*Force Trans.*), *Gates Letters*, I, August 22, 1777. Burgoyne said ruefully that the Vermont and New Hampshire militia were equal to any of the troops under Gates.

[2] *Ibid.*, August 19. Congress had reinstated him, and recalled St. Clair and Schuyler, he informed Stark.

[3] *Ibid.*, September 3, 1777 (Gates to the President of Congress). Nevertheless, Gates had to promise the Governor of Connecticut not to detain his militia one moment longer than was necessary. *Ibid.*, September 4.

Ontario, and minor waterways, to strike terror to the 'Rebels' of the Mohawk frontier, chiefly Dutch and German with a sprinkling of other nationalities. With less than 600 white men, and anywhere from 500 to 1000 Tories and Indians, mostly of the Six Nations, St. Leger arrived before Fort Stanwix early in August.[1] Instead of a ruined fort, garrisoned by sixty men, which the British expected, they found fairly well-restored works, and 550 Continentals under Colonel Peter Gansevoort, short of guns and powder, but full of fighting spirit.

Parading his motley-clad force — the English and Germans in the gorgeous regalia of a European parade ground, the Indians and Butler's Tories in paint and feathers — St. Leger tried to terrify Gansevoort into surrender. Fully informed by his Oneida spies, the Dutch commander refused to be scared by a flourish of tomahawks and scalping knives. A convoy of 200 men with supplies had entered the fort just before St. Leger's arrival, and with 750 men Gansevoort felt strong enough for a siege. Moreover, he learned that General Herkimer, who could fight better than he could spell,[2] was coming with 800 Tryon County militia to the rescue. Molly Brant, the Mohawk 'princess,' and widow of the late Sir William Johnson, took that news to St. Leger, and he sent out 400 Indians and Tory Rang-

[1] Two English regiments, 100 Chasseurs, Sir John Johnson's Royal Greens, Butler's Tory Rangers were with him. Four of the Six Nations favored the British. See Johnson's *Orderly Book* (Stone, ed.), 82.

[2] Herkimer had long before begged of Gates 2000 pounds of powder, lead, and flints to defend his country. Library of Congress (*Force Trans.*), *Gates Letters*, May 7, 1777.

ers, who entrapped Herkimer in an abrupt and wooded ravine, where was fought the desperate battle of Oriskany. Herkimer, wounded so that he died a few days later, sat on his saddle with his back to a tree, directing his men. Both armies fought with knife and hatchet as much as with muskets, and the bloody affray went on until the Indians fled, leaving the Patriots on the dearly bought field. Meanwhile, a sortie from Fort Stanwix had seized and sacked the Tory camp. St. Leger, however, gathered his scattered troops, and was still a menace to the beleaguered fort.

Schuyler, at Albany, August 8, believing that Burgoyne's van was already at Saratoga, heard that Herkimer had been defeated, and took the risk of detaching a force under Benedict Arnold to rescue Gansevoort.[1] The detachment was inadequate. Moreover, the militia of the county were 'borne down by the Tories,' and had laid down their arms.[2] At German Flats, Arnold decided to await reënforcements. Learning, however, that the fort was in desperate straits, he advanced and sent ahead a half-witted spy, threatened with doom if he failed, who scared St. Leger's Indians with a wild pantomime that carried the impression of myriads of men right at his heels. Arnold's name had its terrors, too. The Indians, furious and abandoned, fled, after stealing the liquor and clothes of the British officers.[3] St.

[1] *Cont. Cong. Papers* (*Schuyler Letters*), 153, III, 234–36, 246.

[2] *Ibid.*, 242–43. Though supplanted by Gates he sacrificed his feelings by acting under him because the crisis demanded it. *Ibid.*

[3] Burgoyne, *State of the Expedition* (2d ed.), App. XLVI.

Leger had to follow, leaving even his tents standing. Arnold, finding the enemy gone and all well at Fort Stanwix, hastened back to Gates, now in command of the main army.[1] The news of St. Leger's defeat, coming right after that of Bennington, was a hard blow to Burgoyne, but surely he could still depend upon Howe making a diversion on the Hudson River.

[1] *Cont. Cong. Papers* (*Gates Letters*), August 20, Gansevoort to Gates; August 23, Arnold to Gates.

CHAPTER XX

BURGOYNE ANTICIPATES WATERLOO

Burgoyne, all too confident, seems to have been little concerned, until after Bennington, about Howe coming up the Hudson from New York City. After the defeat of Baum and St. Leger, that relieving expedition was his chief concern. Howe did, in fact, toward the end of July, leave New York, embarked on his brother's fleet with an army of 14,000 men, and after six weeks at sea, landed them at the head of Chesapeake Bay and proceeded to conquer Philadelphia, which he entered late in September.

History from that day to this has sought to fix the blame for this utter lack of coöperation between Howe and Burgoyne. Germain's orders to Howe respecting common action with Burgoyne were pigeon-holed, forgotten, and never sent,[1] is one explanation, but there is no proof. Besides, Howe obeyed or disobeyed Germain's very mild orders at will. They were never more than polite requests which the general in the field often set aside with a courteous excuse.[2] Moreover, before Howe started south, he did receive a copy of the plan of Burgoyne's campaign, wherein it seems plain as Holy

[1] Fitzmaurice, *Shelburne* (1912 ed.), I, 247; Fonblanque, *Burgoyne*, 233; Egerton, *The American Revolution*, 120–21. See also the William Knox story in Hist. MSS. Com., *Knox MSS.*, in *Reports on Various Collections*, VI, 277.

[2] See, for example, *Germain Papers*, June 3, August 30, 1777, Howe to Germain.

Writ that one of the chief props of Burgoyne's success was that the Hudson should be opened from New York to Albany. Burgoyne's junction with Howe was to be his 'principal object,'[1] and Howe, reading the plan, should have seen his reciprocal obligation. Every other military man of note, friend or enemy — Clinton, Carleton, Robertson, Gates, Washington, Heath — could conceive of no other thing for Howe to do. To turn from that and to 'attempt Philadelphia' was, wrote Heath, 'repugnant to every principle of military policy.' If Howe makes that his main object, predicted Gates, it will 'effectually ruin the British army.'[2] Surely Howe's parade and preparation for that expedition must be mere deception. 'Watch with argus eyes the passes of the Hudson,' cried a warning voice.

Clinton, who was in Howe's most intimate councils, could not believe to the very last, even when the fleet sailed away, that his chief really meant to go south. Only 'a feint,' he thought. Clinton said to Howe himself you 'intend to deceive us all.' Howe will, of course, 'return with the first southernly blast, and run up North River.'[3] All except Howe and, perhaps, Cornwallis, saw in the attack on

[1] *Stopford-Sackville MSS.*, II, 60–63. Howe, of course, admitted getting the copy of Germain's letter to Carleton, March 26, but 'without any instructions whatever to myself.' *Germain Papers* (W.L.C.L.), *American*, April 22, 1779.

[2] P.R.O., *State Papers, Domestic, Military*, 19, no. 8, p. 39; Library of Congress (*Force, Trans.*), *Heath Papers*, July 6, 19, 1777; *Ibid.* (*Gates*), April 29, 1777, May 2, 7, 1777; *Clinton Papers* (W.L.C.L.), Clinton Memo., July 6, 1777; Washington, *Writings* (Ford, ed.), v, 501.

[3] *Ibid.*, *Clinton's MSS. History*, 79. That was Washington's idea also. *Writings* (Ford, ed.), v, 502.

Philadelphia no object except to 'draw on a general action with the rebels,' but the same thing could be better done on the Hudson.[1] A move against Philadelphia was a diversion, but not the best diversion; the Hudson was that. Burgoyne was bringing his army for the purpose of reënforcing Howe, and it was the latter's business to give every aid to that end, and then, if he would, go toward Philadelphia. General Robertson believed that Burgoyne would need every succor. Indeed, if he extricated himself from all his difficulties, 'future age would have little occasion to talk of Hannibal and his escape.'[2] Burgoyne's troops were not equal to forcing their way to Albany without coöperation, but if Howe's army and his brother's fleet went up the Hudson, all would be well. Indeed, that should have been done early in the spring.[3]

Howe could urge, of course, that his plan had been approved at home. George III certainly knew as early as May 18 that Howe planned to invade Pennsylvania by sea.[4] On that date, Germain wrote to Howe to go ahead with the Philadelphia plan, but get back in time to coöperate with Burgoyne. The whole Cabinet doubtless approved this letter. Lord North, July 24, was not at all perturbed that Howe was going by way of the Chesapeake against Phila-

[1] *Clinton Papers, MSS. History*, 76. Even Cornwallis refused before the House of Commons to *admit* that he had agreed with Howe as to the wisdom of going down to Philadelphia. P.R.O., *State Papers, Domestic*, 18, pp. 19–20.

[2] P.R.O., *State Papers, Domestic, Military*, 19, no. 8, p. 39.

[3] *Ibid.*, 19, no. 7, p. 140; no. 11, pp. 35, 36; no. 10, pp. 61–63.

[4] *Correspondence of King George III*, III, 436, 446.

delphia.[1] But all that approval in London signified nothing, since the King and his Ministers were not on the ground and were woefully ignorant as to American geography and conditions. Germain wrote Howe, indeed, that the Ministers could not at that distance judge the propriety of measures taken for the public service in America.[2] England not only expected every man beyond the seas to do his duty, but to use some sense about it.

It was true also that Howe had written Carleton, April 5, that he would not be able to 'detach a corps *in the beginning of the campaign* to act up the Hudson river,' and therefore he could give little assistance to Burgoyne's army. Yet, later in the same letter, he said he would try to have a corps open up the way for shipping through the highlands now barred by rebel forts.[3] Such a letter could hardly release him wholly from an obligation to aid Burgoyne. Later, when his back was against the wall, and he was hunting excuses for not coöperating with Burgoyne, either by going up the Hudson or by invading New England that he might keep the

[1] *Correspondence of King George III*, III, 461. See also 439, 441. Members of the cabinet must also have known, indeed, it was asserted in Parliament later that Germain knew Howe's intention of going to Pennsylvania before Burgoyne left England on his ill-fated campaign. *Germain Papers, Military, Dispatched*, no. 11. Also in *Stopford-Sackville Papers*, II, 66–67. True, Howe did not receive this letter until August 16, too late to change, but the point is, he was supported. P.R.O., *State Papers, Domestic, Military*, 18, no. 5, pp. 50–51.

[2] *Germain Papers*, Germain to Howe, August 7, 1777.

[3] *Stopford-Sackville Papers*, II, 65–66. The italics are mine. Carleton showed Burgoyne that letter, of course, but Burgoyne assumed that Howe would get later orders from Germain, and, moreover, Howe gave assurance of the essential thing, the opening up of the Hudson.

militia of that section at home, he conjured up amazing reasons. It would have been said, he argued, 'that I had envied Burgoyne the glory which after taking Ticonderoga, he had reason to expect.' Against an invasion of 'Yankee land,' he talked of absurd numbers of men (53,000) that would have been brought against his 14,000.[1] He never does more than show himself mesmerized by the glitter of Philadelphia, 'the rebel capital,' as an object of capture.

General Clinton saw clearly the folly of the southern expedition. He pointed out the risks, the delays involved in the use of the fleet, the sickness in the summer months in those latitudes, but all in vain. The two men had always quarreled — at Bunker Hill, at Frog's Neck, in the New Jersey campaign, and concerning the Rhode Island expedition. They admitted to each other that they had never agreed on any single question. 'It is impossible for us to live together' in harmony, snarled Howe. They could never pull together. Clinton could not bear to serve under Howe, and the latter knew it.[2] In a cipher memorandum Clinton recorded his lack of esteem for Howe whom he had served so well that his chief 'could not forgive it.' Clinton claimed to have borne the burden of the whole campaign; that he had commanded every first attack, and always succeeded. It was a pity, he thought, that the Ministry were going to lose America, because they had

[1] *Germain Papers, America,* April 22, 1779. (Heads of Howe's speech.)

[2] *Clinton Papers,* Clinton's report of conversation with Howe, July 6, 8, 13, 1777.

not made him the happy instrument of its salvation. Clinton, though advised to 'gulp and swallow,' and not to 'jar' his chief, was always finding slights.[1] Just now he was outraged that everything had been done to 'mark' his 'insignificancy.' Burgoyne had been given a 'respectable command' and the 'planning of his whole operations.' It is all 'your own fault,' retorted Howe, 'you ought to have insisted on that command.' 'Too delicate,' pleaded Clinton. 'You may get it in the future,' said Howe. No, 'Burgoyne will ever be the fitter person,' wailed Clinton. Oh, well, said Howe, 'You had better go home and come out again if a good command is found.'[2] But Clinton could not find peace 'while my junior in rank is placed on the high road to glory.'

On the eve of Howe's departure, the two generals quarreled over every feature of Howe's plan. Clinton growled that he was being left in New York with 'a damned starved defensive,' but his chief swore that he could not spare a man. As soon as Howe was off, Washington, declared Clinton, would assemble ten thousand men in West Chester, worry the British at other points, force a landing at Harlem Plains, 'and then, there we are.' Howe said, nonsense, the men-of-war would stop him; but Clinton replied ships could not face cannon on heights. Moreover, Clinton showed how Washington might take Brooklyn, the Narrows, Staten Island. He would risk everything to take New York, for by

[1] His 'inferiority complex' drove him to follow up the historians (Andrews and Soule) and see that his story prevailed. *Clinton Papers* (*History*, 80), and memorandum, Sunday, 13, 1777.

[2] *Ibid.* (Memorandum of conversation.)

that he 'finished the war.' Nonsense, said Howe, New York is only 'of some little consequence.' Clinton argued that, if Washington did not 'murder' the British at New York, he would send a great force against Burgoyne. Let him go, snapped Howe, he will never come back. Perhaps he cannot come back, said Clinton, but Burgoyne certainly cannot come forward, and on that depends the whole campaign. Howe said he did not wish to see him further than Albany.[1] These were the sentiments, these the relations of the generals whom the British Ministry expected to work together in harmony for the preservation of the Empire.

By the time Burgoyne most needed Howe, that worthy, who always took with him enough soldiers to win his own battles, but who rarely considered the fortunes of those associated with him, was well inside of Chesapeake Bay, and quite unable to render that desperate 'gamester' any assistance. Clinton's masked letter to Burgoyne, on August 10, was more than justified: 'I own to you I think Sir W's move just at this time the worst he could take.'[2] For more than a month, while the toils were gathering about Burgoyne, Howe kept thirteen thousand troops out at sea, broiling on wooden decks under the summer's sun, useless either to Clinton or Burgoyne, and having no effect on Washington except

[1] *Clinton Papers*, Memorandum, Sunday, 13 [1777]. I am under deep obligations to Miss Jane Clark, archivist in charge of the Germain and Clinton Papers, still at Mr. Clements' residence. She has pointed out many valuable documents to me, and I have seen her manuscript, soon to be published in the Am. Hist. Review.

[2] *Clinton Papers* (W.L.C.L.), August 10. The letter, without the mask, seemed to approve of Howe's venture.

to make him anxious. Having promised, July 17, to go north if Washington did, Howe placed himself within a week where he could not possibly keep his promise.[1]

Burgoyne's one comforting hope after Bennington and Fort Stanwix was that Howe would surely send aid. He still had an army of 4350 and some eighty Indian scouts. The morale was high, though supplies were low. Confidence in Tory aid was shaken, and rebellion had new vigor. The Americans had not, however, followed up their victory. There was an unheroic epilogue. The New Hampshire militia drifted home; Stark was ill, his men, many of them down with measles, and all feeling slighted — all resentful of Continental orders. The glory of Bennington was in danger of being 'tarnished.'[2] What Burgoyne called 'the most active and most rebellious race of the continent' was very local in its loyalty. Schuyler had been superseded by Gates, Congress being justified, perhaps, by public policy. It must satisfy either New England or New York, and the four 'Yankee' States had furnished as many soldiers as the other nine. New York, now stirred by the Jane McCrea outrage, would fight anyway, and New England must be coaxed. Gates, with the inherited manners of an upper-class English servant, was rude to Schuyler, who remained during the crisis, though unbidden to the army councils. The new commander had his strong points, good military

[1] P.R.O., *State Papers, Domestic, Military*, 18, pp. 3–6, Howe to Burgoyne.

[2] Library of Congress (*Force Trans.*), *Gates Letters*, I, September 6, 7, 10, 12, 13.

judgment and skill in administration, but he did not hunger for a fight, and now, though under fifty, was writing pitifully home to his wife that he was getting too old to bear the trials of campaigning.[1]

Burgoyne delayed his advance three weeks, while he brought up thirty days' supplies which he had failed to acquire at Bennington. The army had gone back to salt meat and meal, brought from England 'at a kingly price.' There was 'pork at noon, pork at night, pork cold, pork hot,' all brought over lakes, rivers, and mountains, and through forests, though game was all about them and the resources of New England were so near.[2] Before him, early in September, was Gates with about six thousand effectives. Daniel Morgan's famous riflemen from the Pennsylvania, Maryland, and Virginia back-country joined,[3] and Arnold was back from the Mohawk Valley with twelve hundred men. Though a waiting policy might have been best, Burgoyne, ever mindful of Germain's 'peremptory' orders to 'force a junction with Howe,'[4] assumed full responsibility for risking a crossing of the Hudson near Saratoga. It was a hazard; retreat was endangered; further supplies from Canada were out of the question. At once, indeed, 'rebels,' who had hung like a gathering storm upon his left, cut in behind him. A 'consum-

[1] Library of Congress, *Gates Letters*, I, September 22, 1777.

[2] *Letters from America*, 1776–79 (trans. by Pettengill), pp. 86, 95, 99.

[3] Washington spared Morgan to Gates, because he thought for the moment that Howe had gone down to Charleston. Washington, *Writings* (Ford, ed.), VI, 44–50. Library of Congress (*Force Trans.*). *Gates Letters*, Washington to G. Clinton, August 21, 1777.

[4] Fonblanque, *Burgoyne*, 275, Burgoyne to Germain. *Germain Papers*, Burgoyne to Germain, October 20.

mately desperate' move, good if successful, it seemed safe if Howe kept faith about following Washington should he turn north.[1] Anyway, Gage and Carleton had already been rebuked for too much caution. Advance was expected, delay would 'damp the spirits' of the army, and finally Albany, with some five hundred houses, was an alluring place to winter.[2]

On a bridge of boats, September 13, Burgoyne, reënforced by some five hundred men, crossed the Hudson. The boats were later used for transport down the river. Gates had advanced to Stillwater, September 8, and to Bemis Heights four days later. On September 19, Burgoyne, despising his opponent, divided his army, depending on a gun signal to unite the action of three columns, and fought the American army at Freeman's Farm. Gates wanted to make a stand in the entrenchments on Bemis Heights; Arnold was for going out and attacking the detached British column in the woods at the Farm. Arnold prevailed and sent Morgan's sharpshooters, who had a rough time at first, but with support were getting the best of a three or four hour desperate struggle, when Riedesel arrived and saved the day for the British.[3] The jealous Gates seems to have kept Arnold out of the fight, and thus perhaps

[1] Letter of July 17 (Howe to Burgoyne), received August 3. It was a mystery how he could, since he was at sea, but perhaps that was only a ruse, and he might come sailing up the Hudson. Clinton's masked letter, August 10 (*Clinton Papers*), only surmised that Howe had landed. In letters home, however, Burgoyne does not admit expecting any coöperation from Howe, Fonblanque, *Burgoyne*, 276, August 20 letter.

[2] P.R.O., *State Papers, Domestic, Military*, 18, no. 6, pp. 13–15.

[3] *Ibid.*, pp. 16–20.

his own troops from victory.[1] The American loss was three hundred and twenty killed, wounded, and missing, the British five to six hundred. Strategically it was an American gain, though Burgoyne's tactical successes entitled him to call it his victory.[2]

Knowing what we know to-day, we may complacently criticize the British commander for not following up his 'smart and very honorable action.' Gates's army, largely composed of amateur soldiers, was in great confusion. Its military chest was low, the commissariat wretched, the supply of lead and musket cartridges so poor that men were scurrying about Albany, taking all the lead in clocks and window weights, and buying up all the writing paper. Gates was 'inexpressibly' anxious about the lack of flour and other provisions.[3] He and Arnold, quarreling bitterly, each heading a faction of officers, weakened the leadership. Gates, cold, cautious, and calculating, was ambitious and jealous of Arnold's growing fame. Arnold, vain, headstrong, and overbearing, was dashing, impetuous, and daring. They were little fitted to get on together.[4] But all this

[1] But see Nickerson's argument on this question, *The Turning Point of the Revolution*, 473–77.

[2] *Clinton Papers* (Clinton, *History*, 80–88); also Burgoyne to Clinton, September 23; P.R.O., *State Papers, Domestic, Military*, 19, no. 7, p. 86.

[3] Library of Congress (*Force Trans.*), *Gates Letters*, II, Gates to Washington, October 5, 1777, Gates to President of Congress, Gates to Trumbull, Rensselaer to Gates. *Minutes of the Albany Com.* (Flick, ed.). I, 843.

[4] Yet, up to August 20, 1777, their correspondence shows them on the best of terms, affectionately writing of their mutual devotion, but on that day Arnold reported triumphantly from Fort Stanwix. Library of Congress (*Force Trans.*), *Gates Letters*, I, *passim*.

Burgoyne did not know. He saw before him what he believed an army of twelve thousand men, his own army was 'badly shot up,' and he had no word of any relief from New York.[1]

A ray of light came to Burgoyne on September 21 — a cipher message from Clinton. 'No time or place will be difficult for such emissaries as you employ,' chuckled Burgoyne. 'Gates little suspects how near they are to his person.'[2] Clinton asked Burgoyne's wishes about an attack on Fort Montgomery, ten days later, with two thousand men, all he could spare. Burgoyne's reply was wildly eager. 'An attack or even the menace of an attack' would call off Gates. 'Do it . . . directly.'[3] Clinton, mortified that he could do nothing for his country or his own fame, had warned Howe that with the 'fettered and starved defense,' some 7200 men, of whom 2782 were newly enlisted 'Tories,' every move from New York was 'dangerous,' for there was a circuit of one hundred miles to defend. Howe admitted that, until he had landed and engaged Washington's army, it would be 'madness' for Clinton to stir from his station.[4] Yet, when Howe, fearful at last that Burgoyne might fail, and the blame be imputed to lack

[1] P.R.O., *State Papers, Domestic, Military*, 19, no. 7, p. 86.

[2] *Clinton Papers*, Burgoyne to Clinton, September 23, 1777. Clinton's cipher was dated September 10, arrived September 21, and was first answered in cipher that day. Clinton received the answer September 29, yet it was the first messenger who had got through from Howe since early in August, and he knew that two of his own had been hanged. Burgoyne, *State of the Expedition*, App. XLVI, lxxxviii.

[3] *Ibid.*

[4] Clinton, *History*, *MSS.*, 78, 79; *Clinton Papers* (9 queries and 2 answers), Sept. 10; Memorandum, April 20, 1779, Sunday, 13, 1777. A detailed list of Clinton's troops is in *Colonial Office*, 5–253, p. 495.

of coöperation from New York, wished good advice at least to be on record, he wrote, July 30, from off Delaware Bay that if Clinton could make a diversion in favor of Burgoyne, it would have 'utility.'[1] Clinton suspected the motive, but when, September 11, the battle of Brandywine had been fought and won, and, September 24, reënforcements, 1700 men, reached New York, and September 29 came Burgoyne's feverish plea for even the 'menace of an attack,' he resolved upon 'a desperate attempt on a desperate occasion.'[2]

Before following further the fortunes of Burgoyne and Clinton, we should follow Howe's adventures in conquering 'the empty city of Philadelphia.' He had Germain's and King George's consent to this venture, because Pennsylvania was thought to be swarming with Loyalists. From them Howe would raise a force to defend the Quaker province, and then with his 'free army' hasten back to Burgoyne's aid.[3] It was the abiding delusion of the King and his Ministry that the army sent overseas was to 'assist the good Americans to subdue the bad ones.'[4] As a result they were never adequate to subdue America.

The Howes set sail with two hundred and fifty ships, July 23, expecting from the first to approach Philadelphia from the Chesapeake, but with the

[1] *Clinton Papers* (Clinton, *History*, 78, 81, 86); *Germain Papers* (W.L.C.L.), *America*, April 22, 1779; July 30, also. *The Narrative of Sir W. Howe . . . Observations . . .* (ed. 1780), 23.

[2] *Clinton Papers*, January (1778).

[3] *Germain Papers, Military Despatched*, no. 11.

[4] Even some military men shared this idea. P.R.O., *State Papers, Domestic, Military*, 19, no. 10, pp. 21–22.

Delaware route at least in mind.[1] The British had an immense advantage in their control of the sea, and this sea voyage of the Howes had the one virtue of being 'extremely embarrassing' to Washington. Clinton, though admitting he would never agree with Howe, though he served with him twenty years, said of the General and the Admiral, 'separate the two brothers, their equals are to be found in either profession, but together they are irresistible and to be equaled only by two such brothers.'[2] If they were 'irresistible,' it seems to be because they never undertook any venture unless it was a 'dead sure' thing. There was no spirit of daring. It took but two hours off Delaware Bay to decide to go on. They listened to stories of shoals, rapid tides, fire-rafts, galleys, cannon-shot from the shore, and eight or nine creeks and rivers to cross, if a landing was made below New Castle.[3] The loss of time and the fate of Burgoyne seems not to have entered the reckoning. Though the long confinement on shipboard brought great suffering and sickness to the soldiers, Howe actually offered the excuse later that 'the heat was so intense that I was not sorry upon that account to keep them longer at sea.'[4] Yet he must have got a jar, at least, when on August 16, in Chesapeake Bay, he received Germain's letter of

[1] *Clinton Papers* (W.L.C.L.), Howe to Clinton, July 23, 1777. But see Howe to Germain, *Stopford-Sackville Papers*, II, 73, July 16, 1777.

[2] *Ibid.*, 91, January 19, 1778.

[3] Howe, trying to explain going on to the Elk instead of up the Delaware, made a very poor showing before the House of Commons. P.R.O., *State Papers, Domestic, Military*, 18, pp. 2–91, and *passim*.

[4] *Germain Papers, America*, April 22, 1779.

May 18, three months in transit telling him to go ahead with the Philadelphia campaign, but be sure to complete that easy conquest in time to go to the aid of Burgoyne! It took Howe two weeks to reply to this amazing letter, and then he was at the head of the Elk, full of reasons why he could not 'act up to the King's expectations.'[1] As usual heat or cold, ill winds or fate, were good enough excuses for inaction or delay.

Landing at the head of the Elk, Howe was no nearer Philadelphia than he might have been a month before, and with some of the same rivers to cross that he would have had by landing in a safe part of Delaware Bay. Disembarking in a leisurely way, he advanced upon the fleeing inhabitants, not so loyal as he had hoped, and at Chadd's Ford, on Brandywine Creek, September 10, defeated Washington's army, not so much because of that leader's personal fault as because his half-trained staff was bound to show its inherent weakness in such a crisis, and because of the lack of adequate light cavalry to furnish flank protection. Clinton said that Washington's account of the battle was 'the most beaten letter I have ever read,' but, nevertheless, with General Greene's help he saved his army.[2] Howe might have

[1] *Germain Papers, America*, May 18, and August 30, 1777. Two years later, Howe appeared to believe that he did not get this letter until the date of his reply, August 30.

[2] *Clinton Papers* (W.L.C.L.), January, 1778. A Tory newspaper reported 'Washington knocked up — the bloodiest battle in America, 6000 of his men gone.' *Ibid.* Both armies had about 11,000 men. Washington's actual loss, killed, wounded, and missing, was not far from 1200, while Howe's loss was 90 killed, 488 wounded. Howe's *Narrative* (ed. 1780), 100; Greene, *Life of Greene*, I, 447–53.

broken it then and there, but, as ever, having fought his battle like a brilliant and scientific soldier, he wasted hours restoring the perfection of his army machine and lost the golden opportunity. Again, as Galloway sneered, he succeeded only so 'far as he chose to succeed.' Six days later, Washington was ready to strike again on the Lancaster road when rain disarmed his troops, and he retreated over the Schuylkill above Philadelphia. Within a few days Howe entered the city.

Congress, 'very sulky' and determined, early in September, not to move for that 'plaguey fellow of an How,' got over 'scorning to fly,' and, by September 19, having considered and reconsidered four times, was sending baggage ahead across the American Rubicon.[1] John Adams, waked at three o'clock in the morning, learned that others were 'on the wing' at midnight, the enemy at Schuylkill Ford, and no vote for adjournment necessary, since each member was consulting his own safety and crossing the Delaware in haste. Adams fled the Quaker City with a curse, glad to leave 'that mass of cowardice and Toryism.'[2] Fright, almost 'lunacy,' Laurens wrote, put everybody on horseback in flight, first to Lancaster, and then across the broad Susequehanna to York, and even there 'hearts were still fluttering in some bosoms.' Though the distance was only sixty miles direct to Lancaster, members traversed one hundred and eighty miles, hurrying from place to place for days — via Trenton, Easton, Reading —

[1] *Letters of . . . Continental Congress* (Burnett, ed.), II, 486.

[2] *Ibid.*, II, 497–98.

and no business done. The wagons with the papers of Congress, 'of more importance than all the members,' went the longest way round.[1] The previous flight to Baltimore had been 'a trifle in comparison.' There was much criticism of Washington. Loose tongues declared there was no regulation or discipline in the army; that nobody minded who went in or out of the American camp; that the commander's heart was too diffident to take the proper measures.[2] The one consoling thought was the rumor that came to York of a glorious victory by Gates in the North.

Philadelphia fell, and in France, Voltaire mourned that 'the troops of Doctor Franklin have been beaten by those of the King of England. Alas! philosophers are being beaten everywhere. Reason and liberty are unwelcome in this world.'[3] However it may have been with Franklin's troops, the old sage, himself, was not afraid. 'Philadelphia has taken Howe,' was his view of the affair.[4] In Paris, Lord Stormont asked Vergennes ironically to share the British 'pleasure in this happy event,' and the French Minister sent his 'sincerest felicitations' upon this victory 'so satisfying.'[5]

Washington was too stout-hearted to give up even when his enemy had entered 'the capital city.' Clinton had thought him a 'blockhead' to pay any

[1] *Letters of ... Continental Congress* (Burnett, ed.), II, 504. See Preface, xix–xx.

[2] *Ibid.*, 521–22.

[3] *National Geographic Magazine*, Jusserand article, 1917.

[4] For a detailed study of the defense of Philadelphia, the letters and documents collected by W. C. Ford, in *Pennsylvania Magazine of History*, vols. 18–21, will be indispensable.

[5] *Corres. Pol., Angleterre*, 526, F 142, 145.

attention to Howe; he should turn his whole force against Burgoyne or the British post at New York;[1] but Clinton forgot the political factor. Washington had to consider Congress and the natural civilian attitude toward 'the capital.' A few farm wagons could cart off to Lancaster all that was necessary to enable the 'rebel government' to 'carry on,' but there was the general morale of the country to consider. To sustain that, Washington struck again at Germantown, which Howe had made his main camp and headquarters. Though Washington tried to surprise him by a dangerous night's march, it is fairly certain that Howe was not caught napping.[2] Nevertheless, the attack, October 4, was vigorous, and only the morning fog, a chance confusion among the American troops, and some steady fighting by the British and Hessians, saved Howe from a serious reverse. Thinking only of his own precious safety, he at once ordered Clinton to send several thousand troops of his own inadequate force. Washington, seeing the futility of further effort, retired to Valley Forge, a good strategic position for his army, while Howe secured at best a good winter shelter for his troops — but at what a cost! Clinton had truthfully said 'he has ever succeeded,' though his victories have 'cost him dear.'[3]

[1] *Clinton Papers* (W.L.C.L.), August 27, 1777. Indeed, Howe also doubted whether Washington would defend Philadelphia.

[2] P.R.O., *State Papers, Domestic, Military*, 18, pp. 14–21. Howe told Sir George Osborne that Washington would attack next morning at 'the exact time and place they did attack.'

[3] *Clinton Papers*, January, 1778, October 9, 1777, Howe to Clinton. October 8, 1777, Howe to Clinton, writes a full account of the battle of Germantown.

Meanwhile, Burgoyne's troubles were becoming insupportable. Even Clinton's promise of September 21 was, perhaps, his undoing, since retreat to 'his den,' Ticonderoga, was then barely possible. Hoping for Clinton, and bringing up provisions meanwhile, Burgoyne delayed seventeen days.[1] Every day the British army weakened, and the American army grew stronger. Indians, Tories, and Canadians were deserting Burgoyne daily, while to Gates swarms of New England militia were coming as they snuffed the scent of victory.[2] During the days of deadlock, while neither side 'yielded an inch,' Burgoyne's supplies melted down; his officers slept if at all in their clothes; the whole army was harassed by cold, wet, and a pest of insects.

Four days after putting the army on short rations, Burgoyne struck desperately at the American left, October 7, bringing on the second battle of Freeman's Farm. Gates very properly sought to avoid a general battle, but again Arnold's spirit inspired the American troops at the crisis to pierce the British line. Burgoyne, ever in the midst of battle, was more lucky than Fraser, who was killed. Gates reported to Congress a 'warm and bloody' conflict from which the enemy retreated, leaving tents, baggage, brass cannon. 'Great praise' was due, he wrote, to Morgan and his rifle regiment. He also

[1] The Earl of Harrington, when asked (1779) in Parliament whether such a delay was necessary, said all the work on redoubts was necessary, since the British were in inferior numbers, and that the army was working all that time. P.R.O., *State Papers, Domestic, Military*, 18, no. 6, pp. 42–46.

[2] Hist. MSS. Com., *Report, American MSS.*, I, 140–41; Library of Congress (*Force Trans.*), *Gates Letters*, II, October 5.

had the grace to speak of the 'gallant General Arnold,' whose leg was 'fractured by a musket ball as he was forcing the enemy's breastworks.'[1] Indeed, Burgoyne said his defeat was all Arnold's 'doing,' and Germain got from official reports, long before, the impression that Arnold was 'the most enterprising man among the rebels.'[2]

Meanwhile, where was Clinton? After Burgoyne's plea for even the 'menace of an attack,' Clinton with commendable speed prepared, the moment it was reasonably safe, an expedition to take Fort Montgomery, to 'unbar that door,' the Highlands, which was Gates's greatest fear.[3] The combined military and naval stroke was completely successful. Putnam with only one thousand Continentals, four hundred half-armed militia, and 'not one artillery man,' was not surprised, but was outwitted, his main force decoyed to the wrong side of the river. British ships prevented his return, and both forts, Montgomery and Clinton, surrendered, the 6th of October. The 'Loyal American Regiment,' having 'indispensable' knowledge of the country, were of greatest service. All American forts and ships be-

[1] Library of Congress (*Force Trans.*), *Gates Letters*, II, October 12. Arnold, a few days before, had accused Gates of 'neglecting' him, leaving him 'a cypher in the army,' never consulted, his advice ignored — all due to Gates's 'spirit of jealousy' and the 'malice of my enemies.' He warned him that the army was 'clamorous for action' and would go home if he did not let them fight. Gates denied any grounds for all this, and gave him leave to go to Philadelphia. *Ibid.*, I, September 22, 23; October 1.

[2] *Clinton Papers*, Burgoyne to Clinton, October 25, 1777; Hist. MSS. Com., *Report, Stopford-Sackville Papers*, II, 39.

[3] Library of Congress (*Force Trans.*), *Gates Letters*, II, October 5, 1777.

tween New York and Albany were destroyed.[1] Clinton could scarcely credit his own triumph. 'Six days sooner or six hours later, we should not have carried our point,' he declared. It was 'a desperate attempt on a desperate occasion,' everything risked to save Burgoyne; but no sooner done than Howe ordered sent to him 'the very troops' with which Clinton had made the stroke. 'Good God! what a fair prospect blasted,' lamented Clinton.[2] He had to give up the control of the Highlands, won, as he said, by one of those 'extraordinary events which may happen once in a century, and . . . to be attributed to a combination of fortunate circumstances, some tolerable arrangement, and wonderful exertion and spirit in the execution.' [3] Nevertheless, Clinton was too late, and it is hard to see how he could have been blamed.

[1] Library of Congress (*Force Trans.*), *Gates Letters*, I, Putnam to Hancock and Gates, September 29–October 4; *Clinton Papers*, New York, Sunday, 13, 1777. Howe expected his ships to turn the scale. (George Clinton to Colonel M., September 29, 1777.) A return of American prisoners, 26 officers, 237 privates, was signed by Joseph Loring, husband of General Howe's 'Delilah.' (*Ibid.*, October 12.) Clinton, writing to the Duke of Gloucester, October 9, and in his official account written to Howe on that date, gives the fullest and best account of the expedition. (*Ibid.* See also Clinton to Colonel Robinson, October 9; Howe to Clinton, October 9.) During this expedition Clinton was suffering one of his attacks of blindness. In one almost indecipherable letter he says, 'My eyes are out but observe how well I write.' (October, 1777.)

[2] *Ibid.*, Clinton to Burgoyne, October, 1777; Clinton to Carpenter, January (1778); Vaughan to Clinton, October 26, 1777. Governor Tryon had urged Clinton to make 'a dash up the river' with transports enough to take all Burgoyne's army from Albany to New York. He proposed taking and destroying (not holding) all posts and pressing on to save Burgoyne. 'Notify him to attack at same time,' urged Tryon. *Clinton Papers, Fort Clinton*, October 8, 1777.

[3] *Clinton History, MSS.*, 95–97.

All things considered, it is no wonder he treasured up among his papers a memorandum, almost surely of his own composition, not overcomplimentary to his chief. 'Had Sir Wm. Howe Fortified the Hills round Boston, he could not have been disgracefully driven from it: Had he pursued his Victory at Long Island, he had ended the Rebellion: Had he landed above the lines at New York, not a man could have escaped him: Had he fought the Americans at Brunswick he was sure of victory: Had he coöperated with the Northern Army, he had saved it, or had he gone to Philadelphia by land, he had ruined Mr. Washington and his Forces; But, as he did none of these things, had he gone to the D——l, before he was sent to America, it had been a saving of infamy to himself and indelible dishonour to this Country.'[1]

It was Howe who had been entrusted to lead the 'forlorn hope' that forced the entrenched path by which Wolfe scaled the Heights of Quebec. Howe finished that war with a record second to none. He was a master of tactics and strategy, and of all that books could teach him of military science, but no ray of genius ever illumined his activities. Opposed to North's pre-war policy, ashamed to go to Boston because its people had placed a monument in Westminster Abbey in honor of his brother, he went, nevertheless, at King George's bidding, to take Gage's place at that seat of war. He went again with his brother Richard to New York, only to fail

[1] *Clinton Papers, Memorandum* (copied by Clinton's secretary). See T. Pennant, *American Annals* (W.L.C.L.), for a terrible arraignment of Howe.

after brilliant victories. Why did he play cat and mouse with Washington? Was he a tool of Burke and Pitt? Did the Ministry order him to have the sword in one hand and the olive branch in the other? Why did he sit around waiting for rivers to freeze or weather to cool, and fall just short of actually seizing his prey? It is all an historical riddle with many answers, none convincing. The malicious gibe of a major-general that Americans should be grateful that Howe was placed at the head of the British army, not for his merits, but because of his connection with King George through his grandmother's frailty, is no solution of the mystery.[1]

The news of Clinton's victory, sent October 9, reached Burgoyne too late. That very day Burgoyne left the entrenched camp, his refuge after his heavy and fatal losses in the last battle, and retreated toward Saratoga, destroying as he went. Gates, pursuing, chose to regard this military measure as an effort 'to ruin those they could not conquer.' Such conduct, he taunted Burgoyne, 'betrays more of the vindictive malice of a monk, than the generosity of a soldier.'[2] Burgoyne was a rhetorician, too, but he was jaded, almost mad with anxiety, and answered feebly, though justly. Schuyler, whose own house was burned, agreed with him as to military necessity. On reaching Saratoga, Burgoyne called a council of war.[3] Gates was thought to have

[1] Winsor, *Narrative and Critical History*, VI, 291.

[2] Library of Congress (*Force Trans.*), *Gates Letters*, II, October 12 (Letters to Burgoyne and President of Congress).

[3] *Clinton Papers, Minutes of Council of War*, October 12, 1777.

fourteen thousand men, while an 'unknown army' was on the other side of the Hudson between the British and Fort Edward. There were no boats, no materials for a bridge, no retreat possible save by the ford at Fort Edward. Army provisions would last only to the 20th. A height above Ticonderoga had been taken by Lincoln, though the fort held out. The decision for a retreat by night was later cancelled — the army could not move a mile undiscovered. There were three more council meetings and finally a decision to capitulate, unanimously agreed to by 'all the generals, field officers, and captains commanding corps.' [1] Refusing Gates's demand for unconditional surrender, Burgoyne secured what is known as the Convention of Saratoga. Arms were to be given up, but the army was to be returned to England and not to serve again during the war. Gates, however, hardly deserved the gibe that like Hannibal he knew how to win a victory, but not how to use one. Aware of the long sick-list in his army, and of the slack discipline among his militia, he lost his nerve. Moreover, he knew of Clinton's victory in the Highlands. Before the signing, Burgoyne knew it, too, but, a majority of officers agree-

[1] *Clinton Papers, Minutes of Council,* on the 13th, 14th, 15th. *Germain Papers,* Burgoyne to Germain, October 20, 1777. Wilkinson's return of Burgoyne's forces, October 17, 1777, showed 2139 British, 2022 Germans, 830 Canadians: total 4991. Library of Congress (*Force Trans.*), *Gates Letters,* II. Gates's immediate army seems to have been 7716, rank and file, 3382 militia. (*Ibid.*) In a detailed return of Gates's army given by Gates to Burgoyne, evidently to use in explaining his difficulties to the Ministry, the numbers are given as 18,624. P.R.O., *State Papers, Domestic, Military,* 19, no. 8, pp. 2–3; also *ibid.,* 19, no. 7, p. 115. See curious report on Burgoyne's army, *ibid.,* pp. 117–18.

ing that it would be bad faith to suspend the treaty, the arrangements were completed, and mutually signed October 17.[1]

Gates surely agreed with d'Argenson that 'triumph is the most beautiful thing in the world: cheers . . . hats in air and on bayonett ends, the master complimenting his warriors, joy, glory, affection'; but he must have been aware also that 'the groundwork of all this is human blood and the shreds of human flesh.' The 'voice of fame,' Gates wrote to his wife, has told you of our victory. 'If Old England is not by this lesson taught humility, then . . . is she bent upon her ruin.' He gloried over many things, but — as the son of a duke's housekeeper might do — especially over the number of English lords and ladies who were his prisoners. There was Lord Petersham, Major Ackland — 'One of the prettiest fellows . . . but a confounded Tory' — his lady, daughter of Lord Ilchester — 'the most delicate, amiable little piece of quality you ever beheld.' Morover there were some Scotch lords and 'about a dozen members of Parliament.' Finally there was General Phillips, 'who wrote me that saucy note . . . from St. John's.'[2]

Though rumors of the victory lifted Congress 'up to the Stars,'[3] confirmation from Gates did not arrive until October 31, a suspense not borne with good temper. Washington, too, was plainly annoyed at

[1] P.R.O., *State Papers, Domestic, Military,* 18, no. 5, pp. 25, 53, 85; *Clinton Papers,* Tryon to Clinton, October 26.

[2] Library of Congress (*Force Trans.*), *Gates Letters,* II, October 20, 1777.

[3] *Warren-Adams Letters,* I, 373.

having, two weeks later, no direct word of Gates's 'signal success,' but the victorious general, weeks before, had written Congress that, since Washington was south of Philadelphia, would they please transmit copies of his letters to the Commander-in-Chief. He also made a like special request concerning his letter announcing victory.[1]

In Burgoyne's mind the wind, the weather, and the waves — if not the very stars in their courses — had fought against him. His critics, he said wryly, in their easy seats at the fireside, 'travel across the map very fast.' They could not see how wet weather had ruined the roads, until hard toil, incessant effort availed nothing against a thousand difficulties, and he had in store but three days' rations on short allowance. There had been total defection of the Indians, timidity or desertion of Canadians and Tory Provincials, while the Germans were 'disposed to be prisoners rather than endure hard blows.' Had the Germans fought like the British, he declared, he would have won. When too late, he had been disappointed of any timely coöperation from Howe. Moreover, the stringency of his orders had left him no liberty of action, no freedom to retreat until it was too late.[2] Finally, his regular troops were reduced by losses to 3500 fighting men, not 2000 of whom were British, and these invested by an army

[1] Library of Congress (*Force Trans.*), *Gates Letters*, I, September 3, 1777, October 2, 1777.

[2] This plea that his orders were positive, the King endorsed — or at least 'much inclined to' that belief. *Correspondence of King George III*, III, 521, 527. George III was honest, which is more than one can believe of Germain.

of 16,000 men. In short, his army, at last, '*would* not fight, and *could* not subsist.' His own mind, he confessed, was 'broken by agitation, his body with fatigue.'[1]

Expert opinion in general supported much of Burgoyne's exculpation. Schuyler had always believed that the variety of difficulties to be surmounted before Burgoyne could reach a place where his army could be subsisted was too great.[2] Du Coudray, troublesome as he was, had a soldier's eye, and saw the folly of expecting Burgoyne to traverse 'two hundred leagues of a frightful country, almost wilderness.'[3] Clinton had feared, and was not silent, that, if Howe did not aid, such numbers from New England would press on Burgoyne as might overwhelm him. Washington, Gates, and Greene all agreed. Behind all, explaining this as well as other defeats, was the repeated failure of the British Ministry to secure the ships, the men, the provisions, the guns asked for by their commanders in the field. General Grey swore that he never saw a British force in America in any way adequate to subdue it.[4]

In England the opponents of the Ministry rejoiced. Chatham wrote Shelburne that in Bur-

[1] *Germain Papers* (W.L.C.L.), Burgoyne to Germain, October 20; *Clinton Papers*, Burgoyne to Clinton, October 25; Hist. MSS. Com., *Report, Am. MSS.*, I, 140, 141, 144; Burgoyne to Howe, Oct. 20; P.R.O., *State Papers, Domestic, Military*, 19, no. 7, pp. 32–33. King George agreed with Burgoyne that his orders were positive. *Correspondence of King George III*, III, 421.

[2] *Cont. Cong. Papers* (*Schuyler*), 153, II, pp. 308–09.

[3] *Clinton Papers* (1c, 86a), Du Portail to St. Germain, September 12, 1777.

[4] P.R.O., *State Papers, Domestic, Military*, 18, p. 87.

goyne's defeat 'the Will of Heaven seems to open to us some deliverance from the Calamities of the American War.' He would have not a moment lost in forcing an inquiry into 'this scene of imbecility and of horror under Burgoyne's command.' His motion for a publication of Burgoyne's orders was defeated by a vote of 40 to 19. 'What a scene of perdition opens on this country,' he cried in despair.[1] The House of Commons debated 'the State of the Nation.' Conway, we are told 'spoke from the heart, in warm affecting language above the rules of rhetoric,' while Wedderburn, masterly, eloquent, insinuating, but 'artful,' tried to 'smooth with a cold iron' the fire Conway had raised. Burke attacked, Adam spoke wildly, and Fox 'flew at him,' overturning him and his arguments.[2] Fox thought Burgoyne ill-used, and his defeat due to the Ministry. Indeed, the King himself, though he refused North's offer to resign 'if the storm should rise,' favored an inquiry, but Germain's influence in the Ministry prevented that until June of 1779.[3] Horace Walpole reported the King falling 'into agonies' on receipt of the news, and then being 'indecently merry' to disguise his concern. His only comfort was that the 'late catastrophe' 'raised the Lion' in the country, and increased enlistments.[4]

Taunted by Chatham that their 'Spring hopes and vernal promises' had become 'equinoctial dis-

[1] Chatham, *Correspondence*, December 3, 5, 1777, January 15, 1778.

[2] Hist. MSS. Com., *Fourteenth Report, Rutland MSS.*, III, 11.

[3] *Correspondence of King George III*, III, 504, 521, 522, 527; IV, 333, 334, 337, 338.

[4] *Ibid.*, 513; H. Walpole, *Last Journals*, II, 58.

appointment,' Lord North and 'his crew' were desperate, indeed, and grasped at every straw. They even talked of getting repealed the laws which prevented the arming of Roman Catholics in Ireland. They heard from Stormont, their ambassador in France, that Irish Catholic officers, serving in France, because debarred from the British army, were offering to enlist in the imperial forces. Germain sounded the Duke of Buckingham, Viceroy of Ireland, as to whether 'necessity and the public good' did not require such a measure. He wrote plaintively 'the blow which this country has received by the unexpected loss of General Burgoyne's army makes everybody look forward to the fatal consequences that may attend it.' [1] France and Spain, he urged, continue armed, their navies daily become more formidable. Our fleets will do, he wrote, but if foreign war comes, our land forces are deficient and the resources of England are not enough. It had long been augured that the French would join Briton's enemies if the British suffered losses. There had been plenty of friendly assurances from France, but her actions did not correspond with her professions.[2] King George was well aware, through his amazingly efficient spies, that France was violating nearly every duty of a neutral, and furnishing the munitions of war which made American military resistance possible. Yet he hardly realized that nine tenths of the military supplies that made the victory at Saratoga possible came from France or through

[1] *Germain Papers* (W.L.C.L.), December 22, 1777.

[2] Hist. MSS. Com., *Marquess of Lothian*, 305, 312.

foreign merchants whom she secretly encouraged. How did it come about that the oldest monarchy, and the most despotic king in Europe, gave such aid to the rebellious subjects of a brother king? Why did the French people aid the Americans 'to assert a freedom, which they dared not taste themselves'?[1]

[1] Hist. MSS. Com., *Carlisle MSS.*, xxiii.

CHAPTER XXI

FRANCE, HUMBLED, SEEKS REDRESS

THE righteous and conscientious Louis XVI, doomed to die on the scaffold for the manifold sins and wickednesses of his fathers, was led to give, first secret, and then open, aid to the Americans by motives in part peculiar to the age of despots, in part common to all ages. Quite unaware that the waters were gathering which would 'wash the balm from an anointed king,' the Ministers of both the French monarchs whose reigns immediately antedated the French Revolution urged upon them a recovery of prestige and a consequent revenge for the downfall of 1763. By that peace France lost her commerce and credit in India. She lost Canada, Louisiana, Isle Royale, Acadia, and Senegal. She issued from the war deeply in debt. Her allies were disaffected, her ambassadors marched behind those of England at affairs of state in foreign capitals, and all Frenchmen mourned the shame of Dunkirk, where no stone could be turned, no pier erected, without England's consent. Nine years later, her helplessness at the time of the partition of Poland revealed how she was despised in all the courts of Europe. When Maria Theresa wept, but took her share of Poland, it meant that even France's own ally was party to the crime and scorned to ask her advice. In vain Vergennes mourned the absolute scorn of the principles of decency and justice shown in the conduct of the 'bandit powers' who despoiled the richest territory of a feeble and impotent state. He doubted whether posterity would believe that indignant Europe looked on and did nothing. Where is the safety of any state, he cried, if such political brigandage can be consummated before the eyes of Europe? Even England, zealous for the balance of power, turned her eyes away and dared not protest. If force is right and decency a mere name, where is the safety of states? he asked.[1]

That Vergennes should lash himself into fury over this partition of Poland is all the more noteworthy, because the fresh air of moral indignation did not often sweeten the close atmosphere of diplomacy in those days. This Polish affair seemed to complete the effacement of France.[2] Once the center of all European activity, she became, wrote a Frenchman, an unheeded onlooker. None cared for her favor or her wishes. Of all great powers she seemed least considered. England was in the ascendant, France at the nadir, of her power.

France, whose pride had grown with what it fed upon, would not accept her fate. D'Argenson in happier days had looked upon France as sustaining the feeble and oppressed, 'The paternal protector' who gave the law to Europe, 'so it be a just law,' and, though feared by all, had nothing to fear from them.[3] France's greatness, France's antiquity, her

[1] Doniol, *Histoire de la Participation de la France à l'Établissement des États-Unis d'Amérique*, I, 15.

[2] *Ibid.*, 14.

[3] *Journal et Mémoires du Marquis d'Argenson* (Paris, 1859), I, 325, 371; IV, 131.

rôle of leadership, and the tradition of her grandeur were instilled into the minds of all French diplomats as a fundamental principle of their activity in every court of Europe.[1] The Hohenzollern demand in the old grandiloquent days, that 'nothing must be settled in this world without the intervention of the German Emperor,' would have come as naturally from the lips of Bourbon princes or their Ministers in the eighteenth century. That a French king should lead in Europe was a 'dogma consecrated by a thousand years,' cried de Broglie.[2] France in the center of Europe has the right to influence all great affairs, asserted the Count de Vergennes. To him the Bourbon throne was a tribunal set up by Providence to adjudicate the rights of kings.[3] Walpole might think the monarch 'weak, and weak-eyed,'[4] but in the view of a French Minister he was Jove himself.

The great menace to this tradition of grandeur was England. As early as 1740, Maurepas noted the threat of this 'usurping race,' of these 'ancient enemies,' now almost the masters of the fate of Europe.[5] Choiseul in 1764 denounced to his master the intrigues, the jealousy, the 'haughty tone' of England in the world's affairs. This arch-enemy of

[1] A. Sorel, *Recueil des Instructions données aux Ambassadeurs*, etc., I, 356.

[2] Ségur, *La Politique de Tous les Cabinets*, I, 229.

[3] Flassan, *Histoire Générale et Raisonnée de la Diplomatie Française* (Paris, 1809), VI, 134.

[4] Walpole, *Letters* (Toynbee, ed.), VI, 310.

[5] Maurepas, *Mémoires* (Soulavie, ed., 1792), III, 93, 161, 194, 205, 241.

French power aimed, he declared, at supremacy 'in the four quarters of the globe.' [1] There was no peace with such a race. Choiseul put the worst interpretation upon all England's actions in the past and all her plans for the future. The Seven Years' War had begun with a 'scandalous rupture.' All the 'maxims of the rights of nations,' the most 'sacred rules of equity,' were then thrown to the ground. England's true aim had been to rob France of her American colonies and trade. Did she not design to seize all Louisiana, he asked; penetrate thus to New Mexico, and in time follow Cromwell's plan and open the way through Central America to all of Spain's possessions? To this end England aimed to stifle the French marine at its birth and to rule the sea alone.[2] The Abbé Raynal declared that a new power, sea-power, had given the universe to Europe, and Europe to England, whose 'spirit of rapine' had led her to rule the sea and thus dominate the states of the world.[3] Belief in this, added to the age-long traditional enmity of France and England, created a bitterness which made the Treaty of Paris a mere suspension of hostilities.

The pen that signed the treaty for France was not dry before Choiseul began his efforts to reverse the decision of Destiny. Like a Trojan he worked to wipe out that hateful memory. He repaired French naval losses, reformed the army, bettered the

[1] *Archives des Affaires Étrangères, Mémoires et Documents, France*, 581, F 41.

[2] *Ibid.*, 3, 4.

[3] Abbé Raynal, *Histoire des Indes* (1781), v, 203; vii, 208; ix, 80; x, 136.

finance.[1] He thought seriously of an invasion of England, sending agents to seek landing-places and sources of supply.[2] Portsmouth was doomed, at least in Choiseul's mind. He instigated Spain to question the right of English ships to sail the Pacific, though Pitt had said that England would sooner consent to give up the Tower of London than abandon that right. Choiseul's secret agents searched every crevice of British armor in America and so worried Pitt that he cried out against such activities in a world 'infatuated, bewitched.'[3]

The French archives in the period from 1763 to 1775 abound in *mémoires*, diaries, letters, and reports filled with the same purposes, revenge upon England, a death-blow to its commerce, a revival of that of France, and finally the restoration of French prestige in Europe.[4] French spies roamed afar through England and America, keeping the French Government intimately informed as to the state of the British national debt, the size of its navy and its army, the meaning of its political cri-

[1] Rochefort to Shelburne, January 7, 1767 (intercepted letter of Merci quoted), *Shelburne Papers* (W.L.C.L.).

[2] Royal Historical Society, *Transactions* (3d Series), IV, 82.

[3] Royal Historical Society, *Transactions* (3d Series), IV; Stanhope, *Pitt*, V, 247; Coxe, *Memoirs of the House of Bourbon*, III, 298.

[4] The prospects of commerce with free America form the principal theme of most *mémoires* in the French archives. Mr. Corwin, in his 'French Policy' (*American Historical Review*, XXI, 33–61), puts a great deal of stress upon the restoring of French prestige in Europe and seems to belittle the motive of increased trade with America or hoped-for decrease in England's trade. But French statesmen, royal and noble writers of petitions, economists, and all who wrote memorials to the King, urged the trade argument, and often gave as its purpose the increase of power and of wealth which would bring in its train the restoration of French prestige.

ses, and every aspect of its relation with its colonies.[1] Choiseul hoarded every document, every proclamation and revolutionary broadside, every seditious American sermon or clipping from a rebellious newspaper. The surest way to his favor was to report discontent and trouble in the Carolinas or Virginia, as did the crafty Chevalier d'Éon, while nothing so damned an agent, the Baron de Kalb found to his chagrin, as to report that the colonies caressed their chains.[2]

In America these secret emissaries took every means to spread dissatisfaction among the colonists. They took pains to impress Americans with their own importance. The colonial strength was represented as an object of greater magnitude than the British rulers were aware. No insinuation lacked to induce a spirit of discontent.[3] Franklin, in 1767, declared that France, 'the intriguing nation,' was blowing up the coals between Great Britain and her colonies, and he, at that time, hoped to prevent her success.[4]

Scores of reports of French Government spies fill the French archives, but the tritons among the minnows were M. de Pontleroy and the Baron de Kalb. Pontleroy was a well-informed naval officer who for twenty years had been useful to the French Government in a like capacity. His great fault was that when he became gorged with information he

[1] *Archives des Affaires Étrangères, Correspondance Politique, Angleterre*, 474, 475, *passim*.

[2] *Ibid.*, 450, F 392, 410; 451, F 23, 115, 140, 218.

[3] J. Andrews, *History of the War with America*, I, 20.

[4] Bancroft, *History of the United States*, III, 261.

seemed to fall into a state of mental coma,[1] so that he wrote and talked painfully, and only the patient efforts of Durand, acting as agent for Choiseul, drew out his report. In 1764, he had 'journeyed along the New England coast and then passed on to the middle colonies. He gave a fairly accurate account of the economic strength, the population, and the rate of increase. Children in America he found swarming like ants. There was noted the number of men furnished in the Seven Years' War, the fortifications, the number of men in garrisons.[2] Colonial arsenals were located and the *parcs* of artillery. Ports and rivers were sounded, and distances measured between important towns, the state of the roads between them, with full plans for taking and pillaging Boston, New York, and Philadelphia.[3] He estimated that French armies could live long on the country in New York and Pennsylvania, but ventured the unflattering prediction that in barren and rock-ribbed New England they would starve to death. He offered a rosy plan for an attack on the colonial fishing fleet.[4] He reasoned that if France could destroy the fisheries and the fleets of the merchants, the colonists would press the British Government for peace. He

[1] *Archives Nationales, Marine,* C 7, F 255.

[2] *Archives des Affaires Étrangères, Correspondance Politique, Angleterre,* 471, F 8, 9. Durand's report with some omissions is in print in C. DeWitt, *Thomas Jefferson* (2d ed.), 407–17.

[3] August 3, 7, 9, 1766. *Archives des Affaires Étrangères, Correspondance Politique, Angleterre,* 471, F 7–9, 124–25. Three months later, Pontleroy wrote at length to the Duc de Praslin. *Archives Nationales, Marine,* B 44, 111, 11–13, 106, F 14.

[4] *Archives des Affaires Étrangères Correspondance Politique, Angleterre,* 471, F 7–9.

even hoped to corrupt their 'corsairs' so that they would prey on British rather than French trade.

Pontleroy thought that he knew all the reasons for America's unrest. He witnessed their wrath over the Sugar Act, their rage over the British revenue ships sent to stop their illicit trade with the French and Spanish West Indies, and their plaints over the loss of cash once acquired in this illegal trade.[1] He found them boasting of their power, no longer fearing France, less needing British protection. Too rich to be obedient, eager to shake off the fetters and restraints on their commerce.[2] They would be seduced soon or late, he declared, to seize for their own profit the islands near the American continent. It must have been cold comfort for a French Minister to find Pontleroy frank to say that the colonists wished for war with France to the end that they might conquer St. Domingo and St. Pierre de Miquelon, one as a needed market, the other to control the fisheries.[3]

He rejoiced to find the New-Englanders lovers of liberty, always ready to murmur against government. He was told that the colonists would not allow the British to fortify Boston Harbor, lest the forts be used to subject them to acts of Parliament.[4] He found the Germans, Palatines, and Alsatians of

[1] *Archives Nationales, Marine,* B 4, 111, F 13.

[2] Report of another French spy, in 1765, agrees. *American Historical Review,* XXVII, 84.

[3] *Archives Nationales, Marine,* B 4, 111, F 11; *Archives des Affaires Étrangères, Correspondance Politique, Angleterre,* 471, F 7, 8.

[4] Another French spy, 1765, name unknown, agreed on this matter with Pontleroy. *American Historical Review,* XXVII, 84.

Pennsylvania discontented with the British Government, hating the local Presbyterian and Quaker Assemblymen. All were more loyal to Germany than to England. He believed that revolution would be the end of all of England's efforts to better the lot of her colonists. Should it come to war, France might recruit troops in Pennsylvania. The indentured servants would be glad to escape, and he advised getting a leader for such recruits with a name that would recall old German heroes.[1] There is much evidence that the French Ministers not only read these reports, but pondered them deeply.

In the year after Pontleroy's visit, a spy, whose identity is unknown, but who had great gifts as an observer, passed through the colonies at the height of the Stamp Act excitement.[2] He presented credentials to men of Provincial prominence, and had contact with a remarkable number of men, like Dulany, Joseph Galloway, James Christie, and others who later became Loyalists. Though often dined and wined by governors, and others of great prominence, he also mingled with those who 'damned their souls' if they would pay stamp duties. They would fight, he was told, to the last drop of their blood before they would consent to any such slavery. After feasting, the bottle went round and rage against the Stamp Act augmented, until they talked of taking up arms and coping with Great Britain. Even a magistrate who in the early

[1] *Archives Nationales, Marine,* B 4, 111, F 11–15; *Archives des Affaires Étrangères, Angleterre,* 471, F 18–19.

[2] Document in *American Historical Review,* XXVI, 726–47, and XXVII, 70–89.

evening reproved their disaffection admitted, as the night wore on, that if it came to a push, he would take up arms himself in defense of his liberty.[1] The King's health was usually followed by that of the Virginia Assembly, then damnation to the Stamp Act, until, the spy confessed, 'we scarce used to go to bed sober.'[2] In Virginia he heard a great deal about that 'Noble Patriot Mr. Henery,' and all declared publicly that if the least injury were offered they would stand by him to the last drop of their blood.

Besides these observations on the temper of the people, he reported with great fullness and judgment the rural and town economy, the general conditions, and ventured the prophecy that the country would not be long subject to Great Britain. Its extent was too great, its growth too rapid. Not only was there immigration from every part of Europe, but he saw about the farmers' houses children swarming like broods of ducks in a pond. This growing race had around them everything needed, and all things for their own defense. No nation was better calculated for independence, the people were disposed to it, and there was nothing they talked of more.[3]

[1] *American Historical Review*, XXVII, 72–73.

[2] Attending a celebration of the 'King's Birth Night,' he was much disappointed as to the throng he hoped to see, for there was not above a dozen people. *American Historical Review*, XXVI, 746.

[3] *American Historical Review*, XXVII, 84. About the same time, October, 1765, D'Estaing was writing to Choiseul from St. Domingo of one Hopkins to whom he had given the use of his house and with whom he had talked at length. He had a great knowledge of America as to the fortifications, conditions, revolutions in progress, places most

It is very noteworthy that the French, with whom the wish was father to the thought, were much more clear-sighted in foreseeing rebellion in America than the British.[1] Montcalm had dreamed of it just before he fell on the field of glory at Quebec. Choiseul a few years later counseled his royal master, Louis XV: 'There will come in time a revolution in America — but' he added ruefully, 'we shall probably not see it — which will put England into a state of weakness where she will be no longer a terror in Europe. . . . The very extent of the English possessions in America will bring about their separation from England, but, as I have said, this event is yet far off.'[2]

Nearly three years after the Stamp Act, the eager French Minister sent the Baron de Kalb not only to report conditions and resources, but to learn whether the colonists, raging against the Townshend Acts, had a plan of revolt and were rebellious enough to desire trained officers and engineers. What use did they mean to make of the munitions 'they were getting'? Were they sincere in the desire to resist Great Britain?[3] De Kalb, judicious, sensible, able to grasp the real issues, made the mistake of report-

easily attacked. *Archives Nationales, Colonies,* C 9A (St. Domingo), 124.

[1] Yet Englishmen did fear it. See letter in *Archives des Affaires Étrangères, Angleterre,* 474, F 273, Durand to Choiseul: 'Il n'y a personne en Angleterre qui n'avoue que, faute de prévoyance, les colonies qu'elle possède en Amérique formeront un jour un état séparé: c'est la forme de cette révolution que je désirerois de prévoir,' etc.

[2] Bib. Nat. (*Doniol MSS.*), *Angleterre,* 515, F 21; *Archives des Affaires Étrangères Mémoires et Documents, France,* 581, F 41.

[3] Bib. Nat., *MSS. Français, Nouvelles Acq.*, no. 9435, F 352, 353. (The cipher scheme is here.)

ing the truth, rather than what his master wished.[1] He found the Americans complaining of all the ills which Pontleroy had noted.[2] Yet, in spite of all, in spite of a fierce spirit of sedition, De Kalb believed they nevertheless really loved England. There was certainly no disposition to shake off British domination by means of foreign power. Their own divisions would cease at once, he thought, in the presence of a common enemy.[3] Any foreign aid they would deem dangerous to their liberties. Should France attack England, De Kalb felt sure that the British Government could get in the colonies all the needed troops, money, vessels to conquer the French West Indies.[4]

Nevertheless, De Kalb reasoned, soon or late the colonies will be free. The very distance from England made them so. He found the spirit of inde-

[1] It made no difference that De Kalb brought back quantities of letters, public prints, and documents, proofs as strong as Holy Writ; Choiseul resented bad news.

[2] Bib. Nat., *MSS. Français, Nouvelles Acq.*, no. 9435, F 367–70. A translation is in Kapp, *De Kalb*, 62–67 (see also 286–92), but I take this from the original. De Kalb's opinion is valuable because, as an outsider, he was likely to hear the real and not the simulated complaints.

[3] Bib. Nat., *MSS. Français, Nouvelles Acq.*, no. 9437, F 365, 366, 378. All this was wholly opposed to the views of Châtelet (Durand's successor) which Choiseul thought 'profound.' Châtelet (1767) asked if there were a rupture 'could France and Spain remain idle spectators of an opportunity which in all probability would never occur again?' Within six months America would be on fire and her success would depend on a foreign war. Could France and Spain risk the fire going out for want of fuel? DeWitt, *Thomas Jefferson*, (2d ed.), 56–57.

[4] There are many indications that one solution often in the colonial mind for regaining lost trade with French and Spanish West India islands was to conquer them.

pendence everywhere. Though there was more fermentation and vehemence in Boston, the spirit of resistance was elsewhere the same. The New England colonies, peopled in the main by English, were more closely united. Their very privileges, he thought, had only increased their pride and arrogance, and Massachusetts, richest and most populous, gave the cue, the signal for independence.[1] Even there they were fain to blame not so much the Ministry as the Governor, who for personal ends fomented trouble. He found them unable to imagine extreme measures. The colonies were so important, the King so good, their cause so just, that Government must recognize itself in the wrong, and admit their claims.[2] The Baron advised letting them alone, for though fated to be independent, all effort to push would only retard their progress toward freedom — disagreeable advice, he knew, but based on the facts. Choiseul rewarded his faithful endeavor to tell the truth by tiring of the reporter and turning his noble back.

All this intrigue against the peace of Europe took place while perfect amity seemed to exist between France and Great Britain. Cordiality on the surface, suspicion and hate in secret, marked their relations. Each extended the hand of friendship, but consorted and intrigued with the other's enemies. In 1768, the French Minister planned to form a league of Prussia, Russia, Austria, and Spain against the sea-power of England, to take Gibraltar at any

[1] Bib. Nat., *MSS. Français, Nouvelles Acq.*, no. 9435, F 374.
[2] *Ibid.*, F 375.

cost and close the Mediterranean to British commerce.[1] When France was in bad financial straits in 1770, the distresses of France were comfortable objects in British eyes, for, wrote Walpole, 'one tiger is charmed if another tiger loses his tail.[2] Money and arms were openly collected in England to aid the Corsican rebels against France, and the British Government secretly supplied them with ammunition.[3] Choiseul in anger vowed to collect money in France to aid sedition in New York and Boston.[4] The Corsican patriot Paoli was exalted in England, which France could revenge only by waiting eight years to show equal adoration of Franklin. In spite of Dr. Johnson's brutal opinion that the British had drubbed 'those fellows,' the French, into 'a proper reverence for us,' the Ministers of his Most Christian Majesty would never admit it.[5] When in 1770, Choiseul fell from power, the policy of the French Government was not altered.

Throughout the Choiseul régime of plot and counterplot, the American colonies were little responsive. The colonists not only inherited the immemorial English hate and suspicion of France, but they had new reasons of their own for filling their

[1] *Archives des Affaires Étrangères, Mémoires et Documents*, 410, F 115–17. Shelburne to Devisme, December 20, 1766 (*Shelburne Papers*). There is every evidence that France was on tiptoe at this time to spring to the aid of the colonies should there be a rupture with England over the matters in dispute. *Archives des Affaires Étrangères, Angleterre*, 479, F 360–63.

[2] Walpole, *Letters* (Toynbee, ed.), VII, 368.

[3] *Ibid.*, 203, note; Hunt, *Political History of England*, X, 98.

[4] Friedrich von Raumer, *Beiträge zur Neueren Geschichte* (1839), II, 163.

[5] Boswell's *Johnson* (ed. 1901), I, 417.

vials of wrath. War after war with the French in Canada, embittered by the use of Indians to raid the English frontiers, increased the colonial bad blood toward all Frenchmen. The repugnance of Puritan New England to Catholic Canada waxed rather than waned with the decades. All American leaders believed that Bourbon despotism far exceeded anything ever attributed to a British ruler by the most violent colonial demagogue. James Otis, in 1762, declared that the French King was a despotic, arbitrary prince, his subjects very miserable.[1] Yet, odious as France was, there is more than one bit of evidence to indicate that under the provocation of the Stamp Act a mysterious committee of American leaders sent secretly to London a man who under certain political circumstances was to hasten to France to try to get secret aid, ammunition, and guns from the French Government.[2] Durand more than once called that fact to Choiseul's attention, and the mysterious French spy of 1765 heard Virginians mutter between their teeth, let the worse come to worst, we will call the French to our succor.[3] So convinced was Durand of this intent that he urged having an agent in the colonies ready to blow up the fire lying under the ashes, at the moment it is ready to burst out. All there is lacking, he exhorted, is arms, a chief, and courage for these people to make themselves independent. If there were a man in

[1] Tudor, *J. Otis*, 126.

[2] *Archives des Affaires Étrangères, Angleterre*, 475, F 235, 240, 263; C. De Witt, *Thomas Jefferson* (ed. 1861), 432–33.

[3] *Archives des Affaires Étrangères, Angleterre*, 447, F 349, 350; *American Historical Review*, XXVI, 747.

New York with a genius of a Cromwell, he could set up a republic there more easily than did the great Oliver. It is for France and Spain, he urged, to make that man appear.[1] There is good proof that the great leaders in Boston were counting as early as 1769 on help from France, revenge for 'the drubbing' received in the Seven Years' War.[2]

That France, and perhaps Spain would render aid to the American colonies, should they rebel against the mother country, had long been a hobgoblin rising in the darkening path of British statesmen. Lord Shelburne wrote in 1767: 'If the colonies resist, France and Spain would no longer defer breaking a peace, the days of which they already count.'[3] As the open break became more imminent (1774), Burke, Pitt, Barré, the Duke of Grafton, and others sensed the danger. 'You will draw a foreign force upon you,' Burke warned, 'if you get in open war with the colonies.'[4] Foreign war hangs 'over your head by a slight and brittle thread,' cried Chatham. 'France has her full attention upon you. War is at your door'; and he pictured France, like a vulture, hanging over the British Empire, waiting only for the right moment to pounce upon her prey.[5] Barré

[1] *Archives des Affaires Étrangères, Angleterre,* 477, F 349, 350; De Witt, *Thomas Jefferson,* 56.

[2] British Museum, *Add. MSS.,* 30870, F 222. Otis, S. Adams, J. Warren, B. Church, J. Quincy, Jr., R. Dana, all wrote Wilkes to that effect.

[3] Hist. MSS. Com., *Var. MSS.,* VI, 112, 119; Fitzmaurice, *Life of Shelburne,* I, 312.

[4] Almon, *Debates,* IX, 109, 114.

[5] B. Williams, *William Pitt,* II, 305; Chatham, *Correspondence,* IV, 384; Hansard, *Parliamentary History,* XVIII, 159.

bent his fierce looks upon the House of Commons, predicting France would not be quiet.[1] Burke pointed out again and again the reasons why the Bourbons would intervene.[2] Pamphleteers asked the rhetorical question whether France would be a peaceable spectator of British civil contentions.[3] Only the most blind of the ministerial group refused to see the menacing aspect of the French [4] and Lord North himself admitted that the situation was such that if France should raise a finger against England the British Government would be compelled to give the Americans anything they might demand.[5]

Could those who harbored a doubt that France was crouching for a spring have peered into the secret recesses of official desks at the French Ministry, all incredulity would have vanished. From 1774 on, every move in British colonial affairs was chronicled by French spies who gloated over the gathering clouds. Garnier, the French Ambassador in London, informed his royal master that he had solved the problem of acquiring reports of the most secret debates in the House of Commons by getting the French reporter elected to Parliament. A secretary in the Colonial Office gave, for a bribe of five hundred guineas a year, the inside information there.[6] Vergennes, Minister of Foreign Affairs, after

[1] Hansard, *Parliamentary History*, XVII, 1309.

[2] *Ibid.*, XVIII, 967.

[3] *A Letter to Lord M.* (pamphlet), 29; [Arthur Lee], *American Appeal to Justice* (1774), 47.

[4] Hist. MSS. Com., *Var. MSS.*, VI, 116, 117, 122.

[5] April 12, 1776, *Archives des Affaires Étrangères, Angleterre*, 515, F 77.

[6] *Archives des Affaires Étrangères, Angleterre*, 507, no. 84 (November 9, 1774), 511, no. 29.

the accession of Louis XVI, counseled Garnier as to the hired agent, the Jesuit Roubaud, who reported debates in the House of Lords. 'Get what you can from him,' wrote Vergennes, 'but use him as a post-horse which one pays for and abandons at the end of the course.'[1] From these spies Vergennes learned every detail of the British Government's activities, Chatham's and Burke's speeches, Gage's plans, the departure of British troops, while other spies furnished reports of the work of the First Continental Congress, details of every campaign, names of generals, the country's topography, copies of every proclamation of George III, Gage, Carleton, Lord Dunmore, all of which were stored in the French archives, where they lie to-day.

By July of 1775, French agents in America were reporting with ill-concealed joy that 'everybody was running in crowds to the camp of liberty,' that there was not a town or city in America where the majority of the inhabitants in a frenzy of war were not continually practicing military maneuvers. The French agents and the Ministers in Paris were sure that the colonists would never again consent to be subjects of Great Britain.[2] Not even French heroes could have been more highly lauded than were Arnold and Montgomery. All this the British knew, but since it was part of the policy of the Government in the early days of rebellion to make the colonists believe that England was on the best terms with France, this desire to deceive the Americans made

[1] *Archives des Affaires Étrangères, Angleterre,* 515, no. 41.

[2] Doniol, *La Participation* . . . I, 12, 13.

it difficult for the British Government to make effective its complaints that the French were not observing neutrality.[1]

Nor was France the only land that looked complacently upon England's troubles. Vergennes did not greatly exaggerate when he wrote that if England looks outside to the other countries of the world — from Buenos Ayres to New Orleans, from Dunkirk to the Antilles (except Portugal, whose defense is only one more burden) — she sees only enemies.[2] In April of 1774, the British Ministry was greatly alarmed lest a naval force, which France and Spain were apparently preparing to aid Turkey in her war with Russia, were really arming against England.[3] Indeed, during 1775 England seemed on the verge of war with Spain in defense of Portugal. Ralph Izard, traveling across Europe (1774–75), wrote that the cause of America was approved by all. At Rome he found many well-wishers. The Swedish Ambassador told him that he was glad to find that there was still a part of the world where tyranny was not triumphant and where the people dared virtuously to oppose its progress. Izard found the proceedings of the Continental Congress filling the French, Dutch, German, and Italian papers, which he had seen, and he was told that the same was true in Denmark, Sweden, and Russia.[4] Frederick the Great viewed 'this Boston Heroism' with

[1] *Archives des Affaires Étrangères, Angleterre*, 508, no. 129.
[2] *Ibid.*, 507, no. 147.
[3] *Correspondence of King George III*, III, 90–91.
[4] R. Izard, *Correspondence*, I, 46, 82, 126.

interest, pleased with England's troubles.[1] The Dutch were hoping for independence (1774), wrote Henry Ellis, in hopes the Americans would buy from their shop.[2]

And yet the French Government was not wholly happy. Vergennes was aware that the spirit of revolt, wherever it breaks out, is always a troublesome example, a moral malady which might become contagious. He feared that spirit of independence which had made so terrible an explosion in North America.[3] Then there was the fear of the British recouping any losses to their fisheries by seizing the French fishing grounds.[4] But above all was the specter of Chatham, who, 'uniting great talents with a love of glory,' might again arouse the English people to war on France.[5] He, too, might conciliate America. There was the man to fear. And should he to that end yield to the colonies the right of taxation and regulation of commerce, would he not make amends by using British sea-power to seize the French West Indies, and thus regain the lost source of revenue? Louis XVI himself feared, more than anything else, lest Chatham should plunge the world in flames, attack France and Spain,[6] in order to unite England and her colonies against the common enemy. The King of Spain fully agreed with him.

Meanwhile, in America, opinion was veering toward a hope for French aid. Faced with the

[1] Circourt, III, 163. [2] Hist. MSS. Com., *Var. Coll.*, VI, 112.
[3] *Archives des Affaires Étrangères, Angleterre,* 510, no. 127.
[4] *Ibid.*, 515, no. 45. [5] *Ibid.*, 510, no. 118.
[6] *Arch. Nat.*, K, no. 3 (année, 1775), no. 21, no. 22.

prospect of war with the greatest power on earth, ancient prejudices tended to melt away. The wiser a patriot was, the less he was confident of victory without foreign aid. Franklin, while yet in London, found the French Embassy there most attentive, and he did not repulse them lest his country might need them later. He began (1774) to prophesy foreign interference in America's behalf and, indeed, seems to have negotiated with merchants and armorers of Holland and France for such munitions of war as America might want.[1] Patrick Henry, even before Lexington, assured Virginia burgesses that 'A just God who presides over the destinies of nations' would raise up friends 'to fight American battles.' One after another (1775), Hamilton, Arthur Lee, R. H. Lee, Charles Lee, William Gordon, John and Samuel Adams, General Greene expressed confidence in French aid.[2] Arthur Lee thought that France looked upon no part of the world with a more attentive eye than on America. The French posture might well make the British tremble.[3] John Adams, 'forced to seek the friendship of England's enemies,' urged alliances with France and Spain.[4] He admitted doubts whether ambassadors would be

[1] Franklin, *Works* (Sparks, ed.), IV, 396.

[2] Hamilton, *Works* (Lodge, ed.), I, 169; Gordon, *Sermon* (W.L.C.L.), 124; *Letters of R. H. Lee* (Ballagh, ed.), I, 205, 211; *Life and Speeches of Patrick Henry*, I, 383; Force, *American Archives* (4th Series), IV, 1126; J. Adams, *Works*, I, 200; II, 487; Franklin, *Works* (Sparks, ed.), IV, 47; VII, 470; Frothingham, *Siege of Boston*, 263; Burnett, *Letters of . . . Continental Congress*, I, 106, 107, 233, 248; *Greene Papers* (W.L.C.L.), Greene to Ward, June 4, 1775; October 22, 1775.

[3] [A. Lee], *American Appeal to Justice*, 47.

[4] Burnett, *Letters of . . . Continental Congress*, I, 106, 107.

received. He wondered whether he could do more than get introduced to some of the 'misses and courtezans' in keeping of the French statesmen, if his pockets were filled with money, and his person robust and elegant enough. Charles Lee was for feeling their pulse. Hamilton argued that their promises to keep quiet meant nothing, were mere finesse to hide a sinister design, and would never bind longer than the temptation to break. Princes' promises were worth nothing, anyway, and France would, of course, use every means to destroy British power. They might refrain from open rupture, but would use every clandestine method to aid America.[1]

[1] Hamilton, *Works* (Lodge, ed.), I, 169. Late in 1774, John Dickinson was sure that European powers would fall on England as soon as she was entangled with her colonists. Force, *American Archives* (4th Series), I, 947.

CHAPTER XXII

JEALOUS EUROPE, LED BY FRANCE, GIVES SECRET AID

SOON after Lexington the public journals in America contained matter expressing faith in a French alliance. There was published a letter from an American in Paris who wrote that the French to a man were strongly in favor of America — on the 'principle of humanity.' Another thought France would wait until the breach between England and America was irreparable and then would come to aid.[1] Zubly, of Georgia, declared in Congress, October 6, 1775, that a proposal had been made to apply to France and Spain. Though he believed that any one who would propose it would be torn to pieces like De Witt, yet it was only two months later when even Congress moved to explore the likelihood of French aid. The Committee of Secret Correspondence, Franklin, Dickinson, and Jay, wrote to Arthur Lee that Congress wished to know the disposition of foreign powers, but in learning it he must use 'impenetrable secrecy.' Franklin wrote to Dumas to inquire about among the many ambassadors at The Hague whether any power in Europe would enter into alliance with America for the sake of her com-

[1] *Pennsylvania Evening Post*, October 19, 1775; *Essex Gazette*, July 21, 1775; *ibid.*, November 30, 1775; *Pennsylvania Packet*, no. 147; *Continental Journal and Weekly Advertizer*, July 11, 18, 25, 1776; *Letters on the American Revolution* (Willard, ed.), 182.

merce, amounting to some seven millions sterling per annum.[1]

Meanwhile the popular imagination was pleased with delusions and anticipations. Early in 1775, colonial journals spread the tale of forty ships of war building in Sweden for the French Government with an eye to the quarrel between England and America.[2] In May an imaginary French fleet had put to sea to give aid to American ships.[3] By fall the papers carried the rumor that France and Spain had a greater sea force than the British could muster in a year; that superior French and Spanish fleets were in the West Indies; that Choiseul was again in favor and would lead France and Spain at once into war with England.[4] Algiers was attacked, and Gibraltar besieged by the Spanish, ran the wild rumors. By midsummer of 1776, the daily press deluded Americans with a French general and an admiral in the West Indies ready to begin hostilities against England as soon as Congress decided upon Independence.[5] Indeed, so alarmed was the British Ministry, late in June, 1776, that the Cabinet met to discuss the late intelligence, relative to menacing armament in the ports of France and Spain. They agreed to increase the guard-ships to twenty-four,

[1] Burnett, *Letters of . . . Continental Congress*, I, 274 (December 12, 1775); J. Adams, *Works*, II, 459; Force, *American Archives* (4th Series), IV, 353.

[2] *Maryland Gazette*, January 12, 1775; *Pennsylvania Gazette*, January 25, 1775.

[3] *Essex Gazette*, May 18, 1775.

[4] *Pennsylvania Gazette*, September 13, 1775; *Essex Gazette*, September 14, 1775.

[5] *New England Chronicle*, July 11, 1776.

the marines to one hundred per company, and to continue raising volunteer seamen for the fleet, and to impress them if necessary.[1]

Nor were France and Spain the only hope. Soon after Bunker Hill, there were flying rumors of eight German general officers and a ship loaded with artillery and ammunition bound for America.[2] Two months later, three German princes were said to be traveling *incognito* in New England hoping to aid America.[3] There was joy everywhere over the report that the King of Prussia was about to invade Hanover to collect a British debt.[4] In the hour of peril much comfort was derived from embracing these delusive phantoms of hope.

Against the growth of this American aspiration for aid from France, British pamphleteers and American Loyalists fought in vain. The Americans were reminded that 'the English are generous, brave mastiffs; the French have always been sly, ravenous foxes, the Spaniards cruel wolves.'[5] A pamphlet circulated in the colonies at British Government expense offered friendly advice against reliance on France.[6] If America wished the aid of France and

[1] *Correspondence of King George III*, III, 380, 382, 396, 405, 429, 431. It was feared that France and Spain had a larger number of ships in commission than did England.

[2] *Essex Gazette*, June 29, 1775.

[3] *Ibid.*, August 17, 1775.

[4] *Pennsylvania Gazette*, September 20, 1775. Sweden also had interfered and dissuaded Russia from hiring troops. *Letters of . . . Continental Congress* (Burnett, ed.), I, 396.

[5] Moore's *Diary*, I, 356.

[6] [Sir John Dalrymple], *Address by the People of Great Britain to the Inhabitants of America* (1775), 6.

Spain, no doubt it could be got. British felicity is the envy of all nations, the author insinuated. 'Slaves always hate the free.' But can Americans trust such aid? 'Will the despotism of France establish a new Empire of Liberty?' Will French armies conquer for America and not for themselves? 'Will the Inquisition of Spain make a Protestant cause independent?' asked the pamphleteer, appealing to New England prejudice. These dark hints were reënforced by Joseph Galloway's reminder of the 'danger, and all the horrors of French slavery and papish superstition.' In every way he tried to recall the old American hate of France. Her ambition is still alive, he warned. Her power is asleep, but will awake. With her aid America would win independence from England only to become the slave of arbitrary power — of popish bigotry and superstition. Beware of the miseries of a foreign yoke, he pleaded.[1] Indeed, when John Adams first suggested in Congress application to Europe, he got only 'grimaces' and 'convulsions' from the members, for whose nerves it was too much. Paine and Sherman, of Connecticut, in fact, did not approve of employing 'Foreign Papists' in American service. But all warning and hesitancy were in vain. These imagined terrors were nothing compared with the dismay in the heart of every reasoning American as he contemplated war with England lacking the aid of France.

After the news of Lexington and Concord had spread in ever-widening circles over the sea and

[1] Joseph Galloway, *A Candid Examination* (1775), 46.

throughout Europe, the French Government felt pressure from every side to render some kind of aid to the Americans. It was the fashion in France in those days of absolutism for men of influence in the state to sit down and write to the monarch as publicists to-day write to the public in magazines or for the Sunday supplement of a great newspaper, long articles urging their political views. These *mémoires*, hundreds of them preserved in the French foreign archives,[1] written by dukes, counts, nobles of every degree, great ministers of state, and intended solely for the eyes of the King and his Ministers, pressed at this time the argument that the prestige and the fundamental economic interests of the French nation were at stake in the outcome of England's struggle with her colonies. The Duke de Noailles, the Count de Broglie, the Count de Saint-Germain, the Chevalier d'Anemours, de Magnières, and many lesser persons offered the motives of historical example, of French safety, of right or of honor, decorous mantles for everything from secret aid to brutal assault.[2] The sophisticated writers recalled that Carthage once had a navy, now England; that Carthage was destroyed, why not England? Others reminded the King that Queen Elizabeth gave aid to Holland in its struggle with the Duke of Alva. Like the Dutch provinces the Americans were republicans suffering impatiently and trying to shake off the yoke of domination,

[1] Division of *Mémoires et Documents*.

[2] *Arch. Nat.*, K 157 (*Broglie*), F 128–29; K 1340, no. 10, pp. 53–89; *Archives des Affaires Étrangères, États-Unis, Supp.* (2d Series), xv; *ibid.*, *États-Unis*, I, no. 21, F 69–70; *ibid.*, *Angleterre*, 515, F 24.

jealous to excess of their liberty, ready to sacrifice all to preserve it. England, on the other hand, was a nation rich, drunk with its success in the last war, impatient of the least resistance, resembling, indeed, the Romans dictating laws to their colonists.

Such were the arguments that reached the King, but outside the court the expression of sympathy was even more ardent. Joseph de Maistre, fired by Rousseau, cried, 'Liberty, insulted in Europe, has taken its flight to America, another hemisphere,' and there France must protect it.[1] Citizens, philosophers, young nobles, who had found in their classics, and in Voltaire and Rousseau, enthusiasm for the cause of freedom, became patrons of the colonial rebels. Even the meager press, published only with royal permission, gave much space to sympathetic accounts of American events.[2] In the French West Indian islands, it was said, a common toast was 'The Independence of America.' [3]

In the very Cabinet of the King progress was being made beyond what the impatient French society imagined. The Count de Vergennes, Minister of Foreign Affairs, denounced in popular verse as a fool, a dolt, a tool of the British Ministry, used words in 1775 much the same as Choiseul had used ten years earlier concerning England. This 'restless and greedy' nation, the declared enemy of France, seeking 'her humiliation and her ruin,' was haughty, avaricious, jealous, seeking supremacy in the four

[1] Sainte-Beuve, *Portraits Littéraires,* II, 388.

[2] L. Rosenthal, *America and France,* pp. 15–18.

[3] *New England Chronicle,* May 2, 1776.

quarters of the earth. She was powerfully armed and ready to strike in a convenient moment.[1] Here was the time marked out by Providence to deliver the universe from a greedy tyrant. Moreover, French economic interests were at stake. If England engulfed herself in civil war, France might gain her share of American commerce.[2] To this end Vergennes urged, not open war, but secret aid. Count de Saint-Germain, too, proposed secret aid;[3] Turgot, his face set like flint against open war, 'the greatest of evils,' which he declared meant financial ruin, would nevertheless favor aid which was *sub rosa*; he would shut ministerial eyes to the Americans buying ammunition in French ports.[4]

The Ministry advanced far enough to accept, in the fall of 1775, the proffered services of one Bonvouloir to go to Philadelphia.[5] He met there the Secret Committee of Congress, whose five members came to a rendezvous in the dark, by different roads, to find that Bonvouloir had no right, no power. He was only 'a traveler out of curiosity,' but he inti-

[1] *Journal des Savants* (1881), 178; *Arch. Nat.*, K 164, *Dossier III*, no. 22; *Archives des Affaires Étrangères, France, Mémoires et Documents*, 410, F 119.

[2] Corwin, *French Objective in American Revolution*, 40, 41, 48, 50, 54.

[3] *Archives des Affaires Étrangères, Angleterre*, 515, no. 24 (March 1, 1776).

[4] *Arch. Nat.*, K 1340, no. 10, pp. 53–89.

[5] Doniol, *La Participation*, I, 510. When the British suspected this mission, Vergennes instructed Garnier to say that the French Government knew nothing of it, that the King's 'delicacy and sense of justice would prevent such an act,' and that he was anxious to do his whole duty as a good neighbor. (*Archives des Affaires Étrangères, Angleterre*, 515, no. 45, Hist. MSS. Com., *Report, Dartmouth MSS.*, II, 401.)

mated darkly, 'showing his hand only a little,' that Congress could get the sinews of war from France if it would but ask. They asked him about engineers, arms and supplies, and free entrance and exit to French harbors, and whether they should send a deputy. He would say only that France wished them well, was able to furnish engineers, and that getting munitions was only a matter 'between one merchant and another'; that he could give addresses, and *perhaps* French officials at the ports would shut their eyes. Yet he made no advances, gave no guarantee, he assured his French employers, '*absolutely* nothing.' As to a deputy, 'it was slippery business in the face of the English.'[1] Evasive, clandestine, underground as the French approaches were, Congress took heart at last, and on March 2, 1776, sent Silas Deane as an agent to buy supplies in France.[2]

By July 12, Congress chose a committee to draw up a plan of foreign treaties. France was the country most in mind. In committee, Franklin, marking with a pencil some articles in a printed volume of treaties, handed it over to John Adams, who made a draft which was approved by the whole committee. It was a treaty of commerce, aiming to avoid any entangling alliance which might involve America in future European wars. For several days it was debated in Congress by those who held it no sufficient temptation for France, but was at last adopted

[1] Durand, *Documents on the American Revolution*, 2–16.

[2] G. L. Clark, *Silas Deane*, 38 (facsimile of commission). Frenchmen were already bargaining with the Secret Committee to supply military stores 'by Connivance.' *Letters of . . . Continental Congress* (Burnett, ed.), I, 299, 304, 341, 367.

with no changes that troubled John Adams. By August 27, the plan of this model treaty had passed the Committee of the Whole.[1] Time alone would determine whether it would prove a tempting bait to France.

Deane meanwhile had gone on his mission. On arrival in Paris early in July, the British at once knew his name, his lodgings, and the purpose of his visit. Two powerful English diplomats were sent to counteract him, and the city 'swarmed with Englishmen,' it seemed to Deane.[2] When he told Beaumarchais that for fear of spies he did not 'open his mouth before English-speaking people,' the witty Frenchman wrote Vergennes that Deane must be 'the most silent man in France,' for he defied him to say six consecutive words in French. Deane was filled with 'heart-rending anxiety,' for at the head of the French Ministry he found 'no daring genius,' and though pleasantly received saw poor prospects for accomplishing his mission.

Fortunately for Deane and the American cause the cautious French King and his Ministry had already been led across the bridge of doubt, in part by public opinion, in part by the tireless zeal and infectious enthusiasm of Caron de Beaumarchais, who was the spirit of Benvenuto Cellini, reborn in the eighteenth century. Though sharing at times

[1] *Letters of . . . Continental Congress* (Burnett, ed.), II, 16, 62. Harrison, Robert Morris, and Dickinson were the other members of this committee. For the further evolution of the model treaty see *American Historical Review*, XVI, 579–87.

[2] G. L. Clark, *Silas Deane*, 50–51. For Deane's instructions from Congress see *Letters of . . . Continental Congress* (Burnett, ed.), I, 375.

even the moral standards of his prototype, Beaumarchais, with all his love of intrigue, had a certain nobility of character, an heroic fervor for the cause of freedom. This brilliant writer of plays, one of the most fascinating figures that history records, had risen by his own talents from the humble home of a watchmaker to a position of influence even in the superb court of Louis XVI. He had been sent on a delicate mission in 1775 to England to recover from the notorious Chevalier d'Éon papers which in his hands were dangerous to the French State. He was wholly successful, outwitted 'this fiery and deceitful creature,' who confessed to having been in disguise for twenty years, and who now became a 'crazy woman,' crazy over Beaumarchais, who laughed at having to play 'gallant cavalier' to this 'capitaine de dragons,' this woman, who, nevertheless, 'drank and smoked and swore like a German trooper.'

While engaged in this wild romance, Beaumarchais, in the home of John Wilkes in London — a home haunted by friends of America — met Arthur Lee, and through him first touched the pulse of American life. Only a spark was necessary to fire his sympathetic nature. In a moment he became almost idolatrous of the cause of his 'dear Americans,' clapping his hands and triumphing over every victory, trembling lest the pleas he offered in behalf of America be denied. To both Vergennes and the French King he sent letter after letter, amazingly audacious, reminding the King that he was responsible to God, to himself, and to a great people for his decision. He even prayed the Guardian Angel of the State for just a half-hour audience with the King.

In these appeals he exhausted every argument and every sophistry to win Louis XVI from his scruples even against secret aid. Did he owe most to the proud English or to his own people? Beaumarchais asked. Let the King beware of a deplorable excess of equity toward his enemies, urged the author of 'Figaro.' Let him remember that the policy of governments is not the moral law of its citizens. Were men angels, counseled the 'Barber of Seville,' political ways might be disclaimed. Moreover, let the King reflect that a kingdom is a vast isolated body, farther removed from its neighbors by a diversity of interests than by the sea, the citadels, and the barriers which bound it. Beaumarchais appealed to Athens and to Solon — to the wisdom of all the ages. As to his duty, the King must understand that, though strict and vigorous in its performance to his own people, to other nations his duty was only conventional. He taunted the King with Dunkirk, with his impotence before the partition of Poland, with the perfidious British seizure of five hundred French vessels at the opening of the last war. He recalled the lost provinces in America and pointed the danger of further losses. Is France again to become the victim of England and the laughing-stock of Europe? he asked. In the name of the glory and prosperity of his reign, Beaumarchais implored his royal master, let him realize the 'facility of doing, the certainty of success, the immense harvest of glory and tranquillity.' The only really important matter now, he cried, is America and all that pertains to it. Thus he forced on the kingly attention 'the famous quarrel between America and England which is soon going to divide the world.' [1]

Since French finances seemed to preclude open war, secret aid was the one solution indicated. That would bring the fruits of a great victory without the danger of combat. Then, to clinch all other arguments, Beaumarchais, after meeting Arthur Lee in London, audaciously wrote the King: '*We must aid the Americans*,' to save our own West Indies. Lee had declared that the Continental Congress had authorized him to demand a treaty of commerce with France in order that America might get from her the munitions of war without which defeat was certain. Should France refuse, Lee threatened, America must yield to England, and then, that the two parts of the Empire might become reconciled by fighting side by side, they would unite in an attack on the French and Spanish West Indies. It is impossible to determine whether Lee or Beaumarchais invented this amazing threat, but it was just the menace to have the greatest effect with the French Ministry. Over and over again that frightful portent had appeared in reports and *mémoires* familiar to every member of the Ministry. De Kalb prophesied it in his report in 1768.[2] Saint-Germain twice raised

[1] The letters in which these arguments appear are to be found *passim* in Volume I of Doniol, and in Loménie's *Beaumarchais*, but they are most conveniently brought together in Miss E. Kite's *Beaumarchais*, II, 21–90.

[2] Kapp, *De Kalb*, 64.

the specter in his *mémoires* to the King. 'The ease of conquest would suggest the idea,' he wrote, 'the excuses are easy to find.' Only thus could England recoup her losses.[1] Turgot, apprehensive of both France and Spain, had the same vision, fearing most for Martinique and Porto Rico. Only thus could the Government hide its shame from the English nation.[2] Indeed, John Adams had intimated as much in the Continental Congress, though that could not have been known to the French Ministry.[3]

Pressing the Lee story with all his fiery zeal, Beaumarchais urged the King, urged Vergennes. France could escape war only by advancing money for secret aid.[4] On March 17 and again in May of 1776, Vergennes himself proposed 'veiled and hidden aid to appear to come from Commerce.'[5] Beaumarchais promised to prevent such aid becoming 'a firebrand between France and England.' Vergennes, ever plying Spain with reasons for being ready for war would perhaps have plunged France into war with England any time after 1776, could he have induced Spain to join. Without that, he hesitated even to give America secret aid, but yielded at last to fear and importunity. Long before the Ministry made its fateful decision, Beaumarchais had offered his services, and when a million livres was ventured,

[1] *Archives des Affaires Étrangères, Angleterre*, 515, no. 24.

[2] *Arch. Nat.*, K 1340, no. 10, p. 42; *ibid.*, F 5.

[3] J. Adams, *Works*, II, 487–88. Frederick the Great, too, had forecast such an action by the British. Circourt, III, 63.

[4] Doniol, *La Participation* . . ., I, 515.

[5] Flassan, *Histoire de la Diplomatie Française*, VI, 143, 144; *Arch. Nat.*, K 164; *Vergennes Correspondence*, 1776, no. 9.

with the hope that Spain might double the amount, it was Beaumarchais who founded the business of Hortalez and Company, a merchant house, on a boulevard of Paris, which straightway took all the risks of a private merchant and supplied American needs through the risky channels of a pretended commerce. Beaumarchais had furnished the brains, the intellect, the tireless energy which pushed the French Ministry into secret action. His activity was not a fundamental cause, but was the actual occasion.

The resolve of the French Government to give the Americans secret assistance preceded by more than eighteen months the treaty of alliance and open aid. Washington's victory at Trenton and Princeton was, perhaps, made possible by the supplies furnished by the French or through their instigation. As early as July, 1775, Governor Campbell of South Carolina had the 'mortification of hearing' that vessels from the Dutch and French settlements in the West Indies were arriving and smuggling their cargoes of military stores into the neighboring creeks. Indeed, schooners were sent out from Charleston loaded with rice, and having the confessed purpose of exchanging the cargoes at Hispaniola for military stores.[1] Beaumarchais's endeavors did not bear fruit until later, not until late 1776 or early 1777. The battle of Saratoga — won, it is true, by American soldiers — was won with

[1] *Clinton Papers* (W.L.C.L.), Lord William Campbell to the Earl of Dartmouth, July 19, 1775. As early as October, 1774, Lord North was alarmed at a report of arms sent from Amsterdam to America. *Correspondence of King George III*, III, 148, 159, 160.

ammunition and guns of which nine tenths were obtained through French channels. That became itself, as we shall see, the final encouragement and the cause of the French delusion which determined Louis XVI and his Ministry to reach the great resolution to enter the war on the American side.

French secret aid, which involved encouraging her own and foreign merchants to supply America with all those things which a farming people must buy of a manufacturing nation, had begun long before Hortalez and Company set up its mysterious business on a boulevard of Paris. Thereafter, the volume of aid vastly increased. The business was founded upon funds taken from the royal purse, and even the resources of the King's arsenals were at its call. Yet all was so secret that Beaumarchais defied any man in France from the Ministry down to give him the name, cargo, port, or destination of any vessel he had dispatched to America.[1] American representatives agreed to pay in tobacco for all the needed supplies, but the haste to ship them was never slackened in spite of the fact that the delectable weed rarely arrived. To this day invoices lie in the French archives listing every need of an army.[2] There were one thousand tons of brass cannon with King Louis's monogram, and thousands of muskets and cartridge boxes. Music books and snare drums were listed in lots of many hundreds.

[1] Stevens, *Facsimiles*, no. 1517.

[2] *Archives des Affaires Étrangères, États-Unis*, III, no. 128, F 261–72. There were even buckles for belts, silk for regimental colors, sheep-shears, padlocks, duck for tents, shoemakers' tools, tailors' tools, and glyster pipes.

Horse combs and wagon harnesses were to go in huge quantities, and one hundred thousand blankets. Thousands of uniforms were invoiced, and every kind of medical supply, from alum to opium, with the necessary mortars and pestles. Amputating instruments and all the other implements of torture which the army surgeons would need appear in the lists. Indeed, no want of an army was missing from the invoices, and the quantities proposed were far greater than ever actually reached America.

It was in selecting and dispatching these supplies that Silas Deane, first of American emissaries to France, rendered great service. The impossible was no barrier to either Beaumarchais or Deane. Difficulties rose before them 'like the heads of a hydra.' With everything ready, everything waiting, Beaumarchais was 'on thorns,' pleading, imploring, reasoning with Vergennes.[1] Blocked in one port by 'something obscure and inconceivable,' they shipped out at another. As Beaumarchais cried, 'I have devoted my heart, my labors, my time and my strength to serve as best I can the rising Republic.'[2] If ships were wrecked or taken by the enemy, the tireless pair found some new device to meet the desperate needs of the American soldier. In Washington's armies the slightest increase of the dearth and famine in the matter of clothes and guns and ammunition would have brought them to their knees.

This secret aid — long before France entered into diplomatic alliance — saved Washington's armies from complete disintegration, if not from defeat in

[1] Stevens, *Facsimiles*, no. 886, 908. [2] *Ibid.*, no. 1758.

the field, and the two human agents upon whom all this business of secret supply depended were Beaumarchais and Silas Deane. Yet, in spite of this great service, one of these saviors of the cause of American Independence is known to few Americans except as the author of the 'Barber of Seville' or the 'Marriage of Figaro.' The other, Silas Deane, is a name either wholly unknown or vaguely associated with Benedict Arnold. At best the twilight of dubiety has settled on his reputation, and one wonders lazily whether he was a patriot or a traitor.

The truth seems to be that Deane was almost a fanatic in his eagerness to serve his country. He spent his fortune and wore out his energies in the service of the new States only to find at the end that faction and intrigue and inscrutable caprices of fortune made him an object of calumny rather than a beloved and appreciated patriot. A few good and great men vouched for his integrity, and continued for a time to defend his reputation against the rancorous Lees and the oversuspicious Adams. But even these defenders could not remain faithful to the end. Gradually their voices were hushed, and the waters of oblivion seem to have closed over their praise. It appears very clear to-day that Deane was the victim of factions, which themselves were the results of differences in economic interests of sections, and of chance affinities among men, over which the unfortunate sufferer had no possible control.

Little by little the accusations of his enemies came to be accepted as established truths, and as Deane's friends fell away from him, his heart failed him; the very cause of Independence seemed tainted with this injustice, and he lost faith in it. He never betrayed anybody nor was guilty of any treachery like that of Arnold, but injustice like a canker consumed the faith in his heart. An age which was very bitter against all who doubted the wisdom of Independence condemned him for his despair. His past service was forgotten. Imaginations were too dull to understand his sufferings; the charity of his contemporaries was too weak to spread a mantle over his last days. The world hurried on and left this pathetic figure one of the human wrecks upon its path.

CHAPTER XXIII

SARATOGA LEADS TO A FRENCH ALLIANCE

French sympathy, as shown in the aid sent through the agents, Beaumarchais and Deane, did not stop there. American privateers, preying upon British commerce to its great distress, were encouraged in French ports to a degree just short of bringing upon Louis XVI a British declaration of war. Moreover, the British suspected French preparations for war, and rightly, for Vergennes wrote to Louis XVI, October 17, 1776, 'Of course we must keep up our preparations for war of all sorts so that we may be in position to arbitrate peace or war when the time comes.'[1]

The Continental Congress had early given its approval of the fitting out of privateers, under the delusion at first that seamen would there be trained for a proposed American navy.[2] That both navy and army would be robbed by the resulting passion for privateering was not foreseen. The 'plague, trouble, and vexation' that Washington had with the mutinous and complaining crews of privateers was 'inexpressible.' He spoke of the 'disorderly set' as 'our rascally privateersmen.'[3] Their love of Mammon always seemed far to exceed their love of country. Yet they were not wholly bad. The stopping of

[1] *Archives des Affaires Étrangères, Mémoires et Documents, France,* 1897, F 70.

[2] *Journals of Continental Congress* (Ford, ed.), IV, 230.

[3] Washington, *Writings* (Ford, ed.), III, 231, 262.

New England fisheries drove the bold, simple, seafaring folk, not only to the sword for revenge, but to some new way to feed their wives and babes.[1] A lucky cruise, a captured British West-Indiaman, might drive the wolf from the door for years to come. Unfortunately, such honest aims easily turned to greed and insatiable avarice. After seizing enemy's ships, they found it easy to seize those of neutrals. Success brought luxury, extravagance, dissipation, and a loosening of the people's morals. Sailors were easily seduced from the public ships of war to the private ships of prey.[2] By December, 1776, there were, perhaps, ten thousand 'Yankees' aboard the privateers, badly cutting the numbers in the State militia, or the Continental army and navy.[3] Paul Jones was disgusted and dismayed with the mania for privateering, which forced half the American fleet to lie empty and idle in the harbor.[4]

Silas Deane, in addition to his work as American business agent in France, was soon seeking to do 'infinite damage' to British commerce by securing for his countrymen's privateers and their prizes the liberty of French ports.[5] When Franklin came with Lambert Wickes in the Reprisal, he carried from Congress an order to apply at once to the court of

[1] *Letters of the American Revolution* (Willard, ed.), 98; Paullin, *Navy of the American Revolution*, 149.

[2] G. W. Allen, *Naval History of the Revolution*, I, 48–49.

[3] Force, *American Archives* (5th Series), II, 622; III, 1513; Stevens, *Facsimiles*, no. 1397. Morris says the rage for privateering made it hard even to get workmen to cast cannon.

[4] De Koven, *Paul Jones*, I, 123, 236.

[5] Silas Deane, *Papers*, I, 206–07, 398.

France for such protection to American men-of-war, and even to ask if prizes might be sold in France to save the dangerous journey to an American port.[1] It was not long before commissions were actually sent overseas so that privateers might be fitted out in French harbors.[2]

Efforts in these directions were hardly begun before Lord Stormont, the British Ambassador, was assailing Vergennes with proofs that he knew all about it. English spies talked, ate, slept, cruised with the American agents.[3] With the gift of a sword or a brace of pistols they loosened the tongues of the ships' captains who carried American secrets, and Stormont was able to show Vergennes most accurate and disconcerting evidence as to the amazing things that went on in French ports.[4] Spies produced perfect proofs that there were ten boats loading at Bordeaux and Nantes; that three brigs, one snow, and one ship, taken on the very coast of France, were sold in a French port for one hundred thousand livres; but what was the good? Before Lord Stormont's protest could be received and answered, the ships were out again, and off on some new raid on British commerce.[5] He grew very weary of being 'amused with promises.'

At the beginning of the activity by American privateers, the British Ministry seriously considered

[1] Wharton, *Diplomatic Correspondence*, II, 179.

[2] *Ibid.*, II, 249; III, 364.

[3] *American Historical Review*, XXIX, 474–95. This study of the British Secret Service, by S. F. Bemis, is the most interesting account.

[4] Stevens, *Facsimiles*, nos. 187, 235, 670.

[5] *Ibid.*, nos. 46, 171, 246, 670; Hale, *Franklin in France*, I, 114.

hanging as pirates all who might be captured. Perhaps only the fear of retaliations prevented that or shutting them up in Newgate as men guilty of high treason. Lord Mansfield was seriously asked for an opinion. Were they to be committed at once for piracy, or kept in a guard-ship, or should all idea of holding them for crime be abandoned? In an actual case of four captured officers, he advised keeping them on a guard-ship, and looking out for *habeas corpus*. Of course, he said, their crime was piracy, but also they had levied war and that was high treason.[1] When one Captain Lee took five British prizes, and entered Bilbao with captains and crew as prisoners, the British Government demanded his surrender as a pirate, but Deane and Beaumarchais made such an impassioned appeal against such a precedent being set that Lee was protected by the Spanish Government, and the French approved.[2] The English Ambassador got what satisfaction he could by the sneer that no civilized nations ought to give refuge or assistance to 'pirates.'[3]

Louis XVI issued solemn orders perfectly in keeping with international law. Placards went up forbidding the bringing of prizes into French ports. There must be no sales of prizes, and the purchase of them was made a penal offense. Violators would be

[1] Mass. Hist. Soc., *Proceedings*, October, 1911, pp. 17–18. Even Vergennes admitted that, when American privateers sold prizes without securing a judgment in an Admiralty Court, it was a kind of piracy. *Archives des Affaires Étrangères, Angleterre*, 524, no. 188.

[2] Stevens, *Facsimiles*, nos. 589, 899; Wharton, *Diplomatic Correspondence*, II, 174–75, 208.

[3] Stevens, *Facsimiles*, no. 1392.

prosecuted. All privateers must anchor under a fort, obtain provisions and water and then get out, not even entering the port. What more could England ask? If that would not do, Vergennes was ready to give up trying to satisfy a nation so hard to please.[1] Stormont, the 'vivacity of whose apprehensions' astounded Vergennes, was almost deceived. 'Nothing franker than their behavior or readier than their promises.' But, he asked, will they keep their promises? King George, finding French conduct 'irksome,' distressing, whether due to duplicity or timidity, thought the court so generous on one occasion that he wrote Lord North to put a good word about it in his Speech to Parliament. Sometimes French promises were 'good as we can expect,' but 'will the execution be scrupulously observed?'[2] The French Ministers were so sympathetic, too. Maurepas said of course Stormont had reason to be annoyed, so would he be. But the Americans were so persistent; ordered away, they refused to go; and Vergennes wrote in despair, 'I can order them out, but surely I cannot *put* them out' at the mercy of English cruisers. As for Frenchmen sailing with the privateers, Noailles asked, innocently, 'We cannot watch every individual Frenchman,' can we?[3]

Vergennes, trying to pacify the adroit and clever Stormont on the one hand, and the impatient and spirited Beaumarchais on the other, used sounding phrases to the American commissioners. He warned

[1] Stevens, *Facsimiles*, nos. 706, 1670, 1671, 1679.

[2] Donne, *Correspondence of George III and Lord North*, II, 407, 409.

[3] Stevens, *Facsimiles*, nos. 1594, 1597, 1646.

them that their privateers might have refuge and succor, but then they must go away and not come running back with prizes and sell them. Wily captains thereupon paid carpenters for certificates that it would be very dangerous to go out. They stove in water casks to simulate a leak which would need repairs. Vergennes blandly told Stormont to pump them dry and see if they had a leak. Stormont retorted that if a French court wished a boat to be leaky, a leak would be found. By hook or by crook prizes were brought in and sold in French harbors, or a little way out.[1] Signals were made, and the French buyers went out to sea to meet the 'pirates.' Having bought prizes cheap, purchasers passed them off as French boats, taking all the risk as to the legality of the procedure. While officials shut their eyes, workmen painted and disfigured the ships, whose names changed as if by magic. The Clarendon and the Hanover Planter became the Hancock and the Boston. Given by Stormont the very names of the French buyers, Vergennes only rolled his eyes to Heaven, distressed at the 'cupidity of private individuals.'[2] When the British forced an inquiry, the Minister of Marine made much show of investigation. It is hard to credit how slowly the inquiry proceeded, and at last came the verdict that there might have been fraud, but it was hard to trace now![3]

At times the privateers got so brazen that the

[1] Stevens, *Facsimiles*, no. 1574; Hale, *Franklin in France*, I, 115–16.

[2] Stevens, *Facsimiles*, nos. 1766, 1669, 1730; Wharton, *Diplomatic Correspondence*, II, 222–23.

[3] Stevens, *Facsimiles*, no. 1536.

French could not wink at their impudence. One Wickes, accused of loading cannon clandestinely at night, defended himself by declaring that he put them on board at noonday publicly. Some were seized and imprisoned, but the British found that balls and card-parties and reviews were being held for them that detention might not be irksome. If a boat was taken away, it was soon found that a new and larger one had replaced it, and that Frenchmen eked out the crew.[1] One Hodge, having deceived a French official and fitted out a privateer in a Gallic port, was told with a wink that in France it was a serious fault to tell the King a falsehood.[2] After two months in the Bastille he was released. If the British prodded Vergennes, an American captain might for a time get pushed from pillar to post, and would grumble loudly about the indignities suffered in the ports of France, the cat-and-mouse methods of holding them up and letting them go, but the angry Deane would get a hint that all would be right anon.[3] Often orders to stay in port were found to be efforts to protect them from men-of-war outside. Some slipped out without orders or papers. One way or another, they always escaped finally, when the British were off guard. On the whole, Vergennes plainly favored a secret aid that kept short of open rupture with England. His rigor waxed or waned with Stormont's mercurial pressure, with the changes

[1] Stevens, *Facsimiles,* nos. 187, 1541; Neeser, *Cruises of Gustavus Cunningham,* 48.

[2] Wharton, *Diplomatic Correspondence,* II, 377; *Deane Letters,* III, 168.

[3] Stevens, *Facsimiles,* no. 904.

of feeling in the French Cabinet or the varying fortunes of America on the battle-fields.[1]

Even with this care, France came within a hair's breadth of war, again and again. Vergennes was confronted by affidavits, sworn on 'the Holy Evangelists of Almighty God,' that, in the French islands, English sailors, captured by American privateers, were held in French prisons and dying by 'inch-meal.'[2] Yet he never hesitated to trail England along with promises, evasions, and unblushing denials of facts plain as Holy Writ. Vergennes's correspondence with Stormont, the British Ambassador, and with Beaumarchais, the French agent in American affairs, convinces one that had he enjoyed the ambidexterity which tradition attributes to Cæsar, he would not have hesitated to write with one hand to the British Government protesting his regard for the obligations of a neutral, asserting the friendship, good feeling, and peaceful intention of the King of France, while with the other hand he gave written orders to Beaumarchais to render the Americans every possible assistance. When compelled to make some show of rigor against impudent American privateers, he made amends by pleading with Spain to compensate by a gift of money the losses suffered by Americans through this enforcement of the prize laws.[3]

[1] I am much indebted for the material in the last few pages to papers written in my seminar by Miss Helen Bates on *Lord Stormont at the Court of France*, and by Miss Ruth Y. Johnston on *American Privateers in French Ports*.

[2] *Archives des Affaires Étrangères, Angleterre*, 526, F 20, note.

[3] Stevens, *Facsimiles*, nos. 1704, 1734.

On one occasion, Stormont asked the French Government to restore prizes brought into ports by American privateers. Vergennes, finding the warmth of his expressions extreme, answered, 'You cannot expect us to take upon our shoulders the burden of your war; every wise nation places its chief security in its own vigilance.' Stormont retorted, 'The eyes of Argus would not be too much for us.' Whereupon the astute Vergennes replied with unction, 'And if you had those eyes, they would only show you our sincere desire of peace.' Stormont said that even the French officers were hurrying to America. 'Yes,' suavely returned Vergennes, 'the French nation has a turn for adventure.'[1] Told that a French commander had forgotten all dignity and saluted one of the American pirates, Vergennes replied that if he did, it was certainly nothing to be boasted about! Vergennes knew that an emollient answer turneth away wrath — especially when the recipient is chiefly anxious to save his face, and will prefer a palpable lie to an acknowledgment of a truth, which could have no other result than a war which England, just then, was anxious to avoid. English statesmen were never blind to the fact that the population of France was twice that of their own country.

No wonder the British were bitter, for early in 1778, when France was changing from neutral to open enemy, a committee of the House of Lords estimated that American privateers had cost the British £1,800,633. They had seized seven hundred and thirty-three ships, of which five hundred and

[1] Bancroft, *History of the United States* (ed. 1866), IX, 286.

fifty-nine were not retaken. The added danger on the seas had doubled insurance even on convoyed ships, and raised it to six times the peace rates when not convoyed. Seamen's wages, too, had risen from twenty-five to fifty-five shillings per month. Never before had the hardiest enemies so menaced the coasts of Great Britain and Ireland.[1] Even the Irish linen trade had to be convoyed, and, confident of a harbor of refuge on the near French coast, American privateers had seized ships at the very mouths of English rivers. The Harwich mail packet even was seized by Captain Cunningham and taken into Dunkirk. Lord Camden, from the Opposition benches, taunted Lord North with these consequences of his American policy — the seas covered with Yankee privateers, French ports full of them. 'They come to the very mouths of your rivers, and insult you.' Commerce languishes, trade decays, ships, vexed, tormented, torn in every sea, 'rot in your harbours, because merchants are unable to pay the insurance.' The French become your carriers, twenty-six of their vessels actually in the Thames. 'Your West Indian islands ruined,' the plantation owner driven from affluence to poverty and despair.[2] It was little comfort that about an equal number of American privateers had been captured, and that thousands of American sailors from these boats languished in British naval prisons.

After the news of Burgoyne's surrender came over

[1] Hansard, *Debates*, XIX, 708–13; *London Annual Register* (1778), 36. The Register of the Society of Merchants at Lloyd's Coffee House was the source of the data.

[2] Hansard, *Parliamentary History*, XIX, 339, 342, 344.

the sea, France was not long in exchanging peace and secret succor for war and open assistance to the American cause. We cannot know all that went on within the ivory towers of French diplomacy, but the reasons for this alliance must have been very strong, since the King and Cabinet had been obdurate to every argument for eighteen months preceding the day when they seem to have seen a great light. Why did the French Government, already overwhelmed with debt, abandon the policy of secret aid to the Americans, which had been so rich in results, which had cost so little, and which seemed to be entirely successful, for a policy which meant certain war, and probably financial ruin, even if the war were won?

We must remember that Vergennes had been haunted with the bogy, from 1776 on, that as a result of America's struggle for Independence, France and Spain would lose their West Indian possessions. It was Beaumarchais's fine Italian hand which first planted this thorn, which never ceased to worry Vergennes until the war was ended. Though Figaro was only a creature of Beaumarchais's fancy, the intriguing author was a remarkable embodiment of his own imaginary hero. The fears of Vergennes were never allayed, but rather ever augmented by reports from England. Noailles, the French Ambassador in London, wrote as early as November 8, 1776, that the British Ministry would be glad to see a war break out between England and France and Spain over the Portuguese affair. Then they could gracefully drop the American affair, which they were now too proud to do. Indeed, Noailles wrote that Lord Rockingham, calling attention in debate to the growing armaments of France and Spain, had proposed reconciliation with America at any price, and then an alliance with that independent people. The Duke of Manchester and the Duke of Grafton had seconded the proposal.[1] Again, December 31, 1776, he wrote that the news of the American loss of Fort Washington had made London wild with joy. Their madness knew no bounds. This delirious English people were ready to defy all the powers of the world, and 'they talk loftily of attacking France.'[2] In May, 1777, the French spies reported that Lord Camden had shown full knowledge of French aid to America, and of France's preparations for war. 'Let us have war with all the world,' he cried, 'but peace with America.'[3] By August of 1777, Vergennes was so beset with his *bête noire* that he told Stormont, the British Ambassador, flatly, 'Your public papers, your pamphleteers, your orators, and ours, repeat ceaselessly that if you do not regain your colonies, you will fall upon ours.'[4]

This was the state of the French Foreign Minister when the news of Burgoyne's defeat came oversea to England and to France. After all those auguries of war, it is little wonder that trifles light as air seemed proofs as strong as Holy Writ. Simultaneously with the arrival in Paris of the news of Burgoyne's surrender came the news of the French spies in London

[1] *Archives des Affaires Étrangères, Correspondance Politique, Angleterre*, 519, no. 17.

[2] *Ibid.*, no. 123. [3] *Ibid.*, 523, F 155. [4] *Ibid.*, 524, no. 114.

that the Duke of Richmond had proposed in the House of Lords to reëstablish peace with America, and form with it a family compact, in all the force of that term, which would put the two countries out of reach, and render them superior to all other family compacts.[1] Fox, wrote the Duke of Noailles, was occupied with the same object in the House of Commons.[2] Another agent discusses at length the ominous threat that Chatham will be recalled.[3] 'If he reënters the Cabinet he will be the master, and his insatiable avidity for glory will not let him neglect the means which he will have in his hands, if he can, of attacking France and Spain.'

Although Vergennes hastened as early as December 6, at the latest, to assure the American commissioners in Paris that the King contemplated an alliance of some sort with America,[4] yet we know that the French Ministry hesitated until December 17 before committing itself any further, and for a month after that it would probably have withdrawn from negotiation if anything untoward had happened, or if it could have shaken off the fear that America would make peace with England and form such a compact with it that France would be in

[1] *Archives des Affaires Étrangères, Correspondance Politique, Angleterre*, 526. These spies not only reported the debates of both houses of Parliament, but even in some cases the discussions in the Cabinet.

[2] *Ibid.*, F 163, December 5, 1777.

[3] *Ibid.*, F 154, December 5, 1777. Vergennes quotes this exactly, December 5, 1777. *Ibid.*, *Espagne*, 587, no. 102.

[4] Doniol, II, 626. He and Maurepas, he says, 'think there is not a moment to lose in making friends with Congress — useful if we attach it, dangerous if we neglect it.'

danger of attack by both. Vergennes's diplomatic aims for a time appear in passages of his letters, as in that to Gerard (December 10, 1777), where he says he is too tired to see Deane and Grand, who have just called, but 'you see them' and 'encourage them.' 'It is not possible to promise absolutely, but you can put them on the road to give themselves the promise.' [1] On the following day he was writing Montmorin, 'I will study meanwhile in the conference which I am to have to-morrow with the American deputies to so compass my language that I shall nourish their hopes without meanwhile engaging us beyond what is reasonable.' [2] Moreover, he had told the commissioners that France ought not to act without Spain's approval, and had got them to await an answer from Spain.[3] December 6 was not the critical moment when the French decision was made, but rather some later date, perhaps as late as February 4, 1778, when the Spanish letter of January 28, 1778, arrived, and the French Ministry knew of Spain's positive refusal to join with France against England.[4] Therefore, all information which came to Vergennes meanwhile, strengthening his conviction that war was inevitable, influenced the final decision.

Letters from secret agents of France in England continued to pile up the evidence that England sought peace with America, and wished for war with

[1] *Archives des Affaires Étrangères, Correspondance Politique, États-Unis*, 2, no. 175.

[2] Doniol, II, 634–35. [3] *Ibid.*, 750–56.

[4] The drawing up of the treaty, it is true, had gone on, and after December 17, it would have been awkward for France to withdraw.

France.[1] The Duc de Lauzun, writing from London, corroborated their fears, while the Comte de Broglie indited his usual *mémoire* to the King filled with the same idea.[2] Every rumor from London confirmed these fears. The Duke of Richmond in parliamentary debate had declared that it was impossible for England to get peace with America on any other basis than that of independence. He urged a treaty of union like that with Scotland, wherein the two nations would recognize the same king.[3] Chatham was reported to have made the same proposal.[4] Lord North, talking of peace, was known to be working with the greatest zeal to get unlimited subsidies for war. Already sixty thousand sailors were voted, it was said, and it was not difficult to foresee the use they would make of them if they could get their elbows free in America.[5] While French spies in London were daily sending the French Ministry fresh proofs of the reality of their fears, Vergennes knew that the American commissioners were receiving agents sent by the British Government to propose terms for conciliation,[6] and Franklin and

[1] Doniol, II, 648–49; *Archives des Affaires Étrangères, Correspondance Politique, Angleterre*, 526, F 129.

[2] Doniol, II, 649–50, 668–70; *Arch. Nat., Marine*, B 4, 132, F 20 (original of Broglie *mémoire*).

[3] *Archives des Affaires Étrangères, Correspondance Politique, Angleterre*, 526, F 226.

[4] *Arch. Nat., Marine*, B 4, 132, F 20. See also Bancroft, IX, 478.

[5] *Archives des Affaires Étrangères, Correspondance Politique, Angleterre*, 526, F 248, December 13, 1777.

[6] The assiduous Beaumarchais, ardent as ever for intervention in favor of America, brought this news. Doniol, II, 685. Noailles also suggested this. *Archives des Affaires Étrangères, Correspondance Politique, Angleterre*, 526, no. 120; also no. 131 *bis*; Doniol, II, 648, note.

Deane, while seeming very frank in confiding to Vergennes all that went on in these secret interviews, admitted with diplomatic innuendo that America might have to make peace with England, and even to turn on France because the United States got so little support in Europe.[1] It seems to have been the astute policy of the American agents to create a jealousy in the French Government by feigning to be near to a compulsory alliance with England, while at the same time they kept England on the anxious seat by affecting to desire an alliance with France.

Carmichael, one of the American commissioners, put in Vergennes's hands a memoir pointing out that the help France had given thus far in money and arms was regarded by many in America as merely giving a little nourishment to the fire which would consume its enemy. If France, he warns Vergennes, lets England triumph, this force in America, which, united to France, might put England where it could do no harm, will be directed against France. In America the love of conquest might replace that of patriotism. And Spain ought not to forget that England will console America for the loss of its liberty by the pillage of Spain's American possessions.[2] Paul Wentworth, the British spy, reported that Franklin in conversation with him (January 4, 1778), said, 'It was affection to Great Britain which induced him to say that Independency was certain,

[1] Doniol, II, 629–31; also Wharton, *Diplomatic Correspondence*, December 8, 1777.

[2] *Archives des Affaires Étrangères, Correspondance Politique, Angleterre*, 526, F 388.

that a few weeks would evince that he was still the friend of Great Britain, in wishing her to go before France and Spain and avoid a war on her part as well as prevent the colonies from engagements, which must be taken out of England's scale.' [1]

These clever American agents seem to have understood well the art of worrying both England and France to the eternal advantage of their native land. They made capital out of their report to Vergennes on the proposals of England's secret agent. 'He made them understand,' writes Vergennes, December 15, 1777, 'that the British Ministry was ready to grant everything almost to Independence, which they could not risk for fear of losing their places. All was tried, promises, seduction, menaces. The most positive thing was that instructions had been sent to Lord Howe to negotiate in America. The formal proposition is to unite cordially and to fall upon France and Spain.' [2] A fear that haunted Vergennes was that Lord North, taking advantage of the stress of circumstances, would anticipate Parliament's action. 'Give all news on the wings of haste,' Vergennes wrote fervidly to Noailles in London, December 13; 'do not spare the couriers.' 'Tell them to push on in case of urgency even to Versailles. 'Be on the alert, watch Parliament, the Ministry, and the ports. We may expect violent scenes and

[1] British Museum, *Add. MSS.*, 34415, F 27. Franklin had conditioned this interview 'on the understanding that propositions of honor and emolument, if Franklin would bring about a conciliation with England, must not be made.' *Ibid.*, F 18.

[2] *Archives des Affaires Étrangères, Correspondance Politique, Espagne*, 587, no. 105. More fully told, *ibid.*, no. 112.

extraordinary resolutions.'[1] 'In the distress wherein the British Ministry finds itself,' urges Vergennes, 'every means will appear good to it to escape from its straits. Although North has announced the coming January 20, for submitting his plans of peace and of war, I have some reason for believing that he will not wait this time to prepare a reconciliation with the Americans. Orders must have been sent very recently to Howe for this undertaking. . . . If he believed that he had the power to accord Independence, he might have a good chance — all other conditions being more difficult.' He begs Noailles to solve for him the question whether North would dare grant Independence and treat as state with state before having the consent of Parliament. He fears that the Ministry in its desperation may do almost anything. They may well regard a new war as a remedy to the evils which overwhelm them.[2] Even if the North Ministry falls, one under Chatham will succeed, and 'it is the same to us,' cried Vergennes, 'whether war comes from Lord North or Lord Chatham.'[3]

By December 27, Vergennes was using Beaumarchais's argument. 'The question which we have to solve,' he wrote, 'is to know whether it is more expedient to have a war against England and America united, or with America for us against England.'[4]

[1] *Archives des Affaires Étrangères, Correspondance Politique, Angleterre*, 526, no. 84.

[2] December 20, 1777, *Archives des Affaires Étrngères, Correspondance Politique, Angleterre*, 526, no. 110 *bis*; *ibid.*, F. 248.

[3] Doniol, II, 649.

[4] *Archives des Affaires Étrangères, Correspondance Politique, Espagne*, 587, no. 135.

Over two weeks before, Vergennes had used in a letter to Spain the exact words of Beaumarchais, who, Mentor or Mephistopheles, was ever at his elbow during this critical period, whispering suspicions and furnishing him with taffeta phrases which Vergennes never disdained to borrow in his next letters, while he kept a little at a distance and in the background this 'Barber of Seville,' who was too clever not to be used, but of too humble birth to be acknowledged. He wrote in Beaumarchais's words of the day before, 'We must not forget that the power which recognises the independence of the Americans first will gather all the fruits of this war.' [1]

This idea came also to dominate the mind of the king, as we see in his letter of January 8, to his 'dear brother and uncle' the King of Spain. After discussing the effects of Burgoyne's defeat, and Lord North's proposal for pacification, he says: 'It is the same thing to us whether this ministry be in power or another. By different means they unite to ally themselves with America, and they do not forget our ill offices. They will fall upon us as if the civil war had not been. This fact and the griefs which we have against England, have determined me after having taken the advice of my cabinet that it is just and necessary to consider the propositions which the American insurgents make, and to begin to treat with them to prevent their reunion with their mother country.' [2] Toward the end, the British intelligence service informed the Government that

[1] Doniol, II, 632; Beaumarchais's letter, *ibid.*, 684.

[2] *Archives des Affaires Étrangères, Mémoires et Documents, France*, 1897, F 83.

the French thought North's plan of such a nature that the Americans could not refuse it. The French court is so alarmed, declared the spies, that 'it would grant any terms sooner than see America reunited with Great Britain.'[1] Vergennes's fears, expressed in all his correspondence from 1776 to the time of France's momentous decision, make it seem clear that Vergennes did not invent this final incentive to the alliance — the idea that the French Government was confronted by the dilemma of war with England anyway, whether France allied itself with America or not. But whether it is his conviction or his device, the idea of the terrible dilemma remains the occasion for the decision of the France Cabinet.[2] The King's letter of January 8, 1778, seems to dispose of any idea that Vergennes alone of the members of the French Cabinet was possessed of this specter of inevitable war. France entered into alliance with the United States in the spring of 1778, because the King and his Ministry were convinced that France was doomed to a war with Great Britain whether she formed the American alliance or not, but that it was the better policy to join with America and thus win her support than to wait for England to make peace with America, and then make war in company with her upon the House of Bourbon whose insular possessions would lie so completely at their mercy. Back of this immediate occasion

[1] Hist. MSS. Com., *Tenth Report* (*Abergavenny MSS.*), no. 6, p. 20.

[2] Corwin, in his *French Objective in the American Revolution*, disagrees with me in this matter, but I think he has in mind the 'fundamental causes' and does not give proper weight to the evidence which supports this 'immediate occasion' of the decision to make an alliance.

of the decision lay, of course, the age-long enmity of the two powers, the opportunity for revenge, and the dominating motive of restoring French prestige among the nations of Europe. Once the decision was made, the first phase of the War for Independence came to a close. The lone struggle of the weak American colonies against their powerful mother country was at an end. Thereafter the European phase of the war began — a war which was the resultant of many forces, the ambitions of kings, the pride of nations in their prestige, the economic interests of merchants, the follies of ministers, and the unreasoning hate of one people for another. The consequence of that war and of America's own struggles was the birth of a new nation.

THE END

INDEX